The Trojan War
Second Edition

The Trojan War

*Literature and Legends
from the Bronze Age
to the Present*

SECOND EDITION

DIANE P. THOMPSON

McFarland & Company, Inc., Publishers

Jefferson, North Carolina, and London

Maps by Melanie De Cola.

LIBRARY OF CONGRESS CATALOGUING-IN-PUBLICATION DATA

Thompson, Diane P., 1940–
The Trojan War : literature and legends from the Bronze Age to the
present / Diane P. Thompson. — Second Edition.
p.   cm.
Includes bibliographical references and index.

ISBN 978-0-7864-7229-1

softcover : acid free paper ∞

1. Trojan War — Literature and the war.
I. Title.
PN56.T76T46 2013   808.8'03583921— dc23   2013017738

BRITISH LIBRARY CATALOGUING DATA ARE AVAILABLE

On the cover: *background* relief of Trojan soldiers and
inset Trojan Horse images © 2013 Clipart.com

Manufactured in the United States of America

*McFarland & Company, Inc., Publishers
Box 611, Jefferson, North Carolina 28640
www.mcfarlandpub.com*

Table of Contents

Preface

When I was in graduate school, mulling over the amazing unfairness of human suffering, I looked to the past for answers. Seeking wisdom, I studied the three-thousand-year-old tradition of Trojan War stories. I hoped to learn about how human beings could become involved in the destruction of their own civilization, a central theme of most stories of Troy. I thought that I might discover what brilliant people of past times had concluded. Unfortunately there were no answers. Only grief, weary sighs, questions of *what if, if only, why?*

I finished my dissertation ("Human Responsibility and the Fall of Troy," City University of New York, 1981), but I felt bitterly let down by ancient poets' lack of wisdom. I spent several years nursing my disappointment at the failure of great authors to answer my questions about the causes of human suffering and disaster. Gradually, however, I began to accept the fact that, although there were no easy or satisfying answers to the problem of human suffering, there were thousands of years of Troy stories, many by major poets. The true wonder of these stories was not in their wisdom, which was not all that different from ours today, but in their amazing endurance, as generations of poets persisted in retelling the story of a small war for over three thousand years.

My goal in writing this book is to communicate the extraordinary endurance and variety of Troy stories, so that modern readers can appreciate how ancient, how persistent, and yet how contemporary these stories are. Only stories from the Hebrew Bible can compete with the story of Troy for popularity, substance and durability in Western civilization. Each new author retells his or her Troy story in the context of his or her own contemporary values and perceptions, while the ancient events and characters mark the story as from long ago and far away. Thus, Virgil tells the story of Troy as part of the founding story of the Roman Empire, while Benoît tells it as a huge medieval moral exemplum, chock-full of tragic romances. Chaucer uses the ancient pagan story of Troy deliberately to separate the love story of Troilus and Criseyde from his own Christian values. Authors also play against one another to identify their contemporary values, as when Shakespeare takes Chaucer's *Troilus and Crisyede* and transforms it into the bitter political drama of chaos in Renaissance politics — *Troilus and Cressida*.

I have selected a few interesting threads from the enormous number of Troy stories that have been composed over these three thousand years. I chose the story of Iphigenia, Agamemnon's daughter, because her sacrifice has appealed to writers from Euripides to Racine, Goethe, and Sheri Tepper. Over the centuries Iphigenia has been transformed from

1

a young girl who was sacrificed so that Agamemnon could sail to Troy (Euripides), into a lovely young princess too nice to kill (Racine), a perfect woman who can transform humanity (Goethe), and a ghost whose function is to help convince Achilles that there is no use for a dead woman (Tepper). I chose the story of Troilus and Criseyde/Cressida because of the interesting development of the role of love in the story of Troy, from the seizing of Helen and fighting over Briseis and Chryseis in the *Iliad*, to the ambiguous Dido in the *Aeneid*, to the elevated, yet pagan, romance in Chaucer's *Troilus and Criseyde*, to Shakespeare's degenerate Cressida in his *Troilus and Cressida*. I selected the feminist goddess movement of the 1980s because it offers recent examples of the continual reinvention of Troy in new contexts. And finally, I looked at many interesting uses of Troy in the present — on film, on TV, in books, in art, in advertising, and on the Internet.

When preparing this second edition, I added a chapter on the *Historia Destructionis Troia* by Guido delle Colonne, who took Benoit's gigantic poetic version of the story of Troy and transformed it into the accepted prose "history" of Troy that became the main source for many medieval and renaissance versions of the story of Troy. I also added a chapter on James Joyce's *Ulysses,* which is the greatest and best known of the twentieth century retellings of the story of Homer's *Odyssey*, with the Mediterranean recast as 1904 Dublin, and Leopold Bloom as the wandering Ulysses. I revised the chapter on the Bronze Age to reflect the archeological explorations of Troy in the 1990s and early twenty-first century and Troy's connection with the Hittite Empire of Central Anatolia. Finally, I updated the last chapter to reflect some of the newer books published on Troy in the past few years.

The Plan of the Book

After presenting material on the history of Troy and Mycenae in the Mediterranean Bronze Age and the oral transmission of epic poetry, I discuss the primary Troy sources — Homer's *Iliad* and *Odyssey*— offering a detailed synopsis of each. My purpose is to give a general reader enough background to recognize the main characters and story elements in later Troy stories. Then I examine the story of one very bad homecoming from Troy: how Clytemnestra murdered Agamemnon and Cassandra when they reached Mycenae, as told by Aeschylus in *Agamemnon*. Euripides wrote two interesting plays about Agamemnon's sacrifice of his daughter, *Iphigenia at Aulis* and *Iphigenia in Tauris*, which I examine next because the theme of the king sacrificing his daughter became an important thread in Troy stories. I then deal with Virgil's *Aeneid,* which offers an important counter-tradition to Homer. Virgil's Greeks are bad, while his Trojans are noble refugees from Troy who become the founding ancestors of Rome.

After examining some of the transmission materials to the European Middle Ages (Dictys and Dares), I consider two medieval Troy romances: the *Eneas*, updating the *Aeneid* for the world of the crusades, and the *Roman de Troie*, a massive poetic narrative of the intertwining of love and death in the Trojan War. Next I examine Guido delle Colonne's refashioning of the Troy Story into what came to be considered the true history of Troy, his *Historia Destructionis Troiae*. From the *Roman de Troie*, I pick up the tale of the Trojan prince Troilus and his lover, Briseida, and follow it in two major retellings by Chaucer (*Troilus and Criseyde*) and Shakespeare (*Troilus and Cressida*).

Next, I look at the improvements Racine and Goethe each made to the story of Iphigenia in the seventeenth and eighteenth centuries. Then I consider the grandest and most compassionate retelling of the *Odyssey*, James Joyce's *Ulysses*. After that, I pick up Cassandra's story (from *Agamemnon*) in Marion Zimmer Bradley's novel *The Firebrand*, which tells about the fall of Troy from Kassandra's point of view. I compare *The Firebrand* with another feminist retelling of the Troy story, Sheri Tepper's *The Gate to Women's Country*. Finally, I examine the role of Troy stories today, in both literary and popular culture, including the burgeoning wealth of Troy materials on the Internet.

A Timeline of Selected Troy Stories

Ca. 1250 BCE: Fall of Troy
Ca. 750: Homer's *Iliad* and *Odyssey*
Fifth century: Classic Greek dramas about Trojan themes (such as *Oresteia*, *Iphigenia at Aulis*, *Trojan Women*, *Ajax*, *Helen*, etc.)
29–19: Virgil's *Aeneid*
First century CE (or later): Dictys: *Ephemeridos Belli Troiani*
Dares: *de Excidio Troiae Historia*
Twelfth century: Benoît: *Roman de Troie*
Anonymous: *Eneas*
Geoffrey of Monmouth: *Historia Regum Britanniae*
1287: Guido delle Colonne: *Historia Destructionis Troiae*
Ca. 1340: Boccaccio: *Il Filostrato*
Late fourteenth century: Chaucer: *Troilus and Criseyde*
1420: Lydgate: *Troy Book*
Late fifteenth century: Henryson: *The Testament of Crisseid*
Ca. 1602: Shakespeare: *Troilus and Cressida*
1833: Tennyson: "Ulysses"
1914: Hauptmann: *Der Bogen des Odysseus*
1922: Joyce: *Ulysses*
1938: Kazantzakis: *The Odyssey: A Modern Sequel*
1952–54: H.D.: *Helen in Egypt*
1986: Zimmer Bradley: *The Firebrand*
1988: Tepper: *Gate to Women's Country*
2004: Wolfgang Peterson (director): *Troy*

Introduction

Stories

Long before writing developed, people were telling stories around a fire after sharing a meal, or, later, in a home or tavern; or, best of all, at a banquet in a palace with plenty of food and gifts of warm clothes and a warm bed to reward the skillful teller of a wonderful story. Stories not only entertained, they threaded together the experiences of people into history, reminding them who they had been, who they were, how they should behave, and what could happen if they acted badly. Some compelling and enduring stories are even like bad dreams, dreamed over and over again in many variations, as the poets or dreamers try to process difficult experiences in order to make sense of the world.

Individuals similarly tell the stories of their own lives, rewriting the script to suit their present needs. For example, a chance encounter can turn into a happy or painful experience. Later, one can interpret it as chance, fortune, fate or the intervention of a god. The more self-assured may even come to interpret the chance encounter as the outcome of good planning and brilliant insight. Cultures also rewrite historical scripts to suit present needs. Storytellers, the historians of oral cultures, organize the raw stuff of their culture's experience and memory, the imagined past and the possible future. What they do with this traditional material varies with the teller and the time, but key elements of plot and character must remain, so that audiences can recognize the retelling as part of the familiar, often revered, ancient story.

The Troy Cycle

Stories of the fall of Troy are precious both as literature and as historical documents. The original events of these stories are rooted in a real event — the collapse of the Mediterranean Bronze Age Civilization around 1200 BCE. Over centuries the participants in these events became enlarged into mythic figures, the heroic ancestors of later civilizations. The stories told about these heroic ancestors were so wonderful that they lasted far beyond the Greek civilization that created them. Troy stories became foundation stories of European civilization and were later carried to the Americas. Troy stories continue to be told today in novels, plays, poems, and films. Names and myths connected to Troy show up in advertising, in place names and people's names, on the Internet, and in children's cartoons.

The Troy Cycle began as various oral stories about a federation of Mycenaean Greeks who besieged and conquered the city of Troy in the thirteenth century BCE. These stories preserved the Mycenaean Greeks' ancestral history as well as their myths. As oral poets composed and retold the stories, they combined legends of the gods with heroic deeds of Mycenaean Greek kings and warriors. Eventually the various episodes became connected into the Troy Cycle, a series of epics that covered the events of the war in a universal context, from the creation of the world to the first causes of the war at Troy, the war itself, the fall of Troy, and finally the homecomings of the surviving Greek heroes.

Homer's Iliad *and* Odyssey

The *Iliad* and the *Odyssey* are the only complete parts of the Troy Cycle remaining today. Homer composed these epic poems in the eighth century BCE. The *Iliad* tells about the quarrel between two Greeks, Agamemnon and Achilles, in the ninth year of the ten-year siege of Troy. The *Odyssey* tells about another Greek, Odysseus, who struggles for ten years to return home to Greece after the fall of Troy. "Homer" may have been one person or more than one, although we refer to him as an individual. He almost certainly composed the *Iliad* and *Odyssey* orally. *Rhapsodes*, professional performers, transmitted Homer's epics orally for about two hundred years. The *Iliad* and the *Odyssey* were probably first written as fixed texts in the sixth century BCE.

Homer's epics were received by his Archaic Age Greek audience as a source of valuable information about the gods, history, how people should behave, and the consequences of misbehaving. Gradually, other religious and ethical ideas replaced Homer's, but nothing has ever replaced the brilliance of his stories about Olympian gods, ancient heroes, dangerous tempting women, deadly quarrels and the hindsight/foresight wisdom of the underworld.

In the fifth century BCE, Athenian Greeks retold many Trojan stories as dramas. Athenian attitudes toward the Greek heroes of the Trojan War were mixed. The Mycenaean Greeks were the revered ancestors of the Athenians, but they were ancestors who had behaved brutally, and the victims of war were innocent women and children. Euripides' *Trojan Women* is perhaps the bitterest anti-war play ever written. In it he presents the victorious Greek heroes as cruel monsters and focuses audience sympathy on the suffering of the captive Trojan women and children, victims of war.

More serious in the long run was the charge that Homer told lies about the gods. Plato wanted to remove all poets from his ideal state, largely because he felt that Homer, the best of poets, had told lies about the gods, their passions and intrigues, and their cynical manipulations of human beings. Many later writers agreed with Plato that Homer was a liar. Nonetheless, the *Iliad* and *Odyssey* provided source material for endless new stories, plays, poems, sculptures, paintings, and histories far beyond Greece. Trojan War stories remained popular because they were considered basically true history, even if Homer didn't always have the facts straight.

Medieval European knowledge of the Trojan War came not from the Greek Homer, but from Latin sources, including a brief pro–Trojan account by Dares, a supposed "eyewitness," and especially from Virgil's *Aeneid*. The *Aeneid* tells how the Trojan prince Aeneas, a refugee after the fall of Troy, brought his remnant of surviving Trojans to Italy. At first the Trojans fought the native Latins, but eventually they made peace and joined together to become a single people, symbolized by Aeneas' marriage to Lavinia, daughter of the Latin king. Their descendents were the ancestors of Roman civilization. Consequently, in Latin Europe, the ancient oriental losers (Trojans) became the ultimate heroes of the Trojan War and evolved into the revered ancestors of the Europeans.

After three thousand years, stories of the Trojan War are woven into the consciousness of the West. There is a Troy in New York State and a Trojan football team in Southern California; a personal weakness is an Achilles' heel; Helen of Troy is a line of cosmetics; and a siren can be a cruelly tempting woman as well as the blaring scream of a fire engine.

Troy

The ancient city of Troy was perched at the western edge of Asia Minor on the Dardanelles, a narrow sea passage leading from the Mediterranean toward the Black Sea, separating Europe from Asia. This area has been a touch point for contact and conflict between western and eastern cultures for thousands of years. Troy's strategic location on the boundary between Europe and the Orient may be one reason that stories about Troy have held the imagination of Europeans for so long. Trojan stories connect the ancient, brilliant, yet "decadent" East to the foundations of Western civilization.

There is a fascinating parallel between the Troy story as told by Virgil and the movement from east to west in the other great European foundation story — the Hebrew Bible. Abraham, like Aeneas, left the Orient (Mesopotamia) and moved westward. Abraham's descendents founded Judaism and settled in what is now Israel. Christianity had its roots in Judaism, but moved even further west to Rome and then throughout Europe. Such parallelism might seem a stretch to us today, but it is the sort of coincidence that delighted medieval minds, who were aware that their roots were in the ancient Orient, yet did not exactly approve of those roots.

In the fourth century CE, the Roman Emperor Constantine moved his capital from Rome to the city of Byzantium, which he renamed Constantinople. (It is now named Istanbul.) Perhaps this eastward move was at some level a reaching back towards ancestral Troy, whose ruins were near Constantinople, across the Dardanelles. There is a story that Constantine first tried to build his new city on the site of Troy itself, but he had to give it up because the ancient harbor had become too silted up to be useful (Wood 31).

The language and culture of Constantinople were Greek, not the Latin of Rome. After the fifth century, there was no longer a Western Roman Empire at all, just the Eastern Greek Byzantine Empire, whose capital was Constantinople (Cameron 33). Over time, major differences and stresses developed between the western–Catholic-Latin and eastern–Orthodox-Greek churches and cultures. This separation even showed in the choice of Trojan epics: Virgil's *Aeneid* was cherished as the Trojan foundation story of the Latin West; Homer's *Iliad* and *Odyssey* remained, as always, the Trojan War epics of the Greek Byzantine East. But in both cases, the epics were treasured for their purported historical content as well as for their rhetorical brilliance.

Euhemerization: The Loss of the Pagan Gods

Late Antiquity (after the third century CE) became increasingly Christian, and Christians were energetic idol smashers and destroyers of pagan temples because they abhorred the earlier (pagan) gods, who continued to speak their oracles from statues and through seers until perhaps the fifth century (Cameron 144; Fox 679). Homer obviously presented problems.

But Trojan War stories were too good to be missed. Stripped of the gods, these stories endured in supposed "eyewitness" versions by Greek Dictys and Trojan Dares. Actually, both Dictys and Dares wrote long after the Trojan War, perhaps in the first century CE, or perhaps later (Frazer 3). Each dealt with the gods in two ways popular at that time: where possible, eliminate the gods entirely; where the gods had to play a role, present them as historical human beings falsely reported to be gods. This explanation of the ancient gods as human was called euhemerization. Euhemerized stories of the Trojan War endured because they were interesting and not threatening to Christians. They became the main sources, along with Virgil, for medieval European treatments of the Trojan War.

Back to Troy in the European Middle Ages

In the European Middle Ages, ruling families traced their ancestry back to exiled Trojan heroes. Medieval histories might begin their narratives at the Garden of Eden, but they quickly moved on to Troy, the start of secular history in the West (Geoffrey 5; Lawman, 2ff.). Twelfth-century Anglo-Normans enjoyed long complex romances about the matter of Troy; perhaps these stories reminded them nostalgically of their crusades in the East and of the wonderful luxuries and technological marvels they had seen or heard of there (Faral 344–5; Owen 148–9).

Europeans went on the first crusade in 1096 to save Christian Byzantine Constantinople from the Infidels and to free Jerusalem. However, Latin Europe had an ambivalent relationship with the Greek Byzantine East. There were tensions between crusaders and Byzantines during the first and second crusades, especially over camp locations and supplies (Baldwin 486, 502). During the fourth crusade (1204), European Christian soldiers actually sacked Christian Constantinople. Troy offered Anglo-Norman authors a perfect metaphor for European ambivalence towards the Greek Byzantine East — it was an ancient, luxurious, eastern civilization, yet ultimately flawed and doomed to fall because of failures of hospitality, ethics, and right religion.

From Sex to Romance

Sex had been a problem at Troy ever since the Trojan prince Paris ran away with Helen, the wife of the Greek king Menelaus, and their elopement led to the Greek invasion of Troy. Further, the great quarrel between Achilles and Agamemnon, the theme of the *Iliad*, was over who got to keep Briseis, Achilles' war-prize concubine, when Agamemnon had to return *his* war-prize concubine, Chryseis. There were also ancient rumors about the intimate relationship between Achilles and his beloved friend Patroclus. Even Virgil's Aeneas, good as he was, had an unsavory affair with Queen Dido. These were issues of passion, not love, and classical authors presented passion as basically destructive, a form of madness that could lead to disaster.

Along with this ancient disapproval of passionate sexual love, however, ideas of courtly or romantic love were becoming popular in the twelfth century, and poets were inspired by the potential for love interests in the Trojan War material. In the mid-twelfth century Benoît de Saint-Maure composed a major Trojan romance, the *Roman de Troie*, weaving four love stories throughout the huge war poem, each love leading to its own special form of disaster (Lumiansky 410–24).

One of these doomed affairs was between a Trojan prince, Troilus, and his love, the Greek Briseida, who was traded back to the Greeks in an exchange of prisoners. Briseida later had an affair with the Greek Diomedes, destroying Troilus' faith in women. Benoît's romance of true Troilus and faithless Briseida became the source of Geoffrey Chaucer's *Troilus and Criseyde*, a poem that glorifies the beauty and splendor of romantic love, but finally, reluctantly, rejects it for the Christian love of God. A more sober revising of the *Roman de Troie* into moralistic Latin prose by Guido delle Colonna, a Sicilian judge, became the "true" history of Troy for hundreds of years.

The Renaissance: Homer and the Tudors

Although Homer was continuously read and taught in the Greek Byzantine East, few in the Latin West were able to read Greek (Geanakopolos 393, 401; Kazhden and Epstein 134 ff.; Berschin 19). The reintroduction of the full text of Homer via translations was an important part of the Renaissance recovery of ancient Greek culture. In the Renaissance, people no longer found the pagan gods threatening. These ancient gods were easily explained away as allegories for natural forces or as symbols for metaphysical concepts. The gods also could be euhemerized into historical human beings.

The Elizabethan rulers shored up their legitimacy by tracing the Tudor line back to Troy. Consequently, stories about Trojans were welcome. The first book printed in English was Caxton's translation of a French history of the Trojan War, *The Recuyell of the Historyes of Troye* (Sommer viii).

Seventeenth- and eighteenth-century authors made fascinating use of Troy materials, adapting the stories and characters to suit more refined sensibilities. Racine introduced a second Iphigenia character, Eriphile, whose function was to commit suicide, allowing his primary Iphigenia to both obey her father Agamemnon and not be sacrificed. Goethe, too, worked on improving Iphigenia, making her into an idealized perfect woman who could not tell a lie, not even to save her own life or the lives of her brother Orestes and his companion Pylades.

The twentieth century is rich in Troy lore. In World War I the British sent the flagship *Agamemnon* to Gallipoli, near Troy, and poets wrote about that battle in terms of Troy. James Joyce reinvented Ulysses as Leopold Bloom, a clever, non-heroic man who wandered through Dublin instead of the Mediterranean. Derek Walcott placed his Odysseus in the Caribbean. Eugene O'Neill retold the Electra story (she was Iphigenia's sister) in *Mourning Becomes Electra*, a psychological tragedy set in New England. Troy has been popular in films since the beginning of that industry, from *The Return of Ulysses* in 1909 to the present.

In the 1980s, the Troy tradition was taken up by the women's movement. According to some feminist historians, the Trojan War had occurred around the time when the ancient Mediterranean world of mother right and Goddess worship was being overrun and destroyed by the Aryan Greeks, who oppressed women and worshipped male sky gods. Sheri Tepper's fantasy novel *The Gate to Women's Country* is one of the most interesting late-twentieth-century uses of Trojan War material. Tepper writes about the post-nuclear-war relationships of war-loving men and peace-loving women. Within the novel, a startling feminist version of the play *Iphigenia at Ilium* is rehearsed and performed. Marion Zimmer Bradley also wrote a reinterpretation of the Trojan War, *The Firebrand*, from the viewpoint of the Trojan princess Kassandra. During the novel, Kassandra travels from Troy to Colchis, where she meets her Amazon relatives. Kassandra is personally part of both worlds — the matriarchal Goddess-worshipping ancient world and the newly developing patriarchal Zeus-worshipping world of later Mediterranean civilization.

Troy continues to thrive in popular culture as well as in more literary settings. Troy shows up in movies, videos and books of all sorts from the silliest to the most profound. There are all sorts of Troy-related sites on the Internet, ranging from an excellent archaeology course from Dartmouth, to wonderful museum exhibits of Troy related materials to ads for films and games about Troy, to a home page for the city of Troy, New York.

Why Do Troy Stories Endure?

Troy stories offer a body of material that European authors have been drawn to for over three thousand years. Their attraction is based on various factors. Perhaps most important, Troy stories have been narrated by some of the world's greatest poets, playwrights and novelists, including Homer, Aeschylus, Euripides, Virgil, Boccaccio, Chaucer, Shakespeare, Racine, Goethe and Joyce. The Trojan War offered Christian Europeans the first great event in secular history, and it linked the fall of Troy to the founding of Rome, the root of later European civilization. The story of Troy is thus the founding story of Europe. It is also a boundary story: Troy is on the boundary between Europe and Asia, a place of contact and stress between competing cultures over thousands of years.

Troy stories were a marvelous source of plots and characters, centering on major issues of European civilization. Trojan themes included power and war, love and deceit, loss in victory and success in failure, the heroic West and the suspect (decadent) East, the tangled connections between human desires and divine will, the end of the world, and the beginning of a new way of life.

In Christian countries, the fall of Troy offered an alternative secular vehicle for pondering the implications of the Fall of Man. Why did Troy fall? Were the Trojans flawed? Was it Fate? Fortune? The Stars? Amors? The deceitful pagan gods? What caused basically decent men and women to act in ways that led to their ruin? These were all issues of the Fall of Man, but telling stories from the Bible could be an invitation to resistance and repression in Medieval Europe, while telling stories about Troy invited no trouble at all.

Perhaps one reason Troy stories have enjoyed such an incredibly long run of popularity is their antiquity. Another is surely their continuity. Aside from the Hebrew and Christian biblical traditions, we don't have much that endures — especially in America, where the old is continually being torn down to make way for the new. Troy offers recognizable, familiar, interesting stories to people who don't have much of a past. This may be its greatest use in the twenty-first century, offering a common historical perspective to Americans from many different cultures.

Future Troy stories will no doubt tell about future issues, mining this ancient material for wonderful characters, an end-of-the-world scenario, and a framework for tales of cultures clashing. Troy stories provide a sense of substance and continuity, tying the ancient past to the future present.

1

Bronze Age Mycenae,
Anatolia and Troy
The Archaeological Evidence

Before there were myths and stories about the Trojan War, there was almost certainly a Bronze Age city of Troy. Some knowledge of the Mediterranean and Anatolian Bronze Age can help readers to appreciate the world of Homer's epics more fully. Consequently, this chapter will consider Troy in its Mycenaean and Anatolian Bronze Age context, noting possible connections between Troy, Mycenaean Greece, and the great Hittite kingdom in north central Anatolia. It will then discuss various theories about the destruction of Troy as well as the destruction of much of the Mediterranean and Anatolian Bronze Age civilizations.

The Bronze Age city of Troy, or at least the Turkish site of Hisarlik on the northwest coast of Anatolia that most scholars now accept as having been Troy (Bryce, *Trojans* 181), thrived for nearly 2000 years (from roughly 3000 to 1200 BCE), and after the end of the Bronze Age Troy continued its existence as a city in various reduced forms for another millennium. This post–Bronze Age Troy known as Ilion was a destination site for many visitors including Xerxes and Alexander the Great (Bryce, *Trojans* 151–179). We may never know the extent to which Troy was a real city and the extent to which it was a mythic city made unforgettable by Homer's poems. However, Troy has had an extraordinary impact on the cultural history of the Greeks and on subsequent Western civilization. Whatever Troy's reality may have been, its importance to the history, literature, music and visual arts of later civilizations has been unprecedented. Even today Troy is a powerful mythic emblem of a great city destroyed by lust, greed, and foolish errors.

Troy became significant to the Greeks as the site of a final great battle shortly before the collapse of their own ancestral civilization. The heroic Greeks and Trojans who fought at Troy were mythic beings, living before the time of ordinary humans. Some of the Greeks and Trojans were even semi-divine or at least closely involved with the gods. Helen's father was Zeus and Achilles' mother was the goddess Thetis. Paris had been given the dubious honor of judging three goddesses for beauty. Although Odysseus was no god, Athena was his divine guardian and friend while Poseidon was his divine worst enemy. Helen was under the control of Aphrodite. The goddess Calypso wanted to marry Odysseus and make him immortal. Menelaus eventually got promoted to immortality because he had restored his marriage to the semi-divine Helen. Shortly after the fall of Troy, the semi-divine heroes

11

The Eastern Mediterranean in the Bronze Age, from Greece to Egypt.

and heroines left the scene. Their descendents were ordinary human beings, the Greeks who composed wonderful poems and plays about their illustrious ancestors. Consequently, the fall of Troy came to represent the beginning of the Greeks' own contemporary history as a people anciently descended from the gods, but no longer mingling with them.

Although bards probably began telling stories about the Trojan War soon after the actual war (or wars if more than one), the Homeric epics were not organized into their present form until several hundred years later, when many Greeks had already colonized the western coast of Asia Minor (Anatolia). According to Bryce, Homer was "an Ionian Greek who lived on or near the western coast of Asia Minor in the second half of the Eighth century" ("Homer at the Interface" 85). Consequently, while the Mycenaean Bronze Age provides the historical context for the Troy epics, Homer's narratives are largely rooted in the practices and values of the later Archaic Age, and the epics were addressed to the nobility of that time and place, the "prominent family groups of Greek, indigenous and mixed origins, located on or near Anatolia's Aegean coast" (Bryce, "Homer at the Interface" 87). Nonetheless, many elements of Bronze Age culture are reflected in the *Iliad* and *Odyssey*.

To some extent, both the *Iliad* and the *Odyssey* are elegies to the ending of the great

Mycenaean Greek civilization. Homer sings of the fall of Troy, but there are hints of the fall of Mycenaean Greek civilization in the *Odyssey*. On the one hand, the organization of a military confederacy to invade Troy indicates a high degree of civilization and cooperation among the Greeks. On the other hand, the *Iliad* places the Greeks at Troy for ten years, and so long a time without a local ruler would have put a serious strain on any palace state. The surviving heroes returned home to an imploding civilization. The *Odyssey* is haunted by discussions of the terrible death of Agamemnon, murdered by his wife Clytemnestra upon his arrival home. Agamemnon's death echoes the dangerous struggle Odysseus must still undertake when he finally arrives home to find his palace infested with evil suitors. The many tales Odysseus tells describe an insecure world where capture, slavery, even death, can come to any person at any time.

Bronze Age Mycenae

The Troy Cycle is rooted in the real world of the Mediterranean Bronze Age, the bronze-using cultures of the third and second millennium BCE in the lands of the eastern Mediterranean. The Trojan War is set in the later Mycenaean Bronze Age, which refers to Greek areas of the Mediterranean during the fifteenth through thirteenth centuries BCE. During that time Mycenaean Greeks based in and around the palace state of Mycenae dominated Greece and neighboring areas (Redford 242).

Although Homeric and later Greeks considered the Bronze Age Mycenaeans their ancestors, modern scholars found no physical evidence to support this belief until a wealthy amateur named Heinrich Schliemann rediscovered the Homeric cities of Troy, Mycenae, and Tiryns in the late nineteenth century. Unfortunately, Schliemann's unprofessional methods of digging destroyed or confused much of the evidence (Warren 12–18). In the twentieth century, modern methods of archaeology and linguistics finally began to decipher the complex reality of the Mediterranean Bronze Age (Vermeule, *BA* 237).

During the fourteenth and thirteenth centuries BCE, the Mycenaean Greek aristocracy lived in palaces built of huge stones (Vermeule, *BA* 264). Evidence of increasingly strong fortification of these palaces indicates frequent raiding and warfare in the area. Nonetheless, independent warlord kings such as Homer's Agamemnon, Odysseus, Nestor, and Menelaus must have lived quite well in their palaces, gaining wealth from native farm products, crafts and trade, as well as by raiding weaker kingdoms for treasure and slaves. Each palace, with its surrounding city, was a state.

Mycenaean Bronze Age palaces were staffed by highly organized bureaucracies that used a complex form of writing (Linear B) to keep track of every slave, jar of oil, weapon, chariot part, sheep, and piece of cloth. Such detailed records were useful for running the palaces as well as for collecting taxes to keep wealth flowing in. The records were written on clay tablets, some of which were accidentally baked and thus preserved by the fires that destroyed the palaces. Although these records are basically inventories of palace goods and activities, they also include more tantalizing bits of information, such as the names of Greek gods, including Zeus, Hera and Poseidon (Burkert 43). Palace records indicate that the society was organized hierarchically, with each level of leaders and workers firmly set in place (Desborough 131).

Mycenaean palaces were production and trading centers as well as ruling centers. Great quantities of goods have been found in some of them, such as "2,853 stemmed drinking cups" in one room of the palace at Pylos and "850 pots of twenty-five different shapes" in another room (Vermeule, *BA* 264). These goods were manufactured in the palace itself and in attached or nearby buildings (Vermeule, *BA* 161). Grain, wine, and oil were stored in huge containers in the palaces. Storerooms were piled with clothing, blankets, weapons, armor, cooking pots, bowls and goblets — all the requirements of a comfortable life for the aristocracy. The *Odyssey* mentions such storerooms and their treasures many times as Odysseus struggles and feasts his way home. Once home, Odysseus finally destroys the greedy suitors who are consuming the food and drink kept in his own palace storerooms.

Mycenaean palaces were not only wealthy; they were full of beautiful crafts and art. Walls were painted with graceful frescos; pottery, golden jewelry, arms and armor were elegantly designed. Poets played music and sang at feasts. Notable people, their faces covered with golden death masks, were buried with lavish grave goods in massive family tombs (Vermeule *BA*).

Troy and the Hittite Kingdom

Meanwhile, from about 1680 to 1180 BCE the powerful Hittite empire controlled much of Anatolia (Bryce, *Trojans* viii). While there is no writing extant from Troy except for a single seal, and while the Mycenaean Greek Linear B texts do not deal with politics, but rather with possessions, there are Hittite Tablets that refer to the Mycenaeans (called Ahhiyawans by the Hittites) and to Troy, known to the Hittites as Wilusa. These tablets deal with political relationships, and include a treaty between the Hittite Great King Musattalli and "a man called Alaksandu, ruler of the kingdom of Wilusa. ... The treaty makes clear that Wilusa was a vassal state of the Hittite empire, and one of four western Anatolian kingdoms called the Arzawa Lands" (Bryce, *Trojans* 107). Over the centuries, Wilusa-Troy had a fluctuating relationship with the Hittite Kingdom, at times rebelling and at other times functioning as a loyal vassal state (Bryce, *Trojans* 105 ff.).

Bryce remarks that "Wilusa-Troy ranked third amongst the western kingdoms [of Anatolia].... In spite of its remoteness, they [the Hittites] considered it an integral part of the security network that they had built up in western Anatolia" (*Trojans* 114). Troy may not have been a major city state, but it was an important fortified city on the Anatolian coast. Eric Cline explains that Troy was a "'contested periphery' located between the Mycenaeans to the west and the Hittites to the east" (11). As such, Troy had contacts with both the Anatolian Hittites and the Mycenaean Greeks over a long period, because the Mycenaeans were interested in expanding eastward, while the Hittites were interested in expanding westward (13). Troy was a rich trading center that evidently needed its massive fortifications to protect its wealth. Cline notes that "[g]oods found by archaeologists in the ruins of Troy VI ... provide evidence of the city's wealth and of the diverse ethnicity of the visitors to this international emporium" (15). Referring to the recent archaeological discoveries by the Korfmann excavation at Troy which uncovered an extended Bronze Age town surrounding the Troy Citadel, Cline asserts that these findings support "Homer's description that Troy was a large, wealthy and quite probably multi-ethnic city that could have resisted a prolonged siege by a Greek army" (15).

The Collapse of the Bronze Age

For nearly two thousand years the Mediterranean Bronze Age flourished, and during that time Troy was an intact, wealthy, important city, although destroyed and rebuilt more than once. To be sure, there were periods of unrest and warfare due to conflicts among competing Mycenaean palace states as well as among the vassal states of the Hittite Kingdom. There may also have been intermittent wars as well as extensive trade between the Mycenaeans and the Trojans. There must have been times when people suffered from natural disasters such as famines and earthquakes. New populations moved into the Mediterranean basin, which may have created strife with existing populations. Dynasties rose and fell. But the basic Bronze Age existence in highly organized, well-protected palace states continued for many generations.

Life became more dangerous in the thirteenth century. Palace cities added to their fortifications with even bigger walls and underground channels for access to water. The affluent, relatively stable Mycenaean Bronze Age culture ended in the twelfth century BCE, as did the Hittite kingdom in central Anatolia (Bryce, *Trojans* viii–ix). There are many theories about what happened and how. Each theory is built on bits of evidence gathered from the ruins of three-thousand-year-old cities.

The theories include one or more of the following causes:

- Great masses of warlike people migrating into and through the area (the Sea Peoples)
- Interstate warfare
- Climate changes such as prolonged drought
- Volcanic eruption
- Plague
- Earthquakes
- New technologies of warfare
- Overly centralized, over-populated Mycenaean palace states
- Popular uprisings

Probably some combination of these led to the weakening of Bronze Age civilization in the Mediterranean. Taking advantage of the decay, roving bands of piratical "Sea Peoples" looted and destroyed the weakened palace states of the eastern Mediterranean. Donald Redford remarks that this invasion of the Sea Peoples "changed the face of the ancient world more than any other single event before the time of Alexander the Great" (243–4).

Vermeule explains that the "Sea Peoples are one of the historical mysteries of the Late Bronze Age ... a phenomenon, not a race: tribes of coastal inhabitants who profited by the desire of the inland powers to have experienced sailors and mercenary infantry fighting for them. Between mass engagements, they seem to have freelanced" (*BA* 271). The Sea Peoples got as far as Egypt, which has records of their invasion at about this time (Redford 244). Although the Sea Peoples were finally repelled by the Egyptians in two battles around 1187 and 1180, their destructive raids left the Egyptian, Hittite and Greek kingdoms exhausted by the middle of the twelfth century (Vermeule, *BA* 273).

How did these roving barbarians destroy the great Bronze Age kingdoms? Part of their effectiveness may have been due to a shift in technology, part to the sheer numbers of the invaders (Drews 211). Archers riding in chariots were the Bronze Age kingdoms' main defense. Barbarians from various backward lands may have first entered the cities as professional foot soldiers or chariot runners, doing the dangerous, difficult work of hand-to-hand fighting with swords and javelins (Drews 157). Such foot soldiers were much cheaper to train and outfit, and hence more plentiful, than chariot warriors. Drews argues that once the Sea Peoples began their attacks in large numbers, the palace-based chariot warriors of the Bronze Age were unable to repel them (214–215).

There were enough invaders to overrun the main palace states of the eastern Mediterranean within a few years (Snodgrass 213; Desborough 21). The idea of conquest may have driven the Sea Peoples. Poverty, discomfort, hunger, and their own expanding populations probably also drove them (Redford 243). Severe climate changes or major earthquakes may also have precipitated the movements of peoples (Bouzek 172). Since the Mycenaean palace states were heavily involved in self-destructive state-to-state warfare, they may have been unstable politically (Redford 245; Sandars 198). The Mycenaean palace states may have been over-centralized, over-specialized, over-populated, and thus unable to withstand hard times (Sandars 79).

At first there was general unrest. Mycenaean palaces became increasingly fortified; a fortification wall was built at the Corinthian isthmus to keep out northern invaders. In the late thirteenth century, important Mycenaean settlements, including royal centers, were destroyed; some were rebuilt. Not long after, they were again attacked, destroyed and permanently deserted (Vermeule, *BA* 264; 270). The palace sackers were not always content to simply loot the palace wealth, kill the men, and enslave the women and children. They deliberately burned palaces to the ground, setting fires that fed off the timbers used in construction and the storerooms full of oil, leaving only rubble (Vermeule, *BA* 163, 181). Oddly enough, the most famous destroyed palace in Greek legend was not Greek at all, but Troy, sacked by the Greeks. Perhaps it was more comforting to remember the enemy's destruction than one's own.

Troy/Greece

Troy was located on the northwest coast of Anatolia (modern Turkey) within sight of Greek islands in the Aegean. In ancient times the citadel of Troy overlooked a harbor where ships could berth before traveling from the Aegean up the narrow Dardanelles Strait toward the Sea of Marmora, which in turn connected to the Black Sea. In recent years there have been conflicting scholarly opinions about the extent and importance of Troy as a harbor and trading center. According to Korfmann, Troy was a large and important trading city with an extensive population in the "lower city" below the main fortified hilltop citadel (31 ff.; Latacz 15 ff.). However Frank Kolb and others have argued that Korfmann has exaggerated and misinterpreted the data, and in fact Troy was merely an "aristocratic residence" with a very limited population, not an important city (Hertel and Kolb 86). Evidence is still being accumulated to support analysis of this contentious issue.

One reason for so much uncertainty about the nature and importance of Troy in its time is the lack of writing at the site. Certainly the Trojans, like other Bronze Age palace-state peoples, used writing for accounts as well as for correspondence, but none has been

Bronze Age Greece, including the Corinthian Isthmus.

found. It was of course chance that preserved clay tablets by baking them in the fires that destroyed the palaces. But there have been many such troves of baked tablets found at Bronze Age sites. Bryce suggests that if any such tablets eventually turn up at Troy, the language they would be written in would be Hittite, not Greek Linear B. So far, the only example of writing found at Troy is a single seal from Level VIIb1, with an inscription in Luwian, an Anatolian hieroglyphic script (*Trojans* 115–116; 67). Thus written evidence for Trojan culture is totally lacking.

Troy was strategically located at the entrance to the Dardanelles, the narrow waterway between the Mediterranean and the Sea of Marmora which led to the Black Sea. Thus Troy may have controlled this important water route between Asia and central Europe (Mellart 67–8; Mellink 94). However, some scholars doubt that many ships were able to navigate this difficult passage in Trojan times (Bryce 124–6). Hertel and Kolb remark that "Bronze Age commercial vessels were not able to overcome the adverse currents and winds in the straits" (73). It is possible that trade goods were transferred from Troy by land up to the

Black Sea and into Europe via the Danube. Whether or not they passed on to the Black Sea, Mycenaean ships had been calling at the port of Troy for centuries before Agamemnon's war against Troy (Mellink 98; Vermeule, *BA* 274). Mycenaean trade goods have been found at Troy, but it is not entirely clear what Troy exported — perhaps slaves, textiles and furs that would not leave archaeological traces, or the horses the Trojans were famous for raising and taming. People also may have come to Troy to catch or buy the abundant fish that spawned in the Dardanelles (Mee 51). Perhaps more exciting and ultimately more relevant, recent scholarship has been examining Troy within the context of its connections to the dominant Anatolian Hittite civilization of the Bronze Age, as well as its connections with Mycenaean and other Mediterranean peoples. Trevor Bryce's excellent *The Trojans and their Neighbors* (2006) offers a fascinating overview of this more recent way of thinking about Troy.

From its foundation at the start of the Bronze Age (ca. 3000 BCE), Troy had been fortified (Finley 61), evidently for good reason. Troy was destroyed and rebuilt on the same site, using the same materials, many times over. Some Troys were looted and ruined by war; other Troys were destroyed by earthquake or by fire. Ironically, Troy's final desertion, long after the Trojan War, does not seem to have been due to war. In the centuries after the Trojan War, the bay eventually filled with silt, ruining Troy's value as a harbor city (Wood 257; Zangger 216).

Whatever the ultimate truth, Troy was the city sung about in Homer's epics and it has been remembered and re-imagined for more than three thousand years. Troy was close enough to Greece to invite an invasion and rich enough to reward a successful conquest. The Aegean Sea between Troy and the mainland of Greece was full of islands that provided plenty of landfalls on the relatively short trip from Greece to Troy. Indeed, Troy was close enough to mainland Greece that in Aeschylus' play *Agamemnon* Clytemnestra arranges to have signal fires transmitted from peak to peak, quickly carrying news of the end of the Trojan War from Troy to Mycenae.

The Fall of Troy—The Beginning of Greek History

In memory, the Mycenaean Bronze Age became the age of the Greek heroes, the myth time of classical Greek culture. The kings, queens and heroes of the Trojan Cycle are often related to the gods; they blur off into ancient myths, yet they are also the ancestors of Homer's Greeks. For example, one of Helen's manifestations in the Mycenaean world was as the ancient vegetation goddess Helen Dendritis. There were also myths about her being carried away by more than one hero, including Theseus (Butterworth 174). Helen is thoroughly human, however, in book 3 of the *Iliad*, where Homer represents her as a touchingly sensitive, sorrowful woman who regrets having run away from Menelaus with Paris. She is in the grip of Aphrodite, more a victim than a temptress, and certainly not a goddess. However, Menelaus will never die because he is married to the immortal Helen, child of Zeus. Perhaps Helen's myth became attached to the story of the Trojan War as a way of explaining why the Greek confederation invaded Troy. Or, the divine Helen came to be represented as human in order to give luster to Greek ancestors who recaptured her. Mythic origins gave stature to the Greeks' heroic ancestors, even if the stories were not always very flattering.

The fall of Troy came to represent a fall from an illustrious heroic age, remembered and told about for centuries before being written down. Vermeule explains that for "...later Greeks, the Trojan War was the beginning of history, not the end. Their memory reached back only two or three generations before it" (*BA* 274).

A Mycenaean-Trojan Time Line

More than three thousand years have passed since the war or wars between Mycenaean Greece and Troy that were at the core of the Trojan epic cycle. Aside from Homer's poems, which tantalize with all the unknowns of how an ancient poem relates to a still more ancient event, there is scant, difficult-to-interpret evidence for the relations between Mycenaean Greece and Troy in the Bronze Age. The site, the date, and even who attacked Troy are all controversial and will almost certainly remain so. The available evidence is fragmentary — it includes broken bits of pottery, a few beads, grave artifacts, lists of palace contents, some ancient weapons, references to Troy (Wilusa) in ancient letters from Hittite kings, and the rubble of burned-out cities, some in mounded layers representing many re-buildings of the same city (Chadwick 14).

A time line helps show the relationship of the Mycenaean Greeks to the city of Troy. Troy was already an ancient city when the Greek peoples first arrived in Greece in the late third millennium. There were a number of Troys built, destroyed, and rebuilt on the same site before the fall of the particular Troy that Agamemnon attacked.

Table 1
Time Line of Bronze Age Troy and Greece[1]

Troy	Greece
Troy I 2900–2600; settled and fortified	
Troy II 2600–2350	Early Helladic Settlements
Troy III 2350–2200	
Arrival of proto–Greeks ca. 2100	
Troy IV 2200–1900	
Troy V 1900–1700	Middle Helladic 1900–1600
Troy VI 1700–1300; new powerful culture	Mycenaean Period 1600–1150
Ca. 1500 Troy destroyed by war and rebuilt (first Trojan War?)	
Ca. 1300 Troy destroyed by earthquake	
Troy VIIa 1300–1200; Troy rebuilt, smaller and more crowded	
Ca. 1200 Homer's Trojan War?	Ca. 1250 increasing fortification of Mycenaean palaces; invasions of Dorians; invasions of Sea Peoples
Troy VIIa burned (destroyed by war)	
Troy VIIb1 1200; rebuilt still smaller and poorer	Ca. 1200 Bronze Age ends

As the table shows, Troy had been destroyed and rebuilt numerous times before the Mycenaeans may have sacked it in Homer's Trojan War. Probably there was more than one war between the Mycenaeans and the Trojans (Vermeule, "PC" 85–88; Finley 61, 66). There are stories as well as archaeological evidence of a first and second Trojan War. The most powerful Troy (VI) may have been destroyed by a war with Mycenae in the fifteenth, not the thirteenth, century (Vermeule, *BA* 275–6). The second Trojan War may then have come at the end of the Bronze Age, destroying an already weakened, less important Troy (VIIa) (Vermeule, "PC" 87–9; Mellink, "Postscript" 100).

Mycenae and Troy had a great deal in common. Both Mycenaean and Trojan noblemen "were horse-breakers, charioteers, warriors, sailors and soldiers" (Mellink, "Postscript" 98). Wars between Mycenaean Greece and Troy may have occurred as outgrowths of their connections and shared interests. Almost certainly there was contact between Mycenaeans and Trojans, as "Mycenaeans were in constant touch with the Anatolian coast, often aggressively..." (Vermeule, *BA* 276). Trojan Prince Paris could well have visited a Mycenaean kingdom, met Helen there, and run off with her to Troy, providing a compelling excuse for the Greeks to go to war.

Perhaps the Trojan War occurred at the height of Mycenae and Troy, around the fifteenth century, and the sacked city was Troy VI (Vermeule, "PC" 85, 91; Mee 52). Perhaps the Trojan War came at the decaying end of both cultures in the thirteenth century and the sacked palace state was Troy VIIa (the generally accepted estimate). Perhaps the Trojan War itself was a piratical raid instead of the ten-year siege of the *Iliad*. To confuse matters further, there are bits of pre–Mycenaean poetry scattered through Homer's *Iliad* (Vermeule, "PC" 85–6). Does that mean that the Trojan War was even more ancient than the Mycenaeans? Or is it more likely that some parts of the poems were already ancient before they became attached to the Troy Cycle? Since oral-formulaic poetry is composed using many interchangeable "formula" phrases, it is possible that the pre–Mycenaean fragments came from earlier epics about other topics.

Vermeule suggests that perhaps the Trojan War became "the ultimate version" of the ancient epic theme of the great siege of a great city, "...because it was genuinely the last successful siege of a walled city in the old style. After its conquest, the Mycenaean world became too fragmented to undertake another such allied expedition" (*BA* 277). The rapidly decaying palace states no longer had the resources in wealth or political goodwill to gather an army from several allied states. Certainly the sorry tales of the homecomings of the Greek heroes suggest that their world was fast falling apart. Clytemnestra and her lover Aegisthus murdered Agamemnon in his bath shortly after he arrived home. Odysseus had to cleanse his palace of would-be murderous usurpers. Within a few years, the great Mycenaean palaces were destroyed, their Bronze Age civilization at an end.

Fascinating as it is to speculate on these issues, the "facts" that seem fairly reliable are as follows:

- Wealthy, powerful Mycenaean fortified palaces were located at several sites mentioned by Homer, including Mycenae, Sparta, Tiryns and Pylos.
- Troy was an ancient fortified city on the northwest coast of Anatolia that traded with Mycenaean Greeks.
- Conflict between the Mycenaean Greeks and the Trojans occurred at one or more times.
- Oral epics were composed about one or more of these conflicts.

- Great disruption and destruction of Bronze Age palace life occurred in the late thirteenth century BCE.
- Large-scale movements of peoples and armies were frequent at this time, especially of the Sea Peoples.
- Bronze Age civilizations around the Mediterranean ended abruptly in the late thirteenth century.
- Fragments of older Mycenaean poems and themes became interwoven with the Troy Cycle of stories composed after Agamemnon's expedition to Troy.

After the Bronze Age

Soon after the fall of Troy, Mycenaean civilization collapsed. The population crashed at the end of the thirteenth century and the great palaces disappeared; nothing like them was ever built again. By the end of the twelfth century, there were far fewer people and populated sites in the area than in the thirteenth century BCE (Crossland 13; Vermeule, *BA* 257; Snodgrass 365–7). During the centuries after the fall of Troy, waves of immigrants speaking various Greek dialects came down into Greece from the north. Meanwhile, people from the Greek mainland migrated eastward to the islands in the Aegean Sea and onward to the coast of Asia Minor. From about 1200 to 1000 BCE, a so-called Dark Age replaced the Mycenaean Bronze Age. There are few archaeological records from this period, so not much is known about it, thus it is dark to us; it may have been less obscure to the people of that time. Troy was partially rebuilt several times over the following centuries, but never again became the important city it had been in the Bronze Age.

Again, a time line is helpful for understanding the situation.

Table 2
Time Line of Troy and Greece During the Dark Age[2]

Troy	*Greece*
Troy VIIb1, 2 and 3 1200–950 BCE; minor rebuilding	
1100 (Early Dark Age)	Population crash
1000–950 (Later Dark Age) Troy site abandoned	Greek colonies established in Asia Minor; Protogeometric pottery
900	Geometric pottery
800	Greek writing reintroduced — Phoenician alphabet

Continuities from Mycenaean Greece to Later Greek Culture

Later Greeks recognized the Mycenaeans as their ancestors. They considered the Bronze Age their "heroic age," an earlier stage in their own history (Finley 71). Although there were profound differences between the Mycenaean world and that of later Greece, there were also elements that continued. For example, the names of some Greek gods in the Mycenaean Linear B records suggest religious continuity (Burkert 48; Coldstream 328). Although there is no architectural record to show how people lived during the Dark Age, there are continuities in pottery. Also, a number of sites continued to be inhabited, even though the standard of living collapsed (Vermeule, *BA* 270). Indeed Vermeule asserts that there "...was no break between the Mycenaean and Homeric worlds, only change" (*BA* 309).

The change was enormous, however. Partly, it must have been the result of various migrants wandering, warring, and eventually mingling, creating new composite cultures. Another factor may simply have been the relatively greater freedom to innovate that people had once their lives were no longer dominated by the great ancient palace economies (Drews 224; Finley 68). Certainly, there was more room for individual experiment and development once the centralized bureaucratic palaces were gone.

At any rate, the general upheaval during the Dark Age was so profound that when Greek culture again emerged in the archaeological records of the eighth century, the art was different, the writing was different, the pottery was different and the buildings were different. Modern scholars call this emerging, profoundly changed culture the Archaic Age. It is in this period that Homer composed the *Iliad* and the *Odyssey*, epic recollections of the heroic past.

2

Oral Poetry and the Troy Cycle

The Archaic Age

The Mycenaean Bronze Age had been a period of great wealth and immense palaces, but Homer flourished in a period of great poetry. During the centuries between the end of the Bronze Age (ca. 1200 BCE) and the time of Homer (ca. 750 BCE), the civilization of the Greeks shrank and then changed. Meanwhile stories about the past were transmitted orally because writing fell out of use (if indeed it had ever been used to tell stories instead of to count possessions). This means that in order to appreciate Homer, one needs to be aware of the differences between the Bronze Age civilization he told tales about and the Archaic Age civilization that produced the *Iliad* and *Odyssey*.

As the Dark Age lightened, a reinvigorated Greek civilization flourished and expanded. Tribes speaking various Greek dialects had been moving south into Greece, east across the Aegean, and onto the Anatolian mainland since the end of the Bronze Age. What may once have been Trojan territory in the Bronze Age was now Greek. Homer himself probably lived in western Anatolia, nearer Troy than Athens.

Homer composed two great oral epics, the *Iliad* and the *Odyssey*, in the Archaic Age. Writing was reintroduced during this period, and these epics were eventually committed to writing.

Table 3
Time Line of Greece and Troy in the Archaic Age
(Whitman, 65–86; Coldstream, 341–56)

Approximate Dates BCE	*Greece*	*Troy*
700 (Archaic Age)	"Homer" composed epics (stories much older); revived interest in heroic past; reintroduction of writing (from Phoenicians)	Troy VIII; Greek colony of Ilion, "a small market town"
545	Tyranny of Peisistratids	
510	Homer written down and/or organized into the form we have today	

The Troy Cycle: Preserving History and Creating Identity

The heroic stories of the Troy Cycle helped to create and preserve a common history and identity for Greeks everywhere. The Troy Cycle connected the various tribes of Greeks through the magnificent adventures of their quasi-mythic, victorious ancestors. The Troy Cycle also connected the Greek tribes through its language. The traditional epic language that Homer used drew from several Greek dialects and employed many archaic words and formulas. This poetic language was from, and for, all the tribes of the Greeks, not just a single tribe that lived in one place and spoke one dialect (Coldstream 341–357; Vermeule, *BA* 264).

Both the *Iliad* and the *Odyssey* tell of events from the mythical, yet historical, time of the Greek hero-ancestors. These heroic men and women talked with the gods and even mated with them, producing semi-divine offspring that founded human ruling families. The heroes were far stronger than later men and could wield weapons that no common mortal could cope with by Homer's time; Achilles could even battle a raging river god and survive. The heroes were the storied lords of the magnificent ancient Mycenaean civilization. Evidence of these heroes was plentiful in a land containing enormous ruined palaces and wonderful tombs built of stones so massive that giants or gods must have erected them.

Homer's poems may even have inspired the Greeks of his time to re-identify the ancient neglected Mycenaean tombs as the tombs of their own heroic ancestors, semi-divine and capable of helping or harming those who lived nearby. Hero-worship and offerings at these ancient tombs actually increased in the eighth century after Homer's time. Even more odd, in the eighth century Greeks began to burn their dead, something they had not done before and then ceased doing after about fifty years. Perhaps Homer's epics inspired them to recreate their own past by preparing elaborate funerals imitating the fiery pyre of Patroclus imagined and sung by Homer (Coldstream 346–7; 349–51).

Oral-Formulaic Poetry

The studies by Milman Parry, Albert Lord, and others of oral-formulaic composition have demonstrated convincingly that the composition of the *Iliad* and *Odyssey* was oral. For many generations there were no fixed texts. Albert Lord remarks, "the songs were ever in flux, and were crystallized by each singer only when he sat before an audience and told them the tale..." (151). The tales were not original, but each retelling was an original recreation out of traditional story phrases and story materials. Lord argues that Homer was an experienced poet singer who had sung songs about Achilles and Odysseus many times before perhaps dictating them to scribes in the fixed (because written) forms of the *Iliad* and the *Odyssey* (151).

Before they have writing, people transmit their history to future generations orally. Oral poetry employs a large number of formulas, word patterns that can be used over and over again to complete the rhythm of a line. The formulas help the poet to remember crucial information and to compose by plugging in blocks of words instead of having to constantly recombine groups of words into poetically attractive phrases.

Homeric formulas are words and phrases that are used repeatedly to describe a person, place or thing. Each phrase fits into a particular metrical slot in a line of poetry. For example, here are pairs of epithets, each reserved for a single hero with a major role in Homer.

Table 4
Multiple Epithets for Two Homeric Heroes
(Adapted from Parry 92)

Hero's name	Epithet	Syllables	Frequency in Iliad *and* Odyssey
Odysseus	polymetis (of many devices)	4	82
	polytlas (much suffering)	3	38

Hero's name	Epithet	Syllables	Frequency in Iliad *and* Odyssey
Achilles	podus okus (swift of foot)	4	31
	podarkes (strong of foot)	3	21

In each case, the first example has four syllables and the second has three, but the meanings are not much different. Some of these formulas are "fixed" and can be used wherever there is a space in the line that needs a certain rhythm; other formulas are adapted to the particular meaning of an event. They help a poet to compose by providing ready-made or easily adaptable parts for the poetic line. Such formulas can easily be remembered even if their language becomes archaic. A professional reciter, a *rhapsode*, would know the general story outlines of each epic and its many subplots, and he would have a hoard of traditional formulas in his head. Then, depending on the time available for his song, the needs of the occasion, and his audience, he would select story elements to recite and form the recitation out of his own words richly mixed with the oral formulas. This would produce a recitation that was always new and always comfortingly familiar. Homer may have been the best of these *rhapsodes*, or the *rhapsode* whose work has survived, or simply the name attached by tradition to the composer of the *Iliad* and *Odyssey*.

The Troy Cycle

The Greeks of the Dark Age created, preserved and retold many epic stories about the Heroic Age of Mycenae. One major group, or cycle, of these stories deals with the Trojan War, that last burst of glory for the Mycenaean Greeks, shortly before their entire civilization collapsed. I will refer to this group of epics as the Troy Cycle. (It is also called The Trojan War Cycle and the Trojan Cycle.)

There were originally eight epics in the Troy Cycle. Together they dealt with all the matter of Troy, from the conflict at the wedding of Peleus and Thetis that led to the judgment of Paris through the war at Troy, to the death of Odysseus and his sons' marriages (Stanford

82). All except the *Iliad*, the *Odyssey,* and a few fragments of the others are now lost, but the epics were listed and summarized by Proclus in later antiquity:

Table 5
Epics of the Troy Cycle
(Coldstream 342; Stanford 81–6)

Cypria	Marriage of Peleus and Thetis; quarrel of the gods and goddesses; judgment of Paris; rape of Helen; beginnings of Trojan War
Iliad	Quarrel between Achilles and Agamemnon in ninth year of the siege of Troy; death of Hector
Aethiopis	Trojan War to death of Achilles
Little Iliad	Last part of Trojan War
Sack of Troy	End of Trojan War
Returns	Greek heroes, except Odysseus, return home
Odyssey	Odysseus returns home after ten years' wandering
Telegonia	Later adventures of Odysseus and his death at hands of his son by Circe, Telegonus

The Troy Cycle narrated a comprehensive chunk of history that included important events of the Greek mythological and historical world. Zeus had decided on the Trojan War to relieve Earth of its excess human population. To start his plan, Zeus sent the goddess Eris (Strife) to the wedding of Peleus and Thetis (parents-to-be of Achilles). Eris rolled a golden apple, inscribed "to the fairest," into the midst of three goddesses — Hera, Aphrodite, and Athena — and the goddesses quarreled over who should get the apple. This led to the Judgment of Paris, the rape (abduction) of Helen, and then the war at Troy itself ("Eris").

SOME MAIN CHARACTERS OF THE TROY CYCLE

The following alphabetical lists give brief descriptions of some of the important Trojan War characters and their roles in the Troy Cycle.

Greek Deities

Aphrodite: Goddess of love; married to Hephaestus; lover of Ares

Apollo: God of plague for infractions of ritual; angry at Greeks because Agamemnon insults his priest Chryses

Ares: God of war; lover of Aphrodite

Athena: Goddess of wisdom; born from Zeus' head; Odysseus' patron

Eris: Goddess of strife; throws golden apple which starts quarrel among Hera, Athena, and Aphrodite over which one is the most beautiful

Hephaestus: God of the forge; lame; spouse of Aphrodite

Hera: Goddess of marriage; sister and wife of Zeus

Hermes: Messenger god

Iris: Messenger goddess

Polyphemus: Son of Poseidon; man-eating Cyclops; traps Odysseus and his men in his cave; Odysseus blinds him

Poseidon: God of the sea, earthquakes and horses; brother of Zeus; father of Cyclops Polyphemus

Thetis: Sea nymph; mother of Achilles; pleads with Zeus to let the Trojans overcome the Greek armies to assuage Achilles' anger over his loss of honor

Zeus: God of the sky and thunderbolts; chief deity; father of many half-mortal children; final judge of law and order; initiator of the Trojan War

Greeks

Achilles: Son of Peleus, a mortal, and Thetis, a sea nymph; greatest Greek warrior at Troy; leader of Myrmidons; quarrels with Agamemnon over Briseis, a war-prize concubine

Agamemnon: High king of Greece; king of Mycenae; leads Greek armies against Troy; husband of Clytemnestra; sacrifices their daughter Iphigenia to get favorable winds to sail to Troy; killed by Clytemnestra

Ajax: Excellent Greek warrior; vies unsuccessfully with Odysseus to inherit Achilles' armor; goes mad and kills himself

Argonauts: Sailors, including Heracles and Jason, on quest for the Golden Fleece; try to land at Troy, but are rudely sent away by King Laomedon

Calchas: Greek seer; advises Agamemnon to return his war-prize woman Chryseis to her father Chryses to stop the plague sent by Apollo

Clytemnestra: Daughter of Zeus and Leda; sister to Helen; murders her husband Agamemnon

Diomedes: Brave Greek warrior

Helen: Daughter of Zeus and Leda; sister to Clytemnestra; wife to Menelaus; immediate cause of the war: seized by or runs away with Paris to Troy

Heracles: Major Greek semi-divine hero; one of the Argonauts; returns with Jason to destroy Troy after the Golden Fleece quest (also called Hercules)

Iphigenia: Daughter of Agamemnon and Clytemnestra; perhaps sacrificed so that the winds will blow, sending the Greek fleet to Troy

Jason: Leader of the Argonauts; wins the Golden Fleece; elopes with Medea; helps Heracles to conquer Troy to punish King Laomedon for his rudeness

Menelaus: King of Sparta; brother of Agamemnon; husband of Helen

Nestor: King of Pylos; wise counselor

Odysseus: King of Ithaca; father of Telemachus; excellent counselor; devises Trojan Horse strategy; takes ten years to return home after the war

Orestes: Son of Agamemnon and Clytemnestra; avenges his father's death by killing Clytemnestra

Patroclus: Achilles' dear friend; while Patroclus is dressed in Achilles' armor, Hector kills him

Penelope: Faithful wife of Odysseus

Telemachus: Son of Odysseus and Penelope

Trojans and Allies

Aeneas: Trojan prince; not important until Virgil's *Aeneid*

Andromache: Wife of Hector; mother of Astyanax

Astyanax: Young son of Andromache and Hector; killed by the Greeks to prevent his growing up to avenge Hector's death

Briseis: Achilles' war-prize woman; seized in a raid; taken by Agamemnon to replace his war-prize woman Chryseis

Cassandra: Trojan princess; cursed by Apollo to always speak the truth and never be believed; carried off by Agamemnon as a war prize; murdered by Clytemnestra

Chryseis: Daughter of Chryses; Agamemnon's war-prize woman; seized in a raid; returned to her father

Chryses: Apollo's priest; his daughter is wrongfully kept as a war-prize by Agamemnon

Hector: Son of Priam and Hecuba; husband of Andromache; father of Astyanax; Troy's finest hero; kills Patroclus; killed by Achilles

Hecuba: Wife of Priam; mother of Hector

Laomedon: King of Troy when Heracles and Jason conquer it; father of Priam

Paris: Son of Priam and Hecuba; judges beauty of three goddesses; marries Helen after bringing her to Troy; kills Achilles with an arrow after the events of the *Iliad*

Priam: King of Troy when Greek armies under Agamemnon destroy it; husband of Hecuba; father of Hector and forty-nine other children

Troilus: Trojan prince; son of Hecuba and Priam; not important to the story before the European Middle Ages

AN OVERVIEW OF THE STORY OF TROY

Stories tell of at least two Trojan Wars, the first when Laomedon was king of Troy and the second when his son Priam was king. The first Trojan War occurred when Jason, Hercules and the Argonauts were seeking the Golden Fleece. They stopped off at Troy for rest and refueling, but King Laomedon refused them hospitality, forcing them to leave. Other versions suggest that Laomedon tried to cheat Hercules out of promised pay for contracted heroic deeds ("Heracles"). After successfully completing the Golden Fleece quest, Jason and Hercules gathered an army of Greeks and destroyed Troy to punish King Laomedon. Priam, Laomedon's son, survived and rebuilt Troy.

The underlying cause of the second Trojan War is told in the *Cypria*. The burden of too many human beings disturbed the earth and Zeus conceived of the Trojan War to lower the population and relieve the earth. Zeus instigated the path toward war by allowing Eris (Strife) to attend the wedding banquet of Peleus and Thetis, where Eris stirred up conflict among the goddesses Hera, Athena and Aphrodite over who was the most beautiful ("Eris").

The three goddesses asked Paris, a rather foolish, lady-loving son of King Priam of Troy, to judge which of them was the most beautiful. Each goddess offered her own special bribe. Paris chose Aphrodite's bribe, possession of the most beautiful woman in the world. That woman was Helen, married to King Menelaus, one of the regional Greek kings, so Paris set off to Greece with a war party, seized her (perhaps with her cooperation), and brought her (and much of her treasure) back to Troy, where they were married.

Menelaus then went to his brother Agamemnon, the high king of the Greeks, and asked for help retrieving his wife from Troy. Perhaps his main motive for wanting her back was to legitimize his kingship — Menelaus was king of Sparta because he was married to

Helen. Luckily for Menelaus, every eligible king in Greece had wooed Helen. At that time, Odysseus had suggested that they all swear an oath to support and protect her and her chosen husband, which they did. Agamemnon called in this oath and assembled warriors and ships from all over Greece at Aulis. However, the goddess Artemis sent unfavorable winds which prevented the Greek fleet from sailing for Troy until Agamemnon sacrificed his daughter Iphigenia. The Greek army then besieged Troy for ten years.

During the ninth year of the siege, Agamemnon and Achilles, the best Greek warrior, quarreled bitterly over returning Chryseis, Agamemnon's woman war-prize, to her father, the priest Chryses. Then they quarreled over who would possess Achilles' woman war-prize, Briseis. Agamemnon reluctantly returned Chryseis and thoughtlessly seized Briseis from Achilles. Feeling shamefully dishonored, Achilles withdrew his men, the Myrmidons, from the fighting. Many Greeks died because of the absence of Achilles and his troops, but Achilles refused to reenter the war until, by a misadventure (although according to Zeus' plan), Achilles' dearest friend Patroclus was killed by Hector. Achilles finally reconciled with Agamemnon and then reentered the battle, killing Hector, the greatest Trojan warrior. The story of Achilles' wrath is told in Homer's *Iliad*.

In the tenth year of the siege the Greeks pretended to depart from Troy, leaving the hollow Trojan Horse (its wooden belly full of soldiers) on the shore. The Trojans foolishly brought the wooden horse into the city, not realizing that they were bringing Greeks inside their walls. After dark the Greeks came out of the horse's belly and opened the gates to let in the entire Greek army. Troy was burned, many Trojans were slaughtered, and the women and children were taken away as slaves. This was the end of the second Trojan War.

The victorious Greeks began traveling home. Agamemnon returned to his wife Clytemnestra, who conspired with her lover Aegisthus to kill him, at least partially because of his sacrifice of Iphigenia. The murder of Agamemnon is referred to frequently in the *Odyssey* as a warning about the potential dangers of homecoming. Helen returned to Greece and resumed her marriage with Menelaus. They were living more or less comfortably together when Odysseus' son Telemachus visited their palace in the *Odyssey*. Odysseus was the last Greek warrior to return home from Troy. The *Odyssey* tells the story of his amazing voyage as well as his victory over the wicked suitors who were camped in his palace, devouring his cattle and sheep, drinking away his stored wealth of wine, and intimidating his virtuous wife Penelope.

There were also stories about Odysseus' later adventures in the *Telegonia*, a sequel to the *Odyssey* composed by Eugammon of Cyrene in the sixth century BCE. The *Odyssey* ends with the implication that Odysseus' worst troubles were over, but not so according to the *Telegonia*. In that epic, Odysseus continued his infidelities and wanderings until Telegonus, his son by Circe, killed him (Stanford 86–9).

HOMER

The person or persons who assembled Trojan War stories into the *Iliad* and the *Odyssey* remain unknown. There may have been many "Homers," poets who sang the songs of the Epic Troy Cycle (Vermeule, "PC" 86–7). Perhaps one Homer wrote both the *Iliad* and the *Odyssey* (Coldstream 341); perhaps there were two Homers: one composed the *Iliad* and the other composed the *Odyssey* (Finley 82).

Greek tradition says the composer of the *Iliad* and the *Odyssey* was a blind man named Homer who probably lived about 750 BCE in Asia Minor. Homer retold stories about an ancient time, only partially remembered, when gods and humans still mingled and heroes strode the earth. Homer accurately described Mycenaean sites, chariots, artifacts, armor and weapons, but he did not know much about the complex palace bureaucracies of the Mycenaean age that accounted for every sheep, slave and cooking pot. For example, Odysseus' palace at Ithaca was a simple building when compared to the enormous Bronze Age palace complexes that have actually been excavated. Homer also did not seem to be very familiar with writing, mentioning it only once, although the Bronze Age palaces kept extensive records. Homer's heroic age was a mixture of memory and ideals, based more on his own times in Greek colonies in Asia Minor than on the lost actual civilization of the Mycenaean Greeks (Coldstream 341–56; Chadwick 180–186; Finley 82–4; Vermeule "PC").

The very flattering portrait of the gifted blind singer Demodocus in the *Odyssey* may be Homer's self-portrait. Demodocus is a skilled singer who lives at the court of Alcinous, King of the Phaiacians. He is treated with respect, seated on a specially placed silver-studded chair, his lyre nearby, and provided with good food and drink. Odysseus shows his personal respect for the singer by cutting a choice piece of meat and sending it to Demodocus, accompanied by flattering words about how all men should respect singers since the Muse loves them.

Demodocus sings three songs while Odysseus is visiting Alcinous. The first tells about a quarrel between Achilles and Odysseus. The next song accompanies young people dancing; blind Demodocus is led into the center of the dancing circle, where he plays his lyre and sings about the affair of Aphrodite and Ares and how they are caught and shamed by Aphrodite's husband Hephaistos (Hephaestus). The last song is about the Trojan Horse.

Demodocus knows the stories of the gods, such as the tale of Aphrodite, as well as the stories of the Trojan War. He can respond to a request for a particular story, or he can simply respond to the inspiration of his Muse and start singing. He would have spent his life learning his craft, listening to stories and memorizing traditional phrasings, or formulas, as well as the events of the main epic cycles. Each of his performances would be a retelling, never the same, yet always containing the essential actions, the beloved phrasings, of the traditional stories. He could arouse delight or sorrow in his audience.

Similarly, Homer's poems would have been recited by *rhapsodes*, professional singers who accompanied themselves with simple stringed instruments as they sang for their suppers. Eventually, Homer or others wrote down the Homeric poems, and they were probably organized into the form we have today in the sixth century, under the tyrant Peisistratus (Whitman 65–86).

3

Homer's *Iliad*
The War at Troy

Homer is the reason we still know about the war at Troy. He composed two magnificent epic poems about the Trojan War, the *Iliad* and the *Odyssey*, around the eighth century BCE. This was about five hundred years after the war itself. One reason that the Trojan War became so important to later Greeks such as Homer was that they considered the Greek victors their ancestors. Another reason was that the Trojan War, if indeed it occurred, coincided with the collapse of the Mycenaean Bronze Age.

Thus, its fall represented, at least in story, the last great victory of the Mycenaean Greeks before the collapse of their civilization. Homer lived in a less glorious age. Although Greeks had colonized Asia Minor after the Trojan War, they were no longer as prosperous (or, perhaps, as piratical) as during the Bronze Age. However, there still was a town of Troy (called Ilion) in Homer's day, and Homer may have lived in the vicinity, earning his living by telling stories about the glorious past of the Greek conquerors, yet sympathetic to the vanquished Trojans.

Homer was said to be blind, but his vivid images and stories of Troy have survived and thrived for nearly three millennia. Homer's Troy is a mixture of some fairly accurate details of the Bronze Age and other details from his own time, bound together by poetic imagination and elegant, swift-moving language. The *Iliad* and *Odyssey* have been so frequently praised, analyzed, translated, borrowed from, adapted and imitated that a study of Homer and his literary descendents can easily become a study of the history of Western literary culture from Troy to the twenty-first century. People have continued to read and imitate Homer because he was a wonderful poet who told wonderful stories.

The *Iliad* is the poem of Troy; the story takes place in the Greek camp, before the walls of Troy, and within the city itself. It is the ninth year of a ten-year siege. Achilles, the greatest Greek warrior, quarrels with Agamemnon, the greedy, arrogant high king of the Greek army. They fight over women war-prizes, Chryseis and Briseis. Achilles pushes Agamemnon to return his war-prize woman Chryseis to her father, a priest of Apollo, in order to stop the plague in the Greek camp. Agamemnon, furious, takes Achilles' war-prize woman Briseis as his compensation. Achilles, even more furious, vows to stop fighting until the Trojan warriors push through the Greek camp up to their ships at the shore. Achilles also gets his goddess mother Thetis to petition Zeus to keep the Trojans killing the Greeks until this happens. Zeus agrees and the terrible "plan of Zeus" is set.

Many Greeks are killed, Achilles sulks in his tent, Achilles' best friend Patroclus is killed, and then Achilles rampages, slaughtering Trojans. Even the gods get into the battle, fighting one another until Zeus puts a stop to the chaos. The poem ends rather peacefully with two funerals, one for Achilles' dear friend Patroclus and one for Hector, who killed Patroclus. Soon Achilles will die; next year Troy will fall.

Furious short-tempered Achilles and arrogant greedy Agamemnon are not suitable role models for later, more civilized societies, and this became a problem for future generations. Even worse, Homer's stories of the gods quarreling with one another and engaging in wild battles became unacceptable to later generations with different, more restrained ideas of deity.

Homer's vision of the relationship of mortals to gods is chilling. To Zeus, human beings are like the poppies of the field: they bloom briefly and die. The gods are like spectators betting on a violent football game that gets out of hand until Zeus finally calls a halt. But Homer's language, the power of the narrative, and Achilles' heroic character are unforgettable. The *Iliad* has not only survived but flourished, carrying memories of Troy into the twenty-first century.

Homer's Greeks and Trojans

Homer's Greeks are winners, his Trojans, losers. Nonetheless, the Trojans and Greeks share many traits, such as the love of warfare, excellence, gold, adventure, trade, women, and horses. In the *Iliad*, the Trojans often seem more civilized than the Greeks. Priam is a better king and father than Agamemnon, Hector a kinder man than Achilles, Andromache a far better wife than Helen. Nonetheless, Homer's Troy is not Greek. Priam is an oriental ruler with an oriental harem, who has fifty sons and twelve daughters, some by his wife Hecuba and others by his concubines.

There is something exotic and decadent about Troy. The Trojans are not as politically astute, nor as aggressive, as the Greeks. Paris is a no-brain fop, but the Trojans allow him to act in ways that are disastrous for their city. Helen is pure trouble, yet the Trojans let her stay, even though her presence dooms them. Hector is the finest Trojan warrior, yet in his final test of will against Achilles, Hector breaks and tries to run away. Homer's Troy is rich, ancient, past its prime, somewhat effete, an oriental kingdom to admire and plunder.

Even the gods have decided that Troy is ripe to fall. Zeus is ultimately on the side of the Greeks. There are stories of Priam's father, King Laomedon, who was mean-spirited and politically foolish. He tried to avoid paying his debt to the gods and refused hospitality to Jason and Hercules. Troy, for all its power and elegance, has smudges on its reputation. Excellence, and therefore victory, is clearly on the side of the Greeks.

However, the Trojans must display sufficient excellence to provide glory to their conquerors. And so they do. Indeed, they are good enough to inspire later civilizations to make them into *their* ancestral heroes. This is a wonderful irony of the Troy stories — the winners become transmuted into losers and the losers into winners in the great culture wars of later civilizations.

The Iliad

Before considering re-creations of the characters and story of the *Iliad* over nearly three thousand years, it is important to start with a solid grounding in its story. The *Iliad* is about a destructive quarrel between Achilles and Agamemnon over possession of war-prize women. The rest of this chapter will present an overview of the *Iliad*, give a detailed summary of the plot, and consider the characters of Achilles and Agamemnon as heroic in the *Iliad*, yet less than admirable to later generations.

The *Iliad* can be difficult for modern readers, because it tells of an archaic, heroic, violent world whose values are strange to us and whose heroes, by our standards, behave badly. The *Iliad* is a violent poem about brutal men, none more brutal than Achilles. Their excellence is in their pursuit of fame and honor, in their intelligence, leadership and friendships, and in their killing skills. Their anger is passionate, brutal, at times whipped into mad frenzy by the gods. Homer describes battles in carefully anatomical, formulaic detail; the spear goes in the liver and out the nostrils; the body drops to the dust; the corpses pile up; many brave men die over one priceless, worthless woman, Helen, who ran off with the worthless Trojan Prince Paris.

The *Iliad* is about escalating anger and its final bitter resolution. It starts with the pointless, impious anger of Agamemnon at the priest Chryses, who tries to ransom his daughter with appropriate treasure. Next is the righteous anger of Chryses at Agamemnon for refusing to accept the ransom and return his daughter. Chryses invokes Apollo, who starts the plague, which kills the Greeks. Then there is the mutual anger of Agamemnon and Achilles as they quarrel over redistributing war-prize women, the petulant anger of Achilles as he withdraws his men from the fighting, and Achilles' murderous fury when Hector kills Patroclus. The anger eventually spreads to the elements (fire and water) and to the gods, who enter the battle as eagerly violent as the human beings. Only when Zeus declares "enough" do gods and humans let go of their anger and resume an orderly, civil life.

In *The Pity of Achilles*, Junyo Kim argues convincingly that a major theme of the *Iliad* is the way Achilles' wrath gradually and painfully becomes transformed into pity, first for his fellow Greeks, and finally for all human beings. She explains that a central issue in the *Iliad* is the concept of *philotes*, or the connected group of warriors, the friends. It is only this band of friends who are able to confer honor and glory on a warrior, while the group strives to take away honor and glory from their enemies. Thus, when Agamemnon takes away Achilles' honor (by taking Briseis), Agamemnon estranges himself from Achilles; they are no longer bound as friends. Since the Greeks (except for Achilles' Myrmidons) are bound to follow Agamemnon, Achilles feels no further allegiance to them. This precipitates Achilles' wrath at his no-longer-fellow Greeks. Kim explains that Achilles' wrath is finally resolved in two places: first when he sends Patroclus out to help the Greeks in book 16, and second when Achilles reconciles with Priam as a fellow-mortal in book 24 (181–2). Her book is especially helpful for those of us who have real trouble appreciating Achilles as a hero because we tend to be repelled by his incredibly violent behavior.

Although the *Iliad* is about uncontrolled anger and its terrible consequences, the poem itself is remarkably controlled and patterned, both by its elaborate formulaic language and by the organization of its parts in relation to the whole. For example, as Whitman explains, the *Iliad* starts with refusal of ransom, plague, seizure of a war-prize woman, a quarrel and funerals in book 1, and ends with accepting ransom, returning Hector's body, (momentary) reconciliation between Achilles and Priam, and Hector's funeral in book 24 (255, 260).

THE STORY OF THE *ILIAD*

Because the characters (see Chapter 2) and plot of the *Iliad* underlie so many future Troy stories, I am going to present a very detailed summary of the entire epic, book by book. If you are already familiar with the *Iliad*, you might want to skip to the end of this section and start again after the summary of book 24, below.

Book 1. This book introduces the main characters and themes of the *Iliad*. During the ten-year siege of Troy, Greeks keep their fighting skills honed and their supplies replenished by raiding sites around Troy. After a raid or battle, the spoils are divided up among the victorious participants. In the ninth year of the siege, Agamemnon and Achilles get into a major quarrel over woman-spoils from such a raid. Agamemnon has selected the daughter of Chryses, a priest of Apollo, as his share of the spoils. When Chryses brings ransom to retrieve his daughter, Agamemnon rudely rebuffs him with threats. Chryses prays for revenge to Apollo, who obligingly sends a plague to kill the Greeks.

After many Greeks die of plague, the survivors hold a council to decide what to do. Calchas, a diviner, says Apollo sent the plague because Agamemnon refused to release Chryses' daughter. Agamemnon complains that if he gives up his woman-prize, then all the other Greeks will be ahead of him in prizes. Achilles, the greatest of the Greek soldiers, is disgusted by Agamemnon's pettiness and says so. Agamemnon retorts that he will take Achilles' woman-prize, Briseis, to replace the woman he has to return to Chryses. Achilles is furious and ready to strike Agamemnon, but Hera, who loves both Agamemnon and Achilles, sends Athena to stay Achilles' sword.

Agamemnon returns Chryses' daughter and then orders Briseis to be taken from Achilles. Weeping, furious at Agamemnon, Achilles prays to his immortal mother Thetis. He asks her to petition Zeus to punish the Greeks by making many of them die at the hands of the Trojans, until the fighting comes up to the Greek ships beached on the shore. This will increase Achilles' honor, showing that the Greeks cannot thrive without his help. Thetis gets Zeus, who owes her a favor, to agree to this, although Zeus warns that it will create conflict between him and his sister-wife Hera.

Book 1 closes with an ominous foretaste of the consequences of involving Zeus in human affairs. There is an uneasy banquet on Olympus. Hera is angry that Zeus has made a promise to Thetis without consulting her. Zeus replies that he does what he pleases, shares with her when he wishes, and if she does not cooperate, he will harm her. There is an ugly silence until Hephaestus speaks, reminding Hera how, when he once opposed Zeus to save her, Zeus flung him out of Olympus by the heel. At this recognition of Zeus' raw power, the gods smile, eat, drink, and make merry, accepting the authority of Zeus.

All the themes of the *Iliad* are thus laid out neatly in book 1: piety and impiety towards the gods; the absolute and final power of Zeus; the dangerous arrogance of kings and heroes; the inability of humans (or gods) to know what Zeus wills until he speaks it; the rage of heroes and of kings; the quarrels over women; and the danger of involving the gods in what more properly and safely are human affairs.

Book 2. Zeus sends a false dream to Agamemnon, telling him to arm his men because they can now take Troy, since Hera has persuaded the Olympians to be of one mind. Agamemnon responds to this twisted message with his own twist: He tells his council of the dream, but then proposes to test the Greeks by bidding them to flee home to Greece, while the council members try to hold them back. The Greeks start to flee, until Hera sends Athena to hold them. Athena goes to Odysseus and instructs him to persuade the Greeks to remain, which he does using masterful persuasion where possible, threats where useful, and beatings (e.g., of Thersites) where necessary. Then Nestor advises Agamemnon to separate the men by tribes and clans, so that they will fight more fiercely aiding their kin.

The last part of book 2 is the Catalog of Ships, which lists the Greek armies at Troy. This section no doubt interested Homer's audience, who recognized their ancestors in the lists.

In Books 3 through 8, Achilles sulks and fumes in his tent with his best friend Patroclus while the battles rage, until in book 8 the tide turns against the Greeks.

Book 3. This book highlights cowardly Paris, forlorn Helen, the gifts and dangers of Aphrodite, and the futility of humans' efforts to make plans when Zeus plans otherwise. It opens with the Trojan and Greek armies approaching one another. Menelaus sees Paris and approaches to challenge him, but Paris pulls back. Hector accuses his brother Paris of being a coward who caused the war by seizing Helen. Paris does not defend himself but says that it is unwise to scorn the gifts of Aphrodite (e.g., Helen). Then Paris offers to fight Menelaus in single combat, winner take all. The Greek and Trojan armies agree to a truce; they are hopeful that there will be a quick and easy resolution to the war. The goddess Iris fetches Helen to observe the scene below the walls of Troy. Priam tells Helen that he blames the gods, not her, and asks her to identify the Greek champions below. Menelaus and Paris fight. Paris is nearly killed, but Aphrodite intervenes, carries him away to Helen's chamber, and then summons Helen to join him there. Helen tries to resist, provoking Aphrodite's dangerous anger. Frightened by the goddess, Helen returns to her chamber where she and Paris make love, firmly in the clutches of Aphrodite.

Book 4. This book offers more insights into the conflicting wills of the gods behind the human conflict. Back on Olympus, Zeus mocks Hera, suggesting that the war can end right now since clearly Menelaus won the single combat with Paris. Hera and Athena are furious because they desire the destruction of Troy. Zeus agrees to let Hera destroy Troy, although he honors it, but warns that she had better leave him alone when he decides to destroy one of *her* cities. She agrees and asks him to send Athena down to cause the Trojans to break the truce. Athena seeks out Pandarus, a Trojan archer, and tempts him to shoot at Menelaus. Athena then deflects the arrow onto Menelaus' belt, so he is only slightly injured. The Greeks are outraged and the truce ends in bloody fighting spurred on by Athena and Ares.

Book 5. Athena inspires Greek Diomedes to win great glory. He rages on the battlefield, even when shot in the shoulder by an arrow. Athena heals him and she lifts the mist from his eyes so that he (unlike other mortals) can see the gods on the battlefield. She tells him he must not test his mettle against any of the gods except Aphrodite. Diomedes attacks Aeneas, but his mother Aphrodite protects him. Then Diomedes goes after Aphrodite, gouging her wrist with his spear, and she flees the battlefield, retreating to Olympus for solace from her mother Dione, and a little chat among the gods about the pain that mortals can cause to the deathless gods.

Meanwhile, Diomedes again charges Aeneas. Apollo, shrieking, warns Diomedes off and carries the wounded Aeneas to safety. Apollo then asks Ares to get the raging Diomedes off the battlefield. Ares accompanies Hector in a violent Trojan charge against the Greeks. Diomedes sees the god and warns his men to give ground. Hera sees the rout of the Greeks and calls Athena to help. Athena and Hera receive Zeus' permission to attack Ares. Athena approaches Diomedes to ask why he is retreating from the Trojans, and he says it is because she had told him not to fight any god except Aphrodite. Athena assures Diomedes that it is now okay to fight the gods. She climbs into Diomedes' chariot, drives it directly at Ares, and then she rams Diomedes' spear into Ares. The wounded god flees to Olympus, where Zeus shows him little sympathy.

Book 6. This book portrays the irony and pathos of the Trojans, as they pray for succor from Athena, who hates Troy. The Greeks get the upper hand in the fighting, and the Trojans want to retreat back into their city. The Trojan seer Helenus rallies the men. Helenus also wants Hector to tell his mother Hecuba to offer a gorgeous robe and sacrifices to Athena and pray for Troy's safety. Hector leaves the battle to do this, encouraging the Trojans to keep fighting until he returns. The Trojan women pray to Athena, offering her the robe and sacrifices.

Hector then goes to fetch Paris back to the battle. Hector talks briefly with Helen, who condemns herself and Paris. Hector does not disagree, but hurries off to seek his wife Andromache and their young son. Andromache begs Hector to stay in Troy and pull back the Trojan troops to protect the city from the rampaging Greeks, but Hector sees this as cowardly and shameful. Hector tries to embrace his son Astyanax, who is frightened by his father's war gear. Hector prays to Zeus that his son will be a greater warrior than his father, and then Hector and Paris return to the battle.

Book 7. Hector and Paris rush onto the battlefield, inspiring the Trojans to rampage, killing Greeks galore. Athena spies the action from Olympus and hurries towards Troy. Apollo sees the battle and also heads for Troy, intercepting Athena. Apollo says to Athena that although she and Hera will destroy Troy, why not declare a truce today? Athena agrees. Apollo then suggests putting up a Greek to fight with Hector. Athena agrees, and she speaks to the Trojans through Helenus, suggesting that Hector challenge a Greek champion. Hector offers a challenge to the Greeks for a single combat to the death; the winner will strip the other's gear, but return the body for proper burial and lasting fame. Menelaus volunteers, but Agamemnon stops him. Nestor taunts the rest of the Greeks, and nine men offer to meet Hector. They draw lots for the opportunity. Ajax wins. This is a duel for glory. Ajax hurls a boulder that crushes Hector's shield, throwing Hector to the ground. However, Apollo helps Hector up, and then men from both sides call for a truce because night is falling.

The Greeks make a feast and Nestor advises that they should not fight the next day but use the time to gather the dead and bury them properly, heaping stones over the mass pyre. Even better, they can then use this heap of stones to start a wall to protect the Greek camp and make a trench behind it for more protection.

The Trojans gather in council and Antenor urges them to return Helen and her treasures to the Greeks because they are fighting an unlawful war, having broken the sworn truce while Paris and Menelaus fought. However, Paris will have none of this — he won't return Helen, although he will return the treasure. Priam agrees to make this offer to the Greeks, along with a proposal for a truce to bury their dead.

The next day, Idaeus goes to the Greek camp with Paris' offer, which is soundly rejected, but all agree to allow a truce to bury the dead. Both camps feast that night, but Zeus plans new disasters for both sides.

Book 8. Zeus announces to the other gods that *he* could bring the war to an end, and he issues a warning that he is much more powerful than all the other gods together. He orders the gods to stay out of the battle, and goes to Mt. Ida to watch Troy and environs. The Trojans pour out of the gates and attack the Greek army. They fight until noon, when Zeus holds up his golden scales. He places in them two fates of death, one for the Trojans and one for the Greeks. Down goes the Greek side, meaning doom, and Zeus hurls lightning at them from Mt. Ida. The Greeks are terrified and lose heart, except for Diomedes and Nestor, who charge at Hector, killing his driver. Woe to the Trojans, except that Zeus intervenes, hurling lightning at the feet of Diomedes' horses. Nestor warns Diomedes to retreat before the will of Zeus, but Diomedes argues that it would shame him. Nestor says nonsense, no one would believe he is a coward. Since he is driving the chariot, Nestor swings it around, and he and Diomedes flee, pursued by Trojans. Three times Diomedes wants to turn around, but three times Zeus thunders to warn him. This same warning thunder is a sign to the Trojans of victory. Hector seizes the opportunity and rallies the Trojans to storm the Greek ships and set them afire.

Hera and Poseidon are furious at what Zeus is doing, but they fear his power. Hera does impel Agamemnon to arouse his troops to defend the ships. Agamemnon also prays to Zeus to at least spare the men's lives, if not the ships. Zeus pities Agamemnon and sends an eagle sign to encourage the Greeks to fight. But, as the Greeks fight, Zeus again encourages the Trojans, led by Hector, to force the Greeks back to their ships. Hera and Athena are filled with pity for the dying Greeks, and Hera is especially furious with Zeus for fulfilling his promise to Thetis at the expense of so many Greek lives.

Hera and Athena gear for battle and head their chariot toward the battlefield. Zeus spies them and sends Iris to warn the goddesses to turn back and obey the will of Zeus. Hera gives in, and they turn back to Olympus, leaving the course of the battle to Zeus. Zeus then mocks them, saying that if they had not turned back, he would have destroyed their chariot and banished them from Olympus. Zeus says that Hector will not stop killing Greeks until Achilles reenters the battle, fighting over the body of Patroclus.

Night is falling, so Hector has the Trojans make camp to block the Greeks from fleeing in their ships. Hector says that in the morning they will destroy the Greek army.

Book 9. The Greek army is in a panic, and Agamemnon tries futilely to restore their morale. Then Agamemnon, groaning and crying, tells his troops that Zeus had blinded him with madness, deluding him into thinking he could conquer Troy. He urges his troops to sail home to Greece. Diomedes refuses, saying that the Greeks will plunder Troy even if Agamemnon runs home. Nestor has more concrete advice. He suggests that they arrange a secure camp for the night and prepare a feast for the Greek leaders to discuss strategy. The council opens with Nestor blaming Agamemnon for disgracing Achilles and taking away Briseis. That was the fault that led to this rout. Agamemnon agrees, saying that he was mad and blind, but now he is ready to make amends and pay ransom to Achilles in return for his friendship. Agamemnon still does not understand how profoundly he has offended Achilles. Nonetheless, he offers much loot, plus an "untouched" Briseis, and even a daughter of his to wed with an enormous dowry. All this will be in return for Achilles' submission to Agamemnon as the greater king.

An embassy including Odysseus is sent to Achilles with the offer. Achilles welcomes them hospitably. After a feast Odysseus tells Achilles that the fate of the Greek ships hangs in the balance, unless Achilles helps them, and he reminds Achilles of the deadly consequences of quarrels. Odysseus asks Achilles to let go of his anger and accept Agamemnon's apology and bountiful gifts, including the untouched Briseis. Odysseus says that even if Achilles still hates Agamemnon, he should pity the Greeks being destroyed by Hector and the Trojans, and he should think of the glory of killing Hector.

Achilles replies that he hates Agamemnon utterly. While Achilles struggled and fought, Agamemnon, a greedy coward, stayed at the rear, took the best prizes for himself, and tore Achilles' honor from him when he took Briseis. Achilles will take his troops and sail away at dawn. Achilles even rejects the heroic code, saying that it is better to be alive than die fighting for wealth. Achilles' mother had told him he had two choices, a long, but inglorious life at home or a brief life and glory at Troy. He chooses life, telling the other Greeks to go home too.

Phoenix, who had been like a father to Achilles, begs him to let go of his anger, telling stories of the ruin caused by anger. Achilles insists that his honor comes not from Agamemnon but from the decree of Zeus. Achilles then tells Phoenix to stay the night. In the morning they will decide what to do. Ajax accuses Achilles of having lost his human feeling. Achilles still insists that he will not arm again until Hector burns the Greek ships. Achilles intends to stop Hector at his own (Achilles') camp.

Odysseus and Ajax return to Agamemnon, reporting that Achilles still rages with hatred for him. Diomedes says that Achilles will only fight when he is ready, so they should go on without him.

In Books 10 through 15, the fighting continues with the Trojans gaining the upper hand.

Book 10. While the Trojans sleep in camp, Agamemnon and Menelaus worry about tomorrow. Agamemnon sends Menelaus to find Ajax and Idomeneus, while he goes to find Nestor for advice. Nestor advises Agamemnon to wake the main chiefs for a council. When they have gathered, Nestor asks if anyone will volunteer to infiltrate the Trojan camp and gather intelligence. Diomedes offers to go and picks Odysseus as his comrade. They pray to Athena for protection and sneak into the Trojan Camp.

Meanwhile, Hector cannot sleep. He wakes his chieftains and asks for volunteers to sneak into the Greek camp and gather intelligence. Dolon volunteers. He brags of what he will do; Hector offers rich rewards; but we are told that Dolon will never come back. Dolon heads for the Greek camp but is seen by Odysseus and Diomedes, who force him to halt. Odysseus, always clever, manipulates the cowardly Dolon into telling everything he knows about the Trojan situation, while begging for his life. Once Dolon has finished betraying the Trojans, even suggesting which are easiest to kill, Diomedes kills him.

Odysseus and Diomedes then enter the Trojan camp at the place Dolon had suggested, and Diomedes slaughters sleeping Thracian soldiers, while Odysseus pulls their bodies out of the way to make a path for stealing the superb chariot and horses of King Rhesus. Athena urges Diomedes to hurry back to the Greek camp. Apollo arouses a Thracian captain, but the Trojan allies are not able to catch Odysseus, Diomedes and the horses before they reach the safety of the Greek camp.

Book 11. Zeus sends Strife (Eris) to rouse the Greeks to battle. Agamemnon puts on his war gear, while Athena and Hera thunder approval. Zeus rains a shower of blood on the Greeks to arouse panic because he wants many dead that day, giving glory to the Trojans. Agamemnon rampages on the battlefield, killing many Trojans, leading his Greek troops. Zeus draws Hector out of danger, as Agamemnon slaughters Trojans, pursuing them to the gates of Troy. Zeus sends word to Hector, via Iris, that Hector must hold back from battle until Agamemnon is wounded. Then it will be Hector's turn to rage in battle all the way to the Greek ships.

Agamemnon is injured and heads back to the Greek ships. This is the signal for Hector to master the battlefield and win glory. He sweeps the Trojans along with him, slaughtering Greeks, until Odysseus and Diomedes resist. Diomedes injures Hector, who retreats. Paris then wounds Diomedes, who retreats. Odysseus is left on his own, ringed by Trojans. He attacks first, kills some Trojans, and is wounded. He cries out, and Menelaus and Ajax come to rescue him.

Zeus forces Ajax to retreat from Hector, and the Trojans gain the upper hand in the battle. Finally, Achilles pays attention to the battle; he sees the wounded healer Machaon being carried from the battle and asks Patroclus to check out what is happening. Achilles thinks that now the Greeks will grovel and beg him to fight. Patroclus goes to see Machaon. Nestor tells Patroclus of the terrible suffering of the Greeks and asks why Achilles has no pity for them. Nestor also reminds Patroclus that he should be giving Achilles good advice since he is the older one. If Achilles will not fight, perhaps he would send Patroclus into battle wearing Achilles' armor, so the Trojans would think he was Achilles.

Patroclus is moved by Nestor's advice, and he desires to help the Greeks. On his way back to Achilles' tent, Patroclus meets an injured comrade, Eurypylus, cuts out the arrow, and puts medicine on the wound. Patroclus is a kind, responsible man, and he's the next pawn in the plan of Zeus.

Book 12. The Greeks and Trojans are fighting over the trench and wall that protect the Greek ships. Hector is beating the Greeks into the ground, but his horses will not cross the trench, so the Trojans leave their horses and attack on foot, fighting furiously. The Trojans hope to trap the Greeks in front of their own wall, and then, as the Greeks flee inside, the Trojans will try to storm the wall. Amidst the fighting, Zeus sends an ominous sign — an eagle, his symbol, flies past with a serpent in its beak and flings the serpent among the Trojans. Polydamus warns Hector that this means they must stop fighting and return to Troy, but Hector scorns this interpretation of the bird sign. The Trojans start to tear the wall apart, while the Greeks hurl boulders down on them. Zeus drives his own son Sarpedon against the Greek defenses, protecting Sarpedon from Greek arrows as he tears down a section of the wall. There is a stalemate: The Trojans cannot drive the Greeks back to their ships; the Greeks cannot drive the Trojans away from the wall. Finally, Zeus allows Hector to smash the gate in the wall, leading the Trojans through to set fire to the Greek ships.

Book 13. This book tells of the battle for the ships. While Zeus turns his attention elsewhere, Poseidon pities the Greeks. In the form of Calchas, Poseidon first rouses Great and Little Ajax to defend the ships against Hector and then goes through the Greek ranks, inspiring them to organize and fight. Poseidon then takes the form of Thoas and urges more Greeks to brave deeds, offering to help. The gods have divergent interests. Zeus wants the Greeks beaten back to their ships to honor his pledge to Thetis. However, Poseidon feels compassion for the besieged Greeks, but he has to sneak around the battlefield because Zeus is more powerful and wants the gods to stay away. Men die as the gods work out their feelings about these issues. Hector is having a great time killing Greeks, but he has no strategy for winning until Polydamus suggests they draw back a bit and plan their next tactics. Hector goes through the troops, gathering the leaders and meeting a new assault from the Greeks. This is more melee than strategy. Ajax then meets Hector and says that the Greeks are losing because Zeus wills it, not because the Trojans are stronger, and that a day is coming when the Trojans will flee back to Troy. An eagle flies by on the right to seal these words. But Hector, seeking glory, again ignores the sign from Zeus and leads another wild charge against the Greeks.

Book 14. Nestor, Agamemnon, Odysseus and Diomedes take a look at the situation, the broken wall, the marauding Trojans, and worry that not even Zeus could turn the tide in their favor. Agamemnon suggests getting as many ships as possible out to sea and escaping back to Greece. Odysseus is furious, because such a plan would get them all killed while trying to escape. Diomedes suggests that they spur on the Greeks, who until now have hung back from the fighting. Poseidon, in human guise, tells Agamemnon that Zeus does not really hate him and one of these days the Trojans will retreat back into Troy. Then Poseidon utters a huge war cry that inspires the Greek soldiers to fight even harder.

Hera sees this and wonders how to distract Zeus, so he will not see Poseidon helping the Greeks. She dresses herself up beautifully and tricks Aphrodite into giving her the power to be irresistible in love. Then off Hera goes to visit the god Sleep. She offers him a golden throne and footstool if Sleep will put Zeus to sleep as soon as she's seduced him. Sleep refuses at first, because he fears Zeus' anger, but she adds a young Grace to the bargain. Sleep agrees, delighted with the deal. Zeus sees Hera, gorgeous and wearing the Love power of Aphrodite. He desires her immediately, right there on Mount Ida, and wraps them in a golden cloud for privacy. Sure enough, he is put to sleep by Love and Sleep. Then, Sleep rushes off to tell Poseidon that Zeus is temporarily out of the game. Emboldened by Zeus' absence, Poseidon rallies the Greeks to fight back against Hector and the Trojans. Hector hurls his spear at Ajax, but it does not penetrate his armor. Then, Ajax hurls a rock at Hector and knocks him down, but Trojans gather around Hector and take him back to Troy before Ajax can kill him. The Greeks are encouraged by Hector's injury and fight even harder. Ajax leads the charge; the Trojans lose heart and start to flee.

Book 15. As the Greeks are routing the Trojans, Zeus awakens. Zeus sees the Greeks attacking, led by Poseidon, and Hector lying injured on the battlefield. Zeus immediately suspects Hera of having deliberately seduced him and put him to sleep. Zeus threatens Hera, reminding her of when he bound her dangling in mid-air and no other god dared to save her for fear of Zeus. Hera of course denies that she had anything to do with Poseidon's involvement in the battle, claiming that she would advise Poseidon to obey Zeus. This pleases Zeus, who replies that if, in the future, she will always side with him (Zeus), then it will be easy to keep Poseidon under control. He then tells Hera that if she really is on his side, she will summon Iris and Apollo. Iris will tell Poseidon to leave the battle, and Apollo will cure Hector and drive him back into battle, again routing the Greeks so they fall back to Achilles' ships. Then Achilles will send Patroclus into action, and after Patroclus has slaughtered many Greeks, Hector will kill him. Then, in fury over Patroclus' death, Achilles will kill Hector. After that, Zeus will turn the war in favor of the Greeks until they destroy Troy. This is Zeus' plan, which was part of the bargain he made with Thetis when she begged him to exalt Achilles. Until this plan is completed, Zeus will not allow the other gods to again interfere in the war.

Hera hurries back to Olympus, where she announces that Zeus is in total control. Athena gives the angry gods a pep talk about how Zeus will torment them unless they obey his will. Then Hera sends Iris and Apollo to Zeus for instructions. Iris is sent to inform Poseidon that either he will get out of the battle or Zeus will battle him directly and conquer him, because Zeus is the more powerful. Poseidon is furious, claiming that they are equal brothers, but Iris calms him, pointing out that Zeus is the elder and the Furies respect the elder. Poseidon backs down but says that if Zeus ever again interferes with destroying Troy, the breach between them will be permanent. With that, Poseidon leaves the battlefield and returns to the ocean.

Zeus then gives Apollo instructions to panic the Greeks, after which he is to inspire Hector with great courage, breathing strength back into him (he has been nearly killed by a boulder hurled at his chest). The Greeks are terrified at the sight of Hector charging again, as if raised from the dead. The braver Greeks group to resist him, but when Apollo hurls terror into their hearts, they break ranks and flee in panic, as the Trojans, led by Apollo and Hector, pursue and slaughter them. Apollo fills in the trench and tears down the wall of the Greek defenses so the Trojans can storm in. The Greeks huddle by their ships, praying. Zeus hears Nestor's prayer and responds with thunder, but the Trojans misunderstand the sign and keep attacking.

Patroclus hears the fighting around the ships and tries to get Achilles back into combat. Teucer aims an arrow at Hector, but Zeus himself knocks the bow from his grasp. Hector, recognizing that Zeus is on his side, urges his men forward, while Ajax urges the Greeks to resist. The Trojans storm the fleet, with Zeus building up their fury and weakening the Greek spirit to resist. Zeus' purpose is to have the Trojans set fire to the Greek ships, thus completing the "plan of Zeus," based on his promise to Thetis. After that, of course, the Trojans will lose until the inevitable fall of Troy. So Hector attacks, driven on by Zeus. Hector is terrible, like a fire, a flood, a lion. The Greeks are terrified, certain they will all die, and the Trojans are sure of imminent victory. Hector seizes on a Greek ship, calling for fire, while Ajax kills Trojans who try to approach with torches.

Books 16–18 deal with the death of Patroclus and the reentry of Achilles into the war.

Book 16. Patroclus, weeping over the destruction of the Greek army, goes to Achilles to persuade him to relent in his anger against Agamemnon and defend the Greeks. Patroclus says that if Achilles will not fight himself, at least he should send out Patroclus in Achilles' armor with Achilles' Myrmidon army to defend the Greeks. Patroclus does not realize he is begging for his own death, but the narrator makes sure that the audience does. Patroclus asks Achilles if there is some prophecy that keeps him from fighting, but Achilles says no, it is just the terrible pain he feels from being dishonored by Agamemnon. However, he is willing to let Patroclus go. Achilles tells Patroclus just to force the Trojans back from the Greek ships and then return directly.

As the first Greek ship is set afire, Achilles urges Patroclus, dressed in Achilles' armor, out to defend the ships. Achilles calls up all his battalions of Myrmidons and urges them to fight the Trojans. Achilles pours wine to Zeus, prays for glory for Patroclus, and asks that once Hector and the Trojans are repelled from the ships, Patroclus may return safely to the fleet. Zeus hears the prayer, grants one part, and denies the other. The fresh Myrmidon troops pour out of the ships and attack the Trojans. There is much killing on both sides, as the Greeks repel the Trojans from the ships. One poignant battle is the clash of Zeus' son Sarpedon with Patroclus. Zeus knows that Sarpedon is fated to die, and is tempted to save him; but Hera protests that if Zeus acts against fate, so will other gods, resulting in chaos. Instead, Hera suggests an honorable burial in Sarpedon's homeland. Zeus relents and allows Sarpedon to die. The battle continues, with Zeus watching every move, trying to decide how Patroclus should die. Zeus decides that first he'll have Patroclus drive the Trojans back to Troy, killing many. Zeus starts this process by intimidating Hector. Knowing that Zeus has gone against him, Hector leaps into his chariot and yells to the Trojans to retreat.

Patroclus, ignoring Achilles' instructions, goes after the retreating Trojans. What Zeus wills no human can resist, and now Zeus is urging Patroclus on in murderous fury. At this point, if not for Apollo guarding Troy, the Greeks would have taken the city. Patroclus charges the wall three times, and each time Apollo hurls him back. At the fourth attempt, Apollo shrieks at him to go back, because it is not fated that Troy will fall at his hands. Patroclus starts to retreat. Apollo then goes to Hector and urges him to fight Patroclus. Patroclus kills Cebriones, Hector's driver, and then Patroclus and Hector battle over the corpse like two lions over a kill. Patroclus fights brilliantly, killing many Trojans, until Apollo hits him with his hand, striking Patroclus senseless and knocking the helmet off his head. While Patroclus stands stunned by Apollo's blow, a Trojan flings a spear at him. Hector sees Patroclus wounded and rushes him, ramming a spear deep into his bowels. Patroclus, dying, tells the gloating Hector that first Apollo struck him, then Euphorbus, and only third Hector; furthermore, Hector's death is near at the hand of Achilles.

Book 17. This book is about killing, stripping armor and protecting dead bodies. Menelaus tries to protect Patroclus' body, but he is challenged by Euphorbus, whom he kills. As Menelaus tries to strip off Euphorbus' armor, Apollo rouses Hector, who approaches with his troops. Menelaus retreats back to the Greek line, seeking Ajax to help him protect Patroclus' body. Meanwhile, Hector puts on Achilles' armor, stripped from Patroclus. Zeus observes this, pitying Hector, and gives him a moment of glory before his death.

Hector leads the Trojan charge to recapture Patroclus' body, but they are pushed back until Apollo inspires Aeneas to rouse the Trojans to resist. The battle over Patroclus' body rages all day. Achilles' horses weep over Patroclus' death, and Zeus pities them, but Zeus is still determined to give the Trojans glory until the end of the day. Athena, in the guise of Phoenix, chides Menelaus to fight more boldly, protecting Patroclus' body.

Finally, Menelaus sends a fast runner to tell Achilles of Patroclus' death, hoping he will at least help to save the body. But Achilles cannot fight, because he has no armor. Menelaus and Meriones carry Patroclus' heavy body to the ships, while the two Ajaxes defend their rear. Hector and Aeneas lead the Trojans as they pursue the routed Greek army back to their ships.

Book 18. When Achilles receives news of Patroclus' death, he cries out, and in the ocean his mother Thetis hears him. All her Nereid sisters come to comfort her. They accompany Thetis to Troy, where she tries to comfort her son Achilles, telling him that Zeus has granted his wish (for the Trojans to beat the Greeks back to their ships). Achilles replies that Hector has killed Patroclus and now he must kill Hector. Thetis tells Achilles that he must die soon after Hector dies. This does not matter to Achilles, who is ready to die once he has killed his beloved friend's killer. Thetis agrees that this is appropriate but tells him to wait until morning. She will bring him new armor made by Hephaestus, the god of fire. Meanwhile, Hector is trying to drag Patroclus' corpse back to the Trojan lines, and the Greeks are having difficulty preventing him from doing so. Hera sends Iris to urge Achilles to go out to the battlefield and, even though unarmed, show himself to the Trojans to gain a moment of hesitation in the battle. Athena slings her enormous shield over Achilles' shoulder and crowns his head with a burning golden cloud. Achilles goes into the trenches and gives a huge war cry. Athena, too, shrieks, and the noise panics the Trojans. This break in the fighting allows the Greeks to seize Patroclus' body and bring it back to their ships.

Polydamus warns the Trojans that Achilles is back in the war and the prudent thing is to withdraw behind the walls of Troy: They can let Achilles rage below while they are safe within. But Hector scorns this good advice; he wants glory. Athena has removed the good sense of the rest of the Trojans, so they approve Hector's folly.

Meanwhile, Thetis pays a visit to Hephaestus' house. She is very welcome because she healed and hid him for nine years after his painful fall from Olympus. Thetis tells her anguished story to Hephaestus, and he promises to make glorious armor for Achilles. The shield is an amazing artifact, containing lifelike images of the world, the sky, the ocean, and two noble cities. In one city, the city elders are peacefully adjudicating a blood feud. The other city is under siege, prepared for war. Other scenes on the shield depict the joy and variety of human life in lovely natural settings. The river of Ocean goes around the rim, indicating that the scenes on the shield represent the entire world. Hephaestus gives the completed armor to Thetis, who brings it down from Olympus to give to Achilles.

Book 19. Thetis brings the armor to Achilles who is mourning over Patroclus' body. Achilles is roused by the brilliant armor, but worries about Patroclus' body decaying. Thetis reassures Achilles that Patroclus' body will remain fresh, so he should renounce his anger at Agamemnon and lead his troops into battle.

Achilles reconciles with Agamemnon, saying it would have been better if the girl they fought over had been killed by Artemis, because their feud over her has only helped the Trojans and harmed the Greeks. Achilles declares that he has ended his anger, because it is wrong to stay angry forever. Agamemnon responds to this generous speech with a curious claim that he was not to blame, but Zeus and Fate and the Fury who drove madness into his heart when he seized Achilles' girl prize. Agamemnon also blames Ruin, eldest daughter of Zeus, who even collaborated with Hera to blind Zeus once, so how could Agamemnon, a mere mortal, avoid being blinded by a god? Having thus denied his personal responsibility for his actions against Achilles, Agamemnon then offers to compensate Achilles with treasure, but all Achilles wants is to get on with the fighting. Odysseus wisely suggests that they take a break and eat because troops cannot fight all day on empty stomachs. Odysseus then advises Agamemnon to bring the gifts to Achilles and swear that he has not touched Briseis. Odysseus also advises Achilles to accept a feast from Agamemnon.

Achilles is eager to fight and refuses to eat; all he craves is killing and blood. But Odysseus repeats his advice that the troops must eat before they can fight. The treasure is brought out; Agamemnon swears an oath that he never touched Briseis, and Achilles acknowledges that he, too, must have suffered a blinding frenzy sent by some god, or he never would have let Agamemnon arouse such anger in him. Zeus must have been behind it all.

Briseis grieves over the body of Patroclus, as does Achilles, who says he feels this death more than he would the death of his father or of his son. Zeus feels sorry for Achilles' grief and sends Athena to instill nectar and ambrosia into his body because he refuses to eat.

Filled with rage, Achilles puts on Hephaestus' armor, and his chariot is prepared. Achilles then orders his horses to do better than they did when they left Patroclus' body on the field. One of the horses speaks, saying that they will save Achilles' life, but his day of death is very near, and further, it was not their fault that the Trojans were able to strip Patroclus' body of armor — Apollo killed Patroclus and gave the glory to Hector. And away they go!

Book 20. As the Greeks arm around Achilles, Zeus calls for a council of all the Olympian Gods. He tells them that they are free to intervene in the coming battle as they please, while he will watch from Mt. Olympus. Zeus comments that if the gods don't join the fray, Achilles will destroy the Trojans before it is fated. Achilles has been routing the Trojans, but once the gods enter on both sides, the battle becomes more evenly matched. Zeus thunders from above; Poseidon sends earthquakes from below; god battles against god; the river god Xanthus battles the fire god Hephaestus. Apollo then enhances Aeneas' power and drives him against Achilles. Poseidon, Hera, and the other gods who hate Troy sit at one side of the battlefield, while the gods who support Troy, including Ares and Apollo, sit on the opposite side, watching the action, reluctant to get involved in fighting other gods.

Achilles challenges Aeneas, who recites his ancestry and then hurls his spear at Achilles. Achilles hurls his back and is about to kill Aeneas when Poseidon takes pity on Aeneas and proposes that the gods protect him because he is "destined to survive" (*Il.*20.349) and his progeny will rule the descendents of the Trojans. (Centuries later Virgil will pick up the story of Aeneas and his descendents in the *Aeneid.*) Poseidon seizes Aeneas and takes him out of the battle, warning him to avoid Achilles or he will die against "the will of fate" (*Il.*20.383). Hector then wants to fight Achilles, but Apollo warns him off. Achilles plunges into the Trojan ranks, slaughtering all around. After Achilles kills Hector's brother Polydorus, Hector is ready to fight Achilles, even though he knows he is far weaker. Just as Achilles is about to kill Hector, Apollo snatches Hector away to safety. Furious, Achilles rampages like inhuman fire through the Trojan troops, slaughtering them, blood everywhere.

Book 21. This is the book of universal chaos. The gods are now fighting one another, and even the elements become involved. Achilles rages, chasing the Trojans back to Troy, but half of them he chases into the Xanthus River. Achilles then leaps with his sword into the river, slaughtering Trojans. Achilles pulls out twelve live Trojans for sacrifice on Patroclus' pyre and then returns to his fierce slaughter in the river. Achilles is merciless, a butcher, tossing dead bodies into the river, choking it with Trojan dead. The river, outraged, rises up as a man and yells, "'Stop, Achilles!'"(*Il.*21.240) — if he won't stop killing, at least keep the corpses on dry land. Achilles agrees to stop packing the river with corpses but refuses to stop slaughtering the Trojans. The Xanthus River tries to destroy Achilles by burying him in a flood of water and mud. Achilles cannot escape the divine river without divine help, so he prays to Zeus for rescue. Poseidon and Athena come down to encourage Achilles, but Xanthus rages on, pursuing Achilles with a gigantic wave. Hera saves Achilles by ordering

Hephaestus to attack the river with fire. Xanthus cannot resist the fire and decides to stop trying to help Troy. Zeus just observes the chaotic spectacle, and laughs at the conflicts of the gods. Ares charges Athena, who hurls a huge boulder at him. Then Athena beats Aphrodite, who is leading the injured Ares away. Poseidon challenges Apollo, who has sense enough to flee. Artemis chides Apollo for running away, and then Hera attacks Artemis, boxing her ears. Artemis goes off to Olympus to complain to Zeus, who laughs again.

Throughout this chaos, Achilles slaughters on, driving his enemies back to the walls of Troy. Priam orders the gates opened so the retreating Trojans can take refuge in the city. Apollo intervenes to block Achilles, sending Agenor to resist him. Then Apollo takes on Agenor's form to resist Achilles directly, luring him away from Troy by running. While Achilles pursues Apollo/Agenor, the weary Trojans crowd into the city.

Book 22. All the Trojans except Hector retreat inside the walls. Apollo stops running and taunts Achilles — because Apollo is a god, Achilles cannot kill him. Achilles is furious and races back to the walls of Troy, where Hector awaits him. Priam and Hecuba watch from the walls, begging Hector to come inside where he will be safe. Hector considers going in, but remembers that, the night before, when his brother urged the Trojans to retreat into Troy, Hector had refused; and this day many Trojans have died because of his bad decision. Hector feels he must stay and fight Achilles to redeem his honor. But, as Achilles approaches, Hector panics and runs, while Achilles pursues him three times around the walls of Troy.

Zeus watches, pitying Hector, and asks the other gods what they should do now, save Hector or let him die. Athena chides Zeus that they must not interfere with Hector's fated death. On the fourth circuit, Zeus holds up the scales of fate, and Hector's side falls, indicating that it is his day of doom. At this point, Apollo, who has been aiding Hector, leaves him, and Athena rushes up to help Achilles. She disguises herself as Deiphobus, Hector's brother, pretending to help him. This strategy stops Hector, so Achilles can close in for the kill. Hector offers a non-mutilation pact to Achilles, who utterly scorns him. When Achilles' spear thrust misses Hector, Athena returns the spear to Achilles, unseen by Hector. When Hector's spear thrust fails to injure Achilles, Hector turns to Deiphobus for help, but he is gone. Hector realizes he has been deceived and recognizes his fate — he is about to die. Hector's last words after being fatally injured are to beg Achilles to return his body to Troy for burial, but again Achilles scorns him, wishing that his rage were sufficient to eat Hector raw.

Achilles kills Hector, rips off the armor (which Hector had taken from Patroclus), and the other Greeks come up to marvel and stab at the corpse. Then Achilles ties Hector's corpse by the ankles to the back of his chariot and drags him in the dirt back to the Greek ships. Priam and Hecuba grieve from the walls of Troy. Andromache hears the grieving and rushes to the walls where she sees Hector's corpse being dragged away by Achilles. She faints and then gives a pathetic speech about their young son Astyanax, now an orphan.

Book 23. Achilles dumps Hector's body in the dirt next to Patroclus' bier and arranges for the funeral of Patroclus. Achilles prepares a funeral feast for his men and then tells Agamemnon to order his troops at dawn to cut and haul in timber for the funeral pyre. While Achilles sleeps, the ghost of Patroclus comes to him and asks for a quick funeral so that he may be accepted into Hades. Patroclus also tells Achilles that he, too, will die at Troy and requests that their ashes remain together in a single urn.

The next morning, Agamemnon's troops bring timber for the funeral pyre. Achilles asks Agamemnon to dismiss his men and let them prepare a meal. Only the leading captains are to remain. Achilles piles the pyre with the bodies of four stallions, two of Patroclus' dogs, and the twelve captured Trojans, hacked to bits. Achilles refuses to burn Hector's body; he wants it eaten by dogs. (However, the gods protect Hector's body from decay and from the dogs.) The fire burns all night, and in the morning Achilles orders Agamemnon's troops to put out the remaining fire with wine and gather Patroclus' bones.

Finally, Achilles holds funeral games for Patroclus. These games are the civilized counterpart of war; there are rules, competition at martial skills, quarrels, judgments, and prizes, but no one dies. At the end comes the spear-throwing contest, which Agamemnon enters. Achilles, now in control of his anger and sensible of right behavior, tells Agamemnon that he clearly is best and awards him the first prize without Agamemnon even throwing his spear. Agamemnon accepts and then gives his prize to his herald. Agamemnon has learned to be generous, not greedy.

Book 24. The funeral is over, but Achilles continues to grieve, intermittently dragging Hector's corpse around Patroclus' tomb. Apollo, pitying Hector, protects the corpse from damage and corruption. Apollo accuses the gods of allowing Achilles, who has lost all pity and shame, to abuse Hector's corpse. Finally, Zeus wearies of such immoderate wrath and decrees that Thetis must notify Achilles that he will have to accept ransom and return Hector's body to Priam. Thetis delivers this message to Achilles, who agrees to accept the ransom and return Hector's body.

Zeus sends Iris to tell Priam to go alone to ransom Hector's corpse. Zeus assures Iris that Hermes will protect Priam and that Achilles is no madman — he will accept the gods' commands and spare Priam. With great personal bravery, Priam takes a treasure-laden wagon across the battle lines in the night, seeking to ransom his son Hector's body. Zeus sends Hermes, disguised as one of Achilles' men, to help Priam make the journey unharmed. Priam and Hermes exchange a touching dialogue in which each pretends that Hermes is a helpful man, while both know full well that he is a god. When they reach Achilles' lodgings, Hermes puts Achilles' sentries to sleep. He then tells Priam that he is a god, so it would not be fitting for him to be hosted by Achilles, but Priam will be safe.

Priam enters Achilles' lodge, clasps his knees, and kisses his hands, praying that Achilles will remember his own father and pity Priam, who has lost so many of his sons and now kisses the hands of the man who killed his beloved son. Achilles is moved to grieve for his own father and for Patroclus. The two men grieve and weep until Achilles has his fill of grief. Now he feels pity for Priam and asks him to put his grief aside. Achilles tells the myth of Zeus having two jars, one full of blessings, the other of sorrows, and he distributes them to men as he pleases. Men must endure, whatever their fates. He asks Priam to stop weeping, but Priam protests that he must see Hector and exchange the ransom for his body before he can be calm. This angers Achilles, who says he has already decided to return Hector and Priam should not tempt his wrath. The point is that more grieving could lead Achilles beyond his ability to control his wrath. Moderation is necessary, even in grief.

Achilles accepts the ransom and sends his men to bathe Hector's body. Achilles still fears that Priam's grief may lead to anger, which would re-ignite Achilles' own rage, so he might break the law of Zeus by killing Priam. When Hector's corpse is prepared and dressed, Achilles tells Priam that he will see the body in the morning; meanwhile they will eat and rest. Achilles puts Priam to bed on a porch, so Agamemnon's men won't see him. Achilles asks Priam how much time he will need to properly bury Hector and offers to keep a truce for that time. Priam asks for ten days.

Hermes wakes Priam in the middle of the night to sneak him out of the Greek camp with Hector's body. Priam reenters Troy and all the Trojans mourn Hector, led by Andromache, who worries that their son Astyanax will become a captive slave. Then Hecuba leads the cries over her favorite son, and finally Helen mourns for Hector as a kindly friend and wishes she had died before coming to Troy. Finally, Priam orders the Trojans to collect timber, prepare the funeral pyre, and properly bury Hector.

THE PLAN OF ZEUS

The ordering principles for human beings in the *Iliad* are right behavior, piety, human justice, and the plan of Zeus. So long as people behave, the gods stay pretty much out of their lives. But when outrageous behavior begins and gods are foolishly invoked, the gods become involved in human affairs, which can be extremely dangerous. When Agamemnon rudely rebuffs Chryses, a priest of Apollo, the priest prays to Apollo, who sends the plague to kill Greeks. When Agamemnon unfairly seizes Achilles' war-prize woman Briseis, Achilles prays to his divine mother Thetis. She in turn petitions Zeus, who approves the plan of destruction of the Greeks until the fighting comes up to their ships. Achilles has no idea that the price of this plan is the death of his dearest friend Patroclus.

Deals with gods are exceptionally dangerous, their outcomes unpredictable, like all magical bargains. Because Achilles would not fight to protect the Greeks, yet finally pitied them, he sent Patroclus out in his (Achilles') armor, and Hector killed Patroclus. Thus, Achilles lost his best friend, a bitter price for his bargain with Zeus. Further, Achilles must avenge Patroclus by killing Hector, knowing that he himself will die shortly after Hector.

During the period of wrath (and the plan of Zeus), the boundaries between men and gods become unstable, the very elements such as fire and water enter into the fighting, and men even attack the gods. The final outrage is Achilles' bestial treatment of Hector's corpse, dragging it around trying to mutilate it. Finally Apollo, the god of purification, speaks out among the gods against Achilles' behavior. Only Zeus can put a stop to the insanity and chaos. Zeus sends a messenger to Achilles, telling him to accept ransom from Priam and return Hector's body; Zeus sends another messenger to Priam to go and ransom his son's body; Achilles receives Priam graciously, the two men weep together over their separate sorrows, and then Achilles returns Hector's body. The wrath is over. Zeus's plan has been completed.

ACHILLES' HEROIC CHARACTER AND HIS LATER RECEPTION

If the *Iliad* is strange, violent, and heroic, it is largely because of Achilles. His virtues and vices are hard for people in less heroic times to disentangle from one another, and even Homer presents them as a mixed blessing. By classical Greek times, some authors, such as Sophocles, admired Achilles, while others, such as Euripides, criticized his brutality (King xvi–xvii). Achilles' character includes the following virtues, along with their natural flaws:

Intelligence: Achilles recognizes the need to deal with the plague; he knows his future and chooses to die young with glory instead of living a long, ordinary life; he has all the best arguments against Agamemnon; he is finally able to put a stop to his own rage, without blaming it on the gods. Yet he is often remembered for his excesses of passion, vengefulness and fury.

Leadership: He calls the meeting to deal with the plague; he speaks up to protect the seer; yet he pulls his men out of the battle so that other Greeks will die.

Pride: When Agamemnon insults him, Achilles is ready to kill the high king; he does not sufficiently respect rank; yet over and over he is called "the best of the Achaeans."

Friendship: Achilles is totally committed to Patroclus and ready to kill the entire Trojan army to avenge his death; later generations will suspect that this total devotion implies a homosexual attachment.

Integrity: While Agamemnon waffles, Achilles sticks to his principles, but when Agamemnon is ready to make peace with Achilles, Achilles is too rigid in his anger to give in.

Compassion: Achilles is a noble, compassionate host to grieving King Priam, father of dead Hector; yet Achilles' attempts to mangle Hector's corpse are bestial.

Courage: He is fearless in battle; yet he goes, tearful, to his divine mother, Thetis, to ask her to help him get revenge against Agamemnon. Later generations will focus more on his instability and brutality than on his courage; stories are told about how women are sacrificed at his tomb and how he goes mad over his love for Polyxena.

Strength: He is unbeatable in a fair fight, yet in the end the gods interfere on his side, deluding Hector so Achilles may more easily kill him. Achilles will die of an arrow in his heel, shot by Paris.

Fairness: Achilles criticizes Agamemnon's unfair taking of another man's war-prize; however, it was neither thoughtful nor fair for Achilles to let Patroclus wear his armor and go out to do battle in his place. Achilles' plan to withdraw his troops, so other Greeks would die, was also unfair.

There is much to dislike about Achilles; he is passionate to a fault, violent, hugely furious, yet he is unquestionably the greatest hero of the *Iliad*. Later civilizations found Achilles too brutal, too individualistic, too spiteful, too passionate for their tastes, and he became increasingly disapproved of over the centuries as other stories gathered around him; he became an unreliable ally, a slayer of women, sexually suspect, a raging madman, a berserker.

AGAMEMNON — THE BLACK-HEARTED KING

The quarrel between Agamemnon and Achilles is the precipitating event of the *Iliad*. Irrational as Achilles becomes in his wrath, Agamemnon is more responsible for what follows, because he is the high king. Having first insulted Chryses, Agamemnon then insults another seer, Calchas, who has explained that the girl must be returned to her father, Chryses. Agamemnon makes no attempt to control his anger at anyone who gets in his way, whether a foreign priest or his own best warrior. Such behavior by the king is inappropriate and destructive.

The problem, as Agamemnon knows perfectly well, is rooted in the spoils system of Greek warfare. After a raid or battle, all the loot is divided up among those who participate. Consequently, when Agamemnon has to return Chryses' daughter, there is no other woman for him, unless he takes a woman from one of the other soldiers. This is exactly what he threatens to do, infuriating Achilles.

The most essential quality of a war leader has to be his generosity, which makes his soldiers want to follow him even to death. Agamemnon lacks this primary generosity; he is willing to sacrifice his daughter Iphigenia to get favorable winds to sail to Troy, but he is not willing to sacrifice his own greed to the common good. Many later writers focused on the sacrifice of Iphigenia, not one of Agamemnon's best decisions. Although Agamemnon survives the events of the *Iliad* and succeeds in conquering Troy, his wife murders him when he returns home. The murder of Agamemnon is totally disapproved of whenever it is retold, but it is not lacking in poetic justice.

4

Homer's *Odyssey*
The Long Journey Home

Although the *Iliad* dominates the continuing tradition of Troy stories, there are many variants that either use parts of the *Odyssey* or at least focus on the complex and difficult character of Odysseus, a man people have loved to hate for millennia. Like Achilles, Odysseus belongs to a heroic, individualistic and piratical age, not an age of urban communitarian values and well-regulated behavior. While Achilles was unquestionably the greatest Greek warrior and hero, Odysseus was the greatest Greek strategist and survivor. Achilles in his wrath caused the deaths of many Greeks; Odysseus the master strategist was instrumental in the Greek victory over Troy.

It is important to be familiar with the Odysseus of the *Odyssey* as well as the Odysseus of the *Iliad* in order to recognize his multi-faceted, slippery character in future Troy tales. Like Achilles, Odysseus had a bad reputation in Athenian Greece, because he was seen as crafty, devious, and a liar (whereas Homer represented him as a master mariner, brilliantly ingenious and an inspired story-teller). Odysseus' role in Euripides' *Trojan Women* is especially chilling, because he talks smoothly enough, but hurls Andromache's infant Astyanax off a cliff, thus ending the threat of future feuds with the Trojan royal family. Always Odysseus is pragmatic; he is not a cruel man, but he is capable of terrible actions to serve his goal. In the *Iliad* Odysseus' goal is the victory of the Greeks over Troy; in the *Odyssey* his goal is to return home to Ithaca and avenge himself on the suitors who have invaded his palace.

This chapter contains a lengthy, book-by-book summary of the plot of the *Odyssey*. It may be useful if you are not familiar with the story or have not read it recently. I know that although I have read the *Odyssey* many times, I found it very helpful to sit down and write this summary, since it forced me to attend to the sequence of events in their context, independent of any complex analysis. I hope it will be helpful to some readers in a similar fashion. Please skip ahead to the end of the summary if it is not useful to you.

My main focus on the post–Homeric character of Odysseus will be in the chapter about Shakespeare's *Troilus and Cressida*, where Odysseus, called Ulysses (his Latin name), plays a major part. However, Odysseus/Ulysses has had many other fictional lives along the way. There is a wonderful book, *The Ulysses Theme*, by W. B. Stanford, that traces the history of Odysseus from his origins in Homer down to the twentieth century, when his frequently disreputable character is more or less redeemed in James Joyce's novel *Ulysses* (211–240). One charming recent version of Odysseus is Ulysses Everett McGill in the Coen brothers' film *O Brother, Where Art Thou?* This Ulysses is a fast-talking con man as well as a man of constant sorrows and a gifted folksinger in rural Mississippi during the Great Depression. Another unusual contemporary version of Odysseus is as a Caribbean adventurer in Derek Walcott's delightful play, *The Odyssey.*

An Overview of the Odyssey

After the fall of Troy, the men of the Greek armies return home, some quickly, some more slowly, some with great difficulty. The last to get home is Odysseus. The *Odyssey* is the story of Odysseus' ten-year struggle to return home from the Trojan War, where he had been a brave, effective warrior and an exceedingly clever strategist. Odysseus suffers from severe hardships and many temptations during these years, yet he constantly keeps his will focused on returning home and reestablishing his family life. Mortal and divine women find him desirable, but although he enjoys himself along the way, he continually longs for his wife Penelope. Odysseus is the only member of his crew to survive the journey home; the others die, some from the consequences of their own foolishness and greed, others from unavoidable situations. Odysseus is finally washed ashore on Scheria among the friendly Phaiacians, who send him home on one of their magical ships, loaded with rich gifts. Throughout these adventures, the goddess Athena loves and protects Odysseus because he is a steadfast survivor, a brilliant trickster, and an inventive storyteller — a human mirror of herself.

The *Odyssey* is much easier for a modern reader to appreciate than the *Iliad.* The *Odyssey* is a marvelous adventure story, full of amazing wonders, wicked monsters, beautiful women, pathetic ghosts, and lovely palaces. Odysseus is my favorite hero, although some people dislike him, finding him unethical, too calculating, selfish and callous, a philanderer, and a liar. He is all those things, to be sure, but he comes from a culture where these were acceptable qualities in a hero. He is smarter than anyone except Athena, his patron goddess; he is a better husband and father than Agamemnon; he is a better husband than Menelaus or Paris; he has a lot more common sense than the brilliant Achilles; and he tells great stories and respects poets who do the same. Odysseus is brave, endures great hardships, and always lands on his feet, thinking, scheming, and planning. His adventures make a great story.

THE STRUCTURE OF THE *ODYSSEY*

The *Odyssey* as we have it now is divided into 24 books, which can be grouped into four major sections.

- The adventures of Telemachus, books 1–4
- The homecoming of Odysseus, books 5–8 and 13:1–187
- Odysseus' wanderings — told by Odysseus at the Phaiacians court on Scheria, books 9–12
- Odysseus on Ithaca, book 13:187–book 24. (Lattimore 1)

This arrangement is not chronological, since the first section, the adventures of Odysseus' son Telemachus, actually occurs at the end of Odysseus' ten years of wandering, shortly before Odysseus arrives home in Ithaca.

The Story of the *Odyssey*

For a list of characters, see Chapter 2.

Book 1. All the Greeks who went to Troy have either died or returned home from Troy except Odysseus. The nymph Calypso is detaining Odysseus against his will as her lover. The time for Odysseus' fated return has come, but Poseidon is still angry because Odysseus has blinded the Cyclops Polyphemus, Poseidon's son. While Poseidon is away, the other Olympian gods gather to discuss Odysseus' fate. Athena asks Zeus for mercy for Odysseus, and Zeus declares it is time for Poseidon to relinquish his anger and let Odysseus return home. Athena proposes that Zeus send Hermes to tell Calypso that she must release Odysseus. Athena then goes to Ithaca to rouse Odysseus' son Telemachus, to encourage him to show leadership in Ithaca, and then inspire him to travel to nearby kingdoms to inquire about his father and develop a good reputation.

Athena first takes on the guise of the stranger Mentes and encounters the parasitic suitors gambling in front of Odysseus' palace, being served by his people and consuming his food and drink. Telemachus is daydreaming of his father when he sees Athena/Mentes and offers the hospitality of the palace, hoping to hear some word of his father. Athena/Mentes says he's an old friend of Odysseus and has word that Odysseus is alive and on his way home. Telemachus tells Athena/Mentes that Odysseus has been away for twenty years, and now all the local nobles are courting his wife Penelope and devouring all his stores of food and drink. Telemachus worries that soon the suitors will destroy him, because he is heir to the palace, if not the kingship, of Ithaca.

Athena/Mentes advises Telemachus to call an assembly and tell the suitors to leave. Then, Telemachus should tell his mother that if she wants to remarry, she should return to her father's house to do so. Evidently, if Penelope were to remarry in Ithaca, her new husband would be king, but if she returned home to her family before remarrying, then Telemachus would inherit the kingship. Athena/Mentes tells Telemachus that he should outfit a ship and travel, seeking news of Odysseus. If he finds news of his father living, he should come back home and wait another year. If he finds news that Odysseus is dead, he should conduct a funeral and have his mother return to her family and remarry. Then, he should figure out how to kill the suitors and take on the role of a man. Athena flies off, leaving Telemachus greatly encouraged, because a god has been giving him advice.

Meanwhile, a bard is singing of the return of the Greeks from Troy, and Penelope comes down weeping, asking him not to sing that song because it causes her too much pain. Telemachus tells her to harden her heart and go back to the women's quarters because he is in charge of the house. Telemachus then tells the suitors that he wants them to get out in the morning. Telemachus is already weighing his words, lying as needed, and planning strategies. He is starting to become manly, the true son of Odysseus.

Book 2. In the morning, Telemachus calls an assembly, where he speaks as a man, asserting that the suitors are ruining his house and consuming all his worldly goods. Telemachus blames the suitors, but Antinous, one of the suitors, blames Penelope for leading them on, pretending that she will marry one of them when she has finished weaving a shroud for Laertes, Odysseus' father, but secretly unweaving it each night. Antinous says that the suitors will not leave until Penelope marries again. This view of Penelope is ambiguous: Maybe she is innocent of the charges of leading on the suitors, but maybe not.

Telemachus replies that he cannot drive his mother away from home and the suitors must leave if they have any shame. If they refuse to leave, he will cry out to the gods and Zeus will punish them. Zeus sends a confirming bird sign, and the old warrior Halitherses warns the assembly that disaster will strike the suitors if they do not leave, because Odysseus is on his way home. But another suitor, Eurymachus, threatens the old man that if he incites Telemachus, the boy will suffer and the assembly will punish Halitherses. Meanwhile, Telemachus must send his mother back to her father's house to remarry, otherwise the suitors will not leave.

Telemachus asks the assembly to outfit a ship for him, so he can seek news of his father. If he hears that his father is alive, he'll wait another year. If he hears that Odysseus is dead, he'll return home, hold a funeral, and give his mother to another husband. Mentor warns the suitors that they are courting disaster, but another suitor says that even if Odysseus did return, they'd kill him.

Telemachus goes to the beach and prays to Athena, who now appears in the form of Mentor, encouraging him and offering to help prepare a ship to sail. Telemachus tells the housekeeper Eurycleia to secretly prepare wine and barley meal for his voyage. Meanwhile, Athena goes through town disguised as Telemachus, gathering up a crew and getting the loan of a ship. Then she puts all the suitors to sleep, so Telemachus can sail away unnoticed.

Book 3. Telemachus first goes to visit King Nestor in Pylos, where the people are performing a sacrifice to Poseidon. Athena/Mentor encourages Telemachus to question Nestor about Odysseus. Nestor's son Pisistratus gives the gold cup to Athena/Mentor to make the first libation to Poseidon. Athena/Mentor is pleased and prays to Poseidon for blessings on Pylos and that Telemachus may get home safely. (She then will grant what she has prayed for!)

After the prayers, Telemachus tells about himself and his quest for news of his father. Nestor tells of the end of the Trojan War and how a feud then broke out between Menelaus and Agamemnon. Menelaus wanted to sail straight home, but Agamemnon wanted to delay and offer sacrifices to placate Athena. As the brothers feuded, the armies split into sides and began clashing. Menelaus' half of the army set sail for home the next morning, but Agamemnon's half delayed at Troy. Odysseus turned back to help Agamemnon, but Nestor kept on for home, ignorant of the fate of those who stayed behind. However, he has heard rumors of those who made it safely home and those who did not, including Agamemnon who was killed by his wife upon reaching home. Nestor has no news of Odysseus except that Athena loved him greatly and if she loves Telemachus as she loved his father, all will be well. Nestor then tells the story of Agamemnon's murder and how Orestes avenged him. The message is that Telemachus should not stay away from home too long, and, like Orestes, he can avenge the injuries upon his house and family.

Nestor advises Telemachus to visit Menelaus, who was the last home from Troy, because he may have word of Odysseus. Athena/Mentor asks Nestor to send Telemachus there by chariot. She then flies off, leaving the Greeks amazed (and realizing she favors Telemachus, which helps build his reputation). The next morning Nestor arranges a sacrifice and feast in honor of Athena. Afterwards, Telemachus and Nestor's son Pisistratus set off for Lacedaemon in a chariot provided by Nestor.

Book 4. Telemachus arrives at Menelaus' palace as they are celebrating a double wedding. Menelaus quickly invites Telemachus and Pisistratus in as his guests. After they bathe, they join Menelaus in the feast hall. Telemachus is dazzled by the richness of Menelaus' palace. Menelaus explains that he amassed a fortune during the years he wandered home from Troy. But, while he wandered and got rich, his brother was murdered, so the wealth does not bring him joy. He grieves for all his lost and dead comrades, especially Odysseus. Telemachus weeps at this but is not sure whether or not to announce who he is. Menelaus recognizes Telemachus, but does not say so yet. The point is that strangers are from Zeus and true hospitality is due to them without even knowing who they are.

Then Helen enters, gorgeous and luxurious. She settles down and asks Menelaus who Telemachus is because he looks just like the son of Odysseus. Menelaus agrees that there are resemblances. Pisistratus intervenes and introduces Telemachus. Menelaus remembers his love for Odysseus, and they all sit grieving and weeping until Pisistratus again intervenes, praising Menelaus, who then praises Nestor. Helen then slips a drug, "heart's ease," (Od.4. 245) into their wine to cheer them all up. The perfect hostess, she tells a tale of how Odysseus, disguised as a beggar, infiltrated Troy. Menelaus then tells the bitter story of how Odysseus kept the Greeks silent inside the wooden horse while Helen walked around it calling greetings to each of them. Helen must have been inspired by "a dark power bent on giving Troy some glory" (Od.4.308). The talk is getting touchy, so tactful Telemachus suggests that it is time to go to sleep. He is learning how to behave in delicate situations.

In the morning, Menelaus asks Telemachus why he has come, and Telemachus replies it is to gather information about his father because his property is being destroyed and his mother plagued by the suitors. Menelaus says that he has heard of Odysseus from Proteus, the Old Man of the Sea. On the way home from Troy, Menelaus was stranded on an island. With some help from a goddess, Menelaus captured Proteus and held on until he stopped struggling; once this happened, Proteus told him only the truth. Menelaus could not get home because he had not taken the time to sacrifice to Zeus before leaving Troy. Menelaus would have to go back to Egypt a second time and offer a major sacrifice to the gods before he could go home. Menelaus also asked Proteus for news of the other Greeks returning from Troy. Proteus told him who had died, who had gotten home, and how Agamemnon was murdered after getting home. Menelaus learned that Odysseus was still alive but detained by Calypso on an island. As for Menelaus, he will never die, but go directly to the Elysian Fields, because he is Helen's husband again, and thus a son-in-law of Zeus. (No wonder Helen was worth fighting for!)

Menelaus urges Telemachus to stay with him for a few days, but he is eager to return home. Meanwhile, the suitors are still partying at Odysseus' palace. When they discover that Telemachus has actually gotten a ship and sailed to Pylos, Antinous is outraged and proposes ambushing and killing Telemachus on his way back. Penelope discovers their scheme and is so anguished that there is no more doubt where her heart is — with her son, not with leading on the suitors. Athena pities Penelope and sends a phantom in the likeness of a woman friend to reassure Penelope that Telemachus will be all right.

Book 5. This book starts much like book 1, with Athena asking Zeus to pity Odysseus and help him get home. Zeus sends Hermes to tell Calypso that Odysseus will go home on a raft, landing on Scheria at the court of the Phaiacians after much suffering. The Phaiacians will send him home to Ithaca in a ship full of treasure. Hermes flies to Calypso and tells her she must let Odysseus leave. She is indignant, because she had even wanted to make

Odysseus her husband and immortal, but he longs for his family and home. Calypso sadly tells Odysseus that she is sending him home on a raft, but he still doesn't trust her until she swears not to harm him. With some guidance from Calypso, Odysseus builds his raft and sets sail. For seventeen days the seas are calm. Then Poseidon, returning home from Ethiopia, spies Odysseus. Poseidon is furious. Although Poseidon knows Odysseus is fated to land on Scheria, he determines to give him trouble until then. Poseidon stirs up a huge storm that tosses the raft mercilessly. Ino, a goddess who lives in the sea, tells Odysseus to strip off his clothes and leave the raft. She gives him an immortal scarf and tells him to tie it around his waist. It will protect him, but as soon as he grasps the shore, he must untie the scarf and toss it back to the sea. The raft breaks up and Odysseus swims for shore. On the third day he reaches it, but the shore is rocky and treacherous. Athena encourages him, and he finally finds a beach where he can go ashore, nearly dead. He finds a sheltered spot beneath two olive trees, burrows into the dead leaves, and sleeps.

Book 6. While Odysseus sleeps, Athena visits the Phaiacians' city and goes to the room of Nausicaa, the daughter of King Alcinous. Taking on the form of a girlfriend, Athena chides Nausicaa in a dream that she needs to wash all her linens because soon she will marry. Athena tells Nausicaa to take a wagon and mules and go to the washing pools in the morning. In the morning Nausicaa goes to her father and asks him to prepare a wagon and mules for her to take the family wash to the river. Nausicaa and her girlfriends wash the linens and bathe. Then they eat a picnic and play games while the clothes dry.

Odysseus awakens, naked and covered with brine, and sees the girls. He approaches, silver tongued for all his wretchedness, flattering Nausicaa that she is like a goddess, while telling of his escape from the stormy sea. He begs her for compassion and asks for a rag to cover his nakedness. The princess is remarkably composed, telling him that since Zeus gave him pain, he must bear it, but he will be treated as a welcome guest. She tells her frightened girlfriends that all strangers come from Zeus and must be treated well. She orders them to bathe and clothe Odysseus. He is tactful, saying he won't bathe in front of them. Once he is clean and clothed, Athena makes him appear taller and more handsome. After Odysseus eats, Nausicaa tells him to enter town separately from the girls, so there will be no embarrassing talk. She instructs him to go to the palace, directly approach her mother Queen Arête, and grasp her knees in supplication. While Nausicaa goes ahead to town, Odysseus prays to Athena that he may find mercy and love among the Phaiacian people.

Book 7. After Nausicaa has gotten home, Odysseus approaches the city. Athena hides him within a protective mist, and then she approaches him in the form of a young girl. He asks her to guide him to the palace of Alcinous. She advises him that if Queen Arête will favor him, he'll be taken home safely to his native land. The palace is gorgeous, the people wonderfully gifted, the gardens ever-bearing. Still hidden in the mist, Odysseus enters the palace and approaches the Queen. As he flings his arms around the Queen's knees, Athena removes the mist, revealing him. He wishes for blessings for the Queen and her family and pleads for a rapid trip home to his native land. Alcinous raises Odysseus up, seats him next to himself, and orders a feast for Odysseus and libations to Zeus. After the feast, Alcinous says that in the morning they will arrange for his passage home.

Queen Arête notices that Odysseus is wearing clothes that she helped make. She asks him who he is, where he has come from, and how he got the clothes he now is wearing. Odysseus starts his story, telling how he was shipwrecked on Calypso's island, Ogygia. He was there for seven years and in the eighth year the goddess let him leave. He sailed for seventeen days and on the eighteenth a huge storm wrecked his raft. He swam for three days and finally found the river where he came ashore. Then he slept until Nausicaa and her friends awakened him. She behaved with sense and tact, fed him and gave him clothes to wear. The King is annoyed that Nausicaa did not escort the stranger to the palace, and ever-tactful Odysseus says that he chose to fall behind to avoid embarrassing her. The King reaffirms that in the morning he will send Odysseus home to Ithaca.

Book 8. In the morning, King Alcinous and Odysseus go to the public meeting ground beside the ships, and Athena takes the form of a herald to call people to see Odysseus. The King tells the people to outfit a ship and then come to the palace for a banquet. The blind poet Demodocus performs at the banquet, singing a song about Odysseus and Achilles. Odysseus weeps at the song, so tactful Alcinous stops it and announces athletic contests. Odysseus does not want to participate, but one of the men rudely challenges him until he does so. Odysseus flings a heavy discus and Athena, in man's form, announces that his has gone the farthest. Feeling better, Odysseus then cheerfully challenges all the Phaiacians except his hosts. But Alcinous graciously defuses the situation, calling for a dance. Demodocus plays and sings about the affair of Ares and Aphrodite, how Hephaestus caught them in chains while they were committing adultery, and then exhibited them for all the Olympians to laugh at. The Phaiacians dance wonderfully, and everyone has a good time.

Then Alcinous calls for everyone to present rich gifts to Odysseus. Baths are drawn and there is another feast. Odysseus honors the poet Demodocus with a choice piece of meat and warm regards. After the meal, Odysseus asks Demodocus to sing of the wooden horse at Troy. Demodocus sings this with great praise for Odysseus' skill and bravery at the fall of Troy. Odysseus (who has not yet told his name) weeps to hear this, and again tactful Alcinous stops the song and finally asks Odysseus to tell them his name, his family, the land he is from, so they can sail him home. Alcinous also wants to hear about Odysseus' adventures.

Book 9. Odysseus tells his name and asserts that nothing is as sweet as home and family. Then he tells the story of his adventures after he left Troy. Odysseus' travels are drawn from the ancient oral tradition of sailors' adventures to strange places, often beyond the boundaries of the real world. First, they landed at Ismarus, among the Cicones. Odysseus and his men sacked the city, but then Odysseus' men refused to retreat. Reinforcements came and many of Odysseus' men were killed before they got away. After leaving the Cicones, Odysseus and his crew sailed away from the real world and into the world of fantasy. They were blown off course by the north wind and came to the land of the lotus-eaters. Odysseus sent three men to scout the territory; they were not attacked but given lotus fruit to eat. As soon as the men tasted the lotus, they lost all sense of purpose as well as the desire to return home. Odysseus forced them into the ships, tied them under the rowing benches, and ordered his undrugged comrades to set sail immediately.

Next they reached the land of the Cyclopses, who were profoundly uncivilized, not caring for any but their immediate families, having no laws, and eating only what they could gather without planting. They had neither ships nor crafts. Odysseus and his men came to a small island inhabited only by goats, where no Cyclopses lived because they did not have ships to get there. Odysseus, ever curious, proposed to take his own ship and crew across to the Cyclopses' shore. Once there, they saw a cave with a yard around it, the home of the lawless Cyclops Polyphemus. Odysseus took a few of his crew and a skin of wine and set off to investigate. Odysseus' men wanted to steal what they could and quickly leave, but Odysseus insisted on waiting to see the Cyclops and try his hospitality. When Polyphemus saw them, he immediately asked who they were. (This was already very bad form; the best hosts in the *Odyssey* first provide hospitality, food, drink, baths, and beds to strangers, and only afterwards ask their names.) Odysseus replied that they were Agamemnon's men, returning from Troy, blown off course, hoping for a warm welcome and perhaps a gift, according to custom, because strangers were sacred to Zeus. Polyphemus scorned that, picked up two of the men, smashed and ate them, and went to sleep.

Odysseus thought of killing Polyphemus but realized he could not escape the cave because Polyphemus had sealed the entrance with an enormous stone. In the morning, Polyphemus did his chores, ate two more men, and drove his sheep out of the cave, sealing it again with the huge boulder. Odysseus hatched a plan. He and his men cut down a huge club, shaved the tip to a point and then charred it in the fire to harden it. After Polyphemus had his evening meal of two more men, Odysseus offered him some wine. Polyphemus found it delicious and asked Odysseus' name. Odysseus said his name was "Nobody." As a gift, Polyphemus said he would eat Odysseus last. Polyphemus passed out drunk, and Odysseus and his men put the sharpened stake in the fire and then plunged it into the Cyclops' eye. He howled with pain and some of his fellow Cyclopes approached, but when they inquired who was bothering him, the blinded Polyphemus said "Nobody," so they left.

Next, Odysseus figured out how to escape from the cave. He lashed each of his men to the underbelly of a large sheep and bound another sheep on either side. They lay like this, waiting for dawn. The Cyclops let his sheep out, feeling the backs of each, but not the underbellies, so Odysseus and his men escaped. They took the sheep to their boat and left. Once offshore, Odysseus yelled taunts back at the Cyclops and foolishly told him that Odysseus had gouged out his eye. The Cyclops prayed to his father Poseidon to prevent Odysseus from reaching home, or if he was fated to do so, might it be late, alone, a broken man, to a house full of pain. Odysseus sacrificed to Zeus, but did not move him to pity.

Book 10. Next, Odysseus and crew went to the island ruled by King Aeolus, who received them graciously. When Odysseus wished to leave, Aeolus gave him a tightly bound sack full of storm winds and only left the West Wind free to blow them home. They sailed nine nights, and on the tenth night, in sight of land, Odysseus fell asleep. The crew, thinking the sack was full of treasure, opened it, releasing heavy squalls that drove them back to Aeolus' island. This time, Aeolus cursed Odysseus and sent him away with no favoring wind.

They rowed for seven days until they reached the land of the huge Laestrygonians and sent out scouts. King Antiphates promptly ate one of the scouts and the other two ran away. Other giants came running, flung huge rocks down on the ships and speared and ate the crew. Odysseus cut his ship's mooring ropes and sailed away. All his other ships and men were destroyed.

Next, they came to the island of the goddess witch Circe. They rested in the harbor for two days, and then Odysseus, seeing smoke from a dwelling, got curious about who lived there. Although his men wept with fear of more man-eating giants, Odysseus insisted. He divided his crew into two halves and drew lots. The half led by Eurylochus set off to scout the land. They encountered Circe's palace, surrounded by wild animals bewitched by her magic drugs. The men were invited in and all went except Eurylochus who suspected a trap. Circe gave them drugged wine that turned them into pigs but with human minds.

Eurylochus ran back to the ship to report what had happened. Odysseus headed for the palace. Hermes, in the guise of a young man, appeared and offered Odysseus the magic herb *moly* that would enable Odysseus to resist being turned into a pig. Hermes told Odysseus to accept Circe's drink and then, when she waved her wand to turn him into a pig, he should threaten her with his sword. She would be frightened and try to seduce him. Odysseus should play along, but not give in until he got her to swear that she would release his friends and pull no more tricks on them. Odysseus followed Hermes' instructions to the letter. Circe had a banquet prepared for Odysseus, but he refused until his comrades were freed. She freed them and told Odysseus to beach his ship and bring the rest of his crew for a feast.

They enjoyed Circe's hospitality for a year, until finally Odysseus' comrades told him it was time to return home to Ithaca. He asked Circe to let them go and she agreed, but told him that first they would have to travel to Hades to consult the ghost of Tiresias, the only one of the dead who knew the future. Circe explained to Odysseus how to get to Hades and what to do once there. He would have to perform certain sacrifices and rituals and then speak with Tiresias in order to learn how to get home at last. One crewmember, Elpenor, died before they could leave Circe's palace; he was drunk and fell off the roof.

Book 11. Following Circe's instructions, Odysseus sailed to the entrance to Hades and there performed the sacrifices and rituals she had specified. Then, still following her instructions, he sat with his sword, keeping the dead away until he had spoken to Tiresias. However, first Odysseus encountered Elpenor's ghost, who asked him to return to Circe's island and give him a proper burial, which Odysseus promised to do. Odysseus' own mother tried to approach, but he kept her away until after he had spoken to Tiresias, who gave him conditional information about his journey home. Poseidon was still angry about the blinding of his son, but even so Odysseus and his crew might reach home, if they could control themselves and avoid harming or eating the cattle of the sun. If they harmed the cattle, then the ship would be destroyed and all the crew lost, and even if Odysseus got home, he would encounter more troubles in the form of dangerous greedy suitors. Even after killing them, Odysseus would have to leave home again, traveling inland carrying his oar until he encountered people so far from the sea that they did not know what an oar was. Here, Odysseus should sacrifice a ram, a bull, and a boar to Poseidon and then return home. Finally, he would die painlessly in old age, far from the sea.

Odysseus then asked Tiresias how he could make the ghost of his mother speak to him and learned that if he allowed a ghost to approach the blood, it could speak to him and would tell only truth. Odysseus sat and waited for his mother to approach. After she drank the blood, she recognized him, surprised that he had not yet returned home. She told him that his home was still intact, Penelope still waited for him, and Telemachus still had control of his estates, but his father Laertes had retreated to his farm, and she herself had died from grieving over absent Odysseus. He tried to embrace her, but could not because she was a ghost.

Then a crowd of women approached, and Odysseus interrogated each one. They were famous ladies, but most seemed to have had affairs with gods or otherwise been less than faithful to their husbands. Then there was Jocasta, who unknowingly married her son

Oedipus after he unknowingly killed her husband (his father). Clearly, women can't be trusted!

At this point Odysseus finally pauses, saying it is time for sleep. Queen Arête decides that they must give more gifts to Odysseus so he needs to wait another day to collect them. Odysseus graciously agrees. Then Alcinous asks if he saw any heroes in Hades. Alcinous wants more stories, so Odysseus continues. After the female ghosts passed, the male ghosts approached, headed by Agamemnon and his men who were murdered by Aegisthus and Clytemnestra. Agamemnon said that there was nothing worse than a woman bent on murder, and Clytemnestra's deed had tainted all women forever. Agamemnon then warned Odysseus not to trust even his own wife too far, although Penelope would never murder him. Odysseus should sneak into port at Ithaca and be very careful.

Next came the ghost of Achilles. Odysseus praised Achilles as the lord of the dead, but Achilles protested that he'd rather be a slave and alive than Achilles dead. Achilles then asked for news of his son and his father. Odysseus didn't know about his father, but told Achilles about his son's bravery. Then other ghosts approached, except for Ajax, who was still angry with Odysseus for winning Achilles' armor.

Then Odysseus saw some other inhabitants of Hades — Minos who judged the dead, Orion, still hunting in Hades, and Tityus, Tantalus and Sisyphus, who were being tormented because they had offended the gods. He also saw the ghost of Heracles, while noting that the man himself was deathless and feasted with the gods. Finally, thousands of ghosts began to surge around Odysseus, frightening him, and he rushed back to his ship and sailed away.

Book 12. Odysseus and his men sailed back to Aeaea to bury Elpenor on their return from Hades. Circe entertained them for the night and gave Odysseus more advice on how to get home safely. She told him to put wax in his crew's ears as they passed the Sirens. He then must choose a course past the Clashing Rocks and between Scylla, a hungry many-headed monster, and Charybdis, a gigantic whirlpool. It was safer to lose six men to Scylla than be destroyed by Charybdis. Odysseus proposed fighting Scylla, but Circe warned him that Scylla was an immortal so the only choice was to flee. Next, they would come to Thrinicia, where the Sun god kept his cattle. They must leave the cattle alone or the ship and crew would be destroyed and even if Odysseus came home, he would be late, alone, and suffering.

Odysseus and his crew sailed from Aeaea and as they approached the Sirens, Odysseus had his men bind him to the mast, while stuffing their own ears with wax. Thus, he would be able to hear the Sirens, while the ship would get through safely. The ship passed through the Clashing Rocks and entered the straits with Scylla on one side and Charybdis on the other. The men were terrified, but Odysseus, telling them nothing of Scylla, got them to row past her, while she reached out six heads and each head devoured a man. The rest got through alive and soon reached the island of the Cattle of the Sun. Odysseus remembered the warnings of Tiresias and Circe, and he urged his men to keep going. But Eurylochus objected that they were exhausted and needed to land and rest. The rest of the crew cheered, and Odysseus knew trouble was coming. He tried one more plea, warning them to only eat from their stores and leave the animals on the island alone. The crew swore to do so, and they landed.

During the night, a huge storm came up, and then for a month the South Wind prevented them from leaving as their supplies ran out. Odysseus went inland to pray for help from the gods, but he fell asleep. Meanwhile, Eurylochus urged the crew that if they were going to die of hunger anyway, they might as well eat the cattle and die with full bellies. By the time Odysseus awoke, they were feasting on the cattle. The Sun was furious and threatened to go down and shine in the House of Death if he were not avenged. Zeus told the Sun to keep on shining in the sky, and he would destroy Odysseus' ship with a thunderbolt. On the seventh day the wind ceased, and Odysseus was able to sail. Once they were away from land, Zeus sent a squall, breaking off the mast, and then sent a lightning bolt that broke the ship and tossed the crew into the sea. Odysseus lashed the mast and keel together into a sort of raft and held on through the storm. The winds sent him back to Charybdis, where he only escaped destruction by clinging to an overhanging fig tree while his raft was swallowed down and then came up to the surface again. He clung to the raft, unseen by Scylla, and passed through the straits. Then he drifted for nine days and on the tenth was cast up on Calypso's island, Ogygia.

Book 13. Odysseus falls silent at the end of his tale and King Alcinous urges the gathered nobles to add to their rich gifts for Odysseus and tax the people to pay for them. Everyone goes to bed content, and in the morning even more rich gifts are stowed aboard the ship taking Odysseus home. There is one more feast, but Odysseus is eager to leave for home. He graciously thanks Alcinous and the nobles for their kind hospitality and gifts and heads for the ship, where he is bedded down to sleep through the voyage. Just before dawn, they arrive at Ithaca. The Phaiacian crew puts the sleeping Odysseus on the shore beside his pile of treasure and the ship sails for home. However, Poseidon, still angry with Odysseus, wants vengeance. He wants to destroy the ship out at sea. However, Zeus advises Poseidon to wait until the ship is just off Scheria and then turn it into a rock that looks like a ship and pile a huge mountain around the port, so the Phaiacians can no longer have access to the sea. King Alcinous remembers the prophecy that this would happen and advises the Phaiacians to stop carrying people about on their ships and quickly sacrifice to Poseidon, so perhaps he will not pile the mountain in their harbor.

Just then, Odysseus awakes on Ithaca but does not recognize it because Athena has covered everything with mist so she can transform Odysseus privately. Athena approaches in the form of a young man. Odysseus asks where he is and is told he is in Ithaca. Odysseus immediately makes up a false story about who he is and where he has come from. Athena loves the story and changes to her own form, praising Odysseus for his storytelling and his cleverness, just like hers. She assures him that she is beside him to help, but that he must endure still more pain and abuse until the situation is resolved.

Athena lifts the mist, showing Odysseus that he is indeed on Ithaca, and she helps him to hide his treasure. Then they plot the death of the suitors. Athena explains that the suitors are in Odysseus' house courting Penelope, and Odysseus realizes that he, like Agamemnon, might have been killed upon returning home. Odysseus asks Athena for help, which she readily provides. First, she transforms him into an aged beggar so he will not be recognized, and then she tells him to visit the loyal swineherd Eumaeus and ask him for news of the palace and suitors. Meanwhile, she'll go to Sparta to fetch Telemachus home safely.

Book 14. The swineherd Eumaeus receives Odysseus graciously (not even knowing his name), offering him refreshments and asking to hear his story. Eumaeus says that all strangers come from Zeus and it is fitting to treat them well. He prepares a meal for Odysseus and tells him how the suitors are plundering the palace goods. Odysseus asks about his master and Eumaeus tells him what a wonderful, beloved man he was. Odysseus assures Eumaeus that Odysseus is on his way home and will take revenge on the suitors. But Eumaeus does not believe him and continues to grieve for Odysseus.

Eumaeus asks Odysseus (still disguised as a nameless beggar) to tell his story. Odysseus the beggar willingly concocts a tale about having been a well-off Cretan until he sailed for Troy. He survived the war and returned safely home but then sailed for Egypt. His crew went out of control and plundered the area, and the Egyptian soldiers killed or enslaved most of them, but he pulled off his armor and begged the king for mercy. He received it and stayed seven years in Egypt amassing wealth as gifts. In the eighth year, he sailed with a disreputable Phoenician to Phoenicia where he stayed for a year. Then, the Phoenician lured him onto another ship, intending to sell him as a slave. But Zeus struck the ship with a thunderbolt and all the crew died except the beggar. He clung to the mast until thrown up on the beach of Thesprotia where he was treated kindly. And this was where he heard that Odysseus was alive and coming home. The beggar had a few more adventures before landing on Ithaca, poor, old, and wretched. Eumaeus enjoys the story without believing a word of it. Nonetheless, he offers Odysseus-as-beggar a warm bed for the night.

Book 15. Athena goes to Sparta to tell Telemachus to hurry home. She spurs him with warnings that his mother may marry and take away treasures from the palace. She also warns him that the suitors are lying in ambush between Ithaca and Same, so he should take another route home and go to the swineherd's hut. Telemachus should sleep there and send the swineherd to town to tell Penelope he is home safe. At dawn, Telemachus leaves for Pylos, laden with wonderful gifts. He is in such a hurry to get home that when they reach Pylos, he goes directly to the ship, leaving Pisistratus to make excuses to Nestor. As Telemachus is about to sail, the seer Theoclymenus approaches, asking for refuge, and Telemachus takes him on board.

Meanwhile, Odysseus the beggar tests Eumaeus, asking for advice on begging in the town. He'd like to go to the palace for richer pickings, but Eumaeus warns him that would be dangerous because of the pride and violence of the suitors. Eumaeus says that Odysseus the beggar would be better off staying with him on the farm waiting for Telemachus to return home. Telemachus will give him a cloak and shirt and send him on his way. Odysseus agrees to wait and asks about King Odysseus' mother and father. Eumaeus tells him that the Queen died of grief for her lost son and the King Laertes is just waiting to die himself, wracked by grief for his wife and son. Odysseus asks Eumaeus for his own story. He had been the son of a king until a band of Phoenicians landed and one of them seduced his nurse, who agreed to run away with them, taking the child Eumaeus along to sell. They sailed to Ithaca, where they sold Eumaeus to Laertes.

At dawn, Telemachus arrives at the coast of Ithaca and prepares to visit the swineherd while sending his crew ahead to Ithaca. A favorable bird sign appears, which the seer Theoclymenus tells him means that he and his family will rule Ithaca forever. Telemachus asks his trusted friend Piraeus to take care of the seer until he can come home himself.

Book 16. Telemachus arrives at the swineherd's hut and Eumaeus hugs him with love and relief. After they eat, Telemachus asks where the stranger comes from and why. Eumaeus retells the story about how the stranger came originally from Crete, but has suffered many hardships, and now is in the hands of Telemachus. Telemachus replies that he cannot host the stranger because there are hostile suitors in the palace, but he can give him clothes and a sword and send him off wherever he wants to go. Or, if Eumaeus wants to keep him at the farm, Telemachus will send him food and clothing; but it is too dangerous to send a stranger to the palace.

Odysseus the beggar asks why Telemachus is enduring this instead of fighting back. Telemachus replies that he has no means of resisting. Then he asks Eumaeus to secretly tell Penelope that he has returned. As soon as Eumaeus leaves, Athena restores Odysseus to his handsome, more youthful self and tells him to confide in Telemachus, who first doubts and then embraces him. Odysseus asks Telemachus to tell him about the suitors, so they can plan their revenge. Telemachus feels helpless because there are so many, but Odysseus says they will succeed with Athena and Zeus on their side. Then he explains his plot. He will take on the aspect of a beggar again, and Eumaeus will lead him to the city. The suitors may abuse him, but Telemachus must just keep quiet and endure it. When Odysseus is ready to strike, he'll nod, and at that signal, Telemachus should gather up all the weapons from the hall and put them in a storeroom, leaving two swords and two shields for them to use. Athena will befuddle the suitors' wits. Finally, Odysseus warns Telemachus to not let anyone, even Laertes or Eumaeus, know that he has returned. Meanwhile, the two of them can test the servants and maids, seeing if any are loyal. Telemachus agrees to testing the women but says they should leave the men alone for now.

When the ship Telemachus was on comes into port, the crew goes to the palace to announce that Telemachus is back. This upsets the suitors. Antinous proposes that they should waylay and kill Telemachus and split up his property and goods, leaving only the palace for Penelope. However, Amphinomous urges restraint: First, they should ascertain the will of the gods.

Meanwhile Penelope has heard from the herald Medon how the suitors have conspired to kill Telemachus, so, surrounded by her ladies, she goes down to the hall. She cries out at Antinous that he was insane to plot destruction for Telemachus, because Odysseus had saved his father's life. But Eurymachus soothes her, claiming that he would never allow anyone to harm Telemachus (all the while plotting how to kill him!). Weeping, Penelope returns to her chambers. When Eumaeus returns home, Odysseus is again an aged beggar. Eumaeus reports that he has told Penelope secretly of Telemachus' return.

Book 17. In the morning, Telemachus goes to the city to see his mother, and he tells Eumaeus to take the beggar Odysseus to town later, so he can beg his supper. When he gets to Ithaca, Telemachus greets his mother and tells her to go to her rooms and pray to the gods for revenge. Enhanced by Athena, Telemachus strides into the hall, ignores the suitors, and greets his guest, the seer Theoclymenus. They bathe, and then Penelope joins them for a meal. Afterwards, she says she is going to her rooms, but first asks Telemachus what news he has learned of his father. He says he'll tell her the truth and does so up to a point — he relates Menelaus' story of hearing about Odysseus from the Old Man of the Sea. But, like Odysseus, Telemachus keeps the current truth to himself. Then the seer Theoclymenus adds that he saw a clear bird sign indicating that Odysseus is actually now in Ithaca, preparing his revenge on the suitors.

Eumaeus and Odysseus the beggar come to town. They encounter the goatherd Melanthius, who insults them both and kicks at Odysseus, who refrains from killing the man. They come to the palace and Odysseus tells Eumaeus to go on ahead. Just then Odysseus' ancient dog Argos, lying half-dead in front of the palace, senses Odysseus and thumps his tail. Odysseus passes by and the dog dies. Odysseus the beggar enters his own palace and settles down by the doorway. Telemachus sends Eumaeus to him with bread and meat and instructions to go around to the suitors begging from them all. Then Athena comes to Odysseus and tells him to beg from all the suitors to test them (although she intends they should all die).

Some of the suitors give Odysseus scraps, but Antinous is rude and cruel to him. Odysseus goes up to Antinous, asking for scraps, telling him that once he had a life of ease, but his experiences in Egypt and elsewhere have impoverished him. Antinous is unmoved and tries to get rid of him. Odysseus points out that Antinous is eating another man's food and still will not share a scrap. This is the final straw and Antinous hurls a stool at Odysseus, who just goes back to his place by the door and tells the suitors that if beggars have gods, Antinous will die before he marries. Penelope hears of the abused beggar and asks Eumaeus to bring him to her so she can welcome him and ask if he has heard any news of Odysseus. But Odysseus tells Eumaeus that it would be dangerous for him to go through the palace now. Penelope should wait until evening, and then he'll tell her news of her husband.

Book 18. Irus, a real beggar, encounters Odysseus the beggar and tries to run him off his begging turf. They trade insults until Antinous laughs and urges the suitors to set up a fight between the two beggars. He offers a prize of some fresh sausages, and Odysseus requires that the suitors promise not to intervene in the fight. Athena bulks up Odysseus as he prepares to fight. Odysseus restrains his blows, so the suitors will not guess who he is, but he quickly dispatches Irus.

Odysseus the beggar tries to warn one of the more decent suitors, Amphinomous, to go home before Odysseus comes to take revenge on the suitors, but although Amphinomous feels fear, his fate is to die. Then, Athena inspires Penelope to appear and inflame the suitors even more. Athena enhances Penelope's appearance until she is ravishingly beautiful. Penelope descends with two of her women to the hall. The suitors are all wildly lustful for her, but she goes to Telemachus and chides him for the rude reception of the beggar Odysseus. Telemachus replies that he can't control the suitors but wishes they were all beaten or dead like Irus. Eurymachus praises Penelope's beauty, but she replies that her beauty was destroyed when her husband sailed for Troy. However, Odysseus had told her when their son was old enough to grow a beard, she should choose a new husband. She is mortified that the suitors, instead of bringing her gifts, are devouring her stores. The suitors each send for a magnificent gift for Penelope, and they say that they will not leave the palace until she has chosen a new husband. Penelope returns to her quarters and Odysseus orders her maids to follow, but they rudely refuse. Athena encourages the suitors to insult Odysseus even more, which will make their final destruction even sweeter to him. Telemachus urges them to go home to bed instead of making trouble. They do so, leaving Odysseus in the palace, still a beggar.

Book 19. Odysseus and Telemachus now take all the weapons from the hall and hide them in a storeroom. Penelope comes down into the hall with her women, who clear the feasting debris from the hall. While Penelope and Odysseus speak, they may recognize one another, but they are speaking in a public place, and neither acknowledges any mutual recognition. Penelope asks Odysseus who he is and where he comes from, but he evades that question by saying it is too painful for him to recall his past. Penelope says that her life is torment with her husband away, and she yearns for him always. She explains her device of weaving and unweaving the shroud for Laertes while claiming she could not marry until she completed it, deceiving the suitors for three years; but now she has been caught at it and must marry and cannot find a way out. Her parents want her to marry, as does her son.

After telling him this, Penelope again asks who he is and where he came from. Odysseus obliges with a made-up story about his past in Crete and includes a tale of how he actually saw Odysseus and his crew in Cnossos and hosted him for twelve days. On the thirteenth day they sailed for Troy. Penelope is as wary as Odysseus is tricky, and after weeping, she tests him, asking what clothes Odysseus wore, how he looked, and who were his crew. Of course, Odysseus can answer these questions, and he does so in detail. Penelope weeps again, but still keeps her poise and says she will befriend him (he is still in his beggar guise).

Odysseus then tells her some of the truth: He has heard that Odysseus is on his way home, nearby in Thesprotia, with rich treasure. He lost his crew, but came ashore on Scheria and they gave him gifts. But, being Odysseus, he then embroiders the truth, saying that Odysseus would have come home already, but he thought it better to travel more and gain more riches. However, he was also seeking to know the will of Zeus — should he return home openly, or secretly? But, whichever, Odysseus will return this month.

Penelope offers to have Odysseus the beggar bathed, properly clothed and given a comfortable bed, but he says he likes a rough bed and he would only let an old woman bathe him. Penelope tells his old nurse Eurycleia to bathe his feet. While she bathes his feet, she recognizes an old scar received when young Odysseus hunted a boar that wounded him. She starts to speak, but Odysseus grabs her throat and asks if she wants to kill him. She must be silent or he will kill her along with the other women in the house.

Penelope has one last question for Odysseus: should she remain in the palace or should she remarry because the suitors are devouring Telemachus' wealth while courting her? She then tells Odysseus of a dream that an eagle devoured her twenty geese and the eagle said he was Odysseus, back to destroy the suitors. Odysseus says that clearly the dream means that Odysseus is going to destroy the suitors, but Penelope disagrees ... dreams are hard to understand. There are two gates for dreams — one of ivory for empty dreams and one of horn for true dreams. She adds that in the morning she will announce a contest with twelve axes lined up in a row. Odysseus was able to shoot an arrow through all of them. She will marry the man who can string Odysseus' bow and shoot an arrow through all twelve axes. Odysseus urges her to start the contest right away, saying that before it is done, Odysseus will be home. Penelope goes with her women up to their quarters.

Book 20. Odysseus lies awake, listening to the faithless maids, wondering whether to kill them now or after he kills the suitors. He refrains from attacking them but continues to plan his strategy for killing the suitors. Athena pops down for a chat, reassuring him that she will help and he should go to sleep. Penelope, too, has trouble sleeping and prays to Artemis to strike her dead rather than marry a weaker man than Odysseus. At dawn, Odysseus hears Penelope crying, and he asks Zeus for a sign, which promptly occurs as a crack of thunder in a blue sky.

The suitors saunter in as the palace is being readied for yet another feast. As the suitors plot again to kill Telemachus, Zeus sends another eagle omen, this one clutching a dove. Amphinomus realizes that this is a warning that they'll not be able to kill the prince, so they should just enjoy the feast. Telemachus seats Odysseus by the door, gives him food and drink, and announces that this is his house, and he will protect the beggar from the suitors. The suitors are surprised at Telemachus' increasing maturity and assertiveness, but they prefer to feast rather than deal with him. Still, they warn him that he must make his mother remarry if he is to hold on to his father's property. Telemachus says he will gladly let his mother remarry, but he cannot drive her from the palace against her will. Then Athena incites the suitors to laugh crazily, while filled with terror. When Theoclymenus the seer tries to explain what is happening, they laugh at him. He warns that he sees disaster closing in on them; there is no escape. Theoclymenus leaves the palace while the suitors jeer.

Book 21. Athena inspires Penelope to set up the axes and Odysseus' bow. Penelope tells the suitors that the man who can string Odysseus' bow and shoot an arrow straight through the holes in all twelve axes will become her husband. Telemachus lines up the axes. The first to try is the seer Leodes, who fails and warns the suitors that the bow will kill many of them. But Antinous sneers and urges the suitors to grease and heat the bow to make it easier to bend. All but the ringleaders Antinous and Eurymachus try to string the bow, but fail.

Meanwhile, the cowherd and the swineherd leave the palace and Odysseus accosts them, asking if they would defend Odysseus if he appeared, and both assure him that they would. Odysseus then tells him that he is indeed Odysseus and shows them his scar as proof. Then he explains his plan. After the suitors have failed to string the bow, Eumaeus should bring it to Odysseus and then tell the serving women to bolt the doors to the women's quarters. The cowherd should bolt the outer gate of the courtyard.

Then, Odysseus enters the palace and sits on his stool near the door. All the suitors have failed to string the bow, but they propose to feast and try again the next day. Odysseus asks if he can try the bow. They all rage at him, but Penelope intervenes, saying it would be rude to refuse to let Telemachus' guest try the bow. She says if he succeeds, she'll give him nice clothes, a lance and sword, and send him wherever he wants to go. Telemachus interrupts her, saying that he is the one who has the right to say who may try the bow, and he orders Penelope to go back to her quarters. Eumaeus carries the bow toward Odysseus while the suitors heckle and threaten him. But Telemachus shouts at him to continue and he does so. After Telemachus gives Odysseus the bow, he whispers to Eurycleia to lock the doors to the women's quarters.

Odysseus quickly and easily strings his bow, horrifying the suitors. Zeus sends a thunderbolt as an omen. Odysseus takes an arrow and shoots it through all the ax handles, and then he addresses Telemachus as his son and announces that it is time to serve the suitors a feast in broad daylight. He signals Telemachus with a nod, and Telemachus puts on his sword, clasps his spear, and stands beside his father.

Book 22. First, Odysseus shoots Antinous. The other suitors are frantic, but there are no weapons in the room. They still do not want to believe that the shot was not an accident, but then Odysseus announces himself to them and tells them their doom is sealed. Eurymachus tries to argue that Antinous the ringleader is dead and he was the one who incited everyone else. Antinous not only wanted to marry Penelope, but he wanted to kill Telemachus and become king of Ithaca. But he is dead, so spare the rest, and they will all pay abundantly to replace the property they have devoured. But Odysseus is furious and says they must fight to defend themselves because he will kill them all.

Eurymachus tries to rouse the suitors to attack Odysseus in a pack, but Odysseus promptly kills him. Then Amphinomus rushes the king, and Telemachus stabs him dead. Telemachus runs to fetch armor for himself, Odysseus, the swineherd and the cowherd, while Odysseus holds off the suitors with his bow. The goatherd Melanthius runs to the storeroom and brings back armor, which the suitors begin to put on. Following Odysseus' orders, Eumaeus and the cowherd bind Melanthius and hoist him to the ceiling to sway wretchedly from a beam. Then, they put on armor and bolt the door to the storehouse, so the suitors cannot get more armor and weapons.

Athena, in the guise of Mentor, enters the hall. The suitors, thinking she is indeed Mentor, try to lure and threaten her to take their side. Athena, furious, whips Odysseus into action with fierce words and then flies like a bird to the rafters. Six suitors let fly spears all at once against Odysseus, but Athena deflects them. Then Odysseus and his three companions let fly their spears, and each kills its man. Again the dwindling suitors let fly their spears and again Athena deflects them. And once again Odysseus and his men let fly their spears and each kills a man. Athena terrifies the suitors by brandishing her shield, and Odysseus and his men rout the suitors, killing all but two, the bard Phemius and the herald Medon, who successfully beg for their lives and are vouched for by Telemachus as innocent.

Then Odysseus calls for Eurycleia, who wants to cheer when she sees the pile of dead suitors. But Odysseus tells her to keep quiet, not gloat over the dead, and report on the women. He wants her to fetch just the women who have shamed the family by consorting with the suitors. Then Odysseus instructs these women, Telemachus and the two herdsmen to clean out the hall, dispose of the bodies, and wash everything. Once the hall is clean, Telemachus and the herdsmen are to kill the faithless women. After cleansing the hall, the men march the guilty women outside and hang them from a line of nooses. Then they mutilate Melanthius' body, wash and go inside. Odysseus asks for sulfur and fire to fumigate the polluted house. Finally, Eurycleia fetches the loyal women who tearfully embrace Odysseus and welcome him home.

Book 23. Eurycleia now goes to Penelope's room to wake her and tell her that Odysseus has returned. Penelope does not believe her, but the nurse insists it is true. Penelope asks how Odysseus killed the suitors. Eurycleia didn't see that, so she can't answer, but says that all the bodies are stacked outside now and Odysseus is purifying the house with fire. Penelope is still not entirely willing to believe that Odysseus has come home and thinks maybe a god came in his form to destroy the suitors. Again, the nurse tries to convince her, telling her about the scar. Penelope is not fully convinced, but she is willing to go down to her son and see the man who killed the suitors. She enters the hall and sits down facing Odysseus, unsure if he is really Odysseus or someone else. Telemachus thinks her hard, but she tells him she is stunned, amazed, cannot speak, but if this man is really Odysseus, they two will know it through secret signs. Odysseus tells Telemachus to let her test him.

Then, Odysseus asks Telemachus what strategies they should use to deal with the families of the dead suitors, but Telemachus defers to his father. Odysseus then says they should have the maids all dress up and the bard play so any passersby will think there is a bridal party going on. Meanwhile, Odysseus and Telemachus will go to their estate in the country and wait for a strategy from Zeus.

Odysseus is bathed and clothed in fine garments and Athena casts radiance over him, so he looks like a god. Odysseus then confronts Penelope and says she has a hard heart and he will sleep alone. But Penelope replies that he looks like Odysseus did twenty years ago. She then tests Odysseus by telling Eurycleia to move the bed out of their bridal chamber and spread it with fleeces for Odysseus to sleep in. He becomes angry, saying that no one could move his bed because he built it himself. It is fastened to a rooted olive tree and could never be moved. Finally, Penelope believes that he is Odysseus because he knows the secret of their bed. She cries and runs to hug and kiss Odysseus, saying she had often feared that an impersonator would come, pretend to be Odysseus, and create troubles in Ithaca like Helen did at Troy.

Athena holds back dawn, so that the two can have a longer night together, but before they go to bed, Odysseus says that he will have still one more trial and Penelope asks to hear about it. He tells her that Tiresias has said that he, Odysseus, must take an oar so far inland that he will meet a traveler who asks why he is carrying a winnowing fan. At that point, he must plant the oar in the earth and make sacrifices to Poseidon. Then, at last, he can come home for good and live his life to a peaceful old age. They go to bed and enjoy love and telling one another stories of their adventures and experiences for the past twenty years. This time Odysseus tells the same stories that he told on Scheria, so if those stories were true, these are too. In the morning, Odysseus tells Penelope to stay shut up in her quarters with her women and avoid any contact with people. He and Telemachus will go up to their farm where Laertes is living.

Book 24. Hermes takes the suitors' ghosts to Hades. There they encounter the ghosts of the Greek heroes of the Trojan War, grouped around Achilles. Agamemnon's ghost approaches Achilles who greets him. Achilles says that it is a pity he died a wretched death at home instead of a glorious death at Troy. Agamemnon responds with memories of Achilles' death, how his goddess mother Thetis and the sea nymphs mourned him, and the ritual pomp of his funeral and the funeral games. Achilles will always have glory, while he, Agamemnon, died a pathetic death at the hands of his wife and her lover.

Agamemnon recognizes Menelaus' son Amphimedon and asks how he came to Hades. Amphimedon replies that he was one of the suitors courting Penelope. According to him, she led them on, plotted their deaths, and deceived them for three years by pretending to weave the shroud of Laertes, while actually unweaving each night what she wove during the day. In the fourth year they discovered the trick and forced her to finish the shroud, but just then Odysseus returned, and he and his son plotted their deaths. Inspired by a god, Odysseus and his men killed all the suitors. At the time of the telling, their bodies still lie in the palace, unburied. Agamemnon, however, is delighted to hear that Odysseus has returned and avenged his home and family. He praises virtuous Penelope as the opposite of wicked Clytemnestra.

Meanwhile, back among the living, Odysseus and his men reach Laertes' farm. Odysseus now intends to test his father to see if he remembers him. Odysseus sees his pathetic, ragged father working on the farm and weeps, wondering whether he should greet him or test him; being Odysseus, he decides to test him. He goes up to Laertes and tells him that his garden is very well tended but he himself is a shabby, squalid wreck. He then asks whose slave he is and whether this is Ithaca. Then he tells a tale about once meeting a man whose father was Laertes. Laertes weeps, saying that this is indeed Ithaca, but lawless men control it. Laertes asks about when the stranger met Odysseus and tells how he fears Odysseus is dead. Laertes also asks the stranger who he is and where he has come from. Odysseus tells a glib false story, saying that he saw Odysseus five years ago. Laertes begins to cry and finally Odysseus lets go of his story, hugs his father and tells him he is his son, home at last. He explains that he has killed the suitors.

Laertes, true to the family tradition, asks for proof that he is really Odysseus, and again Odysseus shows the scar. He also tells how Laertes gave him the trees in this orchard when he was a boy. Laertes then throws his arms around Odysseus and faints. As soon as he revives he worries about the families of the suitors seeking vengeance. They go to the farmhouse, where Laertes bathes and Athena makes him look younger and more handsome.

Rumor, meanwhile, speeds through the city with news of the suitors' deaths. Their kinsmen gather at the palace and carry away the bodies for their funerals. Eupithes, father of Antinous, urges the families of the suitors to attack Odysseus or they will be shamed forever. But, as Eupithes is haranguing the crowd to violence, Medon the herald approaches and says he witnessed that a god in the form of Mentor was involved in the slaughter, stampeding and panicking the suitors and spurring Odysseus on. Finally, Halitherses, who can see the future as well as the past, tells the families that the slaughter was done because they would not listen as he tried to warn them against letting their sons abuse the household of Odysseus. It is best to let the matter rest. But more than half the warriors prefer Eupithes' plan and arm for a battle.

Athena, seeing this, appeals to Zeus to give peace to both sides. Zeus says that both sides should agree that Odysseus will reign for life, and the gods will wipe out the memories of the slaughter, so they can be friends and the land can be at peace. Then Athena, in the form of Mentor, goes to Odysseus and tells him to let his spear fly immediately. He does so, killing Eupithes, and battle rages between the suitors' kinsmen and Odysseus and his men. (They grab the opportunity to get rid of one more enemy before the peace.) Just then, Athena screams that they should stop fighting and make peace immediately. As the suitors' kinsmen flee in terror, Odysseus is about to pursue and kill them, but Zeus sends a thunderbolt to Athena's feet (a little reminder of their agreement) and she then turns to Odysseus and tells him to halt. He must stop the war and not anger Zeus. Odysseus is glad to obey and Athena creates a peace treaty between the two sides.

HOSTS AND GUESTS IN THE *ODYSSEY*

The *Odyssey* can be read as a poet's travel guide to the imaginary Mediterranean, with plenty of examples of how one ought to treat guests. The first four books of the *Odyssey* are about Telemachus' visit to the mainland, where he is well fed, given gifts and well treated. This is how guests ought to be received. The suitors are slaughtered for the crime of being bad guests who eat their host's cattle, drink his wine and try to marry his wife and kill his son. Adventures in the Odyssey almost all involve some kind of eating or being eaten.

Wrongful food: The suitors devour Odysseus' stores
People are food for: Cyclopses, Laistrygones, Scylla and Charybdis
Blood as food: Shades in the underworld cannot speak until fed blood
Forbidden or dangerous food: Lotus of forgetfulness; Circe's food that turns men into swine; cattle of the Sun
Divine food: Calypso feeds Odysseus, intending to make him immortal

Proper offering of food: Menelaus and Helen offer a proper feast to Telemachus; Nestor offers a proper feast to Telemachus; the Phaiacians provide a proper feast for Odysseus; the Swineherd, Eumaeus, feeds Odysseus; Penelope feeds Odysseus disguised as a beggar.

One can imagine that a traveling poet, such as Homer or the other reciters of the Troy Cycle, would find the arts of good hosting and good guesting extremely important. The narrator gives several accounts of how well the poet Demodocus is treated, including an example of how well Odysseus treats him, sending him a choice piece of meat to show his appreciation. In sum, one moral of the *Odyssey* is: treat your guests well and they'll tell you good stories.

THE UNDERWORLD: FORESIGHT/HINDSIGHT

Books 11 and 24 of the *Odyssey* introduce the Greek underworld, a place where everybody went after they died, no matter what their virtues or vices while alive. The shades, insubstantial remnants of those who have died, can only speak after sipping some blood. The shade of Achilles, the greatest Greek hero, says that he'd rather be a living peasant than dead Achilles. This is not an afterlife to look forward to. However, it does help later readers to understand how precious life was to the Homeric Greeks, since there was no joy after death.

In book 11, the underworld serves as a sort of information clearinghouse where Odysseus learns about what has happened during his wanderings, such as the murder of Agamemnon by Clytemnestra, the death of his mother from grief, and the suitors occupying his palace. He speaks with Tiresias, who knows the future even in Hades. Tiresias advises Odysseus about how best to go home to Ithaca. Odysseus is also warned about what Clytemnestra did to Agamemnon, and he is told that although Penelope is faithful to him, he still should not trust her overmuch, since she is a woman. Guided by Tiresias, Odysseus leaves the underworld better prepared to return home.

The underworld in book 24 is a final gathering of the slaughtered suitors and the other Greek dead. It's a place of retrospection, where the recently dead relate the latest news from life. Hades is a place where nothing more will ever happen. This underworld will serve as an early model for many future underworld journeys by heroes seeking true answers as well as the way home. Virgil will revise it substantially in the *Aeneid* into a more organized, purposive place. Still later, largely following Virgil's redesign, and adding substantial pain and suffering, Dante will fashion Hades into a definitive vision of Medieval European Christian Hell.

THE HERO'S DILEMMA

Homer's heroic men establish their heroic credentials by going out on adventures, trading, raiding and making war. The prizes they seek are fame, treasure, woman war-prizes and slaves, mostly women and children. It seems to be a man's world. However, back home at the palace their women, dependents, slaves and treasures are waiting, vulnerable, never sufficiently protected. Many stories in the *Odyssey* affirm the fragility of the good life in a comfortable palace. People who stay home may be captured by pirates and sold into slavery;

people who travel are also constantly vulnerable to being seized and sold into slavery. This is not a secure situation, either from without or from within.

Control of women is especially difficult while the warlord is absent. Helen leaves Menelaus while he is away. Clytemnestra takes a lover and plots Agamemnon's death while he is away. Suitors invade Odysseus' palace, woo his wife, devour his stores and try to kill his son while he is away. Returning home also can be dangerous for a hero. Agamemnon is murdered in his bath when he returns home; Odysseus has to disguise himself as a beggar to avoid being killed by the suitors when he returns home. Menelaus actually returns home with Helen, and they live in an uneasy truce, she restored to her role as Queen and he anticipating immortality because he is married to a goddess. Luckily, Helen has drugs to help them both forget.

This fragility may well echo the political and social instability at the end of the Mycenaean Bronze Age, when the Sea Peoples were attacking isolated city-states and no palace was secure without a powerful resident ruler and his army. Nonetheless, to be a hero was to roam and plunder. This is the hero's dilemma, epitomized by Achilles' choice — a long dull life at home, protecting his land and possessions, or a short and glorious life at war, hopefully followed by eternal fame in Homer's poetry. Odysseus, however, gets it all — the wandering, the wars, and a final safe return to a faithful wife.

ODYSSEUS' INTELLECTUAL CHARACTER AND FUTURE RESPONSES TO IT

Odysseus is clearly Homer's most beloved hero (although Achilles may be his most glorious one). Odysseus displays the ideals of excellence of his time, a brilliant, versatile man on his own, with no organized authority to turn to, an excellent man, and a favorite of the gods. Yet, some of Odysseus' virtues contain the seeds of what later generations would see as vices.

Intelligence: Odysseus thinks his way through every situation and tests every person he encounters, even his aged father. Later generations will find him too calculating.

Physical courage: He blinds the Cyclops and slaughters the suitors. Later times find him cruel and brutal.

Curiosity: Odysseus gets into scrapes because he is so curious about everything. He has his men explore each unknown place, and this leads to disaster several times, as with the Lastrygonians.

Ingenuity: He has himself tied to the mast to hear the sirens; he ties his men to the bellies of sheep to escape the Cyclops's cave. Later generations will criticize him for devising the Trojan Horse strategy and other too-clever deceptions.

Flexibility: He can, with a little help from Athena, appear young and handsome to impress Nausicaa, or aged and decrepit to remain unrecognized on Ithaca. Later times thought he lacked integrity.

Restraint: He does not warn his men about Scylla; he does not talk to the ghost of his own mother until after he has spoken with Tiresias; he can act like a beggar in his own hall, tolerating abuse; he does not reveal himself to Penelope until after slaughtering the suitors. Later generations will find him too cold and calculating.

Tact: He refrains from holding Nausicaa's knees, the usual posture for beseeching help, because this might embarrass a young woman, especially when the man is naked. Later generations will find him excessively opportunistic, turning every situation to his own advantage.

The will for home: He even leaves the nymph Calypso, who intends to make him immortal (as Helen will Menelaus). Later generations will find Odysseus' will excessive, leading him to adventures beyond the proper boundaries of human endeavor.

Pride: He pridefully, if not wisely, tells his name to the Cyclops he has just blinded. This was not a good idea, since the Cyclops then prays to his father Poseidon to punish Odysseus. However, pride was a necessary heroic virtue for Odysseus as well as Achilles; over the centuries heroic pride evolved into a Christian vice.

Imagination: He makes up endless stories to suit the occasion and achieve his ends. Later generations will call him a liar.

Appealing to women: He appealed to every one of them, it seems, including the goddess Athena. Later times thought him promiscuous. (Lattimore 15–16; Stanford).

As this list indicates, people in later times came to perceive many of Odysseus' heroic, strategic, Homeric virtues as vices. For example, his sense of personal worth could be seen as idle bragging. Had Odysseus not told the Cyclops his name, Poseidon would not have shipwrecked him in revenge. Odysseus's flexibility, which so endeared him to Athena, could be seen as a lack of principled identity. Odysseus' creative imagination, which helped him to tell wonderful stories, could be criticized as the source of lies. His strategic brilliance and ingenuity could be interpreted as devious trickery, as when he devised the wooden horse stratagem to get the Greeks inside of Troy. Odysseus' appeal to women could be seen as faithlessness to his wife by later ages that valued physical as well as emotional monogamy.

Odysseus emerged from the ancient oral world of wandering sailors who have magical adventures, and he never quite fit into the organized, ethical, self-righteous cities of later ages. Odysseus fell swiftly into disgrace; one cannot imagine city fathers and well-fed priests approving his freebooting style. Stanford remarks that by "the end of the fifth century [BCE] the Homeric lion was transformed into a Machiavellian fox, and ... this fox in turn had become the scapegoat of the Athenians" (101).

In a few centuries, Homer's greatest heroes became unacceptable as role models. The world had developed beyond the flux of the Later Dark Age and Archaic Greek civilization. Greek civilization in law-conscious fifth-century Athens had recovered from centuries of migration and chaos when there had been no strict rules of law and order. There was no comfortable place for dead heroes except locked away in their tombs, where they could be safely worshipped and bring blessings to their cities. The Mycenaean Greek heroes of the Homeric poems were as unsuited to Athens as a nineteenth-century gunslinger would be in downtown New York City today. Yet, the heroes were precious as ancestors. Aeschylus' *Oresteia*, discussed in the next chapter, is a wonderful example of how Athenian Greeks transformed their ancestral heroic world into a powerful source for law and order.

5

Aeschylus' *Agamemnon*
Dead Heroes and Wild Women —
Controlling the Past

In the centuries after Homer, Greek attitudes towards the Trojan War and its heroes evolved. The violent, individualistic behavior of ancient heroes such as Achilles and Odysseus was far less acceptable in fifth-century Athens than in Homeric times. Athenians preferred justice under law to the ancient heroic code of revenge. Heroes were best safely buried in tombs, where they could receive offerings and prayers and benefit their descendents without wreaking havoc on their surroundings. Women, especially, seem to have lost ground after Homeric times. The *Odyssey* condemns Clytemnestra and warns that women cannot be trusted, but in fifth-century Athens women were so controlled that they scarcely could leave their own houses after marriage. Nonetheless, the ancient stories remained popular and were put to new uses in Athens.

Greek legends about the Trojan War were plentiful and varied, so different stories about the same event or character might contradict one another, especially in the details. Consequently, although many of the stories used for Greek dramas were based on legends about the Trojan War, the treatment of each legend was up to the individual dramatist (Harsh 6–7). This meant that the Trojan War offered a rich source of important, supposedly historical, story materials along with great freedom to adapt them. The legends of Troy were there for the taking, available to be made into plays that met the needs and interests of Athens's rapidly changing civilization.

A number of plays surviving from fifth-century Athens are based on Trojan War material.

Table 6
Athenian Surviving Dramas Based on the Trojan War

Aeschylus	Sophocles	Euripides
Agamemnon	*Ajax*	*Hecuba*
The Libation Bearers	*Electra*	*Andromache*
The Eumenides	*Philoctetes*	*The Trojan Women*
(Collectively, *The Oresteia*)		*Iphigenia in Tauris*
		Helen

Aeschylus	Sophocles	Euripides
		Electra
		Orestes
		Iphigenia at Aulis

Most of these plays present events before and after the Trojan War. Eight of the plays deal with women. Three plays (*Hecuba, Andromache,* and *The Trojan Women*) center on Trojan women as innocent victims of the war. Two plays deal with Iphigenia before (*Iphigenia at Aulis*) and after (*Iphigenia in Tauris*) the Trojan War. Two plays deal with deceitful, destructive women — Clytemnestra (*Agamemnon*) and Helen (*The Trojan Women*), and one play deals with the odd variant that Helen never really was at Troy (*Helen*).

Eight of the fourteen plays deal with characters from the House of Atreus (the three plays by Aeschylus; *Electra* by Sophocles, and the two Iphigenia plays by Euripides as well as his *Electra* and *Orestes*). Clearly, the cursed yet royal House of Atreus was of great interest to Athenians and their dramatists. The dominant themes of this family history were the cruel, arrogant, impious behavior of the men and the deceitful, destructive behavior of some of their women (Atreus' wife Aerope was unfaithful; Clytemnestra murdered her husband, Agamemnon; Helen, Clytemnestra's sister, ran off with Paris to Troy).

During Aeschylus' long life (525–456 BCE) Athens developed from a city with limited influence, ruled by a family of tyrants, into a maritime empire governed by "the most radical democracy the world has ever seen..." (Rosenmeyer 369). Such radical social changes upset many venerable accommodations of power in Athens, such as those between men and women, and those between the ancient mother goddesses and the more "modern" male deities. A related issue that needed to be redefined was the nature of crime, retribution, and justice in a city where newly enfranchised male citizens freely argued, judged guilt, and established penalties in a court of law. These issues woven together make up the argument of Aeschylus' *Oresteia,* a trilogy, consisting of *Agamemnon, The Choephoroe,* and *The Eumenides.*

The plot events can be summarized as follows:

Agamemnon: Clytemnestra and her lover Aegisthus kill Agamemnon when he returns home from the Trojan War.

The Choephoroe (Libation Bearers): Orestes, the son of Agamemnon and Clytemnestra, kills Clytemnestra to avenge her murder of Agamemnon.

The Eumenides (Kindly Spirits): Orestes must deal with the consequences of his murder of his mother. The Furies drive him mad until Athena initiates a court at the Aeropagus where Orestes is put on trial. The split decision releases him from his bloodguilt.

Modern readers and playgoers often encounter only the first part of the *Oresteia, Agamemnon,* which deals with two women out of control — Clytemnestra, a wife who murders her husband, and Cassandra, a raving girl who had reneged on her promise to a god. The second and third plays of the *Oresteia* deal with bloodguilt and the institution of law at Athens.

The main characters of the *Oresteia* are as follows:

Aegisthus: Lover of Clytemnestra; cousin of Agamemnon

Agamemnon: King of Mycenae; husband of Clytemnestra; father of Electra, Iphigenia and Orestes; sacrificed Iphigenia; murdered by Clytemnestra

Apollo: God of purification; testifies that only the father is blood-related to his child; the mother is merely the vessel in which the child grows

Athena: Patron goddess of Athens; established the court of law at the Aeropagus

Cassandra: Daughter of Priam; war-prize of Agamemnon; speaks truth and is not believed; murdered by Clytemnestra

Clytemnestra: Wife of Agamemnon; sister of Helen; mother of Electra, Iphigenia and Orestes; lover of Aegisthus; murders Agamemnon and Cassandra

Electra: Daughter of Agamemnon and Clytemnestra; sister of Orestes; hates Clytemnestra; cooperates with Orestes to plot their mother's murder

Furies: Ancient demonic goddesses; uphold blood rights

Orestes: Son of Agamemnon and Clytemnestra; brother of Iphigenia and Electra; murders Clytemnestra; driven mad by Furies; cleansed by Apollo; set free by the trial at the Aeropagus

Pylades: Cousin and companion of Orestes

The Story of the Oresteia

The *Oresteia* tells the story of the resolution of an ancient myth — the family tragedy, crimes and recurring bloodguilt of the House of Atreus. Although the complex horrors of this family tree go back to Tantalus, father of Pelops, the conflict presented in the *Oresteia* started with the two sons of Pelops, Atreus and Thyestes, quarreling over the kingship of Mycenae. Atreus became king and banished his brother Thyestes. Atreus then discovered that Thyestes had secretly committed adultery with Atreus' wife Aerope. Hiding his rage, Atreus invited Thyestes to return home for a banquet. Atreus murdered two of Thyestes' children and served their bodies as meat to Thyestes at the banquet. After Thyestes had eaten, Atreus displayed their bloody heads, hands, and feet on a platter. Thyestes vomited and cursed the seed of Atreus (Powell 168–173).

Agamemnon's Family Tree

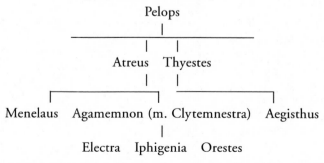

The curse works itself out through the members of Agamemnon's family in the *Oresteia*:

- Agamemnon sacrifices his daughter Iphigenia;
- Clytemnestra murders her husband Agamemnon in conspiracy with his cousin Aegisthus;
- Orestes, Agamemnon's son, murders his mother, Clytemnestra.

The Furies pursue and torment Orestes because he avenges one crime with another, even more forbidden, crime. The Furies are the mythic enforcers of ancient blood-vengeance law, according to which the greatest crime is matricide since the closest blood tie is between mother and child.

Orestes, seeking escape from the Furies and purification of his guilt, petitions Apollo, who advises Orestes to seek help from Athena. She sympathizes with Orestes because she was not born of a woman herself but sprang from the head of her father Zeus. Athena arranges a trial using Athenian citizens as jurors. They will weigh the claims of Orestes' bloodguilt for killing his mother versus Clytemnestra's crime of killing her husband. The Furies agree to abide by the decision of the jury. During the trial, the Furies assert the primary right of the mother, but Apollo insists that the mother is simply a passive vessel; the child is really connected by blood to the father alone (Aeschylus, *Eumenides* 245). This means that matricide is not a bloodguilt crime. Apollo's argument only persuades half the jury, resulting in a tie vote. However, the tie frees Orestes and ends the ancient cycle of murder and revenge in the House of Atreus. Athena then placates the Furies, persuading them to become the Kindly Ladies (Eumenides), benevolent powerful spirits of the city of Athens, tucked underground, safely out of sight.

The *Oresteia*'s stress on violence within the family is not unusual in Greek tragedy. The family was the center of both life and death for the Athenian Greek. As Vickers explains: "The Greek expected to live on not in an afterworld so much as in this world, in the memory and continuous homage of his descendents." Consequently, "the most serious crimes for the Greeks were those which struck against the very basis of family existence: patricide, matricide, all 'shedding of kindred blood,' and incest..." because these crimes interfered with the continuity of the family. Patricide was considered the worst crime because the father was the head of the family in Athenian Greek society (110; 112–13; 377).

Be this as it may, the story of the House of Atreus, like many Greek myths used in the classical tragedies, is full of bloody horrors that both fascinate and repel. Homer generally avoided such horrors. In the *Iliad*, human beings slaughter one another in an above-board, if bloody, fashion. Human wrath, although terrible in its fury and consequences, works itself out with some enthusiastic help from the gods, but there are no demons or furies or dark stories of inherited bloodguilt. Homeric heroes do not die because of what their ancestors did to one another; they die because of their own behavior and that of their living hero peers, lords, and enemies. Although gods may become angry and kill Greek warriors (e.g., Apollo bringing the plague in book 1 of the *Iliad*), even divine retribution in Homer generally ends with death. In the profoundly democratic underworld of the *Odyssey*, the justly slain suitors gather and chat with unjustly murdered Agamemnon and heroic Achilles — all are dead together.

The Story of Agamemnon

The play starts at night with a watchman awaiting a fire signal passed from hilltop to hilltop, from Troy to Greece, indicating that the Trojan War has ended. Clytemnestra has arranged for these signal fires. She is a clever woman as well as a dangerous one, and even worse, she has the heart of a man in her woman's breast, as the watchman tells us at the very start. Clytemnestra, a convincing liar, announces her wifely longing for the return of her husband Agamemnon.

The first half of the play is spent anxiously awaiting Agamemnon's arrival home. The Chorus refreshes the audience's memories about the beginnings of the Trojan War. Although Zeus wanted the Greeks to destroy Troy, Artemis was angered at the prospective slaughter. When the Greek armies gathered at Aulis, Artemis sent winds that prevented the Greeks from sailing to Troy. The Greek seer Calchas prophesied that if Agamemnon sacrificed his daughter Iphigenia, then Artemis would calm the winds and let the Greeks sail to Troy.

Agamemnon, the Mycenean high king, had to choose between sacrificing his daughter or giving up the war. Agamemnon's decision was especially difficult because he was trapped between the demands of two conflicting gods — Zeus wanted the war; Artemis did not (Jones 75–6). The gods were certainly involved, but Agamemnon still made a human choice to sacrifice Iphigenia. According to Clytemnestra (not an unbiased accuser), Agamemnon deliberately chose to sacrifice his daughter and purposively "put on the harness of Necessity" (Aeschylus, *Agamemnon* 41). The gods do not force Agamemnon's choice; neither does his cursed heritage. Aeschylus recalls the old stories about the curse on the House of Atreus but does not make that curse an excuse for Agamemnon's decision.

Agamemnon is not innocent; he sacrificed his daughter to pursue the Trojan War, and now he boldly brings a concubine war-prize from Troy back to his home. Evidently he cannot imagine Clytemnestra effectively rebelling against him. Agamemnon arrives in a chariot with his war-prize woman, Cassandra. Here the real action begins, as Clytemnestra tries to persuade him to walk into the palace on valuable blood-red tapestries, while he objects that this would be an act of excessive pride These tapestries, suggesting the net in which Clytemnestra will trap and kill Agamemnon, are "a symbol of the blood-red destructive woven arts of woman" (Powell 174). Agamemnon and Clytemnestra's argument, which is the only time they appear together, reveals each of their characters in terms of their gender roles. Clytemnestra is a brilliant, manipulative, lying hypocrite; Agamemnon is a proud, insensitive, imprudent hero. As Harsh explains, "the essential weakness of [Agamemnon's] ... character is only too apparent in this clash with the strong-willed Clytemnestra.... In attempting to make Agamemnon accept her base flattery and walk upon the blood-red tapestry, Clytemnestra is attempting to cause him to commit an act of insolence ... which will evoke the disgust and hatred of men and the vengeance of the gods" (69). Agamemnon, who destroyed Troy, surrenders to his wife, who will kill him. Walking on the blood-red tapestries (which are suitable for gods to walk on, not men), Agamemnon enters the palace, shortly to die.

Agamemnon was already famous for his disastrous argument with Achilles in book 1 of the *Iliad*. There, Agamemnon's greed for honor and possessions, his lack of reverence for Apollo's priest Chryses, his capacity for vicious anger, and his insensitivity toward Achilles combined to provoke Achilles' wrath, which nearly destroyed the entire Greek army. Agamemnon remarks later (*Iliad*, book 9) that some god must have blinded him with anger, causing him to quarrel with Achilles. Now, Agamemnon is again blinded, this time by his own arrogance and pride. His argument over whether or not he will walk on the tapestries is, on the surface, a kinder, gentler argument than his quarrel with Achilles because Agamemnon treats Clytemnestra as a mere woman, not a dangerous man. However, Agamemnon is wrong. Clytemnestra has the heart of a man, the murderous rage of a man, but the treachery of a woman. The consequence of this argument will be his death.

Now the most intense scene of the play occurs. The prophetess Cassandra raves outside the palace, predicting horrid murder, while inside, unseen, Clytemnestra murders Agamemnon. Apollo had loved Cassandra, a daughter of Priam, King of Troy. She promised to love him, so he gave her the gift of prophecy, but then she reneged on her promise. Angered, Apollo added to his gift the unpleasant detail that although she would still make true prophecies, no one would believe her. Here, waiting to be killed herself, Cassandra prophesies about the unavoidable connections between the adultery of Thyestes, the cannibalistic murders of Atreus, the curse on the House of Atreus, and the imminent death of Agamemnon. Although the Chorus does not understand much of what she says, the members are inclined to believe her, but not to intervene.

Cassandra does not mention the sacrifice of Iphigenia, although the Chorus told about it earlier. Vickers remarks, "Cassandra's point of view is entirely pro–Agamemnon, anti–Clytemnestra, and her attacks on the Queen are important in establishing that diagnosis of her perversion which Aeschylus is to present as one of the main strands in the motivation of Clytemnestra's crimes" (377). Agamemnon is not innocent, but Clytemnestra's guilt is inexcusable. She is that horror of classical Athenian society, a woman who acts like a man, a woman out of control. Cassandra finishes her raving prophecies and enters the house, going to her own death.

Meanwhile, out of sight, Clytemnestra throws a net over Agamemnon as he bathes and then stabs him to death. Agamemnon's death cries are heard by the Chorus, which still does not want to understand what is happening. When Clytemnestra appears with the bodies of Agamemnon and Cassandra, explaining her actions as just and fated by the demonic curse on the House of Atreus, the Chorus protests her deeds. However, Aegisthus then appears and threatens the members of the Chorus, who quickly back down, and the play ends.

Agamemnon has been murdered, but there will be more murder to avenge his death. Murder is not able to solve the problems of this cursed household; murder begets murder; the ancient, demonic Furies of bloodguilt will punish the murderer, but they do not resolve anything. The punitive, irrational Furies must become integrated into human law in order to stop the series of bloody feuds. This is a message about the need for human law as well as divine punishment (Lloyd-Jones 94), but it is not delivered in *Agamemnon*, which ends in darkness and death. Only in the *Eumenides* does the trial on the Aeropagus prove Orestes to have acted rightly, thus finally breaking the chain of endless retribution (Adkins 185).

Problems with Agamemnon's Character

In the *Iliad* Agamemnon displayed many traits of a bad king. He set off the wrath of Achilles by his own short temper, greed and impetuous behavior. When Apollo's priest Chryses came laden with gifts to petition Agamemnon to give back his daughter Chryseis, Agamemnon could have agreed to return her. Agamemnon also could have respectfully refused to return the priest's daughter (although it was always better to cooperate with men who represented the gods), but there was no reason to threaten the poor grieving father. Similarly, when Achilles called a council to discuss the causes of the plague, Agamemnon might well have resented Achilles' behavior as insubordinate. Agamemnon might have been understandably angry that he had to return his war-prize woman to her father. However, Agamemnon should have had better sense than to seize the war-prize woman of his best warrior.

Agamemnon is too haughty for his own good, and he gets in trouble in the *Iliad* because of his greed, hot temper and pride. This pride is also important in Aeschylus' *Agamemnon*. As Harsh comments: "The pride of Agamemnon ... is ... spectacularly symbolized by Agamemnon's triumphant entrance in his chariot with followers and fanfare. He is ... too proud of his utter destruction of Troy. His conceit ... prevents him from ... understanding the ... warnings of the chorus. From his haughty and contemptuous response to Clytemnestra's hypocrisy, it is obvious that he despises her; but ... he pathetically underestimates his adversary" (19).

Arrogant, imprudent Agamemnon; short-tempered, wrathful Achilles; tricky, murderous Odysseus — these were not ideal Athenian citizens. Live heroes could wreak havoc in a city; dead, however, they provided benefits. Rosenmeyer explains: "According to Greek religious thinking, the great destructive heroes ... can be integrated into the social fabric only after their death. The explosive force, which in their lives compelled them to maim and kill, is later, after they are safely in their sepulchers, thought to be employable for ends beneficial to the society." (347).

Clytemnestra and Other Women Out of Control

Clytemnestra murders Agamemnon. She justifies the murder as vengeance because Agamemnon sacrificed their daughter Iphigenia at Aulis ten years earlier. Clytemnestra, left at home while Agamemnon pursued the Trojan War, took Aegisthus, Thyestes' son, as her lover. Two of Thyestes' children had been killed by Agamemnon's father Atreus and then fed to Thyestes at a banquet. This was cause enough for Aegisthus to crave blood revenge for bloodguilt.

Aeschylus offers no excuses for Clytemnestra — she is presented as thoroughly repulsive, wicked, and dangerous. She is the ultimate horror of the man away at war — a woman out of control, seizing power like a man, taking a lover while her rightful husband is off fighting for loot and glory, and then murdering her husband when he returns home. Powell explains that in "Homer's version of the story, Aegisthus is the principal agent in Agamemnon's murder, and the object of Orestes' wrath. Orestes is therefore a model of heroic behavior, because he defended the honor of the *oikos*, the household. Aeschylus, by contrast, attributes principal responsibility to Clytemnestra, making his drama a powerful study of gender in conflict" (174).

In classical Greek society, women were thought to be unable to control themselves sexually or emotionally. According to Reeder, there "was considerable apprehension in Greek thought that, should her true nature remain unconstrained or become unleashed, a woman would wreak colossal damage on society" ("Women" 26). Young girls were seen as "little bears," wild animals, sexual, energetic and uncivilized; consequently, they needed to be tamed and controlled by the process of marriage at a very young age. Once girls were married, they spent most of their time confined to the women's quarters of their houses (Reeder, "Women" 21–22). Such tight control prevented women from unleashing their terrible emotional powers on men. It also insured that the male head of the family had male heirs who were truly his own (Vickers 110–111).

A man's excellence depended on his position in the public sphere; a woman's on her subordinate position in the household as an obedient, fertile and productive wife (Sourvinou-Inwood 112–113). Some scholars even argue that there was a connection between democracy and the subordination of women since each man's identity as a citizen was based on his role as head of his household of women, children and slaves (Reeder, "Women" 29; Stewart 85).

Girls were married at fourteen to men of about thirty. Husband and society then cooperated to subdue and control the bride, who was by nature emotional, irrational, and unable to control her own sexual desires (Reeder, "Women" 22, 25; Pomeroy 64). An uncontrolled woman was a danger to society since she would act on her animal nature, not as a member of the community (Reeder, "Introduction" 14; "Women" 26). Even worse was a woman who acted unwomanly (that is, like a man). Stories were told about how such women murdered their husbands (Clytemnestra), or children (Medea), rejected a god's advances (Cassandra), rebelled against the rule of law (Antigone), or ran off with a lover, precipitating war (Helen).

Bronze Age Mycenaean Greeks traveled a great deal, pursuing trade, war and piracy, so they may well have felt uncomfortable about the women left at home. Memories or legends of this anxiety are especially notable in Homer's edgy story of Penelope, who is the perfect wife back at home. There are hints in the *Odyssey* that Penelope might have gone wrong, even though, thank goodness, she did not, remaining a model wife to Odysseus. Although Clytemnestra could not wait ten years for her husband, Penelope could wait twenty years for hers. In Homer's representation of the Bronze Age, women were left more or less on their own while the men went off to the Trojan war; some behaved well (Penelope), some did not (Clytemnestra).

However, by the fifth century, Athenian women were supposed to be controlled, primarily by their husbands, and then by the society, which took a strong interest in their containment. Women of childbearing years were largely confined to women's quarters, while the men wandered freely outside. A woman on her own could create a great deal of trouble for society. Evidently this woman problem aroused plenty of interest and anxiety among Greek men, because Athenian dramatists adapted a number of ancient stories about women who were on their own, out of control, and disruptive to society.

Cassandra was a young Trojan princess loved by the god Apollo. First she agreed to accept his love, and he rewarded her with the gift of prophecy. When she reneged on her promise, Apollo cursed her so that no one would believe her prophecies, although they were always true. Young girls were typically reluctant to be possessed by a male; however, they were not supposed to get away with refusing either a marriage or a god. The Greeks believed that young women were prone to serious errors of judgment (Lefkowitz 32) and the consequences could be terrible. Cassandra raves, out of control mentally and emotionally, even though she is a captive slave and the concubine of Agamemnon. She has been removed from her family and the social controls of Troy, which would have restrained her. Agamemnon is unable to restrain Cassandra once he encounters Clytemnestra; he is also unable to protect her.

The Furies, too, are females out of control. They are hideous, ancient, venerable and terribly dangerous. Their ideas of right and wrong are based on blood connection, not law.

They persuade and control by madness, not by reasoned argument. They cannot be denied, their presence is crucial to the city's well being (Lloyd-Jones 93–94); but they have no place aboveground in a well-run city. Athena cleverly persuades them to move into a cave underneath Athens, the underground parallel of the women's quarters in a properly run household.

Demonic gods such as the Furies may have been the remnants of an older, female-centered religion. Certainly, in the *Oresteia* they represent the power of the irrational, the darkness of the unconscious, the kindred blood feud, the necessity of the way things have always been, as well as the fertility of darkness. There was a long tradition of overthrowing gods in Greece; Zeus himself had overthrown his parent generation of gods and ruled Olympus as a model of male power. In the *Oresteia*, however, the ancient demonic Furies of bloodguilt are not overthrown, but placated by Athena and offered a nice new home underground in return for blessing the city of Athens.

The message in all these woman-problem stories is clear: control your women or they will destroy you. After all, the Trojan War was fought over woman problems — goddesses quarreling over a golden apple, the Judgment of Paris, and the consequent abduction of Helen. The curse on the House of Atreus stemmed from woman problems, when Atreus discovered that his wife had committed adultery with his brother. Then there was the incident at Aulis when Zeus wanted the Trojan War, but Artemis, patron goddess of animals, mothers, and infants, did not. In order to appease Artemis, Agamemnon sacrificed his daughter Iphigenia, setting off the wrath of Clytemnestra. Women, out of control, stimulated men to behave in terrible ways; therefore, women must be controlled. This ancient argument is still seen today in cultures that veil and otherwise restrain women, so that men should not be tempted to act badly.

On a more positive note, the message of the *Oresteia* is that the heroic age is over, the heroes are safely buried in their sacred tombs, the Furies are tucked away underground, and the rule of law and order has replaced the demonic madness of feuds and the unending revenge cycle of bloodguilt. The Athenian dramatists' task was not to destroy the heroic past, but to preserve its precious memory and tame its wild energy, rather like building a dam to control a raging river. The dammed water would still be available, but on the city's terms, as a valued resource to be drawn on to meet the needs of its citizens.

6

Euripides' Two Iphigenia Plays
Human Sacrifice and Resolution

More Ancient Violence in the Family Tree of the Atreides (House of Atreus)

Since Greek families were the source of enduring remembrance and fame for their members, it was especially important for ensuing generations to keep the stories of their ancestors in mind. Yet, Athenians of the fifth century BCE found such necessary and pious memories complicated by the bloody history of the Atreides, the rulers of Mycenae (Agamemnon) and Sparta (Menelaus) at the time of the Trojan War. The ancient violence of their ancestors was no simple matter to explain away. The family line of Iphigenia and Orestes had been polluted by the curse on Atreus.

Pollution is a fascinating index of a true difference between our contemporary culture and that of classical Greece. Our current system of morality and justice is based firmly on the idea that each sane person is or can be responsible for his or her own actions, and those actions can be paid for — a robber can pay for his crime by going to jail. We do not accept the notion that a person could carry a moral disease like a virus, without being personally responsible for it, and that this moral disease could sicken others, just as a physical virus could carry the flu from one person to the next. Neither do we accept the notion that a moral disease could descend through a family, as if the pollution were DNA. However, the ancient Greeks believed that the stain of pollution "is not 'within the heart of man.' It clings to a man as something hostile, and from without, and that can be spread from him to others like an infectious disease. Hence, the purification is effected by religious processes directed to the external removal of the evil thing" (Rohde 295). Only divine intervention could purify the cursed Atreides, because human beings on their own could not free themselves of ancient bloodguilt.

An important theme that shows up in both Aeschylus' *Oresteia* and Euripides' two Iphigenia plays is the link between the divinely-aided release of the family of Atreus from the pollution of bloodguilt and the foundation of an important Greek institution. In the *Oresteia*, the Athenian court of law at the Aeropagus is founded; in *Iphigenia in Tauris,* the cult of Artemis at Brauron is founded. Both foundation stories represent the triumphant transformation (with the help of the gods) of ancient violent behavior and bloodguilt into contemporary institutions of classical Greece.

Athens, Aulis, Brauron, Troy and Tauris

The Greek Myths of Iphigenia and Orestes

The Greek armies gather at Aulis, preparatory to sailing to Troy, but the winds fail and the armies are stalled in place. Agamemnon learns that he must sacrifice his daughter Iphigenia in order to placate the goddess Artemis, who will then provide favorable winds to allow the Greeks to sail to Troy. Agamemnon lures Iphigenia to Aulis with a false promise of marriage to Achilles. Iphigenia arrives at Aulis, Agamemnon sacrifices her, favorable winds blow, and the Greek fleet sails.

In some variants of the myth, Iphigenia dies at Aulis. In others, Artemis whisks Iphigenia away from the sacrificial altar, replacing her body with that of a deer. Artemis then takes Iphigenia to Tauris, on the Black Sea, to serve as her priestess. There are also variant myths explaining why Artemis wanted Iphigenia sacrificed. One version claims that Agamemnon boasted that he was a better hunter than Artemis after he had shot a stag. This boast and/or the dead stag angered the goddess. Another version explains that in the year Iphigenia was born, Agamemnon had made a promise to Artemis to give her the loveliest creature born in the year. The false promise of marriage with Achilles had its roots in a tradition that considered Iphigenia to be Achilles' bride. They may even have had a child, Neoptolemus (Lübeck 14, 25).

Years later, Agamemnon's now-adult son Orestes kills his own mother, Clytemnestra, to revenge her murder of his father. Consequently, the Furies pursue him for his bloodguilt crime, driving him mad. Although Aeschylus' *Oresteia* shows Orestes finally freed of the Furies by the court's split judgment at the Aeropagus, Euripides' *Iphigenia in Tauris* presents an alternate version — the half of the Furies that did not vote in Orestes' favor continue to pursue him. Seeking a cure for his madness, Orestes petitions Apollo, who sends him to Tauris to steal a sacred image of Artemis and bring it to Greece. This will put an end to Orestes' suffering.

However, the Taurians, exercising their ancient practice of capturing and sacrificing foreigners, seize Orestes and his cousin Pylades and bring them to Artemis' priestess Iphigenia, who prepares to sacrifice them. Just in time Orestes and Iphigenia recognize one another. They work out a plan to steal the sacred image and escape. Helped by Athena, they succeed and return to Greece, bringing the sacred image with them.

The ancient mythic connections of Iphigenia with Artemis are intriguing. According to Lübeck, the Taurians worshipped a virgin goddess, Parthenos, to whom they sacrificed strangers. When the Greeks began colonizing the Taurian environs, Greek settlers identified the Taurian goddess Parthenos with their own Artemis; however, the Taurians thought that their own Parthenos was identical to Iphigenia, Agamemnon's daughter (50, 55). Evidently, Iphigenia had once been a goddess in her own right. Lübeck explains that Iphigenia, "as a goddess ... was associated with birth and fertility and was invoked by women in parturition: the result could be either beneficial or disastrous. Her cult is considered to have involved human sacrifice" (15).

The sacred image, which Orestes and Iphigenia steal from the Taurians and bring back to Greece, also has ancient mythic origins. According to Lübeck, "Cult places claiming to possess the Tauric image were usually notorious for some bloody and cruel rite which was supposed to have originated in barbaric Taurica. It was also believed that [the sacred image] ... had been brought to these cult places by Orestes and Iphigeneia after their flight from Taurica" (68).

The Plays

The story of Iphigenia is retold by Euripides in two plays: *Iphigenia at Aulis*, which tells of the sacrifice of Iphigenia, and *Iphigenia in Tauris*, which tells the story of Iphigenia as a priestess of Artemis, sacrificing strangers years later in the barbarian land of Tauris. These two plays bracket the Trojan War with stories of aborted human sacrifices, the first of Iphigenia (at the last moment, a deer was substituted for her and she disappeared), and the last of her brother Orestes and their cousin Pylades. These tales of human sacrifice, like the matricide retold by Aeschylus in the *Oresteia*, reflect the cultural importance of the ancient, heroic past, not current events in Athens. Although some scholars argue that human sacrifice was still practiced in classical Athens (Girard 9), archaeological evidence is slim to nonexistent (Hamilton); the theme of human sacrifice in classical Athenian society is probably better considered as analogous to the impact of the biblical story of Abraham and Isaac on contemporary Western civilization. The theme of Abraham's sacrifice is important to many, but we do not practice the sacrifice of young men to Jehovah.

Euripides wrote *Iphigenia in Tauris* first and *Iphigenia at Aulis* a few years later (Harsh 219, 246). This complicates the modern desire to see an orderly progress towards civilized values in the two plays because the earlier *Iphigenia in Tauris* presents a divine "solution" to the ancient problems of blood feuds, bloodguilt, and human sacrifice. The later *Iphigenia at Aulis* raises the problems of blood feuds, bloodguilt and human sacrifice but does not offer a satisfactory solution. This leaves opportunity for modern readers to question whether Euripides had changed his mind about the validity of solutions to violence, perhaps in response to his own war-troubled times, or whether he was just telling the first part of the story a few years after the second. Perhaps he did not believe in ultimate solutions to human violence any more than many of us do today.

Iphigenia at Aulis

This play involves the following main characters:

Achilles: Ag. falsely announced he would marry Iphigenia

Agamemnon: King of Mycenae; brother of Menelaus; husband of Clytemnestra; father of Iphigenia; leader of the combined Greek fleet preparing to sail to Troy

Calchas: Greek seer; says Artemis wants Iphigenia sacrificed

Clytemnestra: Wife of Agamemnon; mother of Iphigenia

Iphigenia: Daughter of Agamemnon and Clytemnestra; demanded by Artemis as a sacrifice

Menelaus: Brother of Agamemnon; king of Sparta; husband of runaway Helen

THE STORY OF *IPHIGENIA AT AULIS*

Agamemnon explains the origins of the Trojan War, starting with Helen's father Tyndareus, who had Helen's many suitors each promise to defend the man who won Helen. She chose to marry Menelaus. When Helen fled with Paris to Troy, Menelaus called in the pledge and gathered an army to invade Troy. The army, composed of Helen's former suitors (mostly kings in their own rights) and their followers, selected Agamemnon as their leader.

The Greek army has become stalled at Aulis by unfavorable winds that prevent their sailing to Troy. The priest Calchas announces that Agamemnon must sacrifice his daughter Iphigenia to Artemis or the fleet will not be able to sail. Agamemnon writes a letter to his wife Clytemnestra, telling her to send their daughter to Aulis to marry Achilles. Vacillating, Agamemnon then writes a second letter telling Clytemnestra to keep Iphigenia at home. Agamemnon sends this letter via an old trusted servant, but Menelaus intercepts the man and seizes the letter. Menelaus and Agamemnon then quarrel bitterly, rehashing one another's considerable faults.

Iphigenia arrives, along with Clytemnestra and Orestes, and Agamemnon decides fatalistically that she must be sacrificed. Now Menelaus changes his mind and tells Agamemnon not to kill Iphigenia, but Agamemnon says he must because the army will force him to sacrifice her in order to go to Troy. All Agamemnon wants is to keep Clytemnestra ignorant of the sacrifice until it's over.

Iphigenia lovingly greets Agamemnon. He equivocates, speaking of sacrifice while she speaks of marriage rites. Agamemnon tries to persuade Clytemnestra to return home and let him deal with the wedding, but she insists on staying.

Clytemnestra encounters Achilles, who knows nothing of the wedding. The old servant enters and says that Agamemnon is going to sacrifice Iphigenia. Clytemnestra begs Achilles to help Iphigenia, and he agrees, not out of any compassion for Iphigenia, but because he feels personally misused. Achilles complains that if Agamemnon had asked to use his (Achilles') name to lure Iphigenia to Aulis so that the Greeks could go to Troy, he would have agreed. What angers Achilles is that his name was used without his permission. Achilles vows to save Iphigenia, but first he wants Clytemnestra to try persuading Agamemnon. Mostly Achilles wants to protect his reputation.

Agamemnon comes to fetch the weeping Iphigenia, who by now has heard of the planned sacrifice. Clytemnestra asks Agamemnon if he will kill Iphigenia. He equivocates and bemoans his fate. Clytemnestra furiously recites Agamemnon's crimes against her. Agamemnon had seized her by force, killed her former husband Tantalus and their infant, and then married her. Despite that, she was a blameless wife to Agamemnon, bearing him three daughters and a son. Now Agamemnon wants to kill her daughter so Menelaus can have Helen back. Clytemnestra threatens Agamemnon that if he forgets his duty, she will forget hers, and she makes not-so-veiled threats about his future homecoming if he harms Iphigenia.

Iphigenia pleads with Agamemnon that she has nothing to do with the guilt of Paris and Helen. However, Agamemnon takes refuge in patriotism, saying he must kill Iphigenia for Greece's sake to protect Greek women from being carried off by barbarians. Agamemnon also says that the Greek army will kill him and his family unless he kills Iphigenia. With that, he leaves the scene.

Achilles enters, complaining that the army is angry with him and he is in danger of having stones thrown at him. This is a degraded, cowardly unhomeric Achilles, but he still says he will defend Iphigenia if she wishes it.

Iphigenia realizes that there's no point in resisting and makes a rather sudden about-face. She affirms the glory of Greece, saying she will die for the common good and arguing that it would not be right for Achilles to fight alone against all the Greeks and die for a woman's sake, because a man is more worthy than thousands of women. She exults: I give my life to Greece.

> Take me, kill me,
> and bring down Troy. That will be my monument
> for ages to come. That will be my wedding,
> my children, the meaning of my life.
> Mother, it is the Greeks
> who must rule the barbarians,
> not the barbarians the Greeks.
> They are born to be slaves; we
> to be free [*IA* 1886–95].

Achilles admires and thoroughly approves Iphigenia's resolution of the problem. She has willed to do what she has to do. Indeed, she is making her sacrifice sound downright glorious.

Iphigenia then tells Clytemnestra not to mourn, promising that her sacrifice is blessed. Iphigenia happily performs sacred rites and goes offstage to die, saying she will bring victory to Greece and destruction to Troy. The Chorus is cheery too, hoping that Iphigenia's sacrifice will indeed result in victory over Troy.

A messenger arrives to announce that during the sacrifice, as the priest grasped the knife, suddenly a wonder occurred. The knife struck, but the girl vanished, and a slain deer lay on the altar. Iphigenia is now with the gods. Agamemnon wishes Clytemnestra farewell, and the Chorus wishes Agamemnon a joyful return and wonderful spoils.

THE ENDING OF *IPHIGENIA AT AULIS*

The ending of *Iphigenia at Aulis* is questionable. The extant text ends with a messenger announcing that during the moment of her sacrifice, Iphigenia disappeared and a dying deer replaced her. Clytemnestra doubts the news, but Agamemnon, remarking that their daughter is with the gods, cheerfully sets sail for Troy. The play may have been left unfinished by Euripides and completed by someone else (Harsh 246–7), or Euripides' ending may have become corrupted, or at least illegible (Dimock, "Introduction" 3). This leaves open the question of whether Euripides intended Iphigenia to die at Aulis or to be rescued by the goddess Artemis, who substituted a deer for the girl's body. There are also questions about whether Iphigenia understood that the sacrifice would lead to her death or believed that it would in some fashion transform or elevate her to another, higher existence (Lübeck 33).

Furthermore, Iphigenia's sudden glorification of her own sacrifice seems unmotivated to many people. The problem is in her sudden change from a frightened girl pleading to live to a willing, even joyous, sacrificial victim. Aristotle long ago criticized Iphigenia's about-face for its lack of motivation (Lübeck 30–33). Various modern readers seek to understand what could have brought about such a radical change in her attitude toward her own death. Rabinowitz points out that a "central and peculiar feature of Greek practice with respect to sacrifice was 'willingness': the victim had to seem to walk up to the altar of its own volition, and various tricks were used to gain the appearance of consent.... The appearance of consent transformed what would have seemed a slaughter or murder into a sacrifice" (35). Perhaps Iphigenia had to change her mind in order to make the sacrifice effective. That might have made sense to Euripides, but it makes less sense to us.

Partially because of Iphigenia's sudden change in attitude, and partially because of the questioned ending (did she die or was she divinely rescued?), modern critics can put forth radically different interpretations of Iphigenia's sacrifice at Aulis — some think she is a pathetic, helpless young woman, fooled into cooperating with a horridly corrupt system (Michelakis on Aretz, BMR; Dimock, "Introduction" 4). Others think she willingly asserts the virtues of a Homeric hero as she dies for the glory and freedom of Greece (Lefkowitz 95; Foley 124; Rabinowitz 42). Iphigenia did indeed choose to die, but what is the meaning of a choice when there are no options? What is the meaning of a choice when one is forced or fated to die?

Iphigenia in Tauris

In addition to Iphigenia from *Iphigenia at Aulis*, this play includes the following new main characters:

Athena: Resolves the situation in Tauris

Orestes: Son of Agamemnon and Clytemnestra; younger brother of Iphigenia; killed Clytemnestra after she murdered Agamemnon; pursued by Furies

Pylades: Cousin to Orestes and Iphigenia

Thoas: Barbarian ruler of Tauris

THE STORY OF *IPHIGENIA IN TAURIS*

Iphigenia recites her genealogy as a Tantalid (Tantalus was an ancestor of the Atreus family). She identifies herself as Agamemnon's daughter and gives a synopsis of the events at Aulis, where her father sacrificed her (or so he thought) for the sake of Helen. Artemis replaced Iphigenia at the altar with a deer and brought her to the land of the Taurians, ruled by King Thoas. Iphigenia now is the priestess of Artemis at Tauris and officiates at sacrifices of captured stray Greeks. Iphigenia has dreamed of the House of Atreus collapsing. She interprets this as the death of her brother Orestes, the last male of the family. She exits.

Orestes and his cousin Pylades enter. Orestes had asked Apollo how he could bring an end to his madness, which was caused by the Furies to punish him for killing his mother Clytemnestra. Apollo sent Orestes to Taurus to steal an image of Artemis that had fallen from the sky into the temple of the goddess. After Orestes brings this image back to Greece, his suffering will come to an end. Pylades suggests they hide in a cave until dark, when they can try to seize the image.

Meanwhile, Iphigenia mourns for Orestes and the end of the House of Atreus. The Chorus wails that this is fate punishing the House of Atreus for their crimes. Iphigenia bitterly responds that she has been cursed since conception, ill-fated since birth. First she was deceived and sacrificed by her father. Now, she lives a joyless, lonely existence sacrificing others.

Herdsmen enter with news of two Greeks, freshly captured for a sacrifice to Artemis. One of the young men is mad and was rampaging at the shore, killing cows as if they were monsters. Iphigenia will officiate at their sacrifice. Iphigenia recalls how she used to be kindly to strangers instead of sacrificing them with a hard heart. If only she could kill Menelaus or Helen as revenge for her father's sacrifice of her at Aulis. Yet, Iphigenia denies that either the gods or the Tantalids are evil; instead she blames the Taurians for their evil practice of human sacrifice.

Bound, Orestes and Pylades are brought to Iphigenia. Orestes avoids naming himself but tells the latest news from the Trojan War: Helen is back in Sparta, Calchas dead, Odysseus still wandering. Agamemnon is dead, killed by Clytemnestra, who in turn was killed by Orestes. Electra is still alive, but Iphigenia was sacrificed. Iphigenia proposes to save the still-unrecognized Orestes. She wants him to take a letter back to Greece to her brother Orestes, while she sacrifices Pylades. Orestes refuses to betray his companion and insists that he be sacrificed instead.

Iphigenia narrates the letter's contents, so Pylades can deliver the information even if the letter is lost. The letter tells how she did not die, but was taken off to Tauris by the goddess. Orestes and Pylades realize who she is, and Orestes reveals his name. Iphigenia wants proof of his identity, which Orestes provides by reciting memories of their childhood home and family experiences. They have an intense reunion, talking about the horrors of their lives. Orestes tells his bitter story. After killing their mother, he wandered about pursued by the Furies until he stood trial in Athens. Apollo testified for him, and Athena somehow arranged the jury vote to come out evenly divided, so he was released after the trial. However, while some of the Furies settled in Athens, other Furies, who had voted against him, continued to pursue him with madness. He prayed to Apollo for release from his torments. In response, Apollo told Orestes to travel to the sanctuary of Artemis in Tauris, steal the sacred image that fell from the sky, and bring it back to the land of Athens.

Iphigenia devises a scheme to escape with the image. She tells King Thoas that she cannot sacrifice the two Greeks until she purifies their pollution since they were matricides. She also has to purify the image since they had touched it. Thoas agrees, and Iphigenia goes to the shore with Orestes, Pylades and the image.

However, a messenger soon informs Thoas that Iphigenia has tricked him. Iphigenia, the Greeks and the image are aboard a Greek ship, struggling to escape through the rocky passage to open sea. Thoas starts to pursue them, but Athena appears aloft and tells Thoas that Orestes was obeying Apollo, who sent him to Tauris to bring his sister and the sacred image back to Greece, thus ending his madness. Athena ties up all the loose ends: Orestes will build a temple for the image in Attica; Iphigenia will be a priestess of Artemis at Brauron; Thoas must return the Greek captive women to Greece; in the future, equal votes will prevail, as in Orestes' trial at Athens; and Thoas should not be angry, since this is the will of the gods. Thoas heeds the goddess, and all the Greeks, along with the image, set off for Athens.

Myth and Human Sacrifice

Euripides drew on the ancient mythic material that connected Iphigenia with Artemis and human sacrifice. To be sure, human sacrifices were far more frequent in fiction than in fact (Lübeck 113). Furthermore, Euripides does abort the human sacrifices in both of his Iphigenia plays, moving the interest of the ancient myth into a more modern, less bloody dimension. Nonetheless, along with cannibalism, fratricide and matricide, human sacrifice was definitely among the horrors committed by the cursed Atreus family.

According to René Girard, the "common denominator [of all sacrifices] is internal violence — all the dissensions, rivalries, jealousies, and quarrels within the community that the sacrifices are designed to suppress. The purpose of the sacrifice is to restore harmony to the community, to reinforce the social fabric" (8). Certainly Euripides presents Iphigenia's sacrifice at Aulis in this light. Her willing sacrifice quiets the dissent in the Greek camp, makes peace between the brothers Agamemnon and Menelaus, as well as between Achilles and Agamemnon, and allows all the Greeks to pursue a common goal — war against Troy to protect Greek interests.

Although Iphigenia's sacrifice (and possible death) does bring about favorable winds that allow the Greeks to sail to Troy, it is not free of consequences. Girard remarks that all "sacrificial victims ... are invariably distinguishable from the nonsacrificeable beings by one essential characteristic: between these victims and the community a crucial social link is missing, so they can be exposed to violence without fear of reprisal. Their death does not automatically entail an act of vengeance" (13). Because Iphigenia is the unmarried daughter of Agamemnon, the highest-status member of the Greek army, it should be possible for her father to sacrifice her without reprisal. Certainly, her sacrifice heads off the burgeoning feuds between Agamemnon and other major characters — Odysseus, Calchas, Achilles and Menelaus, and it also calms unrest in the army.

While the men in the story do reconcile their differences over the sacrifice, Clytemnestra will revenge the death of her daughter. So, although the sacrifice of Iphigenia makes the Trojan War possible, it also leads to Clytemnestra's murder of Agamemnon upon his victorious return from Troy. This leads in turn to Orestes' murder of his mother Clytemnestra, continuing the family tradition of bloodguilt. The female Furies then punish Orestes for his bloodguilt by driving him mad. In Euripides' version of the myth, not even the trial at the Aeropagus ends the persecution of Orestes, because the Furies who voted against Orestes refuse to accept the verdict to free him. When he goes to Tauris to fetch the sacred image and end the Furies' pursuit, Orestes is nearly sacrificed by his (unknown) sister Iphigenia. Such killings, whether sacrifices or murders, do not produce ultimate social harmony. Not even a court of law can produce ultimate social harmony. Only the final intervention of the goddess Athena can put an end to the chain of murders and revenge murders that plagues the descendents of Tantalus.

One might say that Euripides' message about human sacrifice is, "Don't bother; it won't work — see what a mess came from the sacrifice of Iphigenia." That, however, was probably not a particularly useful message in his day. The more interesting message, if one can speak of a message in such complex material, is that human beings cannot clear up the messes they create (and those messes may be instigated by the gods). It is true that the gods make excellent theatrical devices, especially when descending in their machines from the sky (actually cranes from the roof of the theater) to untangle the web of human confusions. But, as we understand so well today, in the absence of those helpful gods in their handy machines, we humans on our own don't do a very good job of clearing up the messes we get ourselves into.

Euripides' Enigmatic Gods

The roles of the gods in Euripides' Iphigenia plays are complex and contradictory — especially that of Artemis, who protects women in childbirth, yet demands human sacrifice. Iphigenia (in Tauris) ponders these contradictions but insists that the gods do no evil. Human beings do not understand the wills and actions of the gods, nor are humans able to "solve" situations created in relation to the gods.

Grube asserts: "No one would maintain that Euripides believed in the literal existence of the gods such as he represented them on the stage, as definite personalities with human shape..." (48). However, Grube also argues: "It can hardly be denied that a good deal of the divine apparatus in Euripides must be so accepted.... The question whether Euripides does or does not believe, or wish us to believe, in the gods, does not arise, at least while the play is going on. He wants us to accept the divine framework as part of the story" (49).

Each of Euripides' two Iphigenia plays is resolved by a *deus ex machina* (a god in a machine) coming down from the sky to intervene at the end, although the actual event is only shown in *Iphigenia in Tauris*. At Aulis, we are told (but not shown) that after demanding that Agamemnon sacrifice his daughter, Artemis (presumably) rescues Iphigenia from the altar. Similarly, Athena rescues Orestes, Pylades and Iphigenia from Tauris. These ancient, god-involved situations are too tangled and dangerous for human beings to deal with effectively. Thus, in the ancient Greek religious context, the *deus ex machina* ending makes sense: Only the gods can solve such problems.

The Literary Afterlife of Iphigenia

Many later writers were attracted by the power of Euripides' Iphigenia plays, especially *Iphigenia at Aulis,* but they had problems with various elements of the play, including the demands of the ancient gods for human sacrifice, the lack of clear motivation for Artemis to demand the sacrifice at Aulis, the vacillating character of Agamemnon, Iphigenia's sudden shift from wanting to live to affirming her own sacrifice, and the extreme barbarism of the Atreus family and their ancestors. The *deus ex machina* ending also became uncomfortable for later Christian writers, who thought in terms of human free will, impulses and actions, rather than the pagan gods as the causes of events. Nonetheless, there are many retellings of the stories of Iphigenia. I will examine two modernizations of Iphigenia's story, by Racine and Goethe, in Chapter 12.

7

Virgil's *Aeneid*
Roman Transformation of Homeric Myth

In the first century BCE, the Roman poet Virgil wrote the *Aeneid*, an epic poem linking the Trojan War to the founding of the Roman Empire. Aeneas was a Trojan prince who fled from burning Troy with a group of Trojan survivors. After much painful wandering, the Trojan refugees arrived in Italy, where they fought a bitter war against the indigenous people of the area. Finally, the Trojans and the Latins made peace, Aeneas married the Italian princess Lavinia, and their descendents founded Rome.

The *Aeneid*, and with it Troy, were considered part of the history of Latin Europe. Because of the predominance of Rome, first as the capital of the Roman Empire and later as the seat of the Catholic Church, the *Aeneid* became widely accepted as the foundation story of Latin Catholic European civilization. In the Renaissance, ruling families in several European countries proudly claimed Trojan Aeneas as their ancestor.

Virgil (70–19 BCE)—A First-Century Roman Citizen

Not much is known about Virgil's life. He was born in 70 BCE and raised in a rural area near Mantua, Italy; he was well educated; his family farm was seized as a political spoil. From his thirty-first year on, Virgil lived either in Rome or near Naples, associated with his patron Maecenas, Emperor Octavian's minister of internal affairs. Virgil was a court poet whose livelihood depended on pleasing powerful members of the ruling class. He evidently did this quite well. Maecenas and other wealthy patrons supported him financially, allowing him to spend his life writing poetry (Starr 171–2; Camps, "Aelius Donatus" 115–120).

During Virgil's lifetime, Rome was the ancient capital city of a huge empire made up of diverse races, religions, and cultures. However, a generation of bitter civil wars had made life precarious. Octavian finally ended the civil wars at the Battle of Actium in 31 BCE, when he defeated Antony and Cleopatra. Octavian, who took the name of Augustus in 27 BCE, thus became the single master of the Roman world. People felt greatly relieved by the end of the civil wars. They credited the gods for the peace because just as war was explained by divine anger, peace also came by the will of the gods (Starr 37; Olgivie 7–8).

Written in the decade or so after the Battle of Actium, the *Aeneid* celebrates Rome, the Battle of Actium, and the Augustan peace, while illustrating the horrors and brutality of war. The *Aeneid* tells about the piteous fall of Troy, the painful struggles of a small band of Trojans to locate their ancestral and future homeland, and the terrible suffering of the unavoidable war they had to fight in order to establish themselves in Italy.

The gods willed the fall of Troy. Jupiter (the chief Roman god), Destiny and Fate all willed the creation of a new Trojan/Latin people in Italy, who would give birth to the ancestors of Rome. In the underworld, Aeneas sees a vision of the future Roman rulers, leading up to Augustus himself. At the very center of Aeneas' shield is the Battle of Actium. In brief, out of the fall of Troy came Rome; what Aeneas founded, Augustus completed.

Virgil worked on the *Aeneid* for a decade, until his death in 19 BCE. He died rather suddenly, just as he was beginning a planned three-year revision of the *Aeneid*. Virgil had left instructions for his friends to destroy the manuscript, but fortunately they did not burn it; perhaps he had changed his mind (Knight 12).

Even though Virgil died before Christ was born, Christian Europe adopted Virgil as a sort of honorary Christian, a gentile prophet. He was often considered a magician, and books about his magic and miracles were popular. People even prophesied the future by opening the *Aeneid* at random to a passage, which was then used as an omen or fortune (Knight 23–24).

The Transformation of the Greek Past into the Roman Future

Virgil's *Aeneid* consciously parallels Homer's *Iliad* and *Odyssey*. However, Virgil transformed Homer's individualistic, crafty Greek heroes into the villains, and Homer's Trojan losers into the noble, pious, community-minded, heroically suffering, finally victorious ancestors of Rome. Virgil even reformed the irrational, passionate Homeric gods, by giving their leader, Jupiter (the Roman analogue of Zeus), Roman purpose. The *Aeneid* is full of raging gods, especially Juno (Hera) and Allecto (one of the Furies). The *Aeneid* also has plenty of raging humans such as Dido, Amata, and Turnus. However, all the events in the poem ultimately serve the purposes of Destiny, Fate and Jupiter, whose shared ultimate goal is the foundation of the Roman Empire.

The individualistic Homeric heroes, even at their best, support only themselves and their comrades. Their goals are limited: fetch back Helen, gain glory, destroy the enemy, and return home. There is no future in Homer — the Trojan War is fought at the end of the Greek Heroic Age. The Greeks leave Troy with treasure and slaves; many never make it home. Aeneas, on the other hand, leaves Troy bearing his past into the future. On his back Aeneas carries his aged father, who holds the Trojan and household gods. Aeneas' young son Ascanius walks by his side. A few Trojan survivors join them. For Aeneas the fall of Troy is only the beginning of the struggle to found a new civilization that will eventually become Rome. Through trial and suffering he gradually evolves into father Aeneas, the ancestor of future generations of Romans.

There is no future after death for the Greek heroes. The Homeric dead all mass together in a vague limbo-land, shades with faint memories and no passion. Nothing ever changes in Hades except the shades of newly fallen heroes who arrive and tell their stories. Even the shade of Achilles, greatest of Greek warriors, says he'd rather be a live peasant than a dead hero.

Virgil's underworld, while echoing Homer's, is a place where past and future meet. The dead go there, not to languish forever, but to be punished if necessary, cleansed, and improved. Then, the purified dead rest and play in the Elysian Fields; most are eventually reborn. It is in this underworld that the living Aeneas, guided by his dead father Anchises, views the procession of yet-to-be-born Roman rulers. In Homer's underworld, Odysseus receives useful advice that helps him to get home safely. In Virgil's underworld, Aeneas receives the true knowledge of his destiny, which encourages and guides him through the coming wars in Italy.

The Main Characters in the Aeneid

Quite a few of the Greek and Trojan characters in the *Aeneid* come directly from the Homeric tradition, which is not surprising, considering that Virgil is retelling a Homeric tale. Other characters in the *Aeneid* are modeled on Homeric characters (e.g., Turnus is modeled on Achilles) but given different names. The gods mostly parallel the Homeric gods, although the names are usually different, and in some cases they behave differently.

Roman Deities (and their Greek parallels)

Allecto (a Fury): Instills irrational rage in her victims
Apollo (Apollo): Sun god; son of Jupiter; god of prophecy
Cupid (Eros): Son of Venus
Iris (Iris): Rainbow goddess; Juno's messenger
Juno (Hera): Wife of Jupiter; chief goddess of Carthage
Jupiter (Zeus): Chief deity; husband of Juno
Mars (Ares): God of war
Mercury (Hermes): Messenger god
Venus (Aphrodite): Mother of Aeneas and Cupid; goddess of love
Vulcan (Hephaestus): Husband of Venus, god of the forge and fire

Greeks

Pyrrhus: Son of Achilles; also named Neoptolemus
Sinon: Lies to Trojans about Trojan Horse
Ulysses (Odysseus): Devises Trojan Horse

Trojans

Aeneas: Trojan prince; son of Venus; father of Ascanius
Anchises: Aeneas' father
Andromache: Widow of Hector
Ascanius (also called Iulus): Son of Aeneas and Creüsa
Camilla: Female warrior; ally of Turnus
Creüsa: Aeneas' wife; dies during the flight out of Troy
Euryalus: Trojan warrior; friend of Nisus

Hecuba: Queen of Troy; wife of Priam
Helenus: Son of Priam; a prophet
Laöcoön: Trojan priest
Nisus: Trojan warrior
Priam: King of Troy
Polydorus: Trojan ghost; warns Aeneas to flee from Thrace

Tyrians

Anna: Dido's sister
Dido: Queen of Carthage; widow of Sychaeus; also called Elissa
Sychaeus: Dido's dead first husband

In Italy

Amata: Queen of Latium; wife of Latinus; mother of Lavinia
Evander: King of the Arcadians; Aeneas' ally; father of Pallas
Latinus: King of Latium, husband of Amata, father of Lavinia
Lavinia: Daughter of Amata and Latinus
Pallas: Young warrior; son of Evander; ally of Aeneas; killed by Turnus
Sibyl: Apollo's priestess; guides Aeneas into the Underworld
Turnus: Rutulian king; heads opposition to Aeneas in Italy; kills Pallas; killed by Aeneas

THE STORY OF THE AENEID

Virgil deliberately patterned the *Aeneid* on the *Odyssey* and the *Iliad*. The first half of the *Aeneid* (books 1–6) adapts the plot of the *Odyssey*: the fall of Troy, hostile gods, lengthy wandering, woman troubles, the underworld, seeking home. The second half (books 7–12) mirrors the wrath and warfare of the *Iliad*.

Book 1. Aeneas struggles to find his ancestral homeland, but Juno opposes him. She hates the Trojans for three reasons: the Judgment of Paris, which insulted her beauty; the theft of Helen, which violated Juno's position as the goddess of marriage, and the future fall of Carthage, her favorite city. After seven years of confused wandering, Aeneas nears his goal of Italy, but Juno interferes. She arranges for a storm to drive him toward North Africa and Carthage. Dido, founder and queen of Carthage, welcomes Aeneas and his companions. Although Jupiter assures Venus that her son Aeneas will prevail, Venus worries that Dido might harm him, so she sends Cupid to poison Dido with love for Aeneas.

Book 2. Dido is gracious to Aeneas and his companions and interested in the story of Troy. Aeneas tells her how the Greeks created the Trojan horse. When the suspicious Trojan priest Laöcoön struck the Horse with his staff, serpents promptly devoured him, suggesting to the Trojans that the gods were angry with the priest. The Trojans consequently brought the Horse into Troy. Sinon, a deceitful Greek, released the Greeks from the Horse, and the slaughter began. Aeneas tells of the final battle. He fought furiously, until his mother Venus revealed to him that the gods themselves were destroying Troy. Venus instructed Aeneas to leave Troy with his father Anchises, his son Ascanius, and the household gods of his family and of Troy. While fleeing Troy, Aeneas' wife Creüsa fell behind and was killed.

Book 3. Aeneas tells Dido how he and his band of Trojans have been searching for a new Troy. First they went to Thrace, where they encountered the dead Trojan Polydorus in the form of a bleeding bush that warned them of treachery. The Trojans performed funeral rites for Polydorus and quickly left Thrace. Next, they traveled to an island where a prophetic voice advised them to seek out their ancient mother. However, they were unsure what place was their "ancient mother." Anchises thought it was Crete, so the Trojans tried to found a city there, but soon they started dying of pestilence. The household gods appeared to Aeneas to tell him that Italy was their true ancient mother. On their way again, the Trojans encountered the horrid Harpies in the Strophades. The Harpy Caelano threatened them, saying that when they got to Italy, the Trojans would be so hungry they would eat their plates. Next they landed at Actium in northwest Greece, where they held Trojan Games. After the games, they sailed to Buthrotum, where the Trojan Helenus, Apollo's priest, directed them to Italy. However, first Aeneas would have to visit the Cumaean Sybil and the underworld. They safely sailed past the Cyclops's island and the dangers of Scylla and Charybdis. But, before the Trojans could reach their goal of Italy, Anchises died, and then a storm drove them to Africa, where they came ashore at Carthage.

Book 4. Dido had been married to the Tyrian Sychaeus, who was treacherously killed by her brother. Dido fled Tyre with a band of followers and came to North Africa, where she acquired land to found the city of Carthage. Poisoned by Cupid, Dido falls madly in love with Aeneas. Juno and Venus strike a deal, each thinking to further her own cause. Juno wants to keep Aeneas from founding Rome, which will eventually conquer Carthage; Venus wants to keep her son safe from Dido's potential treachery. So Juno and Venus set up a "marriage." While Dido and Aeneas are out hunting, a storm begins, so they seek refuge in a cave. Here they make love, while Juno sets off lightning and nymphs cry out. Dido calls it marriage; Aeneas does not. The lovers are neglectful of their duties: Dido ceases working on her city; Aeneas forgets his destiny.

Finally, Jupiter sends Mercury to chide Aeneas about his neglected duty to his son and their future descendents in Italy. Immediately dutiful to the will of the gods and Destiny, Aeneas secretly arranges to leave Carthage. When Dido discovers his plans, she begs him to stay. He cannot, will not, so she raves and rages, curses the Trojans, and kills herself on a pyre heaped with Aeneas' belongings and items of witchcraft. Meanwhile, Aeneas and the other Trojans are in their boats sailing away.

Book 5. Aeneas goes back to Sicily where he arranges memorial games for Anchises, who has been dead for a year. Aeneas displays his skills as a leader, carrying out rituals, presiding at the games, encouraging his men, restraining anger, and preventing injuries. Meanwhile, Juno has been biding her time. She sends her messenger Iris to inflame the Trojan women with fury, encouraging them to burn the Trojan ships, so they will not have to travel any further. A torrential rain saves all but four of the ships. Aeneas leaves the reluctant behind; the remaining Trojans continue on toward Italy and the underworld.

Book 6. The Cumaean Sibyl gives prophecies about Aeneas' future in Italy and leads Aeneas into the underworld. Unlike Homer's dim and wretched Hades, Virgil's Hades is a place of remediation and rebirth, where the lifetime deeds of the dead are examined and judged. Some excellent souls seem to go straight to Elysium, the groves of blessedness, while flawed souls are punished and purged until they are purified. Then these cleansed souls can wander happily in Elysium for a thousand years, until it is time to be reborn. Aeneas meets the shade of his father Anchises in Elysium. Anchises tells him about the World Soul and rebirth, and shows Aeneas a procession of his descendents over the centuries, culminating in Augustus. Aeneas now knows his destiny — to found the Roman people.

The second half of the *Aeneid* (books 7–12) tells the story of the escalating wrath inspired by Juno, forcing Aeneas to go to war in Italy.

Book 7. Aeneas finally arrives in Latium, where he is welcomed by King Latinus, whose only child is Lavinia. Turnus, King of the Rutulians and a powerful neighbor, wants to marry Lavinia. However, omens and oracles have foretold that a stranger would become her husband, so Latinus decides to marry his daughter Lavinia to Aeneas. Juno is not ready to give up her struggle against Destiny, although she knows she cannot win. She fetches the Fury Allecto from the underworld and urges her to stir the Latins into frenzy. Allecto instills poisonous rage in both Lavinia's mother Amata and Lavinia's suitor Turnus. Then she sets up Ascanius (Iulus) to shoot a pet deer belonging to Sylvia, a local peasant girl. Next, Allecto blows her hellish horn, inciting the local farmers to attack the Trojans. Latinus tries to avoid the conflict, but Juno opens gates of war. Lines of alliance are drawn and the troops start to gather.

Book 8. Seeking an ally, Aeneas travels to Evander, the king of the Arcadians. Evander welcomes Aeneas and offers to supply him with troops led by Evander's son Pallas. Meanwhile, Venus persuades her husband Vulcan to make new armor for Aeneas. The designs on the shield illustrate "the occasions when Rome was saved from the threat of extinction" (Starr 178). At the center is the Battle of Actium: The shield connects the beginning of Roman history in Aeneas to its culmination in Emperor Octavian's decisive battle at Actium that ushered in the Augustan peace.

Book 9. While Aeneas is away seeking alliances, a battle rages at the Trojan camp. Two best friends, Nisus and Euryalus, make a foray into the sleeping enemy camp and slaughter many before being killed. Ascanius gets his first real taste of battle and kills his first man. Turnus gets into the Trojan stockade and rages furiously, slaughtering many men. Finally the Trojans rally and Turnus, exhausted, jumps into the river and escapes.

Book 10. Jupiter wants peace, but Juno and Venus are still bickering, so Jupiter allows the battle to continue, since "'the Fates will find their way'" (*Aen.* 10.162). Aeneas finally returns with numerous allies. Turnus and Aeneas both rage in battle. Pallas fights bravely, but is finally killed by Turnus, who strips off Pallas' heavy decorated belt as a trophy. Juno recognizes by now that the battle is about over, but she begs Jupiter to let her spare Turnus' life for a little while. He agrees and Juno fashions a phantom resembling Aeneas, which lures Turnus out of the battle onto a ship that then drifts away, carrying the bewildered Turnus to safety while the battle continues without him.

Book 11. Aeneas learns that Pallas has died, and he prepares to send Pallas' body back to his father, King Evander. Both sides bury their dead. The Latins hold a quarrelsome council over whether or not to sue for peace. King Latinus wants to make peace and share his land and rule with the Trojans. Turnus is in favor of continuing the war, which resumes. Camilla, a woman warrior ally of Turnus, enters the fray, fights bravely, and is killed.

Book 12. Turnus challenges Aeneas to a duel to settle the war. Meanwhile, Juno tells the nymph Juturna, Turnus' sister, to help him if she can, because Turnus is no match for Aeneas in single combat. Juturna provokes the Latins into battle. Aeneas seeks Turnus, but Juturna, disguised as Turnus' charioteer, races around, not letting Turnus stop and fight.

Aeneas is now furious. He starts to burn down King Latinus' city to root out the resistance once and for all. Queen Amata hangs herself. Turnus tells his sister to stop interfering, because Fate has won, and he wants to fight Aeneas honorably before he dies. Finally, Turnus and Aeneas begin to fight, and Jupiter holds up his scales to confirm their fates. Turnus' sword breaks; he panics and runs away, Aeneas pursuing. However, gods are still interfering: Juturna hands the fleeing Turnus a sword, while Venus pulls Aeneas' spear free from a tree it had lodged in.

Jupiter is fed up by now and confronts Juno, who finally gives up, asking only that the merged races be called Latins and that the Trojans lose their identity. Jupiter agrees to create a single Latin race from the two warring peoples. Jupiter sends two Furies to chase Juturna away from Turnus, and Aeneas throws his spear, wounding Turnus. Turnus begs for his life, but Aeneas sees the belt of dead Pallas on Turnus. Enraged by the sight of the belt, Aeneas kills Turnus. The story ends abruptly at this point.

A New Kind of Hero

Aeneas' dominant trait is piety. Pious Aeneas is the man chosen by Fate and Jupiter to play a key role in the destiny of Rome. Piety, to Aeneas, did not mean faith so much as obedience and careful attention to the will of the gods, especially Jupiter. Piety meant doing the right thing in the right way. This piety expressed itself in right relations to the gods, to one's family, and to the state (Bailey 80). Piety also involved performing complex rituals precisely and with a devoted spirit (Veyne 213).

It was not always easy to know what was the right thing to do, however. The gods sent omens and signs, usually in the form of extraordinary natural phenomena such as an unusual flight of birds or weirdly shaped intestines of a sacrificed animal. Romans believed that these signs could be correctly interpreted (Olgivie 53–4). Although Aeneas' world is full of divine signs and portents, their meanings are usually ambiguous. Nonetheless, to the best of his ability, Aeneas obeys the gods, performs the necessary rituals, and struggles to understand what the gods and Fate want him to do so that he can comply.

Aeneas was a new kind of hero with new kinds of virtues. Achilles, Agamemnon and Odysseus became unacceptable as heroes in later centuries because of their intractable individualism and lack of community spirit. Aeneas, however, became a paragon, an ideal hero, for the European Christian Middle Ages. Aeneas was ideal for civilizations that valued community-minded heroes who put aside personal desires in order to struggle for the greater good.

Aeneas has the following characteristics.

Piety: He carries his household gods from Troy to Italy; he holds memorial games for Anchises; he immediately obeys Mercury's message to leave Dido.

Steadfastness: He feels Dido's grief, but is unswayed from his purpose.

Compassion: He stops the boxing match when Entellus is overwhelming Dares; he grieves for his dead soldiers; he soothes his weary followers after the storm in book 1.

Fairness: He awards the prizes fairly during the memorial games.

Courage: He fights bravely at Troy as well as in Latium.

Favored by Destiny: He learns the future in the underworld and acts willingly to bring it about.

Paternal Responsibility: It is Aeneas' fatherly duty to Ascanius to leave Dido and found a new nation for his descendents.

Decisiveness: He forms alliances in Italy and leads the fighting.

Sensitivity: He is exquisitely aware of the "tears of things," the pain of human life.

Emotion: He narrates the fall of Troy with great feeling in book 2.

These were virtues that European medieval readers could appreciate, even if they might not choose to emulate them. Virgil was so admired that in the fourteenth century, when Dante needed a guide through the Inferno, he selected Virgil, the most virtuous and poetically gifted of ancient pagans, to lead the way.

Despite (or perhaps because of) Aeneas' Roman virtues, many modern readers find him a cold fish. The main charge against him is that he callously leaves Dido, who kills herself for grief. People who value personal love over religious or communal duty have difficulty understanding such behavior. Worse, Aeneas' striving to obey Destiny and found an empire makes modern readers uncomfortable, especially after World War II and the expansive totalitarian empires of the twentieth century. Virgil saw the Roman Empire as bringing peace and civilization to humanity; we tend to view expansionist empires as suspect if not evil.

PASSION IN THE *AENEID*

Post-Romantic Western civilization generally approves of strong emotions and admires powerful, sincere feelings. Of all the passions, people are fondest of love, the mutual attractive force that leads to relationships between two people. In Virgil's time, however, such love was not much appreciated. It was generally seen as a source of disruptive behavior, a kind of antisocial, self-destructive madness (Camps, *Introduction* 29–30).

Thus, people today have a hard time with Aeneas' love affair with Dido. She is portrayed so sympathetically that modern readers hate Aeneas for leaving her. One of Virgil's greatest strengths, his sympathy for almost all of his characters, adds to our confusion. Not only does Virgil explain that Cupid poisons Dido with love, but he also gives plenty of hints about Dido's potential for danger to Aeneas, such as her fury when she is about to kill herself:

> And could I not
> have dragged his body off, and scattered him
> piecemeal upon the waters, limb by limb?
> Or butchered all his comrades, even served
> Ascanius himself as banquet dish
> upon his father's table? [*Aen.* 4.826–30].

This sinister echo of Atreus feeding Thyestes' children to him does not suggest that poor Dido is merely upset over her disappearing lover. Indeed, Dido's funeral pyre itself is chockfull of elements of witchcraft.

Nevertheless, Virgil portrays Dido's love for Aeneas with such sympathy that modern readers appreciate her love, hate Aeneas for leaving her, and mostly ignore the negative undertone. One problem is that Dido is modeled on two ancient bad women that people don't know much about anymore. They are the historical Cleopatra and the fictional/mythic Medea in the *Argonautica* of Apollonius Rhodius (Camps, *Introduction* 80).

Cleopatra was the Egyptian queen who fought alongside Mark Antony against Octavian at the Battle of Actium. Virgil presents her as the epitome of the decadent, treacherous Orient (as opposed to the noble Roman West). She and Antony, with their barbarian troops and barbaric gods, are part of the center of the shield of Aeneas. Antony and Cleopatra oppose Octavian and the people and gods of Italy (Starr 178; Bailey 4). Aeneas' affair with Dido echoes Antony's with Cleopatra. Dido serves as the crucial divide between East and West — Aeneas has left the Orient (Troy), and is delayed by one last Oriental experience (decadent passion), before going forth to become the Latin ancestor of the Roman people.

Medea, in the *Argonautica*, falls quickly and madly in love with Jason and betrays her father to please him. Medea uses trickery and witchcraft to help Jason acquire the Golden Fleece. Afraid of her father's anger, Medea runs off with Jason; she also lures her half-brother Apsyrtus to Jason, who kills him. When Jason eventually leaves her, Medea kills their two children to punish Jason. Her echoes in Dido are not auspicious.

The other passionate characters in the *Aeneid* are mostly deplorable. The raging goddess Juno and the raging warrior Turnus head the list. Other negative passionate characters include the Harpies, Allecto, Amata, the Trojan women burning their ships, and the Latins in general when in battle frenzy. Even Aeneas is touched by passionate fury twice — during the sack of Troy and during the battle in Latium, especially at the final moment when he kills Turnus. Passion spreads like a disease. Venus uses Cupid to infect Dido with the passion of love. Juno uses Allecto to infect Amata, Turnus and the Latin masses with the passion for war. In every case except Aeneas' final passionately righteous killing of Turnus, passion opposes the will of Jupiter, Destiny and Fate.

GODS, THE WILL OF JUPITER/DESTINY/FATE

Many of the gods in the *Aeneid* are Roman parallels to the Greek gods of Homer. Greeks had been settled in Italy for centuries by Virgil's time. Over the years, Italians identified Greek deities with Italian counterparts that had more or less similar functions. Gradually, the myths of the Greek gods also became attached to their Italian counterparts. Roman poets, deeply steeped in Greek literature, naturally took up these Greek gods and myths as they created their stories of the gods of Rome (Bailey 88).

Consequently, when Virgil used Homer as his main structural source for the *Aeneid*, he adopted Homer's gods and many of their myths, using their Roman names. However, the relationships of the gods to one another and to human beings are different. In Homer, there is Zeus, who knows and affirms Fate, the way things must be. In Virgil, Jupiter also knows and affirms Fate. But there is also Destiny, the notion that there is a necessary future to strive towards. This is the Fate that Jupiter upholds, a pattern that is not a simple working out of conflicts.

Juno and Venus act in opposition to the necessary path of Fate. They know perfectly well what must come to pass, because Jupiter tells them, but each has her own passionate agenda. Venus is motivated by intense love for her son, Juno by raw frenzied hatred of the Trojans, whose descendents will destroy Carthage. Both goddesses must finally lose, gracefully, as goddesses lose, finally accepting the will of Jupiter. Similarly, on a human level, Dido, Amata and Turnus resist the Fates, acting counter to the will of Jupiter. They must be destroyed, just as Octavian destroyed Antony and Cleopatra.

Aeneas, who spends his life trying to do what he should, not only has many painfully confusing experiences as he misinterprets omens and follows wrong leads, but his final cooperation with Fate leads him to relinquish every shred of personal happiness. He has lost his beloved wife, his city, almost everything he cared about at Troy. He has left his comfortable liaison with Dido. He will marry a woman he does not choose, whose people he has slaughtered. He will create the foundation for the next twelve hundred years of Roman history, but will die, rather like Moses, still outside the promised land of Rome.

Why Read Virgil?

Virgil's *Aeneid* was considered the best poem and the most important secular book in the West for almost two thousand years. The influence of the *Aeneid* on the arts, literature, and philosophy of European and American civilization is immeasurable. For this reason alone, a student of history, literature and the arts should read Virgil. But reading Virgil is not always easy.

The main problem is the Latin. For many centuries, Latin was the international language of educated people in the West. From Virgil's time until the European Renaissance, serious books were almost always written in Latin, not the author's spoken vernacular, which might be Italian, German, English, Spanish or French. Until World War II, children in European or American schools regularly studied Latin, and the *Aeneid* was one of the main Latin texts studied. The *Aeneid* was the premiere schoolbook of the Western world. From it, students learned not only Latin, but a system of values and a sense of the divine purpose of history that were curiously compatible with Western Christianity as well as with Europe's recurring dreams of empire.

Unfortunately, the *Aeneid* does not translate well. Augustan Latin, the language of Virgil, is very difficult. A brief example of Virgil's Latin, from the opening sentence of the *Aeneid,* shows how the words are arranged more like a mosaic than in the linear fashion we are used to nowadays.

Arma	*virumque*	*cano,*	*Troiae*	*qui primus*	*ab oris*
Arms	the man and	I sing	of Troy	who first	from coasts
Italiam	*fato*	*profugus*	*Laviniaque*	*venit*	*litora*
to Italy	by fate	exiled	Lavinian and	came	shores

(I sing of arms and of a man: his fate had made him fugitive; he was the first to journey from the coasts of Troy as far as Italy and the Lavinian shores [Aen 1.1–4].)

In Latin, each word has a meaning that may not become clear until several more words have been read. This is an elegant, complex, literary language that does not lend itself to translation. Even when the meaning is translated, the sound, the mosaic-like quality of the language, the constant back and forth referencing of the words, cannot be easily carried into another language. Consequently, the best way to learn to read the *Aeneid* is in a Latin class;

next best is to read a good translation slowly, aloud if possible. The great qualities of the *Aeneid* are in the intermeshing of its complex details, not in the rush of the plot.

The *Aeneid* is also difficult to read because it is a literary epic, not a folk epic like the *Iliad* or *Odyssey*. The *Aeneid* was written for a highly educated audience that was familiar with the Greco-Roman literary traditions and could recognize and enjoy subtle allusions to other works and events in that tradition. The complexity and allusions added to the value of the *Aeneid* as a schoolbook. By studying the *Aeneid* (with plenty of footnotes), students could learn not only Latin, but also the entire classical literary tradition. Needless to say, this sort of study took years and was a key element in the kind of classical education that very few students receive today.

Modern readers who do like the *Aeneid* are divided between those who find Virgil a positive voice for the glories of the Roman Empire and those who hear his anguish for the human suffering underlying the rise to power of that Empire (Harrison 1–20). It is a tribute to the solid quality and complexity of the *Aeneid* that two such opposing viewpoints can be honestly argued by highly competent critics.

A fair answer to the question "Why read Virgil?" is that it's worth a try to see what so many people, for so many centuries, thought was the best poem, the best secular book. For the first fifteen hundred years of its existence, the *Aeneid* was one of the most widely known books in Europe. After the invention of printing, one or more print editions of the *Aeneid* were published each year for the next five hundred years (Knight 23). A book so well thought of, for so long, by so many people, and with so many echoes in later literature, is worth some effort to get to know.

8

Transmission of Troy Stories
to the Middle Ages

In the gradual transition from the classical pagan world of Augustus and Virgil to the solidly Christian world of the European Latin Middle Ages, two major world-historical events affected the continuing tradition of Troy stories. The first event was the establishment of Christianity as the official religion of the Roman Empire in 312 CE. Christians hated the pagan gods and Homer's *Iliad* and *Odyssey* were full of pagan gods, so Homer's version of the Trojan War did not appeal to an increasingly Christian civilization. The second event was the division of the Roman Empire into the Greek-speaking East and the Latin-speaking West in 395 CE. This split of the Roman Empire left the Greek East still reading Homer as part of their own cultural heritage, while Virgil's *Aeneid* and a so-called eyewitness account of the Trojan War by Dares became the main versions of the Troy story transmitted in the Latin West. Oddly, the pagan gods in the *Aeneid* did not seem to bother medieval European Christians, who adopted Virgil as a sort of honorary almost–Christian.

In the Greek-speaking Christian East, Homer continued to be studied in the schools, along with other classical Greek literature. Homer's deceitful, wrathful heroes and lies about the gods were tolerated because he was such an important figure in Greek literary history (Geanakoplos 393–403). In the Latin-speaking West, however, Homer was increasingly disapproved of and/or forgotten, especially as people no longer learned to read Greek (Berschin 18–19).

The Latin *Aeneid* continued to be read in the West, but its narrative of the Trojan War was incomplete because it started at the fall of the Troy. Furthermore, Virgil explained the importance of the fall of Troy in terms of the rise of Rome, but in the early European Middle Ages, Rome gradually ceased to be seen as the center of the civilized world. It was left to two supposed eyewitnesses, Dictys the Cretan (a Greek) and Dares the Phrygian (a Trojan), to transmit the central stories of the Troy Cycle to the Latin Middle Ages (Baswell 18).

The Roman Empire Split into East and West

By the end of the third century CE, the Roman Empire usually had two senior emperors, one for the West and one for the East. Each emperor, or "Augustus," had a "Caesar,"

Rome, Constantinople and Troy

or junior emperor, who was his adopted son and heir apparent. This system of four rulers was called the Tetrarchy. In 324 CE Constantine eliminated his co-emperor Licinius and became the single ruler of both East and West (Millar 175–77; Chuvin 23). In 330, Constantine founded Constantinople, the New Rome, on the European side of the Bosporus, a narrow water passage between the Mediterranean Sea and the Black Sea (Cameron 7). Constantine chose an ancient city, Byzantium, as the site for Constantinople; it was only a few miles away from the site of ancient Troy.

After the death of Constantine, the separation between East and West increased, and in 395 the Roman Empire was officially divided between the two sons of Emperor Theodosius, Honorius and Arcadius. While the government of the East grew stronger over time, the government of the West grew weaker (Cameron 12–16). The fifth century was a disaster in the West. Rome was sacked by northern barbarians in 410 CE. After the sacking of Rome, the "Western Empire underwent a brutal collapse, during the course of which the great cities disappeared. ... [W]ith the cities a culture was destroyed" (Chuvin 84). In 476 CE the last Roman emperor, Romulus Augustulus, was deposed, which officially ended the Roman Empire in the West (Cameron 33). Over the next few centuries, the so-called Dark Ages, life in the West became still poorer, less urban, less civilized. This left the Greek-speaking Byzantine East as the only "Roman" Empire, although far east of Rome itself, with its capital at Constantinople. The Byzantine Roman Empire remained, thriving more or less, until the Ottoman Turks finally conquered it in 1453 (Geanakoplos 13).

Christianity and Culture, East and West

The not-yet-divided Roman Empire had officially become a Christian empire in 312 CE, after Constantine converted to Christianity (Boardman et al. 860). While the Greek East and Latin West were separating politically, they also were diverging religiously over various questions of doctrine and practice. Once Christianity became the state religion, bitter disputes over correct doctrine became increasingly matters of state and could be punished not just as heresy, but also as treason (Cameron 22).

One major point of contention was the question of "whether, and if so, how, Christ had two natures; the Monophysites held that he had only a divine nature, while Nestorius, and 'Nestorians' after him, emphasized the human" (Cameron 23). Both of these positions about the nature of Christ were officially condemned, but in the East many Christians were Monophysites, while the Papacy far away in Rome was not interested in compromise. Other differences between Christians in the East and the West included the liturgy (Greek in the East, Latin in the West) and various customs such as the use of unleavened bread (West) or leavened bread (East) in the Eucharist (Geanakoplos 3, 5).

Political, religious and cultural separation between the Greek East and Latin West intensified over the centuries. Alienation and hostility between East and West also intensified. These East-West conflicts reached a peak in 1204, when European Christians sacked Christian Constantinople during the fourth crusade (Geanokoplos 5). One interesting consequence of the increasing split between East and West was that Homer remained known and admired in the Greek East, while his poetry became increasingly unavailable in the Latin West.

Although the Latin West had few educated people except clergy in the European Middle Ages, the Greek East had always had a number of educated laymen. Lay education in the East was based on study of the ancient Greek classics within a Christian framework. For example, students could profit from the examples of noble men performing noble deeds, while avoiding the bad examples of wicked men and ignoring false tales of pagan gods and other such evils. Children began their schooling by studying classical Greek grammar, and Homer was central to this study (Geanakoplos 393–4, 401). Consequently, the Greek-Byzantine East maintained cultural continuity with its Homeric and classical Greek past.

Meanwhile, in the Latin West people ceased to read Greek and rejected pagan stories such as those told by Homer (although they continued to read and approve of Virgil's Latin *Aeneid*). Following Virgil's pro–Trojan point of view, people in the Latin West condemned Homer's Greeks as the villains of the Trojan War. When Homer was read in the West, it was in the form of the *Latin Iliad* or *Ilias latina*, "a crude condensation of the *Iliad* in 1070 hexameters, of the first century A.D" (Curtius 49). Consequently, Homer became "lost" for a thousand years in the West, until scholars in Italy began learning Greek from Byzantine travelers in the fourteenth century (Highet 16).

Pagans and Christians

Christianity increased in adherents and influence for several centuries before becoming the state religion of the Roman Empire under Constantine. During those centuries Christians were surrounded by an ancient pagan world. Every freshwater spring had a local divinity, every city had a patron god, and every temple contained statues of gods. Pagan gods were everywhere, and they generally got along with one another, although they could be dangerous to humans if not paid proper homage. It was actually wise for a prudent pagan to participate in offerings and rituals for various gods, as the occasion arose. "Coexistence remained the hallmark of pagan divinities, from the age of Homer to Constantine" (Fox 35).

The many pagan gods were readily available to their worshippers. Pagan gods had interacted with humans in Homer, and they continued to do so into late antiquity. The presence of pagan gods was often strongest in their temples, and especially in their plentiful, enormous, gorgeous statues. Some statues were known to speak; some could even be animated, by means of secret rites that drew the divine presence down into the statue. Christians could not deny the disturbing presence of the statues or even their occasional animation. Consequently, a Christian theory developed asserting that the statues contained not gods, but demons that hid under the statues and created illusions to trap and destroy humans (Fox 24–6).

Christianity did not so much refute the reality of the pagan gods as reclassify paganism "as a demonic system; it was most misleading when it seemed to be most effective. To deceive people, these demons worked mischief by curing and occasionally predicting the future, yet, finally, they would go bankrupt, however impressive their interim results" (Fox 326). As Christianity gained power, the pagan statues and temples became major targets of Christian-inspired destruction and looting (Chuvin 69).

The struggle of developing Christianity against surrounding paganism intensified the old problem with Homer — he told pagan lies about pagan false gods. There was already a long tradition, going back as far as to the sixth century BCE, of explaining away the "gods" in Homer. The myths of the gods could be interpreted philosophically as allegories, veiling deeper truths, or rationalized as historical stories of human beings (Ehrhart 28).

The most influential rationalizer of myths was Euhemerus, a third-century BCE Greek. Euhemerus claimed to have found a column inscribed by a human being named Zeus. This column explained that the Homeric gods were really historical human beings and only the ignorance of their worshippers made them seem divine. After Euhemerus, the practice of explaining ancient myths as confused history became known as euhemerism. The historical explanation of ancient myths allowed future authors to deal with the Homeric gods and their deeds as confused history. The challenge was not to deny the existence of the gods, but to locate the true history lurking behind the false myth. This euhemeristic stance helped later Christian authors deal with Trojan War stories as part of their own universal history (Ehrhart 28–9).

Dictys and Dares

Luckily a supposed eyewitness, Dares the Phrygian, had left a pro–Trojan journal, *de Excidio Troiae Historia*. Dares retold the events of the war from the Trojan point of view, while omitting the disturbing pagan gods. There was also a pseudo-eyewitness account of the Trojan War, the *Ephemeridos Belli Troiani* by Dictys of Crete, that narrated events from the Greek point of view. Dares and Dictys replaced Homer's authority in the Latin Middle Ages, because Homer had not been an eyewitness to the war. Dares and Dictys were also important to medieval Europeans because, while Virgil's *Aeneid* only told of the end of the second Trojan War, Dictys and Dares together provided a narrative of the entire Trojan history from the first Trojan War to the fall of Troy.

Dictys and Dares wrote their "eyewitness" accounts of the Trojan War in Greek during the first or second century CE. Both of these false histories were translated into Latin at some time in the early Middle Ages. The original Dictys in Greek was the basis for some later Byzantine versions of Troy stories, but in the West Dares in Latin was more popular because he presented the Trojan (now European) point of view (Frazer 3; Ehrhart 32). Some authors, such as Benoît de Ste. Maure, used both Dictys and Dares as sources for their Troy stories (Thompson 168, n. 2). Ironically, the original easterners (Trojans) had become the ancestors of the westerners (Europeans), while the Greeks, originally west of Troy, had become the easterners (Byzantines).

DARES' VERSION OF THE TROJAN WAR

Dares' version of the Trojan War opens with a letter by Cornelius Nepos, who claims to have found Dares' Greek manuscript and translated it into Latin. Cornelius points out that Dares' version is better than Homer's because Homer was not an eyewitness to the war, and, furthermore, Homer was thought to be mad because he told stories about gods fighting with men.

The remainder is divided into forty-four brief numbered sections, each a paragraph or two long. Dares' narrative is worth summarizing in detail because many medieval authors used material from Dares to supplement the information about the Trojan War in the *Aeneid*.

1. King Peleus is jealous of his popular nephew Jason, so he arranges to get rid of him by sending him in quest of the Golden Fleece.

2. While seeking the Golden Fleece, Jason enters the port at Troy. King Laomedon rudely sends him away.

3. Hercules, a member of Jason's crew, wants revenge for Laomedon's rudeness. After the Golden Fleece adventure is completed, Hercules gathers an army and attacks Troy. They kill Laomedon and most of his sons (Priam is away), plunder Troy, and give Laomedon's daughter Hesione to Telamon as a gift.

4. Priam returns to Troy with his children, rebuilds and fortifies the city, and sends Antenor to Greece to ask for the return of Hesione, his sister.

5. Antenor is treated rudely by the Greeks, returns to Troy and urges war.

6–8. Priam calls a council, seeking revenge. Priam's son Paris/Alexander urges sending the Trojan fleet to Greece and offers to lead it. He tells about his dream of judging the beauty of Venus, Minerva, and Juno. In it, he selected Venus and she promised him the most beautiful woman in Greece. Consequently, he thinks Venus will favor his expedition. Helenus predicts woe if they go to Greece; Troilus urges war. Antenor tells how he was treated badly in Greece. Panthus warns of disaster if they go to war. The people want war, and Priam orders the fleet to go to Greece. Cassandra foretells disaster if they go to war.

9. The Trojans sail for Greece. They come to the island of Cytherea, where Paris sacrifices to Diana in the temple of Venus. Meanwhile, Menelaus has gone on a trip, leaving Helen to her own devices.

10. Helen decides to go to Cytherea to visit the temple of Apollo and Diana. Paris goes to see her at the temple. They are greatly excited by one another's beauty. Paris and his men, after a fight with the Cytherean citizens, steal away Helen and despoil the temple.

11. Priam is delighted; maybe he can trade Helen for Hesione. He gives Helen to Paris as his wife. Cassandra prophesies disaster, but Priam has her locked up. Meanwhile, Agamemnon and Menelaus decide to declare war on the Trojans.

12–14. Eyewitness descriptions of the main Greeks and Trojans and catalog of the 1,202 Greek ships.

15. Agamemnon and the Greeks send Achilles to Delphi to consult Apollo. The oracle says that the Greeks will capture Troy in ten years. While there, Achilles meets the Trojan seer Calchus, sent there by the Trojans to consult the oracle. The oracle tells Calchus to sail with the Greeks against Troy and encourage them to keep on fighting until they win. Calchas and Achilles meet, become friends, and sail together to Athens, where the winds delay the Greek fleet. Calchas does an augury and explains that they first need to go back to Aulis and sacrifice to Diana, which they do. Then they go to Troy, destroying two Trojan towns along the way.

16–17. Agamemnon sends Diomedes and Ulysses (Odysseus) to Troy asking for the return of Helen and the booty Paris had stolen, but Priam recalls the Greeks' offenses, refuses to return Helen, and declares war on the Greeks.

18. List of Trojan allies.

19. The Greeks land at Troy and start fighting. Hector rages, kills Patroclus, and the Trojans are almost victorious over the Greeks, until Hector encounters his Greek cousin Ajax Telamon. Hector calls off the firing of the Greek ships and parts in a friendly manner from his cousin.

20–23. Battles, truces, and burials.

24. Andromache dreams that Hector should not fight that day. Priam and others try to keep him back, but Hector insists on fighting. Achilles kills Hector.

25–26. More truces, more fighting. Palamedes complains about Agamemnon's command; finally he is chosen to replace Agamemnon as commander of the Greeks.

27. On the anniversary of Hector's burial, Priam, Hecuba, and Polyxena go to Hector's tomb. Achilles sees Polyxena there and becomes obsessed by love for her. Achilles sends a message to Hecuba, saying that if she gives him Polyxena as his wife, he will return to Greece with all his Myrmidons. Priam responds that first there must be a treaty of peace. Achilles argues unsuccessfully for peace.

28. Achilles refuses to fight. There is more fighting. Paris kills Palamedes, the Greeks flee, and the Trojans start to burn the Greek ships.

29. Agamemnon is again chosen as the Greek commander. There is another battle, and Troilus kills many Greeks.

30. Agamemnon sends Nestor, Ulysses, and Diomedes to ask Achilles to fight; he refuses, because of Polyxena, and argues for peace. Calchas urges the Greeks to keep fighting.

31–32. Troilus is now the major Trojan warrior. The Greeks are doing poorly, and Agamemnon again asks Achilles to fight. Achilles still refuses, but agrees to let his soldiers fight. Troilus and his Trojans kill a lot of Achilles' Myrmidons.

33. Achilles finally leaps into combat. Troilus wounds Achilles; then Troilus' horse falls wounded and Achilles kills Troilus.

34. Hecuba plans revenge for the deaths of Hector and Troilus. She has Paris prepare an ambush in the temple of Apollo. She invites Achilles there, supposedly to discuss his marriage to Polyxena. Achilles goes to the temple, where he is ambushed and killed.

35. Agamemnon and the Greeks consult the gods, who answer that the son of Achilles,

Neoptolemus, will end the war. They send for him. There is another battle and Paris and Ajax kill one another. Helen mourns Paris.

36. Penthesilea and her Amazons aid the Trojans. She wounds Neoptolemus and he kills her. The Trojans flee into the city.

37. At a Trojan council, Antenor urges that they return Helen and make peace. Aeneas agrees. Another son of Priam, Amphimachus, urges more war.

38. Priam is angry with Antenor and Aeneas, since they had incited the war in the first place. Further, Aeneas had been with Paris when they carried off Helen and the booty. After dismissing the council, Priam asks Amphimachus to kill Antenor and Aeneas before they betray Troy.

39. Antenor and others plot along with Aeneas to betray Troy. They send one of their group, Polydamus, to meet secretly with Agamemnon.

40. Agamemnon calls a secret Greek council, and they agree to keep faith with the Trojan traitors. The Greeks agree to protect the families and goods of the Trojan traitors. Polydamus then leads the Greek army at night to the Scaean gate of Troy, which is decorated with an image of a horse's head. Antenor and Anchises will open the gate for the Greeks and signal them with a light.

41. Antenor and Aeneas open the gate and signal the Greek army. Neoptolemus kills Priam; Hecuba gives Polyxena to Aeneas to protect. The Greeks ravage Troy.

42. Agamemnon and his army having agreed to keep faith with the Trojan traitors, Antenor asks for safety for Helenus, Cassandra, Hecuba and Andromache. The Greeks agree and let them go free with all their goods.

43. However, Calchas makes an augury and declares that the Infernal Powers are unsatisfied. Neoptolemus recalls that Achilles, made foolish by his love for Polyxena, was lured into a Trojan ambush and killed. Consequently Neoptolemus orders Antenor to fetch Polyxena from Aeneas and bring her to Agamemnon for sacrifice so that the Greeks can leave Troy. Neoptolemus kills Polyxena on Achilles' tomb. Agamemnon is angry with Aeneas for hiding Polyxena and orders him to leave Troy. Helen returns home with Menelaus.

44. Dares had been a member of Antenor's faction. Aeneas leaves Troy in the ships that Paris had used to fetch Helen from Greece.

DARES' TROY STORY: A SUITABLE VERSION FOR THE LATIN MIDDLE AGES

Dares begins with King Peleus' human jealousy of his nephew Jason, not the divine element of Zeus' judgment. Then Dares turns to Laomedon, king of Troy, who refused hospitality to Hercules and the other Argonauts because Laomedon feared future Greek incursions. Laomedon's inhospitable behavior led to the first destruction of Troy by Hercules and to the theft of Priam's sister Hesione. Priam first sends Antenor to negotiate with the Greeks to retrieve Hesione. When the Greeks refuse to return Hesione, Priam sends Paris to war on the Greeks in order to recover her. Thus, when Paris seizes Helen, it is a justified act of warfare, and Priam is delighted because he hopes to trade Helen for Hesione. Nonetheless, Priam gives Helen to Paris as his wife.

Dares' characters are attractive contemporaries. For example: "Agamemnon was large and had a white body and mighty limbs; he was noble, eloquent, prudent. Menelaus was of medium build, ruddy, handsome, gracious, pleasing. Achilles was great-chested, and had a charming mouth, large and mighty limbs, and well-curled hair; he was most fierce in battle, smiling-faced, generous, and myrtle-haired" (Dares, "Tale of Troy" 257). These are not the attributes of ancient warriors or semi-deities, but of excellent familiar people.

The oracle at Delphi and the auguries of Calchas are practically the only contacts with the sacred that Dares mentions. Dares may be deliberately suppressing pagan elements because he disapproves of them. Even the famous episode of Achilles' quarrel with Agamemnon and subsequent wrath no longer includes divine involvement. In the *Iliad*, Achilles' wrath against Agamemnon (which motivates Achilles to withdraw from fighting) occurs in a complex situation where men and gods interact. Dares gives Achilles a different motive for withdrawing from battle — Achilles falls in love with Polyxena, Priam's daughter. When Achilles asks Hecuba for her daughter Polyxena as his wife, he is told that first the Greek army must leave and peace be sworn. Achilles withdraws from battle and tries to convince the other Greeks to do so. Achilles eventually lets the Myrmidons fight, but he refuses to do so himself. Finally, Troilus' battle rage against the Greeks spurs Achilles back into battle. Dares omits Achilles' wrath, his connection to the gods, and his love for Patroclus, as well as the story of Patroclus' tragic death wearing Achilles' armor.

Homer's Achilles engaged in a spiteful fight with Agamemnon over their concubines and exhibited intense love for his male friend Patroclus; Dares' Achilles is ruined and finally killed because of his love for a woman and female treachery. Hecuba is angry because Achilles has killed Hector and Troilus, her two bravest sons. Hecuba instructs her son Paris to set an ambush for Achilles, and she baits the trap with a promise of marriage to Polyxena. Achilles fights bravely but is overwhelmed and killed. Dares' diminished, realistic Achilles was more acceptable to a medieval audience than Homer's gigantically heroic Achilles. Dares' Achilles provided perfect material for future romances that cherished the love/death connection for doomed knights.

Treachery was a popular medieval theme. Dares' version of how Aeneas betrays Troy and then escapes was not admirable, but it was more realistic than Virgil's. A taint of suspicion clung to Aeneas in medieval Europe. If Aeneas had been so noble and brave, why didn't he die fighting in Troy? Medieval Christians no longer heard the voices of the pagan gods warning Aeneas to flee. Consequently, they were not inclined to accept Virgil's explanation for Aeneas' flight from the sack of Troy. Furthermore, Venus was not exactly the ideal mother and patron deity for a soldier.

Dares removed the divine, the questionable, and the irrational from the Troy story. Instead, he provided a bare narrative, including many famous episodes in skeleton form. In fact, the very minimal quality of Dares' narrative made it an excellent source for future Troy stories, for only the names and events are present. There are no obscure details, powerfully complex emotions, or pagan gods to interfere with the inclination and inspiration of future authors. Dares offered future poets a bare, spare, narrative of the most famous war in secular history, practically a college outline of the Trojan War.

DICTYS' GREEKS AND TROJANS

Dictys' pro–Greek, anti–Trojan presentation of the events at Troy is more negative than Dares' version. Dictys opens his story of the Trojan War with the rape of Helen, ignoring the preceding events of the first Trojan War. Dictys' Paris performs many atrocities, including slaughtering Trojan civilians who disapprove of his behavior. Dictys makes no excuses for Paris, whose horrid behavior is motivated only by his personal desires and fears. Paris is a monstrous man, allowed free rein by Priam, who is blamed finally for the behavior of his terrible son.

Dictys condemns both Greeks and Trojans. Dictys presents the ancient corruption of Agamemnon committing sacrilege at Aulis and quarreling with Achilles over the return of the daughter of Apollo's priest Chryses. Ulysses and Diomedes treacherously murder Palamedes, and the Greeks in general behave badly. Dictys offers, overall, a coherent narrative in which corrupt people fight one another and the winners then struggle amongst themselves. The narrative is consistent and shows treacherous people killing and being killed, usually for reasons related to their unsavory behavior, or because of technical acts of sacrilege, as when Agamemnon shoots the goat sacred to Diana.

Dictys presents the Trojan nobility as "murderous, lustful, lying, and deeply treacherous," contributing to the ambiguous "counter-tradition" of Aeneas in the European Middle Ages (Baswell 18). The treachery of Antenor and Aeneas was appreciated in the European Middle Ages as a reasonable explanation for how a heavily fortified city such as Troy could have been sacked by a pack of scurvy Greeks. Dictys relies solely on that treachery to explain the fall of Troy; he does not even mention clever Ulysses' Trojan Horse scheme. As in Dares' version, the horse is replaced by a mere image of a horse's head above the Trojan gate that Aeneas and Antenor open for the Greek army. Antenor became an important metaphor for treachery in the European Middle Ages because he betrayed Troy to the Greeks. Dante even named a section of the ninth circle of Hell the "Antenora," the area for traitors "who betrayed their country or party" (Singleton 595. n. 88).

Medieval European authors such as Benoît de Ste. Maure and Guido delle Colonne, following Dares and Dictys, wrote about the fall of Troy as a human historical event caused by human failings and human atrocities. Fortune, or Amors, or the baleful planets, might have played a part. However, in the final analysis Troy fell because the Greeks and Trojans were not able to come to their senses and make peace. This naturalistic, historical and very discouraging explanation was passed on to the Renaissance. The lesson medieval and Renaissance historians and poets learned from the Trojan war was that even the greatest civilizations fall because human beings are never sufficiently good, smart, thoughtful, courageous, trustworthy, and pious to preserve them.

9

Love Redeems Eneas;
Love Destroys Achillès
Troy as Romance

Amors at Troy

Amors, the Lord of Love, arrives at Troy in the twelfth century. He is a dangerous, irresistible, ambiguous force who can act on lovers for good or for ill. Sexual passion was always a problem at Troy. Paris absconded with Helen. Achilles and Agamemnon quarreled over who got to keep Achilles' war-prize concubine Briseis when Agamemnon had to return *his* war-prize concubine Chryseis. There were ancient rumors about the intimate relationship between Achilles and his beloved friend Patroclus. Even Virgil's pious Aeneas had a tainted affair with Queen Dido. These were issues of passion, not love. Classical authors presented passion as basically destructive, a form of madness that could lead to disaster. The Greeks and Romans thought of passionate love as either a punishment inflicted on men by the gods, akin to madness, or as mere sensual gratification (Parry iv).

Homer's Helen and Paris were in the grip of Aphrodite. Virgil explained how Venus and Cupid, Aeneas' mother and half-brother, instigated Aeneas' love affair with Dido. Although most of the pagan gods had been eliminated in the Christian European Middle Ages, the god of love, variously known as Cupid, Eros, Venus, or Amors, managed to survive in an ambiguous yet powerful role. The philosophical underpinning of this double role was the medieval concept of the two Venuses. Economou explains that within the context of earthly love "the two Venuses represent two different dispositions ... the one, legitimate, sacramental, natural, and in harmony with cosmic law; the other, illegitimate, perverted, selfish, and sinful" (20).

Venus had two aspects; so did her masculine representatives, Cupid, Eros and Amors. These male representatives of Venus carried bows and shot arrows at hapless people, forcing them to love the first person seen after being shot. The consequence of such a shot could be wonderful — true love between worthy people; or it could be painful — true love for a person who would never reciprocate; or it could be profoundly destructive — obsession for an enemy who would destroy the lover's life.

This chapter will explore the role of Amors in two twelfth-century Trojan romances, the anonymous *Eneas* and the *Roman de Troie* by Benoît de Sainte Maure. In the *Eneas*, the good Amors (creature of the good Venus) intervenes by shooting Lavine so she will love

Eneas. This love will help Eneas to rapidly evolve into a better, more loving and loveable human being, which will enable him to conquer Turnus and marry Lavine. In the *Roman de Troie*, the bad Amors (creature of the bad Venus) willfully destroys Achillès by forcing him to love Polixena, daughter of the Trojan King Priant (Priam). Amors viciously strips Achillès of reason, sense and humanity as he hurries to his death, lured by the false promise of marriage to Polixena.

Back to Troy in Medieval Europe

Medieval histories of the world began with the Garden of Eden but quickly moved on to the fall of Troy, the beginning of secular history. The ancient Trojans had been heroic, noble, ideally tragic, always interesting, yet pre–Christian and hence eternally doomed. Trojans were such excellent ancestors that European ruling families proudly claimed descent from exiled Trojan heroes. In the eleventh century, Dudo of St. Quentin claimed that the Norman Vikings descended from the Trojan Antenor. In the twelfth century, Geoffrey of Monmouth established descent from the Trojan Brutus for the Britons in his *History of the Kings of Britain* (5). Thus, the twelfth-century Anglo-Norman nobility could claim Trojan ancestry on both sides, Norman and Briton (Blacker 163). Since a general principle for ruling families was the older the line, the more legitimate the rule, descending from Trojans conferred a distinct advantage. Trojan ancestry must have especially appealed to the twelfth-century Anglo-Normans, since the Norman William the Conqueror had conquered England only a century earlier, in 1066.

Troy and the Crusades

In 1095, Pope Clermont preached a sermon urging the faithful to organize the first crusade to protect Christian Constantinople from the Infidel and to free Jerusalem. Western knights responded enthusiastically. The resulting first crusade in 1096 was a great success, despite frequent tensions between crusaders and Byzantine Christians, especially over camp locations and supplies (Baldwin xxii, 366, 486, 502). When Eleanor of Aquitaine accompanied her first husband, Louis VII of France, on the second crusade of 1147 to 1149, they were welcomed in Constantinople and entertained lavishly (Owen 218–225; Baldwin 469–490). Unfortunately, the experiences of Eleanor, Louis and the crusaders went swiftly downhill after this initial welcome. The second crusade suffered many hardships, losses and treacheries in the East, which led Louis and the French to mistrust and hate the Byzantines. The second crusade was a terrible failure that "represented a tragic shattering of high hopes" to Christian Europe (Baldwin 511, 532; Owen 26).

Nevertheless, returning crusaders brought back to Europe many tales of the oriental splendors of Constantinople and a revived interest in its near neighbor, the site of ancient Troy. Troy lay in the ancient past and distant East. Troy was also close to the twelfth-century present, because ruined Troy lay near the crusader routes to Jerusalem, across the Dardanelles from Constantinople. Troy offered Western authors a perfect metaphor for European ambivalence towards the Greek-Byzantine East. Troy represented an ancient, luxurious, Eastern civilization. Yet, it was ultimately flawed and doomed to fall because of failures in hospitality, ethics, and religion. The fall of Troy may have offered an echo of the degenerating relations between Byzantine Constantinople and the crusaders. In 1204, crusading soldiers actually sacked Constantinople, which the first crusade had set out to protect.

Eleanor in England: The Birth of Romance

Eleanor of Aquitaine's marriage to Louis VII was annulled in 1152. A few weeks later she married Henry Plantagenet. In 1154, Henry and Eleanor were crowned King and Queen of England. They presided over a cultured, French-speaking Anglo-Norman court, which nurtured the beginnings of romance literature (Owen 219, 37–38). In response to the interests of their courtly audience, educated clerics transformed classical legends into medieval romances. These romances were long, intricate tales that wove together historical and mythical themes, mechanical and magical wonders, exotic locales, supernatural creatures, challenging knightly adventures, and high-risk love affairs.

The three major romances that survive intact are the *Roman de Thèbes*, the *Roman de Troie*, and the *Eneas*. Two deal with the matter of Troy: Benoît de Sainte-Maure's enormous *Roman de Troie* and the anonymous *Eneas*, which followed Virgil's *Aeneid* most of the way, but added a major love interest at the end (Owen 38). All three of these early romances on classical themes deal with the fate of nations and the destined rise of the West. The lesson was: "When men acquiesce in their destiny, they succeed in finding love and empire, as in *Eneas*; when they resist or violate the will of the gods, they destroy such hopes, as in *Thèbes* and *Troie*. Empire passes ultimately from East to West" (Kelly 9). Surely the Anglo-Norman crusaders would have appreciated such a message.

Eleanor's court evidently enjoyed these long complex romances; perhaps the stories reminded them nostalgically of their crusading experiences in the East and the wonderful luxuries and technological marvels they had seen or heard of there, especially in Constantinople (Faral 344–5; Owen 148–9). The romances were filled with descriptions of the wonders of the Orient, land of fantasy and illusion. These marvels, narrated in loving detail, included remarkable buildings and tombs, incredible automata, amazing sorceries and exotic monsters (Faral 411–16). It is certainly possible that "the new and exotic marvels imported by the Crusaders [were] a factor" in such new interests (Cormier 66, n. 53).

From Sex to Love in the Twelfth Century

While classical antiquity had disapproved of passionate love between men and women, medieval Christianity deplored it, at least partially because of the even lower status of women. Women were considered inferior and tainted because of their descent from Eve, who was inferior to Adam because she was created from his rib. Eve was also more sinful than Adam because she initiated the disobedience of the Fall, the cause of all later human woes. The Church considered even passionate love between spouses theologically sinful, if unavoidable, until the thirteenth century when the Church began to modify its attitudes on this issue (Parry v; Fiero et al. 62).

However, medieval audiences also cherished Ovid's *Art of Love* and *Remedy for Love*, two cynical books about how to catch a lover and how to cure oneself of passion (Allen 38). People continued as always to fall in love, and some wrote passionate lyrics about their experiences (Dronke 1–56). Arab love poetry praising lady worship and sexual delight was also available to European poets in Spain and southern France. How exactly these threads of passionate love lyrics, Ovidian love cynicism, Arab love poems and Christian disapproval of physical love combined to form the poetry of courtly love is immensely controversial, yet something new did evidently occur (Menocal 71–88).

This something new seems to have started with the troubadour poets, who flourished between 1100 and 1350 and were attached to various courts in the south of France. They wrote almost entirely about sexual love and developed the concept and the literary — if not actual — practice of courtly love. "The principal features of the love extolled by the troubadours were: an attitude of subservience and fidelity to a cold and cruel mistress, exorbitant and quasi-religious praise of the lady's beauty, and a requirement that love be extramarital. Though [this] ... love was sensual, their ideal of "pure" love prohibited sexual intercourse between the lovers at least in theory" (Preminger 871).

Courtly love made three unique assertions: human love was an ennobling force; the beloved was elevated above the lover; and love was an insatiable, ever-increasing desire (Denomy 20–21). This power of transformation, of ennobling the character of the lover, was the distinguishing characteristic of courtly love. Such love was something new in twelfth-century Europe, and became a major source of later ideas about romantic love.

However, Anglo-Norman authors such as the *Eneas* poet developed more domestic, ethically conservative models of ideal conjugal love (Jones 167–8). The Anglo-Norman romances also examined both the destructive and the ennobling possibilities of love. Love could debase and destroy a noble lover such as Achilles; love could ennoble a debased lover such as Eneas. But all agreed that love was an experience that happened to the lover. When the lover-to-be saw his or her beloved for the first time, Amors struck him or her with an arrow. Once struck, the lover must love.

Love Redeems Eneas

The twelfth-century Anglo-Norman poem *Eneas* is a translation/revision of Virgil's *Aeneid*. It follows Virgil's epic until book 12, when Aeneas is preparing to combat Turnus (Yunck 209).[1] At this point the *Eneas* poet adds a surprising twist: Amors causes Lavine and Eneas to fall in love. Aeneas had a debased reputation in the Middle Ages; in various stories he was presented as effeminate, oriental, decadent, greedy, a coward and a traitor (Wigginton 37; Cormier 228). But in the *Eneas*, the love of Lavine, acting under the influence of Amors, redeems Eneas. Amors transforms timid, girlish Lavine into a courageous woman. Lavine is then able, through her love, to transform Eneas into a paragon of bravery and excellence who conquers his enemies and marries her to found the Roman line.

THE LOVE STORY OF ENEAS AND LAVINE

The story involves the following main characters:

Amors: Lord of Love; representative of the good Venus; forces Lavine to love Eneas

Eneas: (Aeneas in *Aeneid*) Trojan prince; flees from Troy to Italy; kills Turnus; marries Lavine; ancestor of Roman people

Lavine: (Lavinia in *Aeneid*) daughter of Latin queen; promised to Turnus; falls in love with Eneas; marries Eneas

Pallas: Young Arcadian ally of Eneas; killed by Turnus

Queen: (Amata in *Aeneid*); Latin mother of Lavine; close friend of Turnus

Turnus: King of the Rutulians; wants to marry Lavine; violent temper; kills Pallas; killed by Eneas

The *Eneas* love story begins when Aeneas is camped outside of the city of Latium. Shortly before the final fight between Eneas and Turnus, the Queen attempts to instruct her daughter Lavine about love. Lavine is ignorant of love. She neither knows what it is, nor does she want to experience it. Her mother talks of love and points out why Turnus, a local noble who wants to marry Lavine, is worthy of being loved, while Eneas is not. According to the Queen, Turnus loves Lavine, while Eneas will never love her but merely wants her land. The Queen instructs Lavine to direct her heart away from Eneas and toward Turnus. Because Turnus has behaved well toward Lavine, she has a duty to love him. The Queen's advice to choose whom one loves displays her total ignorance of Amors, who strikes in the most unlikely places and is absolutely victorious when he does so.

Amors can only be communicated by experience. Thus, when Lavine asks what love is, the Queen can only describe it indirectly, saying that Lavine's heart will teach her to love. The Queen goes on to describe the pains of love, which she remembers as something like a fever. But, the Queen insists, Amors is more than just pain, as his representation in the temple shows:

> Love is painted there alone, holding two darts in his right hand and a box in his left; one of the darts is tipped with gold, which causes love, and the other with lead, which makes love alter. Love wounds and pierces often, and is thus painted figuratively to show clearly his nature. The dart shows that he can wound, and the box that he knows how to heal [Yunck 213].

Love injures, love heals. Helen and Paris started the Trojan War; Lavine and Eneas will end the suffering of the Trojans. This is the ultimately constructive role of Amors in the *Eneas*, where the destruction and pain caused by lawless love are finally cured by lawful love.

Lavine's mother not only tells her to love Turnus but also threatens to kill her if she loves Eneas. So far, Lavine has heard only of the pains of Amors and assures her mother that she does not wish to love at all. Once her mother leaves, Lavine looks out the window at the Trojans camped below. They look better than previously, and the Latins all agree that the Trojans are the handsomest people in the world. Lavine sees Eneas, the handsomest and most noble Trojan, and she hears everyone praise his bravery and beauty.

Eneas is substantially improved already. He is decked in moral qualities of beauty, nobility and bravery, not the gold and purple of his decadent days in Troy or Carthage. Where did Eneas get his new good looks? Some of Eneas' improved looks come from the new armor given him by his mother Venus, who herself has returned to married love. Better mother, better son, by the moral logic of the poem. Another source of improvement comes from Eneas' alliance with noble young Pallas, whose bravery Eneas incorporates when Pallas dies. This medieval Eneas exists in a moral universe where outer phenomena mirror interior events. When Eneas becomes morally better, he will naturally look better.

Amors now shoots his arrow, hitting Lavine, forcing her to love Eneas: "Now she has fallen into the snare of love: whether she wishes it or not, she must love" (Yunck 215). Once struck, love she must: "When she saw that she could not escape it, she turned all her desire and her thought toward Eneas" (Yunck 215).

Amors can force Lavine to love, but he cannot force her to act. Her heart hopelessly conquered by Amors, Lavine observes the painful behavior of her heart and worries that she is the only one who loves. Lavine knows that Eneas will not experience love for her until she chooses to act and send him a message of love on an arrow.

Amors has given Lavine an instant education, which could only come from loving: "'Now I know enough about love; my mother spoke the truth indeed; I could not learn about love from anyone else as well as I could from myself'" (Yunck 217). Until now, no one in the *Eneas* has known anything about love. Lavine now knows about the force that controls both her heart and her body.

Lavine realizes that it would be smart to wait until after the battle between Turnus and Eneas and then love the winner. But she now knows the laws of Amors: "'He who would love more than one does not satisfy Love's precepts or laws: Love does not wish to be thus divided'" (Yunck 220). Lavine affirms the laws of Amors by freely choosing to die if Turnus wins the battle. Lavine, radically changed by love, now prepares a message announcing her love. This message, sent wrapped around an arrow, is her equivalent of Amors' arrow. Lavine understands that if Eneas realizes she loves him, he will be braver and stronger in battle. Of course, she does not directly shoot Eneas with a real arrow. The arrow is shot towards the Trojans and brought to Eneas, who reads the letter. Once he realizes that Lavine loves him, Eneas turns to look at her and is then struck visually by love as Lavine sends him a kiss. Eneas is now under the power of his brother Cupid or Amors, and he complains bitterly, "'Love is doing me a very great wrong, treating me in such a manner'" (Yunck 233). Eneas, like Lavine, suffers the physiological pangs of love.

Eneas asks his tormented self what good this love is going to do him in battle, and he responds that it will make him hardier. Certainly Eneas, as a Trojan, always needed more courage and strength in battle. However, never having truly loved before, Eneas distrusts women and suspects a trick, but then he decides that the letter told the truth because of the way that Lavine told him in it about her love pains. He comments that he should have recognized her love sooner, but he did not yet know about love.

Love improves Eneas. First he perceives a new beauty in the land that he had not seen before; then he perceives his greatly enhanced courage and strength:

> This land is now much more beautiful to me, and this country pleases me greatly; yesterday became an extremely beautiful day when I stopped beneath the tower where I gained that love. Because of it I am much stronger and more high-spirited, and will very gladly fight for it [Yunck 236].

Amors helps Eneas because Eneas has already helped himself, accepting responsibility for Pallas' death, and actively seeking revenge, which he had failed to do at Troy. Eneas has become worthy of love, so he can be loved and consequently become even more loveable. He gets some help from Venus — her gift of the armor, and some help from Amors — the shot at Lavine. But finally Eneas is redeemed by the feelings and reason of Lavine, her judgment of Eneas' worth, and her willingness to take a risk for his sake.

Conversely, although Turnus has the legal right to marry Lavine, he never wins her love, despite a seven-year courtship. He lacks the beauty and nobility that stimulate love. He also lacks the help of Amors. Turnus does not express affection toward Lavine; he merely claims her as wife and property. Because Turnus does not love, he becomes weaker and more cowardly, while Eneas, loving Lavine, becomes stronger and braver. When the truce breaks, Turnus fears Eneas, blames Fortune, and flees. Turnus never understands that he has failed to deserve Lavine.

Love has strengthened Eneas; lack of love has weakened Turnus. As in the *Aeneid*, it is the burning of Latium that finally convinces Turnus to stand and fight Eneas. Belatedly recognizing that he is at fault for many deaths, Turnus offers to combat Eneas. This will be the final test of Turnus and Eneas. Eneas is dressed in the armor brought to him by the reformed Venus; he has vowed to avenge Pallas; he is braver and stronger because of Lavine's freely given love. Turnus has only cared for the Amazon Camile, now dead; he has shirked his responsibility to his men; no one, except perhaps Lavine's mother, loves him. Turnus has lost the battle of love before he comes to the battlefield. Because this is a moral world, the ability to win must come from the moral, internal value of a person, not from the decree of a god. Eneas will win because he is the braver, stronger, more beloved, and better man.

Turnus' sword breaks and he flees, calling for help, but no one will help him. Eneas, who had once fled Troy, chides him: "'You will never conquer by fleeing, but by giving combat and striking blows'" (Yunck 249). Wounded, Turnus begs Eneas for his life. However, Eneas kills Turnus to pay his debt to Pallas. This is where the *Aeneid* abruptly ends; but the *Eneas* continues.

After the battle, the story of Eneas returns to the private agonies of the lovers, who must wait an entire week before being married. The battle of love is not quite finished. Lavine worries at first that Eneas may now have the upper hand and control her. But then she realizes that the woman, too, has her ways of maintaining mastery, or at least equality; Eneas can win during the day, while Lavine wins at night. Thus the battle of love comes to a proper resolution. A conjugally peaceful Venus and her lawful son Amors will bless the marriage of Eneas and Lavine with a balance of male and female, love and marriage.

Eneas and Lavine are married and crowned, and their conjugally correct happiness is contrasted to the relationship of Paris and Helen: "Never did Paris have greater joy when he had Helen in Troy than Eneas had when he had his love in Laurente" (Yunck 256). The *Eneas* has come full circle, from the illegitimate, destructive love of Paris for Helen to the legitimate, constructive love of Eneas and Lavine. Eneas and Lavine unite the conjugal aspect of Venus and the lawful aspect of Amors, which together represent the potentials for love within the human spirit.

Love Destroys Achillès

Benoît de Sainte-Maure's *Roman de Troie* traces the unavoidable destruction of men and women by the forces of the irrational, Fortune and Amors. Benoît weaves four tragic love stories into the ancient history of Troy: Jason and Medea, Paris and Helen, Troilus and

Briseida (new in Benoît) and Achillès and Polixena (Lumiansky 411). The entire *Troie* focuses on how the passions of love and war, along with the inexplicable malice of Fortune, cause unavoidable degradation and disaster (Adler 24).

THE STORY OF ACHILLÈS' LOVE FOR POLIXENA

The main characters in the story of Achilles in the *Roman de Troie* are:

Achillès: (Achilles); Greek hero of Homer's *Iliad*; shot by Amors; destroyed by conflicts between honor and love
Amors: Lord of Love; represents the bad Venus; destroys Achillès for betraying love in favor of honor
Ecuba: (Hecuba); Queen of Troy; wife of King Priant; mother of Polixena; wants vengeance on Achillès because he killed her sons Hector and Troïlus
Paris: Trojan Prince; stole Helen; brother of Polixena; arranges ambush to kill Achillès
Polixena: Trojan Princess; daughter of Priant and Ecuba
Priant: (Priam); King of Troy; father of Polixena; husband of Ecuba

Benoît uses the story of Achillès' love for Polixena to display the terrible power of Amors, who destroys Achillès' rational will, senses, personality, and finally his life. Although Achilles was the most excellent warrior in the *Iliad*, his wrath had long been suspect. Other unsavory aspects of Achilles in post–Homeric times were the intimacy of his relationship with Patroclus and the sacrifice of Polixena at his tomb. Passionate intensity of one sort or another always was Achilles' dominant attribute; in the *Troie*, the passion of love destroys him.

Achillès' destruction by Amors begins on the anniversary of Hector's death, when the Greeks enter Troy during a truce to attend a festival at Hector's tomb. Achillès goes, ignorant of what the day will bring, and thus unable to avoid the situation in any rational, responsible way.

> It is too bad that his feet carried him there, since before he may turn around or come back from the festival he will be so misguided that he will have taken his own death into his heart. He saw Polixena there, a clear view of her face. This is the occasion and the means by which he will be snatched from life and his soul parted from his body. Hear what destiny did! Now you will hear how he was totally destroyed by *fine amor* [Benoît 17535–47].[2]

A tiny, unavoidable event — the sight of Polixena — and Achillès has met his death. There is never any doubt in the *Troie* that Amors is a force beyond human control, leading inevitably to disaster and death.

Achillès "will be seized by Amors and death" (Benoît 17568). The very image of falling in love as being wounded by Amors, so literal in this poem as in the *Eneas*, denies that a person could avoid the injury. Lavine argued in the *Eneas* that she could not be at fault because, if she fell in love by merely seeing, then the only solution would be never to look at a man, or to fall in love with every man she saw. Reason and free will have nothing to do with falling in love, although in the *Eneas* Lavine could freely choose whether or not to act on her love. There is no such freedom for Achillès in the *Troie*.

While Amors was a healing force in the *Eneas*, Benoît stresses the absolute destructive irrationality of Amors, who can force love and hate to focus at the same point. Once wounded by Amors, Achillès has no chance of surviving: "Neither strength, virtue, nor courage are worth anything against Amors" (Benoît 17565–68). Achillès' virtues as a warrior are useless against Amors. The values of the warrior (honor, loyalty, bravery, courage, trust-worthiness) are in conflict with the values of the lover (total obedience to the beloved and to the laws of Amors). This conflict between two kinds of values torments Achillès, destroying his personality and even his senses. Under the control of Amors, Achillès degenerates into a bestial creature who hacks up a dead body and finally dies himself in a well deserved though treacherous ambush.

Achillès knows that Amors has caught him and that he will never escape. Achillès also knows that Polixena would like him to be killed because he killed her brother Hector. Unfortunately, in the world of the *Troie*, knowledge does not bring freedom. Once Achillès is trapped by Amors, he loses his free will to choose and act according to a rational under-standing of what is good for him. Aware of being trapped and unable to free himself, Achillès can only act out the deadly process of Amors. He recognizes that he is in love with a visual image since he has had no personal contact with Polixena. Achillès knows that his love will be his death: "'I love my death and my injury'" (Benoît 17696).

Achillès' mind will degenerate later; at first it functions with a heightened consciousness stimulated by Amors. He catches himself in self-deception right away.

> Isn't she my deadly enemy? Yes, but now she will be my lover. Truly, I've chosen well. I delude and deceive myself, I fool myself, in my opinion, for I know surely that she would like to have me killed [Benoît 17657–63].

Rapidly, knowledge of what is happening to him flows into self-deception. After all his talk of illness and death, Achillès ends with a prayer to God for advice to help him win Polixena's affection. According to the most rational Benoît, Achillès' dilemma is a perfect example of the ineffectuality of reason. Although Achillès understands that Polixena must hate him because he killed her brother, Achillès' reason quickly becomes harnessed to his captured will, which craves only the satisfaction of his love for Polixena.

Achillès promises the Trojans that he will return to Greece with his troops if he can marry Polixena. However, her father King Priant replies that the Greeks will all have to leave in peace before Achillès can marry Polixena. Achillès then tries to persuade the Greeks to abandon the war and go home. Achillès gives excellent reasons why the Greeks should leave Troy, but all of his apparently logical reasons stem from his corrupted will, which is in thrall to Amors. The Greeks are at war because of Heleine; Achillès wants them to quit the war because of Polixena. Achillès says that it is folly to war over a woman, but Thoas retorts that the war is not for the sake of a woman, but for honor and glory (Benoît 18331). When the Greeks reject Achillès' anti-war arguments, he becomes furious and withdraws himself and his troops from combat. Achillès has utterly forgotten his honor. Honor requires that Achillès remain loyal to the Greeks and support their goals and glory; however, Amors demands that Achillès betray the Greeks.

Homer did not present his Achilles as having betrayed the Greeks, although his wrath and his petition to Zeus caused many of them to die. Achilles was the leader of his own troops, in a rather loose confederation under Agamemnon. When Agamemnon quarreled with Achilles, Achilles withdrew from combat. The weakness of the Greek armies without Achilles actually served to increase Achilles' prestige by showing how important he and his

Myrmidons were to the Greek armies. Achilles' situation in Homer contrasts sharply with his situation in the *Troie*. Benoît's concept of honor is grounded in loyalty, fidelity, and trustworthiness. These are knightly chivalric virtues, not the virtues of a Homeric hero. In the *Troie* Achillès withdraws from the battle because of love for the enemy woman Polixena. Achillès' withdrawal from the Greek army is treasonous; in Homer's *Iliad* his withdrawal was justified by his righteous anger at a bad king.

Benoît traces Achillès' perfidy carefully and yet points out that Achillès has no real choice: "If he does wrong, what can he do about it? ... who is wise about Amors? He isn't, nor is he able to be; he has too severe a master in Amors" (Benoît 18444; 18448–50). Benoît's Amors is a totally destructive force, undermining all the necessary social institutions best summed up in the word "honor"; yet, people cannot avoid falling in love. Benoît does not present Amors as a justification for Achillès' increasingly bad behavior, but he does present Amors as an adequate explanation of why Achillès could not avoid behaving as he did. Typically, Benoît takes pains to point out that Achillès' behavior is wrong, but he is equally at pains to excuse him on the grounds that he is trapped by Amors and cannot escape.

Amors destroys Achillès' will; Amors also destroys Achillès' honor. Amors imposes on Achillès an alternative value system, which negates the value system of chivalry as the honor of the warrior. When the Greek army sends ambassadors to Achillès, accusing him of dishonorable behavior, he replies by demeaning the institution of chivalric warfare.

Under pressure from the Greeks, who are being killed and desperately need his support, Achillès refuses to fight, although he eventually allows his troops to go into battle. Here, acting to help his own people, Achillès breaks his promise not to fight against the Trojans. Achillès has now committed an unpardonable sin against Amors, who accuses him of having broken his law.

> You have violated my law. You should not have sent your Mirmidoneis into battle.... This deed will be paid for dearly. Justice will have its way. You must pay terribly, the penalty will be very hard. I know certainly that you must die of her beauty and her appearance [Benoît 20715–17; 20720–25].

Amors forces a complete reversal of the morality of chivalric honor, which demands that Achillès defend his own side loyally. Amors and honor are irreconcilable absolutes; each is betrayed by allegiance to the other.

Amors, delighted that Achillès has ruined himself by both codes — honor and love — explains that the very love that led Achillès to lose his men will now destroy him.

> I wish that she may cause her desire to kill and torment you, that she may take away from you drink and eating, sleep, rest and relief, without hope or expectation. Now it's all arranged how she may overcome you in her bonds [Benoît 20768–74].

This deadly beloved woman is not exactly Polixena herself, but rather a personification of her beauty, which operates on Achillès without the conscious will or cooperation of either Polixena or Achillès.

Achillès responds to Amors' threats not with regrets for his lost men but with regrets for his now unavailable love. Achillès gives an ecstatic love-death speech, claiming that love is a transcendent experience and the beautiful Polixena an absolute value transcending any earthly code of social morality. Achillès blames himself for having sinned against love and then addresses the now and forever unattainable Polixena.

Other than you, nothing can have any value for me....

Ah! sweet, pure, fresh flower, above all the beautiful spirits and above all the angels, how I lose my life for you, without having help or aid! Work of divine nature, queen above all other beauties, my spirit goes to you, but alas, it will never be received there. I know and see how Amors has injured me. He will never release me. Polixena, I dedicate myself to you [Benoît 20793; 20798–809].

Achillès understands Amors as a transcendent value, beyond all earthly concerns with right and wrong. Achillès has lost because he has sinned against the standards of that transcendent value. Polixena is an idealized embodiment of the absolute principle of love and beauty. Amors, using Polixena as his vehicle, destroys all of Achillès' earthly values except love. And that is unrequited: Achillès has lost Polixena forever, although he cannot and will not lose his love for her until the end of his life, when his memory and senses are destroyed. Transcendent love, without an attainable object, can only lead to death, and Achillès accepts death as the price of his experience.

Certainly Achillès is not yet a coward or a fool. He must, however, be destroyed, which is accomplished by a systematic breakdown of his personality. Composed of conflicting parts, Achillès will now be literally taken apart, his senses removed and his personality broken down and robbed of its basic elements. Achillès degenerates from a man to a beast to a senseless, unperceiving monster as he hurries to his death.

Achillès declines from his peak of love-death ecstasy and renews his conflict about whether to fight or not to fight.

He wants to go there, but soon Amors, for his part, so overwhelms him that he doesn't dare lift a foot. Bravery and reason, all love and courage and knighthood, are quite destroyed in his heart. He is no longer master of himself, since Amors holds him fast in his net [Benoît 20851–58].

Loss of self-mastery is the key to Achillès' destruction. He refuses to fight to aid his own troops and remains firm until the Trojans have carried the battle to his own tent. The Greeks cry out that not only are his men being slaughtered, but he too is in danger. Finally Achillès responds to save himself. Achillès has completely lost his self-control: "He's very upset and grieved by what he hears and sees; he's in such anguish and so distraught that he has neither reason nor memory" (Benoît 20168–71).

Achillès is already under the control of Amors; now he is swept up by his own wrath: "He's so enraged that he doesn't remember either lover or love" (21083–84). Achillès' mind has ceased to function; he is no longer a man, but a beast.

Just as the starving lion sweats among the lambs.... Furious and mad and swept away by wrath, he charged amongst his enemies. He wrought among them like a wolf among sheep. He made more than two hundred bloody heads among them in a little while. He is a wolf that devours all [Benoît 21089–90; 21097–102].

Achillès lost his will to Amors; now he has lost his mind to wrath. Forgetting his love for Polixena, Achillès fights against the Trojans, breaking his oath to them. Priant, hearing of this, swears that Polixena shall never marry Achillès.

Achillès has his men surround and unhorse Troïlus before killing him. Benoît remarks disapprovingly, "He committed great cruelty, great treachery" (21444–5). Achillès attaches Troïlus' dead body to the tail of his horse and drags him along the ground. While rescuing Troilus' body, Mennon wounds Achillès. Achillès now craves violent revenge against Mennon. After killing Mennon, Achillès chops his body into so many pieces that the parts must be gathered together before he can be buried. Benoît emphasizes Mennon's excellence in order to stress Achillès' debasement.

Ecuba arranges to lure Achillès into an ambush and have him murdered by Paris and a gang of Trojans. Polixena, unwitting, is used as the bait, and a messenger promises Achillès that if he comes into Troy he will be given her as his wife. Fresh from his butchery of the Trojans, Achillès again switches allegiance. He tells the messenger to inform Ecuba that he will now deliver Troy from the Greeks. Achillès' mind is so devastated by Amors that he does not even suspect a trick. He hurries to the temple, where he thinks he is to marry Polixena: "Amors destroys his reason for him; he doesn't know or see or perceive. He doesn't fear death; he doesn't remember it. Thus wrought Amors, who fears nothing" (Benoît 22117–20). Achillès can no longer judge right and wrong. He cannot even judge whether or not a situation is dangerous. His mind, his senses, have been destroyed by Amors.

> He doesn't fear danger or interference, because Amors has caused his mind to change, who makes a man deaf, blind and mute. Amors has so overcome and deceived him that he no longer has any desire except to go to his woeful martyrdom and grievous destiny [Benoît 22129–35].

Amors has destroyed Achillès, reducing him from a valiant man to a creature without will, judgment or even perception. Yet, rather than blame Achillès, Benoît expresses compassion, pointing out that it was the sight of Polixena that destroyed Achillès; he was stricken by beauty, by Amors, and his very senses have been ruined. Achillès is deaf, dumb, and blind to the pre–Amors "reality." Since Achillès can no longer perceive correctly, he cannot judge or "know" what is true and what he ought to do. One may regret that Amors destroyed Achillès, but his death should not be regretted. Achillès' chivalric and human value has been so degraded by Amors that he has become a monster, not a human being.

After Achillès is ambushed and killed, Agamemnon eulogizes him: "'He was so valiant and brave, and lord and master above all others'" (Benoît 22391–2). Benoît wants his readers to remember Achillès as a great man who suffered a terrible fate, not as a man responsible for choosing to do wrong. Amors is something that happens to people, not something people cause to happen.

Amors Elevates a Decent Man; Amors Destroys a Violent Man

Eneas was a basically decent man whose reputation had soured in the European Middle Ages, especially because of Dictys' version of how Eneas helped Antenor betray Troy. Cormier explains that Eneas had a double reputation in the Middle Ages: "brave, undaunted hero and effeminate, homosexual coward (228)." Such a man needed to be improved if he were to survive and found the Roman Empire. Amors, that favored pagan god of twelfth-century Europeans, was up to the task of improving Eneas, with willing help from Lavine.

Achillès, however, was quite another sort of person. His wildly individualistic virtues were those of an ancient heroic age. Urbane, educated medieval people could not relate to Achillès. His lack of loyalty to the Greek expedition was treason in their minds. His wrath was terrifying and not rooted in any just cause. Achillès already carried within his character the seeds of his own destruction. Amors did not change Achillès from a man into a beast; there already was a beast within Achillès, just waiting to emerge.

10

Guido delle Colonna's
Historia Destructionis Troia
Fate, Fortune, Demons and the Restless Heart[1]

Guido Transforms the Story of Troy into History

Guido de Columnis, a Sicilian judge, completed a prose adaptation of Benoît's *Roman de Troie,* the *Historia Destructionis Troiae,* in 1287.[2] Guido did not mention Benoît's romance, and he claimed that he had followed the more respectable historical sources of Dictys and Dares.[3] The *Historia* became the standard version of the Troy story thereafter and was widely accepted as historically true until the eighteenth century.[4] It became a source for many future versions of the Troy story, including Raoul le Fevre's *Le Recueil des Histoires de Troie,* which Caxton translated into English and printed, and which then served as a source for Shakespeare's *Troilus and Cressida.*[5]

Guido modifies the Troy story to express a world-view rather different from Benoît's. Guido is intent upon understanding why people behaved as they did and why disasters overwhelmed them. He analyzes relentlessly where Benoît merely sighs. Guido struggles with the conflicts between the fates that destroy human beings and the free will which ought to be able to protect them, and yet he reaches no solution to this dilemma, any more than did Benoît a century earlier.

Guido's *Historia* is important for three main reasons: (1) it represents itself as a true history of the Troy story, not a poetic version of the events, and was accepted as true history for several hundred years (Meek xi; Benson, 4–5); (2) it contains a detailed account of all the Troy cycle material available at that time, from the story of Jason and Medea and the first fall of Troy to the death of Ulysses in an unfortunate encounter with his unknown son by Circe; (3) it analyzes the various fatalistic causes of the greatest disaster known to humanity since Noah's Flood, and this profoundly pessimistic tone permeates many subsequent Troy stories.[6]

This chapter is in two parts. The first deals with Guido's analysis of the complex and unavoidable causes of the fall of Troy. The second provides a detailed synopsis of the entire *Historia,* including some parenthetic comments of my own on points where Guido's version is substantially different from the ancient Homeric narrative of the events at Troy; like other medieval versions, Guido's includes a corrupt Ulysses, an Achilles driven mad by love for Polyxena, one of Priam's daughters, and a traitorous Aeneas.

Part I: Guido's Analysis of the Causes of the Fall of Troy

In the European Middle Ages the destruction of Troy was seen as a pre–Christian ana-logue to the Fall of Man. As such, it provided a non-biblical model for analyzing why bad things happen to rather decent men and women. Different versions of the Troy story focus blame on various causative factors, including the gods, demons, stars, fate, Fortune, and Amors, as well as human folly, more or less freely exercised. The *Historia Destructionis Troiae* is particularly interesting because of its complex, undigested mixture of fate and free will. Guido was a judge and poet associated with the Sicilian Court of Frederick II, a place where newly translated Greco-Arab theories of scientific determinism coexisted with Christian ideas about free will. A man of his time, Guido struggled with the conflicts between the fates that destroy men and women and the free will which ought to be able to protect them, but he reached no satisfactory resolution.

Guido, like many Europeans of his time, was stimulated by the new learning dealing with the physical universe, and he attempted to describe the causes of events in terms of natural phenomena, produced by a cause and effect series.[7] There is a tendency, when looking backwards to see the events that lead up to a subsequent event as inevitable; after all, Troy did fall, therefore, the causes of its fall were inevitable. Such thinking lends a darkly fatalistic tone to the *Historia*. Guido did not, however, accept the implications of such determinism, but insisted that people could also be held accountable for their actions. Therefore, while he described deterministic causative factors such as the fates and Fortune as practically all-powerful, he also criticized human beings for not withstanding these forces.

Greco-Arab Science

Sicily was one of the main centers for the introduction of Greco-Arab science into Europe. Arabs had ruled Sicily from 902 to 1091, and a large Muslim element remained in the population under the Norman rulers, who were exceptionally tolerant of cultural and religious diversity.[8] Under the Normans, especially Roger II and Frederick II, Greco-Arab learning began penetrating Europe from Sicily.[9] The influence of the new learning can espe-cially be seen in Guido's interest in the stars, which meant astrology as well as astronomy, for at that time they were two aspects of the same science. The impact of astrology lay in its underlying premise of stellar determinism, a position utterly opposed to the Christian doctrine of free will. However, this opposition was not immediately a problem, and a world-view developed in Guido's time which could include both free will and the inexorable processes of the stars.[10] This is the world view that dominates the *Historia*.

The Greco-Arab thinking which reawakened European interest in the natural sciences was permeated with a deterministic philosophy concerning the nature of the universe. Aris-totle's works reached Europe "accompanied by Arab commentaries which stressed their absolutely determinist character. ... When such commentators as Alkindi, Alfarabi, Avicenna and particularly Averroës (1126–98) introduced from the Mohammedan religion into the Aristotelian system the idea of creation, they interpreted this in such a way as to deny free will not only to man but even to God himself" (Crombie, 57). However, this deterministic thinking was quite undigested in the thirteenth century. Indeed as Crombie remarks, "It was the search for means of finding an accommodation between Aristotelian philosophy and Christian theology that gave rise to the most interesting and critical developments in philosophy and in the conception of science in the 13th and 14th centuries" (60–61).

Causation in the Historia

Causation, in the *Historia*, can be divided into two basic categories: external, generally deterministic controls, such as demons, fates, Fortune and the stars; and internal sources of motivation which could be either determined, or free. Insofar as human beings were made of matter, they could be affected by matter, and Guido never seems sure that human will is sufficient to resist human passions, which are easily governed by the stars.

First I will look at the physical and/or external sources of causation in the *Historia*—the demons, gods, stars, fates and Fortune, and then I will consider Guido's analysis of the restless human heart, which exposes men and women to the malicious workings of these external influences.

Demons

Guido insists that the idol of Apollo itself is merely a powerless, inanimate thing, a euhemerized memorial to a mortal man named Apollo. However, although no god inhabits the idol, a demon does. So when Agamemnon sends messengers to the idol of Apollo asking for advice, a demon responds (*Historia* X, 93). This was standard Christian thinking about the nature of idols and the demonic character of the pagan gods.[11] But set into a pre–Christian context, what was a well-meaning pagan to do? The gods seemed real, the idols spoke, but truth did not come out of them, only demonic wiles.

Planetary Deities

Consistency is not Guido's strong point, and along with his demons disguised as gods, he uses the more ordinary planetary deities. Mars protects the Golden Fleece (*Historia* II, 21); the gods punish Jason for deserting Medea (*Historia* III, 24); Helenus knows the future by the favor of the gods (*Historia* VI, 63); and the Greeks returning home after the war are shipwrecked by the power of Minerva (*Historia* XXXI, 245). These gods are powerful, although not omnipotent, and can be thwarted, at least temporarily, by magic, as when Medea aids Jason with magical devices to use on his quest for the Golden Fleece.

Once demons become confused with the planetary deities, it is an easy step to conceive of the processes of causation as a sort of astrological hodgepodge, demonic and planetary, malicious and inexorable, yet acting *sine causa* (for no reason), as would a physical process such as the motion of the planets.[12] Seznec comments that there is a relationship between astrology and the belief in demons, and even when the Fathers condemn astrology for its fatalism, "They leave untouched the underlying belief in demons in which it is rooted.... It is through the stars and through astrology that these demons often act" (44–5).

Hostile Fates

The demon/gods in the *Historia* blend by insensible degrees into another level of causation that is far more ubiquitous and inexorable, the fates, which Guido uses to explain why things happen as they do, both in the physical universe and in human interactions. Guido first introduces the fates at the opening of Book II, when Jason and Hercules seeking refreshment, not trouble, try to land at Troy. Influenced by his own impulsive anger, and by the fates, King Laomedon refuses them hospitality, setting off the chain of events that leads to the final destruction of Troy. Guido explains: "The envious course of the fates, which always troubles the repose of mortal men, for no cause drew causes for enmity and offense out from unexpected hiding places" (Meek 9). This description of the envious course of the fates (*inuida fatorum series*) acting for no cause (*sine causa* [*Historia* II, 11]) is crucial to the world view of the *Historia*.

The very term *inuida fatorum series* carries the implication of an inexorable, hostile process. The Trojan Council decides to send Paris to Greece, and Guido comments, "But because the inevitable fates establish future calamities, it pleased everyone that Paris should go to Greece with the navy" (Meek 64). In the same section, although Cassandra warns the Trojans of disaster, they persist in their course, and Guido remarks, "But after the inexorable Fates decree that misfortune and evils shall happen, they represent the opposite and contrary in the minds of men and commend them as favorable" (Meek 65). The operation of these hostile, inexorable fates is so subtle that not even caution and prudence will suffice to protect men: "it attacks the mighty, through unperceived and obscure snares, and leads them to misfortune, taking its cause from trivial and unthought-of matters" (Meek 42).

Thorndike remarks that for Boethius, "Fate may be exercised through spirits, angelic or daemonic, through the soul or through the aid of all nature or 'by the celestial motion of the stars.' It is with the last that Boethius seems most inclined to identify the *fati series mobilis*. That series moves sky and stars, harmonizes the elements with one another, and transforms them from one to another" (Vol. I, 621).[13] The *fati series mobilis* (the moving course of fate) has become transmuted, in the *Historia*, into the *inuida fatorum series* (the hostile course of the fates). Both describe the processes of causation as celestial in nature; however, Guido generally leaves out the Divine Providence which rules the *fati series mobilis* according to Boethius.[14] Somehow, in Guido's worldview, an abstract and orderly conception of fate has become infused with the persona of the devil, an active, intelligent agent who represents not lawful causation, but malicious destruction, and who acts by means of the planetary motions, which in turn influence the behavior of human beings and control the outcome of events.

Malicious Fortune

Guido also presents an image of the fates as governed by a malicious Fortune: "that envious dispenser of men's fates can cause tares to grow from the slightest sliver of a root. While she begins her approach secretly and stealthily, later a huge amount of evil follows, until a most wretched conclusion follows, and her final departure is rounded off by perpetual losses" (Meek 42–3). Guido's Fortune, like his fates, is demonic, and unlike the more traditional Fortune figure turning a wheel which both raises and lowers the human beings riding on it, this Fortune only brings men and women down to ruin.

Fortune and the fates are so devious, and act by means of such trivia, that not even caution and foresight will suffice to protect a human being from their destructive wiles. Guido expresses pity, not blame, for Laomedon: "And so, when the first Troy was destroyed by the fates acting under this pretext, such was the very unfortunate end of the very noble King Laomedon" (Meek 42). Guido even questions whether Laomedon's "crime" of refusing to let the Greeks land "can be called a crime" (Meek 42). What Laomedon did was so trivial that any king might easily have done the same.

Guido treats Priam as he does Laomedon, as an impulsive, even foolish, but not wicked king, trapped by the inevitable processes of the hostile fates. Cassandra, who knows and speaks the truth, asks, "'Ah, unfortunate King Priam, what crime will it be said you committed to cause you to bewail the death and perpetual servitude of yourself and your men?'" (Meek 65). Cassandra implies that it was not really any crime of Priam's, but the inexplicable hatred of the fates that will destroy Troy. It is true that Priam is not innocent; he chose to involve his kingdom in a very risky undertaking and his judgment was poor. But, to prevent placing too much blame on Priam, Guido comments: "But the opposition of Fortune, who had already in her course given voluntary impulses and unfortunate inspirations, hastened toward the end by ordaining the rapid progress of events thereafter" (Meek 65).

False gods that are really demons; fates that are demonic and control human destinies beyond the ability of men and women to perceive the snares and evade them — this is a terrible world indeed. Of course, Guido is deliberately describing and analyzing a post–Fall, pre–Christian world, in which there is no means of salvation from demons and evil fates. Nonetheless his conception of the universe as malevolent in its most basic causative processes is striking and not relieved by assurances that there is now a heavenly alternative. Although he does insist on the traditional notion that the demon-idols were destroyed at the coming of Christ, Guido never suggests that the demonic fates are not still with us.

Astrological Opportunity

There were conflicting theories about the fates available in the thirteenth century, and while astral determinism was one possibility, there was also the conception of the fortunate opportunity, which a man could seize and exploit. Guido blames the fates, but he also blames men in some situations, as in the encounter between Hector and his cousin from the Greek army, Ajax-Telamon. They meet on the battlefield, recognize one another, and Hector agrees to call off the fighting for the day, a decision which proves disastrous to the Trojans. First, Guido blames the fates for the situation: "But the fates, who arrange for future adversities to happen, destroy everything by hidden snares, by which they complete those adversities which they have arranged for the future" (Meek 140). How can we blame Hector, if the fates have arranged it all?

Yet Guido is not sure. As he contemplates the tiny cause of such woe, the day's truce, Guido shifts from the notion of fate as inevitable to a different conception of fate, one based on the astrological moment of opportunity. Using this model, he then criticizes Hector for failing to seize the opportunity offered to him by the fates: "For the fates, if the good they present is not received at once by some ungrateful person, afterward refuse to give it to him, as one who had lost it through the fault of ingratitude" (Meek 141). Hector was offered a chance by the fates, and he failed to take advantage of it. Guido does not explain why basically demonic fates should also offer good opportunities to human beings, any more than he explains why the fates generally seek to destroy them. What Guido does stress here is the matter of timing. There is one favorable hour, no more. A man is lost forever if he does not respond to the offer of fortune, "by taking that which in one hour the favorable event presents to him" (Meek 140). Either one seizes the opportunity, or fails forever.

Elections

Alongside of deterministic astrology was the doctrine of elections, which, as Thorndike explains, involves the astrologer applying "his knowledge of the movements and effects of the stars and their relationships to inferior bodies to the selection of a favorable hour for beginning a contemplated action. This doctrine of course implies and requires freedom of election and will, and shows that astrology is an operative as well as a divining art" (Vol. II 587). It is this aspect of astrological thinking that seems to influence Guido at this point in his narrative. Having first assured us that the fates had planned the fall of Troy, he now criticizes Hector for not seizing the one hour of opportunity offered him by the fates. Guido also criticizes Medea who, despite her knowledge of the stars, is unable to predict her own awful future if she commits herself to Jason (Meek 23).

The Restless Mind and the Unquiet Heart

Just as Guido includes both determinism and free will in his analysis of the external, physical processes of causation he also interprets human psychology both as determined and as free. The key to wrong human behavior in the *Historia* is the restless heart.[15] Emotional agitation precedes each action that leads to disaster, beginning with King Peleus, who hated his nephew Jason and sent him on the fateful quest for the Golden Fleece. Guido explains that Peleus "raged inwardly and was in turmoil lest Jason despoil him of the kingdom of Thessaly on account of his courage" (Meek 4). There is no mention of gods or the fates here. The initiating action occurs because a man is angry and acts on his anger.

Medea's passion for Jason develops somewhat differently. Her father seats her next to Jason at a banquet, and she is unable to control her developing emotions: "still she could not control the glances of her eyes; in fact, when she could, she turned their glance with sweet looks toward Jason, so that by gazing with eager imagination at his face and at the features of his face, his blond hair, and his body and the limbs of his body, she suddenly burned with desire for him, and conceived in her heart a blind passion for him" (Meek 16). To a very real extent, Medea is innocent, at least so far as the initiating events of her passion are concerned. It is her father who places her next to Jason, and once there she cannot control herself. She is not blamed for falling in love, because in the quasi-deterministic psychological system of the *Historia*, people cannot control falling in love once they **see** the person to be loved. It is Medea's uncontrollable restlessness of emotion, expressed by the uncontrolled glances of her eyes, that causes her to see Jason and then fall in love with him because she has seen him.

After Priam has rebuilt Troy, it is his unquiet mind and restless heart that touch off the troubles of the second Trojan War: "with firm resolve he turned his restless thoughts back to the serious injuries which had been offered him a while ago by the Greeks. He became impatient with inactivity, and earnestly enjoined his solemn assembly to convene in that city" (Meek 48). Thus he initiates the council that will send Paris to Greece. Priam's behavior stems from personal emotion and is actualized by his restless mind.

Helen's path into love and misbehavior stems from her emotional response to rumors heard about the beauty of Paris: "the eager appetite of changing desire, which is wont to seize the hearts of women with sudden lightness, excited Helen's heart with an ill-advised passion, so that she wished to go to the ceremonies of this festival in order to see the festive celebrations and to look at the leader of the Phrygian nation" (Meek 68). Helen goes to the temple where Paris sees her: "As soon as he saw her he coveted her, and while being easily kindled from the torches of Venus in the temple of Venus, he seethed with intense desire" (Meek 70).

Restless human hearts, given opportunity, perceive objects of desire, and that is sufficient to inflame them with destructive passion. Helen and Paris freely enter the temple of Venus; after they see one another, they are no longer free not to love. When Guido chides Helen for not staying at home and avoiding Paris, he comments, "for the sight of this man was the venom by which you infected all Greece" (Meek 69). Sight alone causes passion once the restless heart has led its possessor into a situation of temptation. There seems to be no suggestion that people are able to resist temptation once it occurs; the only hope is to avoid it entirely. The inclination to emotion precedes the compulsion of emotion. This seems to be the general law of behavior that controls Guido's erring characters. If they had been calm and peaceful and had stayed at home, they would have stayed out of trouble. Thus, the inclination for change, for emotional experience, precedes the experience itself.

Free Will?

The point at which free will can be exercised is **before** the experience occurs. Guido criticizes Helen for going to see Paris: "But you, Helen, loveliest of women, what spirit seized you so that in the absence of your husband you left your palace on such a frivolous account, and went through its gates to look at an unknown man, when you could easily have restrained the rein of the bridle so that you would have preserved your modest abstinence within the palace of your kingdom?" (Meek 69). There was definitely a time when Helen could have controlled her behavior — before she left her own home. And yet Guido also asks, "what spirit seized you?" It is not clear that he is merely using a metaphoric mode of speech. Guido gives women so little credit for being able to control their behavior that it is tempting to wonder whether that "spirit" was indeed some external demon or merely the whim of an emotionally excitable woman. Guido's solution to the problem of female instability is simple — women ought to stay at home. However, rather than condemning Guido for excessive sexism, it is fair to note that his general solution for dealing with the world is: avoid it. In this he does not discriminate between men and women; both are prone to disaster once they depart from the shelter and stasis of a quiet and withdrawn existence and expose themselves to the whims and malice of Fortune, the fates, the gods, and their own unquiet hearts.

Guido is deeply pessimistic about the human ability to resist the effects of the fates, even though he claims to believe in free will and attempts to blame the unhappy Trojans for the disasters that overcome them. When Priam is burning with emotion over the insults offered to Antenor's expedition, which had attempted to recover Hesione by peaceful means, Guido addresses the overwrought king: "But, say, King Priam, what unhappy quirk of fate incited your peaceful heart to such unfortunate boldness, so that you were not able in the least to restrain the impulses of your heart by mature counsels (although, granted, these impulses are not in the control of man), so that while it was possible you might have withstood evil counsels?" (Meek 54–5). If a "quirk of fate" incited Priam's heart from rest to excited emotionalism, and if a man cannot control these impulses of involuntary excitation which are controlled by the fates, then how can Priam be blamed or considered responsible for what he has done? "Mature counsels" are the only possibility for restraining these destructive emotional impulses, and Priam is evidently not mature enough to employ them to control his impulses, which are stimulated by the fates. Priam might have been a better man; but as he is, he is not able to control his emotional impulses, and this is true of all the characters in the *Historia*. Free will ought to be able to control the impulses of fate; in fact it rarely seems adequate to the task.

The conception of humans being controlled by the fates or the planets by means of their passions was not unorthodox in Guido's time, and Saint Thomas has a very interesting passage that might be used as an exposition of Guido's attitude toward Priam: "the sensitive appetite is the act of a bodily organ. Therefore there is no reason why man should not be prone to anger or concupiscence, or some like passion, by reason of the influence of heavenly bodies, just as by reason of his natural temperament. Now the majority of men are led by the passions, which the wise alone resist. Consequently, in the majority of cases predictions about human acts, gathered from the observation of the heavenly bodies, are fulfilled. Nevertheless, as Ptolemy says, *the wise man governs the stars*, as though to say that by resisting his passions, he opposes his will, which is free and in no way subject to the movement of the heavens, to such effects of the heavenly bodies."[16] Unfortunately, there do not seem to be any wise men or women at Troy.

Ever ambivalent, Guido having just pointed out that Priam's emotional state was beyond his control, chides him for wishing "to submit yourself to the fickle fates" (Meek 55). This submission to the fates is the primary cause for disaster in the *Historia*. War, love, and adventure all make one more vulnerable to the action of the fates, and Guido's repeated advice is stay home, don't act rashly, accept what you have, be careful. Priam's desire to submit to the fates by means of warfare is similar to the restless emotions of Helen, Medea and Achilles. Each, emotionally unstable by nature, craves experience of a stimulating sort, and each leaves the safety of the status quo to gain such experience; in each case the situation is soon completely beyond the person's ability to withdraw or control the course of events.

Yet, is inaction really an effective means of evading the baneful influences of the demons and fates that control the world of the *Historia*? After all, the fates are represented as inexorable and acting by means so slight and trivial that none of Guido's characters seem able to perceive the consequences of their actions, except for certain seers who are given this power by the fates, the gods and the stars. Is the solution then inaction? Not necessarily. Hector loses the Trojan War by his failure to act boldly when Fortune offers him an opportunity. Is prudent action really possible? Agamemnon is as prudent as a ruler could probably be. He has excellent reasons for going to war against Troy after Paris has seized his sister-in-law Helen. Agamemnon, being pious as well as prudent, wants to be sure that his actions are pleasing to the gods, and consequently he sends messengers to the idol of Apollo at Delphos to inquire whether the war they are about to undertake is pleasing to the gods. But there is the problem: the gods that Agamemnon worships and obeys are demons. The advice they give their worshippers is naturally diabolical, even when truthful. There is no true god at Troy, so there is no point in expecting piety to be of any final value, except that these demonic gods do punish people who thwart their wills, as when Minerva causes Ajax-Telamon to shipwreck, or when Mars punishes Iason.

Action is terribly dangerous; however, Guido does not represent inaction, when it actually occurs, as leading to safety. Not only did Hector lose the war by failing to seize Fortune when he had the opportunity, but he is represented more than once as contributing to the downfall of Troy by failing to act. When the Greeks are storming the beach at Troy, Hector fights to repel them, but he does not fight long enough; he tires and leaves the battlefield. With Hector gone, Achilles and his men turn the tide of battle easily and achieve the landing needed to establish the siege of Troy. Hector, although very good, is not quite good enough. Hector also avoids proper action when the Greeks request a truce that is in their own best interests. Hector does speak up in the council, objecting to the truce, but he does not persist in resisting the will of the council and Guido criticizes him for this. In the truce which follows, Antenor is exchanged for Thoas. Later Antenor betrays Troy and steals the Palladium. Guido clearly disapproves of Hector's behavior, not because of his action, but because of his inaction.

How, in a world where demons answer prayers to the gods, and the fates hate you, can you make an attempt to protect yourself and control your own destiny? Free will may exist, but its effectiveness in a world influenced by demons, fates and the stars is of questionable value. You can and should be as careful as possible, but even then the fates will trick and deceive you by means of the slightest trivia, and even inaction can prove disastrous. Piety could not protect Agamemnon, since his gods were demons who hated men; magic and astrological skills could not protect Medea from the perjury of the man she loved.

Guido accepts the ability of fate to incite emotional impulses in human beings and then chides them for not opposing their passions by means of their will. However, Guido seems less sure than Saint Thomas about the actual ability of men and women to control their passions, since he stresses the inexorability of the fatal influences and the extreme trickery of the demonic gods. The entire *Historia* can be viewed as a moral lesson on what can happen to you if you do not control your passions. The combination of free will and the uncontrollable passions which incite the heart produce a conception of human behavior which may have satisfied Saint Thomas, but distresses Guido, who is more concerned with actual human behavior than with theory. In the world of the *Historia*, men and women are never wise enough to do what they ought to do.

However, in his area of professional expertise, judicial analysis, Guido seems more comfortable with a conception of responsible action. He modifies the character of Achilles to emphasize the role of free will. While Benoît, Guido's main source, had developed a situation of courtly love where Achillès was driven to the point of such emotional and ethical conflict that he literally had to suffer memory and personality destruction so that he could forget his love for Polixena and fight against the Trojans, Guido's Achilles can fight against the Trojans merely by becoming angry enough. This Achilles is vicious, brutal, deadly, but not insane. He is also not passive, a dominant quality of Benoît's Achillès in love. Benoît's passive Achillès, caught in the nets of Amors, is changed by Guido into an emotionally turbulent man who can love and hate, and who can be considered responsible for his behavior, at least in the sense that his behavior stems legitimately from his true nature. In order to emphasize his rejection of the Amors-psychology which controls Achillès in the *Troie*, Guido criticizes Homer for praising Achilles (who has just abused the body of Troilus). Achilles could not have been made into a brute by Amors unless he had already been one. Guido asserts that people cannot be so affected by external controls, whether the stars or Amors, that they can be changed into something that was not really already in them. They can definitely be influenced; the stars work on the passions, as do demons and the fates. But Guido insists upon a concept of human responsibility for behavior that must utterly reject the external controls of Amors, such as operates in the *Troie*, which can change a human being from one **kind** of person into another. Guido cannot accept a noble Achilles who was changed by love into a brute; he observes that Achilles did indeed behave like a brute and concludes by denying that he was ever anything but a brute.

Guido is a judge, and does not question the responsibility of people for committing crimes under certain circumstances, as when he approves of the brutal slaying of Clytemnestra by Orestes: "For she was guilty of homicide, since she had had such a man and such a great king as the illustrious Agamemnon killed while he slept under her protection, and she had done injury to her husband and son by disgraceful adultery, and had violated both nature itself and behavior befitting noble women. Hence it was right that on account of so many evils she should have met with much evil, especially through him upon whom she had inflicted so many evils with the marks of dishonor" (Meek 245). Crime is a clear and simple issue for Guido and does not present the strained ambivalence which he experiences when dealing with those tiny actions, difficult to call "crimes" at all, which seem to be the actual causes of the Trojan War. A wicked person commits a crime. An emotional person, influenced by the fates or the stars, can perform actions that destroy an entire civilization, without ever suspecting that the initiating action was any crime at all.

It is the complexity, not the clarity, of Guido's vision of the Fall of Troy, which remains significant. He uses all of the contemporary intellectual tools available to him as he tries to understand why basically decent men and women were destroyed. Consequently, his text displays the many ways of understanding causation available to a thoughtful, educated man of thirteenth century Sicily. Equally interesting are his occasional assurances of the ultimate control of the Christian God and his troubled awe at the malice and hostility of the material universe; his insistence upon the Christian doctrine of free will and his sad doubts about the ability of the human heart to resist the malevolent impulses of the envious fates.

Part II: Synopsis of the Historia

Prologue — Guido claims his book is a "complete" history of the Trojan War, based on the versions of Dictys and Dares (actually, a majority comes from Benoît). "In the contents of this little book, therefore, will be found written everything that took place according to the complete history, both in general and in particular; that is, what was the origin of the enmities and of the cause for offense which aroused Greece against the Phrygians" (Meek 2).

Book I — King Peleus of Thessaly hates his nephew Jason, fears he will seize the kingdom from him, and pretending to love Jason, sends him to seek the Golden Fleece which is guarded by hostile magical powers, so that anyone seeking it will surely die. Peleus lures Jason into the quest promising to make him his heir if he returns with the Golden Fleece. Jason undertakes the quest with a band of valiant heroes, including Hercules. Peleus orders a huge ship, the Argo, built to carry them to Colchis, where the Ram with the Golden Fleece is waiting.

Book II — The Argo arrives at the Trojan coast and the heroes wish to land for rest and resupplying the ship. King Laomedon rudely refuses them permission to stay at Troy and commands that they leave immediately. Jason is furious, but is focused on his quest for the Golden Fleece. Hercules says that within three years they will return for vengeance. They continue their voyage and arrive soon at Colchis, where they are politely received by King Aeëtes, who invites them to a feast where Aeëtes' daughter Medea joins them. She is educated in the liberal arts and in magic. She is gorgeous and falls passionately in love with Jason. She tries to warn him away from his dangerous quest, but he refuses to comply. Then she secretly offers to help Jason overcome the perils of approaching the Golden Fleece if he will marry her and take her away from Colchis. He promises to do so.

Book III — Once everyone is asleep, Medea invites Jason to her room. She has Jason swear that after she helps him to win the Golden Fleece, he will marry her and cherish her faithfully. He swears to do so (but we know he will be false). Making love only increases Medea's passion for Jason. Before morning, Medea teaches Jason how to overcome the perils of approaching the Golden Fleece. She gives him various magical items to counteract the dangers of the ordeal and specific information about how to proceed. Jason returns secretly to his room and the next day he approaches the King to ask for permission to seek the Golden Fleece. Jason rows over to the little island where the Ram with the Golden Fleece lives, and Medea waits with bated breath. Jason follows Medea's instructions to the letter and returns successfully with the Golden Fleece. Medea and Jason hide their affair, and after a month they secretly leave Colchis together and return to Thessaly, where King Peleus rewards Jason as promised. But Jason now thinks about the insult that Laomedon had given him earlier, and thirsts for revenge.

Book IV — Hercules assembles the Greeks from the various kingdoms to take vengeance upon Laomedon, and the combined Greek armies set out for Troy. They land and Hercules offers a strategy for destroying the Trojan forces. A vigorous battle ensues. Laomedon nearly conquers the Greeks, but when he gets word that the city has been destroyed, he gives up the battle, allowing the Greeks to surge forward, killing Laomedon and totally destroying the army and city of Troy. This is the first destruction of Troy. Among the spoils the Greeks take away is Hesione, a daughter of King Laomedon. She is given to King Telamon as a war-prize.

Book V — Laomedon's son Priam has been away pursuing another war during the destruction of Troy. When he learns of the fall of Troy, he returns and rebuilds the city larger and grander than before. Once this has been done Priam thinks about the injuries and insults done to the Trojans by the Greeks, and he especially focuses on his sister Hesione ignobly held as a concubine by King Telamon. Priam sends Antenor to Greece to negotiate the return of Hesione. Antenor first goes to King Peleus who threatens and insults him. He then goes to see King Telamon who is angry and rude and orders him to leave instantly. Antenor continues on to other Greek Kings who treat him with similar hostility. He returns to Troy and reports how he has been refused, threatened and insulted by the Greek Kings. Priam is dismayed.

Book VI — Priam wants to send a Trojan army to punish the Greeks, so he holds a council to discuss this matter. Hector, Priam's eldest son, warns of the possible consequences, but then Paris, another of Priam's sons, tells about his remarkable dream in which he judged that the fairest of three goddesses was Venus and she promised him the most beautiful woman in the world. He considers this a sign that he will go to Greece and seize this most beautiful woman. Deiphobos, another son of Priam, suggests that they can exchange the beautiful woman Paris has been promised for Hesione. Helenus, Priam's son who can foresee future events warns them of disaster if they pursue this plan. Then Troilus, Priam's youngest son, urges them to prepare the military expedition against the Greeks in the name of honor. Priam eagerly sends Paris and Deiphobos to gather up knights for their attack on Greece. Panthus warns Priam of a prophecy that if Paris goes to Greece in order to seize a wife, Troy will be destroyed. But the council sides with Priam, so Paris and Deiphobus are sent off to gather knights for the attack on Greece.

Book VII — Paris and Deiphobos return to Troy with 3,000 knights and a fleet of 23 ships, and Priam orders them to go to Greece with the fleet to recover Hesione. On the way, the Trojan ships cross the path of the ship of King Menelaus without recognizing it, nor do the Greeks recognize the Trojans. The Trojans come to the island of Cythera and go ashore. There is a temple of Venus on this island and her festival is underway. Paris goes to the temple and rumors of his good looks spread widely, until Helen hears of him and desires to see him. Helen sets out for Cythera to visit the temple of Venus and see Paris. Paris sees Helen in the temple, admires her great beauty, and his appearance delights her. Paris then proposes to his knights that they seize Helen instead of trying to fight Telamon for Hesione, so that they will be able to exchange Helen for Hesione without a battle. That night the Trojans invade the temple of Venus, seize Helen and many captives and treasure, and set sail for Troy. Helen is despondent. Paris comforts her and says he will marry her, evidently forgetting entirely about Hesione. Cassandra tries to warn everyone that this marriage will lead to disaster, but as always, no one believes Cassandra. She is so annoying that King Priam has her put into prison.

Book VIII — When King Menelaus hears of the kidnapping of Helen, he is devastated and sends to his brother King Agamemnon and others for help. Agamemnon advises Menelaus to be calm and prepare for revenge. Next is a long section describing the appearances of the Greek and Trojan leaders.

Book IX — A catalogue of the Greek ships.

Book X — The Greeks send Achilles and Patroclus to the Delphic oracle to learn the outcome of the war they propose against Troy. There is a long digression on the origins of idolatry, the point being that the idols are inhabited by demons who pretend to be gods. The oracle of Apollo tells them that they will be victors against Troy in the tenth year of the war. A Trojan priest Calchas is also at Delphos and is warned by the oracle to not return to Troy, but to go to the Greek side, because the Greeks will win the war against Troy. The Greeks welcome Calchas.

Book XI — Encouraged by Calchas, the Greek army leaves Athens. A storm arises and Calchas says that the goddess Diana is angry because they have not sacrificed to her. So Agamemnon goes to nearby Aulis and performs a sacrifice of "certain offerings" (98) to Diana (no mention of Iphigenia). The storm ends and they have smooth sailing to Troy. After looting one Trojan town, the Greeks arrive at the port of Tenedos near Troy, and after a fight take over the town and destroy the castle.

Book XII — Agamemnon, being prudent, suggests sending messengers to King Priam offering to leave Troy in peace if he will return Helen and make compensation for the destruction and looting at Cythera. If he refuses, then the Greeks will be justified in attacking Troy. So, the Greeks send Ulysses and Diomedes to negotiate the return of Helen. Priam rudely and utterly rejects their proposal.

Book XIII — Agamemnon arranges for the Greeks to obtain supplies for the army. Achilles and Telephus go to Messa with many warriors, intending to conquer it and organize a constant stream of supplies. They conquer Messa and as its king Teuthras is dying he appoints Telephus to be his heir. Telephus takes over the government of the kingdom and Achilles loads the ships with provisions for the Greek army. Telephus will stay in Messa and provide a steady flow of provisions to the Greeks. Next is a list of the Greek and allied war leaders at Troy.

Book XIV — The first battle. Palamedes arrives. The Greeks have been at Tenedos for a year. Meanwhile, the Trojans have been fortifying Troy. The Greeks sail for Troy and fight the first battle of the Trojan War to capture the plain in front of Troy. The battle is described in medieval terms, with knights on horses wielding lances. The Greeks establish their camp and settle in for the night.

Book XV — The second battle. The siege of Troy begins. The second battle is described in great detail. Helen and the daughters of Priam watch the battle from the walls of the city (as in *Iliad* 3). Hector kills Patroclus and tries to strip his armor, but is prevented by the Greeks. (In the *Iliad*, Patroclus is not killed until well after Achilles has withdrawn from combat and Hector does strip him of the armor he wears, which belongs to Achilles.) There is an extended violent battle, and the Trojans nearly defeat the Greeks. However, Hector encounters his cousin on the Greek side, the son of Hesione and Telamon, called Ajax Telamonius. They happily recognized one another and Hector invites him to visit Troy. Ajax refuses, but asks Hector to call an end to fighting for the day, and Hector does so. This is Hector's greatest error. By his poor decision, Hector throws away the last opportunity for the Trojans to win the war. If the fates offer a good opportunity and it is rejected, they will never again offer it. From then on, the fates are against Troy.

Book XVI — The third battle. The siege of Troy continues. The Greeks ask for a truce of two months; Priam, Hector and the council agree. The dead are buried in fancy tombs. Cassandra again tries to warn the Trojans of their doom if they continue fighting the Greeks, so again Priam locks her up to gain peace and quiet. In the third battle, Hector and Achilles fight but are separated. Troilus is captured by Diomedes but rescued. The Greeks have to flee from the Trojans at the end of the day.

Book XVII — The fourth battle. The Greeks plot to kill Hector by treachery. The fourth battle begins. Achilles and Hector fight, but neither wins. Menelaus tries to kill

Paris, but Paris wounds Menelaus with a poisoned arrow. Again the Greeks have to flee at the end of the day.

Book XVIII — The fifth battle. The Trojans had previously captured King Thoas and Aeneas suggests keeping him for a prisoner exchange. Aeneas visits Helen in the Chamber of Beauty, a luxurious space for the royal Trojan women. The Greeks are despairing of their fortunes. The night is stormy. In the morning, the fifth battle begins. King Epistrophus brings a powerful centaur to fight for the Trojans, but he is killed by Diomedes. Antenor is captured.

Book XIX — The sixth battle. The Greeks and Trojans fight all day. A three month truce is declared. Thoas is exchanged for Antenor and Calchas, who asks that his daughter Briseida be sent to him. Hector visits Achilles in the Greek camp, and they try unsuccessfully to arrange that the war be decided by a duel between them. Neither the Greeks nor the Trojans agree to such terms. Achilles is furious at Hector for killing Patroclus and Hector hates Achilles for his pursuit of the war against Troy and the times he has tried to kill Hector. (Shakespeare uses this scene in his *Troilus and Cressida*.) When Troilus learns that Briseida (later Chaucer's Criseyde and Shakespeare's Cressida) is being sent to the Greek camp, he is devastated because he adores her. But although Troilus remains faithful to his love, Briseida will soon find another love (Diomedes) in the Greek camp.

Book XX — The seventh battle. Again Hector and Achilles battle with no outcome. Diomedes unhorses Troilus and sends the horse to Briseida. The fighting ends at dusk, as usual, but picks up again at dawn and continues for thirty days. Hector is wounded and Priam asks for a six month truce, which is granted.

Book XXI — The eighth battle. Hector recuperates from his wounds in the Chamber of Beauty. Diomedes is in love with Briseida, who leads him on. The eighth battle starts and goes on for twelve days. Then there is a truce for thirty days and the battle resumes. Andromache has a terrible dream that if Hector fights that day, he will be slain. Hector is angry that she tries to prevent him from going out to battle and he goes anyway. Priam orders Hector back to Troy. But then another son of Priam, Margariton, is killed by Achilles and Hector, full of fury, goes out again to battle. Achilles kills Hector.

Book XXII — Hector's body is preserved in a wondrous jeweled tomb, with special liquids flowing through the body to keep it lifelike. Palamedes has been complaining about Agamemnon's leadership and he is elected to replace Agamemnon as the leader of the combined Greek forces.

Book XXIII — The ninth battle. After a two month truce, fighting resumes, but there is another truce by the end of the day. During this truce, there is a period of mourning for Hector and the Greeks enter the city in safety. Achilles goes to the temple of Apollo, where Hector's body lies. While at the temple Achilles sees Priam's lovely daughter Polyxena. Achilles falls passionately and totally in love with her. Cupid's arrow wounds Achilles, who becomes "…intoxicated by the great ardor of love" (177). He knows it is a no-win situation, because he has killed her beloved brother Hector, but he is totally obsessed with his love.

Book XXIV — Achilles comes up with a mad plan: if he can marry Polyxena, he will persuade the Greek army to withdraw from Troy. He sends a message to Hecuba, Polyxena's mother, proposing this deal. Hecuba agrees to ask King Priam whether he will accept the arrangement and he does. Achilles tries to persuade the Greek army to withdraw, but they are outraged by his suggestions. (This medieval explanation of how Achilles will come to die sidesteps the possible homosexual relationship with Patroclus suggested in the *Iliad*, replaces it with a more acceptable heterosexual love/death scenario, and also reinforces the idea that Achilles was a brute and a traitor rather than the greatest Homeric hero.) Meanwhile, the Greek army is resupplied from Messa.

Book XXV — The tenth battle. When the truce period ends, the battle resumes. The Trojans kill King Palamedes and start to set the Greek ships on fire. Achilles refuses to fight because of his love for Polyxena. The battle rages on and many Greeks die, but Achilles ignores them. A truce is called to bury the dead. Agamemnon sends Nestor, Ulysses and Diomedes to persuade Achilles to reenter the fray and save the Greeks. Achilles advises that they make peace with Troy, which they refuse to do.

Book XXVI — The (eleventh) and twelfth battles and following (numbers are no longer regularly specified). After a two month truce, there is a short battle. Troilus dominates the field. The twelfth battle begins the next morning. Troilus wounds Diomedes, furious at him for loving Briseida. The Greeks rescue Diomedes. Because of many losses, Agamemnon asks for a six month truce. During the truce, Briseida visits the wounded Diomedes, realizes she cannot get back to Troilus, and decides to yield to Diomedes when he has recovered. During this truce, Agamemnon asks Achilles to return to the battle; Achilles agrees to send his Myrmidons, but not fight himself (unlike the *Iliad*, here it is his oath to Hecuba to win Polyxena, not his anger at Agamemnon, that keeps him out of the battle). Many Myrmidons are wounded and killed in the sixteenth battle. Achilles grieves over his men and is torn between his love for Polyxena and his need to avenge his troops. The seventeenth battle rages for seven days, and many Greeks die while Achilles struggles with his conflicting desires. There is a short truce for the Greeks to bury their dead.

Then, the eighteenth battle begins. Achilles learns that the Trojans are vanquishing the Greeks who are fleeing the battle. Achilles can take no more; he returns to the fighting, he and Troilus wound one another, and Achilles plans with his Myrmidons to kill Troilus treacherously. The Greeks isolate Troilus from the other Trojans, attack him, and then Achilles kills him, cutting off his head. Then Achilles ties the headless body of Troilus to the tail of his horse and drags it through the battlefield until the Trojans recover it (in the *Iliad* it is Hector's body, head still on, that Achilles drags around, and the Trojans do not recover it until Priam comes in the night to ask Achilles to return his son's body). King Memnon, disgusted by Achilles' behavior, seriously wounds Achilles. When Achilles recovers, he tells his Myrmidons to surround Memnon on the battlefield and then he rushes up and kills him treacherously, as he had killed Troilus. The Trojans are forced back into the citadel.

Book XXVII — The burial of Troilus and the death of Achilles. There is a truce to bury Troilus. Hecuba wants to avenge the deaths of her sons, so she arranges for Paris to ambush Achilles at the Temple of Apollo. She sends Achilles a message inviting him to meet her there to speak about his marriage to Polyxena. He is deluded by passion, agrees to go, and is treacherously killed by Paris and his knights. Agamemnon and the Greeks send for Achilles' son Neoptolemus, because it has been prophesied that without him they could not achieve victory. The twentieth battle begins at the summer solstice. Ajax goes out to battle without armor (maddened by the sun, perhaps). He kills many Trojans with his sword until Paris shoots him with a poisoned arrow, but Ajax manages to kill Paris before he too dies. Helen grieves piteously for Paris.

Book XXVIII — Penthesilea and the Amazons arrive. Priam keeps Troy shut up until

Penthesilea arrives with her troops. They fight the Greeks, and would have routed them if not for Diomedes' fierce resistance. They continue to fight until Menelaus brings Neoptolemus (also called Pyrrhus) to the Greek camp. The Greeks knight Pyrrhus, give him his father Achilles' armor and other possessions, and celebrate his new knighthood. Pyrrhus and Penthesilea fight bitterly, with no immediate victor. The battle continues for a month. Penthesilea finally wounds Pyrrhus and he kills her and hacks her body to pieces (a true son of Achilles). The Trojans can no longer compete so they withdraw into Troy and bolt the gates.

Book XXIX — Aeneas and Antenor betray Troy. The Trojans can no longer battle the Greeks, but they feel safe locked up in their city and they have adequate provisions. The Greeks surround the city so no Trojans can go out. Anchises, his son Aeneas, and Antenor plot to betray the city to save themselves. They persuade Priam to offer peace, the return of Helen and restitution for the damages on Cythera. Priam is very angry, since it was they who first suggested the attempt to get Hesione back from the Greeks and then to send Paris to Greece, which set off the second Trojan War. Priam realizes that Aeneas and Antenor will betray Troy and asks his son Amphimachus to kill them. However, Aeneas and Antenor find this out and keep armed men with them for protection. Despite his misgivings, Priam eventually sends Antenor on an embassy to the Greeks to negotiate peace. Antenor secretly promises the Greeks to betray the city to them so long as he and Aeneas and their families and possessions are not harmed. Helen goes secretly to Antenor, asking him to negotiate a peace between her and Menelaus, which he does. Then Antenor explains to Ulysses and Diomedes that there is a divine object, the Palladium, in Minerva's (Athena's) temple, and until it is removed Troy cannot fall. However, Antenor has already bribed the guardian priest to let him take the Palladium, and he will send it outside the city walls.

Book XXX — The destruction of Troy. Antenor explains to the Trojans that peace has been agreed on and they need to pay a great deal of gold, silver and grain as tribute to the Greeks. Meanwhile, Antenor brings gold to the priest who gives him the Palladium, which he transfers to Ulysses. The strategy is for Ulysses to get credit for its theft, so that Antenor and the priest will not be blamed. Then the Trojans sacrifice to Apollo and receive two signs that the gods are against them.

Meanwhile the Greeks sacrifice to Apollo and the priest Chryses advises them to make a very large bronze horse that can hold one thousand knights. The Trojans go outside Troy and swear peace with the Greeks and return Helen. The Greeks ask Priam to take the bronze horse into Troy as an offering to Minerva, and Aeneas and Antenor agree to arrange it. They have to demolish part of a city wall to bring it in, because it is so large. Inside the horse are Greek knights and one man, Sinon, who has keys to open the door of the horse. When the Trojans are asleep, Sinon opens the horse, releasing the knights and he ignites a fire signal, so that the Greeks outside the city rush in. They kill every Trojan they can find and loot the city. Pyrrhus kills Priam at the altar of Apollo. Hecuba asks Aeneas to hide Polyxena, which he does. The Greeks destroy and burn down Troy. When the Greeks are ready to leave Troy, they cannot because of a winter storm. Calchas says they have to sacrifice Polyxena before they will be able to leave. Antenor seizes her from her hiding place and brings her to the Greeks. Pyrrhus sacrifices her on Achilles' tomb and cuts her body to pieces. Hecuba seeing this, goes mad, and is stoned to death.

Book XXXI — The death of Ajax Telamonious, the exile of Aeneas, and the dismissal of Antenor from Troy. Ajax Telamonious angrily complains that the Palladium has unfairly been awarded to Ulysses, although he (Ajax) is much the greater warrior and has done more to conquer Troy. Ulysses says his intelligence has helped to conquer Troy. Agamemnon and Menelaus agree that Ulysses should keep the Palladium. The next morning, Ajax is found hacked to pieces in his bed. Ulysses, fearing revenge, leaves Troy stealthily at night with his ships. (This explains part of Ulysses' bad reputation in the middle ages and later.) The Greeks are angry with Aeneas because he had hidden Polyxena, so they sentence him to exile from Troy. He is allowed to repair some ships and must leave in four months. Antenor acquires ships and leaves Troy too, but he is not actually exiled until Aeneas persuades the Trojans to banish Antenor, who then successfully establishes his own city in Gerbondia. Many Greek ships loaded with treasure from Troy are destroyed in a great storm on their way home.

Book XXXII — Deceit and trickery destroy many Greeks returning home. Malicious people stir up trouble by creating a strange twisted mass of lies about the treacherous death of Palamedes at the hands of Agamemnon, Menelaus, Ulysses and Diomedes. In fact, Palamedes had died honorably in battle. These lies are conveyed to Palamedes' father, King Nauplius, who seeking revenge sets bonfires on the cliffs of his kingdom, luring more than two hundred Greek ships onto the rocks. Oectus, the son of King Nauplius sends letters to Clytemnestra warning her that Agamemnon has married a daughter of Priam and will kill Clytemnestra when he arrives home. So, although Agamemnon avoids the shipwreck and arrives safely home, he is murdered by Clytemnestra (who was already intending to kill him since she was having an affair with Aegisthus). Agamemnon's young son Orestes is spirited away to King Idomeneus of Crete for safety. Oectus also tricks Diomedes' wife Egea into exiling Diomedes, who actually ends up helping to protect the remaining Trojans. Aeneas and his father go into exile with many surviving Trojans. Eventually he reaches Italy and various Greek kings go home and rebuilt their cities.

Book XXXIII — Orestes avenges the death of Agamemnon and regains his kingdom. When Orestes is twenty-four he is made a knight by King Idomeneus. Then Orestes sets out to avenge his father and regain his kingdom. Idomeneus gives him one thousand knights and another thousand knights join his army and they besiege Mycenae. The city is not fortified and on the fifteenth day it is taken. Orestes has Clytemnestra and her co-conspirators seized and then captures Aegisthus as he is bringing reinforcements. Orestes has his mother brought out naked and he cuts her breasts off, kills her with many blows, and then has her naked body dragged out of the city and left for the dogs and birds to devour. Orestes has Aegisthus and the other conspirators killed, fully avenging the death of Agamemnon. Clytemnestra was guilty of homicide of a great man, so her end was just.

When Menelaus hears what Orestes has done, he is furious and brings his army to Mycenae, trying to prevent Orestes from becoming king. Arguments are presented pro and con, but in the end Orestes takes the throne and marries Hermione, daughter of Helen and Menelaus, to seal the peace. Meanwhile Erigona, the daughter of Clytemnestra and Aegisthus, hangs herself when she hears that her brother Orestes has killed her parents and is now king of Mycenae.

Meanwhile, Ulysses has all sorts of problems on his way home. He is seized by the people of Ajax, and although he escapes them, he then falls into the hands of King Nauplius who hated Ulysses because he mistakenly thought he was responsible for the death of

Palamedes. Ulysses escapes once again. He arrives in Crete and tells King Idomeneus of his adventures (mostly the same tales Odysseus tells during the banquet on Scheria, but adapted to a medieval audience — e.g. he blinded one of Polyphemus' eyes, Circe and Calypso were sisters, he escapes Calypso using his magical arts, etc.). While Ulysses is with Circe, she becomes pregnant (unknown to him) and gives birth to a son after he leaves her island. By the end of his adventures, Ulysses has lost all of his possessions and is reduced to poverty. Idomeneus pities Ulysses, gives him two ships and many gifts and sends him on his way. Next, Ulysses visits King Antenor in his new kingdom, where he hears stories about Penelope being plagued by many princes. Telemachus arrives and confirms the rumors. So Antenor accompanies Ulysses back to Ithaca to help him. They invade the houses of the traitors at night, killing all of them, and then Ulysses and Antenor go to Ulysses' palace where Penelope is thrilled to see them. Telemachus marries Nausicäa, here the daughter of King Antenor, and Ulysses rests at last. (This section is a free mixture of the *Odyssey* and various other tales about Ulysses.)

Book XXXIV — Pyrrhus gains the kingdom of Thessaly, but falls in love with Hermione, daughter of Helen and Menelaus, and wife of Orestes. Pyrrhus abducts her, brings her to Thessaly and marries her. He then goes off to Delphos to give thanks to Apollo, but his pregnant wife Hermione writes to Menelaus asking him to save her, which he attempts to do, but he does not succeed. Orestes takes troops to Delphos, kills Pyrrhus, and recovers his wife Hermione.

Book XXXV — Ulysses has a bizarre dream that is interpreted as meaning he will be killed or exiled by his son. Ulysses then fears Telemachus and has him imprisoned so he cannot harm him. However, Circe, long before, had borne a son named Telegonus to Ulysses, unknown to him. At fifteen, Telegonus longs to know who his father is and Circe reluctantly tells him. Telegonus travels to Achaia to see Ulysses. However, the guards are rude and rough with him and Telegonus ends up killing them. Ulysses hears the uproar and comes with a spear which he hurls at Telegonus (not knowing he is his son). Telegonus, not recognizing Ulysses, picks up the spear and kills him. Telegonus is devastated when he realizes he has killed his father. Telemachus wants to kill Telegonus, but Ulysses, dying, urges Telemachus to befriend his brother instead, which he does. Circe dies and Telegonus rules her kingdom for sixty years.

11

Chaucer's *Troilus and Criseyde*
The Christian Synthesis

By the fourteenth century, the Trojan War was a story from the distant past. The matter of Troy had become the stuff of romance, although Troy was still considered the root of European civilization. Troy was ancient, pagan, full of wonders, and possessed the delicious poignancy of the irretrievable past. Troy was the perfect setting for a tale of the delights of earthly love, which was wonderful in its own right as part of the created world, but could not legitimately compete with the higher, truer, Christian love of God.

Troilus and Criseyde, by Geoffrey Chaucer, a fourteenth-century English poet, tells how the Trojan prince Troilus scorned love, was struck by Amors, and then fell in love with a charming yet unreliable woman, Criseyde. The lovers have a time of bliss but are parted when Criseyde is sent to the Greek camp in exchange for the Trojan Antenor. Fickle Criseyde soon selects a new lover, the Greek Diomede. Troilus suffers from her loss and betrayal, fights valiantly against the Greeks, and is killed by Achilles. Once Troilus is dead, his soul goes to the eighth sphere, an afterlife locale in the sky for ancient pagans. From this vantage point, Troilus can finally see the folly of all unstable earthly attachments compared to the divine structure of the universe.

Troilus thus suffers a double sorrow and a single joy: the agony of love longing for Criseyde, the bliss of love fulfilled, and finally the despair of love betrayed. This fall, rise and fall of one man's life becomes an analogue for the ups and downs of the difficult ride all human beings take, bound as they are to the wheel of Fortune or arbitrary change. For Chaucer, as a medieval Christian, the only solution to this problem of change and pain is faith in the Christian God. Unfortunately, pagan Troilus does not have that option.

Troilus and Criseyde addresses other important philosophical issues as well, including the delights, purpose and limits of earthly love; why human beings are elevated and then destroyed by Fortune; the tensions between free will and destiny; and why the fall of Troy must be understood in terms of the Providence of God, not the arbitrary malice of Fortune or the Fates. In short, as C. S. Lewis explained, Chaucer medievalizes the story of the Trojan War, combining ancient pagan history and medieval interest in love within a Christian philosophical framework (17).

Troilus and Troy

There was always a Troilus at Troy, but he had not been a major character. Legend claimed that Troilus had to die before Troy could fall (Windeatt 174). Troilus functioned in the Troy tradition as a secondary Hector, who, like Hector, was killed by Achilles (Carpenter 17). Troilus was not part of a love story until Benoît created the tale of Troilus and Briseyde as one of his four destructive love stories in the *Roman de Troie* (Adler 24). The Troilus story nicely fit the accepted medieval tradition that Troy was destroyed by "criminal lust and foolish pride" (McCall 67). The Italian poet Boccaccio used Benoît's Troilus tale as the source for his *Filostrato*, a cavalier story of Troilo and his love and loss of a Trojan woman, now called Criseida. Chaucer in turn used the *Filostrato* as the main source for his long poem of love and loss, *Troilus and Criseyde* (Gordon xiii–xv).

Chaucer's Troilus stands for Troy. Troilus is handsome, courteous, wealthy, noble, valiant, loyal and truthful. Troilus is the best of the Trojans after Hector. Chaucer makes Troilus' personal experience of two sorrows bracketing one joy parallel Troy's experience. In the medieval tradition, Troy is destroyed twice but has a period of prosperity in between, while Helen stays at Troy. In the end, Troy is betrayed and then destroyed. Similarly, Troilus is conquered by Love and suffers greatly. Then Troilus wins Criseyde and spends a blissful time with her. Finally he loses Criseyde, who betrays him; and soon after, he is killed in battle.

Troilus's weaknesses are also those of Troy. He is curiously passive and fatalistic in love, like his fellow Trojans who lack the will to send Helen home to Greece despite the siege destroying their city. Instead of acting, Troilus talks a lot, which is typical of medieval representations of Trojan behavior, especially in Benoît's *Roman de Troie*, where endless councils end up deciding nothing, or worse, coming to foolish, self-destructive conclusions such as sending Paris to Greece to steal Helen. Chaucer's Troilus, like Troy, although valiant in battle, seems more interested in loving and partying than in fighting (Stroud 133).

Constructing such parallels between individual experience and larger meanings is typically medieval. At its most formal, this parallelism is called allegory and can seem stilted and forced because the characters do not behave as human beings, but as the expressions of abstract ideas. In *Troilus and Criseyde*, however, the characters appear alive and emotionally valid, fully "real." Yet, at the same time, they are acting out a situation analogous to the fall of Troy, and their fall suggests or prefigures that larger fall of an entire city and civilization (Robertson 9–17). Historically, Troy's fall always was about lust and bad decisions. Chaucer, more interested in the consequences of love than in the politics of the Trojan War, develops *Troilus and Criseyde* into a complex and subtle exposition of love — courtly, natural, and divine.

Courtly Love

Courtly love is a useful term for discussing the literary expression of love as a blend of spirituality, nobility, and lust among the upper classes in medieval Europe. Courtly love was a literary theme and perhaps a courtly game, not a way of life. The concept and possible practice of courtly love was already controversial and condemned by the Church in the thirteenth century (Denomy 153). Many critics today insist that there never was such a thing as courtly love, while others have argued for the existence of rather systematized adultery among the medieval upper classes. Kaminsky provides a thorough overview of the debate over courtly love in *Chaucer's "Troilus and Criseyde" and the Critics.*

Adulterous love, whether platonic or physical, was a frequent topic of popular European love poetry. Chaucer was thoroughly familiar with sophisticated European courtly love poetry, which he read, translated, adapted and finally surpassed (Wallace 19–37). Many people feel that *Troilus and Criseyde* is the greatest love poem of the European Middle Ages: as well designed, comprehensive, and elegantly patterned as a gothic cathedral.

Boethian Influences on Troilus and Criseyde: *Divine Order versus Blind Chance*

Troilus and Criseyde is rooted in the European literary tradition of romances and love poetry. However, Chaucer deepens his love story by drawing on the Boethian philosophical concept of Love as the divine law of Nature that makes the world go round, the law of attraction and generation that creates and maintains all life in a system of constant, inevitable change. This "law of Love governs death as well as birth, corruption as well as generation, and will eventually restore all created beings to their first cause [God]" (Steadman 70). Troilus loves and loses Criseyde according to the practices and errors of human love; he also loves her, loses her and dies according to the inevitable laws of natural and divine love that finally lead him, after death, to a better understanding of the limits of "this world."

The *Consolation of Philosophy* was written by Boethius, a sixth-century statesman and philosopher who was wrongfully charged with treason, thrown in prison, and executed in 524 CE (Stewart xi). During his imprisonment, expecting to die, Boethius wrote the *Consolation*, which asked questions about how individual suffering from the arbitrary malice of blind chance could be reconciled with cosmic order and the ultimate goodness of God (Mann 78). The problem posed by Boethius is: If God is good, how can the world he created be so full of pain and evil? Boethius explores this and related questions from his prison cell in a dialogue with Lady Philosophy. Instructed by Lady Philosophy, Boethius eventually comes to understand how the local pain of each person's life does indeed fit into the great and good plan of God. Below is a schematic, based on Curry (35–37), indicating how Boethius presents the chain of Universal Causation, starting from a perfect God and descending through the world of time and change, to the uncertain events in human lives.

God is the perfect, stable, benevolent center of the universe. God plans the overall workings of the universe, and transmits his will (the plan) to
  Providence, which is God's whole and perfect plan for the universe. Providence implements this plan in time and matter through
    Destiny, which is a blind force (that is, destiny has no understanding of what Providence's goals are or why they need to be achieved). Destiny uses various blind agents to act out the plan of Providence in time and matter through
      Fortune, which is changeable, unstable, unsympathetic and irrational.

Fortune is represented as a lady with a wheel; people rise and fall, inevitably, for no reason.

Fortune implements the plan in two spheres:

Common	Personal
All the world	One's personal life
Bound by the Chain of Love	Birth chances
Nature as Destiny	Affected by erratic stars

The keys to Boethius' problem are time, matter and change. God's plan, Providence, is outside of time. Providence is perfect and changeless. But as the implementation of the plan descends into the world of time, matter and change, the agents that act out Providence are increasingly unreliable, ending in the fickle, cruel, blind chance of Fortune, which is what people experience as causing their joys and their woes.

This descent into the vagaries of matter fits nicely with the ancient Ptolemaic model of the universe, generally accepted as true until Copernicus put the sun into the middle of the universe in the sixteenth century. The Ptolemaic model has the Earth at the center. The moon, sun and planets revolve around the Earth, while the "fixed stars" are outside the realm of motion and change. God, or the primary cause, is out there, beyond the fixed stars, unmoved, yet starting the motions of the universe; and humans are down here, near the bottom of the universe, where the motion is most unpredictable.

An interwoven problem that Boethius and Lady Philosophy discuss is human free will. If God knows everything that has happened, is happening, and will happen, what room is there for human choice and free will? Time is the key here. Outside of time, God knows everything that happens, since it is all in the present for Him. However, human beings exist and know events in time. They make their choices freely at a particular moment, even though God, outside time, knows what choices they make (Mann 78–79).

Troilus and Criseyde weaves together ancient Trojan and more recent Boethian traditions about Troy and the gods, Providence and Fortune, love, and Fate and free will. Amors shoots Troilus, forcing him to participate in the common Fortune of the Chain of Love that binds all creatures together. Troilus responds, in part, by constant complaints about Destiny, Fortune and his lack of free will. However, Troilus also acts freely to pledge his love to Criseyde and he keeps his pledge, or troth, even though she does not. Unfortunately, in the greater scheme of things (Destiny), Troy must fall, and there is nothing Troilus can do to prevent it.

The Main Characters

Troilus and Criseyde concerns four central characters, their experiences of love, and what, if anything, they learn from love.

The Narrator: A medieval Christian
Troilus: A noble Trojan knight
Criseyde: The woman he falls in love with
Pandarus: Criseyde's uncle and Troilus' friend

THE NARRATOR

At the opening of the poem the Narrator is an enthusiastic worshipper (but not practitioner) of the rites of the pagan God of Love (Cupid or Amors). He says that he has learned of Troilus and Criseyde from an old book. He narrates the experiences of the lovers with close sympathy until Criseyde betrays Troilus. Then, the Narrator begins to withdraw from the situation. Eventually, the Narrator comes to recognize the lack of justice, mercy, and stability within the pagan love religion and turns, enlightened and freely, to the Christian God.

TROILUS

Initially Troilus scorns lovers, angering the god of love, who shoots him; Troilus then looks over the ladies, sees Criseyde, and falls totally, permanently, in love. Although he is a brave and handsome knight, Troilus is a timid, despairing lover. His response to being struck by love is to go home and suffer. By nature, Troilus is passive, a fatalist, born to despair; he interprets every event as caused by Fate or Destiny. It takes Pandarus' activism to get Troilus moving. Troilus has no idea how to pursue a love affair. Pandarus helps Troilus at every stage of the affair.

Although he suffers from love, Troilus is improved by it and becomes a nicer man and an even better fighter. His joy with Criseyde is as perfect as any joy in life can be. But inevitably the wheel of Fortune turns. Criseyde leaves Troy and then she betrays Troilus with the Greek Diomede. Troilus' most noble quality is his troth, his pledge of love that lasts until his death, despite Criseyde's betrayal. Troilus, being a pagan, cannot know the resolution to his pain until after he dies and sees from the sky how small, insignificant and brutal the world really is.

PANDARUS

He is an empathic, friendly man, who is easy to like, easy to despise, unforgettable. Pandarus is Troilus' friend, Criseyde's uncle. Pandarus is an unsuccessful lover, in love with love, a clever impresario who arranges his friends' lives; a "pander" and a voyeur. Pandarus says he means well, and he probably does, but some of what he means is morally disturbing. Above all, Pandarus is an opportunist. He sees each event as opportunity — Fortune creates possibilities, and he exploits those possibilities ingeniously. Pandarus does not understand Troilus' troth at all: When Fortune's wheel turns down, Pandarus is only able to suggest that Troilus find another love.

CRISEYDE

She is charming, lovable, fearful, unstable, and fickle, like the world itself. She is a widow who wants to stay that way because she enjoys her freedom. Her father Calkas is a seer. Because he knows that Troy must fall, he changes allegiance and goes over to the Greek camp. Calkas has already left Troy when the story opens, and eventually he arranges for Criseyde to leave Troy for the Greek camp and safety.

Criseyde is always looking out for her own interests. She is subtle, clever — attracted to Troilus, but not willing to commit unless she can preserve her reputation. She is fond of Pandarus, but cautious, and plays coy manipulative games with him as he maneuvers her into bed with Troilus. She loves Troilus, no doubt about it, but once she is forced to leave him for the Greek camp, she soon pledges her love to Diomede.

MINOR CHARACTERS

Various minor characters are already familiar from older Troy stories. They include Greeks such as Achilles, Helen and Diomede, and Trojans such as Deiphobus, Antenor, Hector, Priam, Cassandra, Paris, and Calkas (Calchas).

The Story of Troilus and Criseyde

BOOK I. LOVE STRIKES

Prologue: The Narrator introduces himself and his purpose, which is to tell of the double sorrow of Troilus, who suffers for love unfulfilled and then suffers for love betrayed. He asks lovers to pity and pray for despairing lovers.

The story proper starts with brief background on the Trojan War and how the priest Calkas knew that Troy was doomed, so he fled to the Greek camp. He left behind his lovely, innocent daughter Criseyde, who feared for her life at the hands of the angry Trojans. Criseyde sought and received Hector's protection and continued to live in Troy.

Criseyde, beautiful even in widow's black, attends the Feast of Pallas. Troilus is also there, scorning lovers. Troilus' scorn angers the god of love, who shoots Troilus with an arrow. Troilus had tried to deny the law of Nature that creatures must love. Love softens hard hearts, ennobles lovers and teaches fear of vice and shame. No one can or should refuse to love. Troilus, now a slave to love, looks around, sees Criseyde, and is struck with love for her. Suffering from the fires of lovesickness, Troilus goes home to bed. He does not have a clue how to pursue his love.

Fortunately for Troilus, Pandarus visits. He is sensitive to his friend's suffering and offers to help. After some prying, Pandarus discovers Troilus' secret. No problem! Criseyde is Pandarus' niece, so he's delighted to help. Pandarus will speak to Criseyde; he leaves Troilus cheered. Now, Troilus is improved by love. He becomes friendlier, noble, generous and a better knight; gone is his arrogance; he no longer makes fun of lovers.

BOOK II. PANDARUS PLOTS

Prologue: The Narrator asks lovers to be tolerant of Troilus' slowness in love, since each person is different.

Pandarus visits Criseyde and teases her that he knows a secret. He praises Troilus and eventually reveals his secret: Troilus is in love with her. Criseyde is timid and worries that her protector is acting against her best interests, but Pandarus assures her that he means well. They banter about love and then Pandarus leaves. Criseyde sees Troilus pass in the street and is impressed: he is a perfect knight. She likes him, perhaps she already loves him, but she vacillates about getting involved, and worries about her reputation. Then she hears her niece Antigone sing a song about how love leads to bliss and virtue. The song persuades Criseyde that loving Troilus might be desirable.

Pandarus tells Troilus to write a love letter to Criseyde. Pandarus delivers the letter and persuades Criseyde to reply. Troilus still does not know how to proceed. Pandarus schemes to arrange a rendezvous between Troilus and Criseyde. Pandarus concocts the story that there are people in town who want to harm Criseyde. He asks Deiphebus (Troilus' favorite brother) to meet with Criseyde to offer her his protection. Deiphebus offers to bring Helen along. Pandarus then scares Criseyde with his story about her enemies. He invites Criseyde to meet with Deiphebus, so she can seek his protection.

Meanwhile, Pandarus tells Troilus to go to Deiphebus' house, pretend he does not feel well, and go to bed, so he will be there naturally when Criseyde arrives the next day. Criseyde, her nieces, and Pandarus all show up the next day at Deiphebus' house for dinner and the meeting. Deiphebus and Helen reassure Criseyde of their protection. Then Pandarus suggests that Criseyde should go in to Troilus' chamber, where he's sick in bed, and tell him about her concerns. Pandarus maneuvers Criseyde into lovesick Troilus' room.

BOOK III. LOVE'S JOY

Prologue: A beautiful song invokes the power and joy of love that binds together all creatures in the world.

Meanwhile, Troilus lies in bed trying to decide what to say. When Criseyde actually approaches, he begs Criseyde's mercy and pledges his soul to her. Criseyde accepts Troilus as her lover, so long as her honor is safe. She kisses Troilus and leaves, while Pandarus assures them he will arrange for them to meet again at his house. Troilus swears his secrecy and honorable intentions. Pandarus now assures Troilus that Criseyde will do whatever Troilus wants. Pandarus hastens to add that he has only arranged this meeting in order to comfort Troilus. Pandarus begs Troilus not to abuse his trust by harming her honor. Troilus and Criseyde meet casually and exchange letters, while Pandarus schemes to bring them together at his house.

Having invited Criseyde to dinner, Pandarus hides Troilus in a closet before she arrives. The weather is dark and stormy. Pandarus persuades Criseyde to stay for the night, and then he concocts a story about Troilus being jealous and suffering terribly. Criseyde is persuaded to let Pandarus bring poor suffering Troilus into her bedchamber. She explains to Troilus that he has no reason to be jealous, but he is so distressed by his own falsehood that he faints. Pandarus tucks Troilus into bed with Criseyde, where Troilus revives, and they consummate their love.

Troilus and Criseyde pursue a joyful, discreet affair. Love makes Troilus better and braver, and he and Criseyde are ecstatically happy for quite a while. Near the end of Book III, Troilus sings a beautiful song about the Bond of Love that rules all nature and regulates the heavens and earth and the harmonious relations of all creatures.

BOOK IV. FORTUNE'S WHEEL DESCENDS — CRISEYDE MUST LEAVE TROY

Prologue: The Narrator invokes the downside of Fortune, which is loss; the story will now tell how Criseyde left Troy, betrayed Troilus, and pledged her love to Diomede.

The Trojans lose a battle and the Greeks capture Antenor. A truce is arranged and a prisoner exchange is negotiated. Calkas reminds the Greeks that Troy will fall and he has left Troy for the Greek camp. However, he left behind his daughter Criseyde, whom he asks the Greeks to exchange for a Trojan prisoner. The Greeks agree to exchange Antenor for Criseyde, and the Trojan Council votes to make the exchange. Troilus is desperate, but he does not dare to speak out because he is pledged to preserve Criseyde's honor.

Troilus retreats to his room, where he despairs and rails against pitiless Fortune. Pandarus, ever the opportunist, tries to comfort him with insensitive suggestions such as finding another woman or running away with Criseyde. Destiny is now taking over; Troilus cannot run off with Criseyde because Troy is at war, and his own father (Priam) has pledged her exchange. Any step Troilus might take to cling to Criseyde would compromise her honor, which he has pledged to protect. Pandarus says if it were his choice, he would run off with her. Pandarus arranges for Troilus and Criseyde to meet and talk over their options. Criseyde, learning of the exchange, is grief stricken but does not know what to do. Troilus debates with himself over Boethian free will versus God's foreknowledge. Troilus rejects free will in favor of necessity, because if God has foreknowledge of everything, what's a poor fellow to do?

Troilus and Criseyde meet for the last night; he urges they flee together; she faints; he laments and starts to kill himself; then she revives and they embrace. Criseyde now wants to rely on her cleverness to manipulate the situation. She says she'll go to the Greek camp but return within ten days. The Narrator assures himself that she meant well. Troilus and Criseyde part.

BOOK V. CRISEYDE BETRAYS TROILUS

Prologue: The Narrator bitterly invokes fatal Destiny and the Furies.

Exchanged for Antenor, Criseyde leaves Troy. Diomede immediately starts to woo Criseyde as he escorts her to Greek camp. Waiting for Criseyde to return, Troilus agonizes for ten days. Pandarus tries to comfort Troilus, but Troilus is inconsolable. Criseyde longs for Troilus and plans to return to Troy, but meanwhile Diomede plans to win Criseyde. Here, the Narrator gives portraits of Troilus, Criseyde, and Diomede that he found in old books. The Narrator is distancing himself from his characters, as he becomes increasingly unhappy with the way the story must end. Diomede woos and wins Criseyde, who gives him a brooch that Troilus had given to her. On the promised tenth day, Troilus goes with Pandarus to the gates to wait for Criseyde, but she does not come, and Troilus despairs, knowing there is nothing left for him but death.

Troilus dreams of Criseyde embracing a boar. Pandarus has Troilus write to Criseyde, who replies ambiguously that she will come, but she doesn't know when. Troilus then sends for his sister Cassandra, who explains his dream: the boar is Diomede, who is now Criseyde's lover. Troilus angrily rejects Cassandra's explanation. Hector is near his fated death and Troy is near its doom. Troilus continues writing to Criseyde, who finally replies with a letter that implies that the reason she will not return soon is that there are rumors about herself and Troilus and she wants to protect her reputation. She assures him of her friendship (not her love). Troilus finally has to face the truth when he sees the brooch he had given Criseyde on Diomede's coat.

Now Troilus fights furiously against the Greeks. Achilles kills Troilus, whose soul then rises to the eighth sphere (where pagan souls undergo penance and purification). At last Troilus understands the harmony of the universe and the trivial foolishness of all mortal life and blind desire. Troilus' liberated soul laughs at the mortals mourning his death. The Narrator, too, has learned the limited value of earthly love, and he recommends that young people pursue the Christian love of God instead of cursed pagan rites.

The Literary Afterlife of Troilus and Criseyde

Although Chaucer hesitated to blame Criseyde and Pandarus, later writers were quite willing to do so. Pandarus' name became the term for a person who arranges for the gratification of others' desires, and Criseyde became the type of the faithless woman. Robert Henryson's *Testament of Cresseid* (a fifteenth-century Scottish poem) continues her story after Diomede tired of her and she returned to her father's house in the Greek camp. She then denounces the gods of love, Venus and Cupid, so they punish her with leprosy. Gordon concludes his overview in *The Story of Troilus*: "By the time of Shakespeare, Criseyde had become a mere wanton, and Shakespeare in his play [*Troilus and Cressida*] left her such" (xviii).

Because Chaucer was able to be so compassionate towards his characters and so understanding of their situations, modern readers have found it difficult to separate what Chaucer believed from the various ideas and attitudes expressed by the characters in the poem. Nothing is simple in *Troilus and Criseyde*. Human love is wonderful; however, only divine love is certain. As Peter Christmas puts it, "Courtly love reconciled with the certainties of the eighth sphere is the whole truth..." (293). However, that "whole truth" is only apparent at the very end of the poem, after Troilus has died and his soul has left earth for the eighth sphere. Possibly, like other pious endings tacked on to worldly poems, this philosophical ending is a sop to the Church, not a summing up of Chaucer's heartfelt belief. It is finally up to the reader to decide.

12

Shakespeare's *Troilus and Cressida*
Human Beings Alone[1]

Chaucer presented human beings and the world they live in as flawed and unstable; however, he placed this unstable world in the context of a perfect, stable universal order, with God firmly at the center. This perfection projected down into the world via a hierarchical chain of being, from highest (closest to God) to lowest (farthest from God). In a pre–Christian world such as that of Troy, this God-centered hierarchy could not be well understood, so until Troilus died, he was not able to understand the true order and sanctity of the universe. Only the post-revelation Christian Narrator was able to learn during his lifetime about the true nature of the unstable world and its place in the perfect divine universe.

Shakespeare, like Chaucer, retells the story of doomed Troilus and his flawed lover Cressida, presenting a world that is treacherous and unstable. But Shakespeare, unlike Chaucer, does not offer a context of universal order as the ultimate solution. In 200 years, the way people viewed the world had changed considerably from the medieval concept of a God-centered great chain of being. Elton explains that the Elizabethan world view featured "complexity and variety, inconsistency and fluidity." Consequently, while Shakespeare's "dramas assert the 'great chain of being' … and the hierarchy of order, they also as frequently act out the opposite, the reality of disorder" (180). This "reality of disorder" governs both the Greeks and Trojans in Shakespeare's *Troilus and Cressida*.

The Story of Shakespeare's Troilus and Cressida

The general situation and characters of Shakespeare's *Troilus and Cressida* are similar to Chaucer's, but the focus is quite different.

ACT I

Troilus tells Pandarus about his love for Cressida and asks him to arrange a meeting. Pandarus then praises Troilus to Cressida.

The Greek Council meets. Agamemnon complains that after seven years of siege, Troy still stands. Ulysses blames Achilles and Patroclus, who are hanging around in their tent

150

making fun of the Greek leaders and destroying Greek morale. According to Ulysses, the behavior of Achilles and Patroclus is causing a failure of degree, the proper ordering of rule among men as well as in the universe.

Aeneas enters bearing Hector's challenge to the Greeks to provide a champion to meet him in single combat. Ulysses (Odysseus) gets an idea: Why not set up dull Ajax as the Greek champion in order to snap Achilles back into line?

ACT II

The Trojan Council meets and debates. Should they keep Helen or let her go? Good reasons are given for both options, but in the end they decide to keep her.

In the Greek camp, Ulysses explains to Agamemnon that he wants to break down Achilles' pride, which is damaging the Greek army. Ulysses praises Ajax to make Achilles jealous.

ACT III

Pandarus makes arrangements for Troilus to spend the night at Pandarus' house (with Cressida). Pandarus brings Cressida to Troilus. They announce their love for one another, and Pandarus promptly sends them to bed.

In the Greek camp, Calchas asks to have his daughter Cressida brought out of Troy in exchange for the Trojan Antenor, who is a prisoner in the Greek camp. Agamemnon sends Diomedes to fetch her. Ulysses persuades the Greek leaders to snub Achilles to diminish his pride. Ulysses warns Achilles that his fame is based only on his actions, and if he does not act like a hero, he will become less of one, especially if he lets Ajax become the Greek champion and conquer Hector. Achilles decides to invite the Trojan lords to dinner after the fight between Ajax and Hector.

ACT IV

Diomedes comes to Troy to fetch Cressida. Troilus and Cressida have just finished their night of love. Aeneas enters with news of the exchange. The lovers give parting speeches. Diomedes enters, scorns Troilus, and takes Cressida back to the Greek camp.

Hector and the Trojans enter the Greek camp for Hector's combat with Ajax. Hector and Ajax fight to a pause, and then Hector says he'd like to stop the fight because Ajax is his cousin and half Trojan. Hector visits the Greek tents for a friendly dinner.

ACT V

Achilles plans to get Hector drunk so that he'll be easier to kill the next day. Polyxena (Hector's sister) sends Achilles a letter asking him not to fight. Achilles loves her, so maybe he won't fight.

Troilus and Ulysses go to Calchas' tent where they watch as Cressida flirts with Diomedes. She lets Diomedes have Troilus' sleeve, which Troilus had given to her as a love token. Troilus is devastated: She was his Cressida; now she is Diomedes' Cressida.

Back in Troy, Priam and family try to keep Hector from going out to fight for the day. No luck. Diomedes and Troilus fight, and Diomedes gets Troilus' horse, which he sends to Cressida as a gift.

Hector kills Patroclus, and Achilles vows revenge. Hector goes after a Greek in gorgeous armor, kills him, and then takes a break from fighting. While Hector is disarmed, Achilles and his gang ambush and kill him. The bitter ending has Troilus mourning Hector and craving more war, while Pandarus gets in the last word, a speech about corruption.

What Is a Man (or Woman)?[2]

In ancient times, the Trojan War and its events had been motivated by various causes, such as the will of Zeus (to reduce human overpopulation), the Judgment of Paris (Aphrodite awarded Helen to Paris as a prize), Roman Destiny (the *Aeneid*), the goddess Fortune and the destructive impulse of Amors (*Roman de Troie*), or the positive influence of Amors (*Eneas*). Shakespeare, however, wrote in a time when all these ancient deities, semi-deities, and causative elements were mere decorative illusions. Nonetheless, Troy had fallen. That was history. Therefore, the questions of how and why Troy fell became more puzzling and important than ever, because only human beings could have caused the fall of Troy. Shakespeare's *Troilus and Cressida* asks an inevitable question: What are human beings, who can destroy a civilization?

What and who are frequent questions in *Troilus and Cressida*. The answer to these questions is generally the name of the person observed; characters tell one another who someone is, or that someone is a man of such a sort. For example, in the second scene of Act I, Cressida, watching the Trojan warriors passing by, asks her manservant Alexander, "Who were those went by?" He mentions Ajax, saying, "They say he is a very man per se, / And stands alone." To which Cressida retorts, "So do all men, unless they are drunk, sick, / or have no legs" (*Tro.* 1.2.1–18). No man (or woman) in the play will prove to be any more than a very man, who stands, or falls, alone.

Cressida then comments, "Hector's a gallant man." Alexander replies, "As may be in the world, lady" (*Tro.* 1.2.38–39). Whatever a man may be, he is alone and limited. Hector is as good as a man can be, which is not nearly good enough to save Troy. When Cressida rejects Pandarus' comparison between Troilus and Hector, Pandarus retorts, "What, not between Troilus and Hector? / Do you know a man if you see him?" (*Tro.* 1.2.63–64).

> *Cressida.* Ay, If I ever saw him before and knew him.
> *Pandarus.* Well, I say Troilus is Troilus.
> *Cressida.* Then you say as I say; for I am sure he is not Hector.
> *Pandarus.* No, nor Hector is not Troilus in some degrees.
> *Cressida.* 'Tis just to each of them; he is himself [*Tro.* 1.2.65–69].

This banter is typical of the radical questions the play asks about the nature of human beings. A man is limited, as well as identified, by his name; he can be no more than himself, as well as no other than himself. As to the nature of that self—the play offers no answers.

When Pandarus and Cressida observe the Trojan warriors returning from battle, Pandarus exclaims, "'Tis Troilus! there's a man, niece! ... O admirable man!" Cressida remarks that Achilles is a "better man than Troilus" and Pandarus replies, "Why, have you any discretion? / have you any eyes? do you know what a man is? Is not / birth, beauty, good shape, discourse, manhood, learning, / gentleness, virtue, youth, liberality, and such like, the / spice and salt that season a man?" (*Tro.* 1.2.228–256). Qualities such as birth, learning, virtue, and so on are merely the seasoning; they do not answer the basic question, what is a man? When the Trojans visit the Greek camp, Hector protests to Achilles, who is surveying Hector's body like a butcher looking for the place to begin cutting, "But there's more in me than thou understand'st" (*Tro.* 4.5.240).

Human Motivation and the Hierarchy of Values

If humans exist alone and act freely, uninfluenced by the stars and the gods, the actions people choose will determine the fall of Troy. Consequently, the question of how people choose actions is crucial. Generally, people act to get what they desire and to avoid what they dislike; however, different people desire different objects and outcomes. Desire is the heart of the problem in *Troilus and Cressida.* A person has value because other people place that value on him or her. An action has value because it will lead to a desired end or express a desired value such as love or chivalry. People choose actions in terms of personal and social values, which allow them to decide that it is better, for instance, to keep Helen than to return her, or that it is better to fight than to stay at home.

Hierarchical value, the worth of one goal, object, or person in relation to another, is a central problem characters struggle with in *Troilus and Cressida.* The question, "What is a man?" is related to the question, "How does he rank in value in relation to other men?" Simply being Achilles is not sufficient to produce value, because value is based in social interaction. Thus, Ulysses is able to concoct a scheme to dampen Achilles' pride and value by snubbing Achilles and promoting Ajax.

Discussions of human identity and value culminate in the paradox of Troilus' statements when he observes Cressida being unfaithful: "This she? No; this is Diomed's Cressida," and "This is, and is not, Cressid!" (*Tro.* 5.2.137, 146). If a man (or woman) exists in relation to others, then Diomedes' Cressida is not the same as Troilus' Cressida. If a woman is herself and no other (if the name of a person uniquely identifies and defines her), then Cressida is and is not herself, since the Cressida that Troilus *knew* by that name and identity was different from the Cressida he now observes.

Three Kinds of Values in Troilus and Cressida

Characters in *Troilus and Cressida* struggle with three kinds of values — absolute, relative, and the direct objects of appetite. Hector argues for absolute value. He insists that worth is intrinsic to a person, not dependent on what he/she does. Ulysses explains and manipulates relative value, claiming that each person is worth more or less only in relation to other human beings. Troilus, Pandarus and Cressida express the value of appetite. For them, value is a function of desire. The more a person desires something or someone, the more value that object of desire acquires.

The question of value develops around the issue of whether to return Helen. The

Greeks have given the Trojans an opportunity to end the war by returning Helen, and the discussion centers on the value of Helen: Is she worth a war? Hector argues for absolute value, or intrinsic worth, so he decides that "she is not worth what she doth cost / The keeping." Troilus, who believes that a man can create value by his choices, objects: "What's aught, but as 'tis valued?" and Hector replies, "But value dwells not in particular will: / It holds his estimate and dignity / As well wherein 'tis precious of itself / As in the prizer" (*Tro.* 2.2.51–56).

Troilus, however, claims that his own choice, although based in desire, can create value. Honor then requires him to treat the chosen person or object as having fixed value. The scene continues:

> *Troilus.* I take today a wife, and my election
> Is led on in the conduct of my will;
> My will enkindled by mine eyes and ears —
> Two traded pilots 'twixt the dangerous shores
> Of will and judgment — how may I avoid,
> Although my will distaste what it elected,
> The wife I chose? There can be no evasion
> To blench from this and to stand firm by honour [*Tro.* 2.2.61–68].

There is no way to reconcile the kinds of values represented by Hector and Troilus. Hector argues that objects have intrinsic or absolute value; Troilus believes that one can assign value to objects by an act of will and choice based ultimately on perception, a mode of appetite. Paris goes even further, saying, "I would have the soil of her fair rape / Wiped off in honourable keeping her" (*Tro.* 2.2.148–49). Paris' claim that the value of an action can actually be changed by future actions shows even more extreme relativism than Troilus' position.

Hector has asserted that moral laws of nature and of nations require that Helen be returned to her husband. Nonetheless, Hector then recommends that the Trojans keep Helen, "For 'tis a cause that hath no mean dependence / Upon our joint and several dignities" (*Tro.* 2.2.192–93). Hector's recommendation contradicts all that he has said so far, since if value is absolute, it could not be dependent upon what one did. Given the choice between his faith in absolute values and his desire to be perceived as having value (his dignity), Hector chooses to act to enhance his perceived value.

Shakespeare portrays Hector as a chivalric hero who has some bad moments. Hector has high ideals, but he does not follow through. In single combat, Hector lets weary Ajax go because he is kin. Hector also courteously lets Achilles get away when they are fighting. Despite his chivalric ideals, Hector dies because he has pursued and killed a Greek to seize his gorgeous armor and Hector then disarmed to rest in the midst of the battle. At this moment Achilles and his men arrive. Hector objects to their evident intent to kill him, saying, "I am unarmed; forgo this vantage, Greek" (*Tro.* 5.8.9). His appeal to chivalry and fair play is unheeded, and the Greeks kill Hector. Hector's chivalric value system leads him to behave nobly and talk eloquently of reason and human feelings. But in the end, Hector chooses glory over good sense, kinship over successful combat, and greed for gorgeous armor over prudence. Absolute (chivalric) values end with the death of Hector.

Ulysses is the exponent of relative values, which he explains most fully in his famous speech on degree. At first degree appears to be the same as the medieval great chain of being or great chain of love that was thought to bind all elements in the universe into an unbreakable, harmonious hierarchy of beings (Lovejoy 59). However, Ulysses' conception of degree is political, not universal, although he compares it to the orderliness of the heavens with the sun properly dominant (*Tro.* 1.3.85 ff.). Ulysses warns that if degree is not observed among men, the outcome will be as chaotic as "when the planets / In evil mixture to disorder wander" (*Tro.* 1.3.94–95). He warns:

> O, when degree is shaked,
> Which is the ladder of all high designs,
> The enterprise is sick! How could communities,
> Degrees in schools, and brotherhoods in cities,
> Peaceful commerce from dividable shores,
> The primogenitive and due of birth,
> Prerogative of age, crowns, sceptres, laurels,
> But by degree, stand in authentic place? [*Tro.* 1.3.101–08].

For Ulysses, place or position is the key to the problem of values. Ulysses is very concerned with the need to maintain degree and order in political relationships, and he warns: "Take but degree away, untune that string, / And hark what discord follows!" (*Tro.* 1.3.109–10). Ulysses not only identifies Achilles as being out of his place, but plots and maneuvers to put him back in his place. Miskimin comments that Ulysses' "affirmation of ideal order is subverted by its speaker and our knowledge of his cunning, and the destructive purpose to which his wisdom is to be put" (162). To be sure, Ulysses omits the "angelic end of the chain of being" (Tillyard 84); yet one could also argue that Ulysses is not destructive, but is attempting rather to reconstruct, or hold together, a world that is falling apart.

Ulysses' conception of degree is not the natural order of the cosmos, the medieval great chain of connected being, but the orderliness of a hierarchical state, where the elements in the hierarchy must be kept in their proper places by means of policy. The alternative to such order is the universal wolf of appetite, self-willed indulgent disorder. Value in such a system is *not* intrinsic or absolute, but a matter of the position of a person, action, or object relative to the other elements in the hierarchy. Thus, to know where a person is in the hierarchy is to know what he is worth; however, as time passes, his deeds, his position, and hence his value, can change. Consequently, Achilles can change from a man of great value to a man of little value, depending on his relation to other men.

Keeping the chain of command in an orderly hierarchy is the "specialty of rule" which Ulysses charges has "been neglected" (*Tro.* 1.3.78). An army that does not observe proper degree descends into chaos.

> The general's disdained
> By him one step below, he by the next,
> That next by him beneath; so every step,
> Exampled by the first pace that is sick
> Of his superior, grows to an envious fever
> Of pale and bloodless emulation [*Tro.* 1.3.129–34].

There is a universal order that people ought to pattern their lives upon, but they will not unless their leaders set an example for them to follow. In short, a man is not a natural member of that universal hierarchy of being, but only belongs to it if other men assign him to his place.

Although there are many references to men as beasts in *Troilus and Cressida*, a man is not a beast, a natural member of the natural hierarchy of being. A man is something else. Just what else is a question constantly asked, but never answered, except by the empty retort that any particular man is himself and not any other man. A person's position in the hierarchy is based on his value. However, his value is a function of how he appears to other men, not an intrinsic and absolute quality such as the scales of a fish or the mane of a lion.

A man's attributes locate him in the social hierarchy. But these attributes are vulnerable to change, since they are based on men perceiving another man. When Ulysses begins his manipulations of Achilles' self-esteem in order to put him back into his proper place in the hierarchy, he first attacks Achilles' attributes.

> Much attribute he hath, and much the reason
> Why we ascribe it to him; yet all his virtues,
> Not virtuously on his own part beheld,
> Do in our eyes begin to lose their gloss... [*Tro.* 2.3.115–18].

Ulysses snubs Achilles, sets up Ajax to fight Hector, and pretends that Ajax is the better man. This strategy begins to strip away Achilles' honor, which depends on other men perceiving his attributes as heroic. Initially, Achilles thinks that only Fortune could strip away his attributes, but then he encounters Ulysses, who instructs him

> That no man is the lord of anything,
> Though in and of him there be much consisting,
> Till he communicate his parts to others;
> Nor doth he of himself know them for aught
> Till he behold them formèd in th'applause
> Where they're extended... [*Tro.* 3.3.115–20].

A man cannot control or even judge his own attributes, except in the responses his actions elicit from other people. All the qualities that would place a man in the chain of degree of human society are dependent upon his actions and other men's responses to his actions. There is no absolute or intrinsic value of a man in the social world described by Ulysses.

According to Ulysses, a man isolated from society has no value. Furthermore, the value generated by honorable deeds is not value forever, but only value for a brief time. A man's value must be renewed by actions, or it will decay into valueless oblivion. As Ulysses explains to Achilles,

> The present eye praises the present *object*:
> Then marvel not, thou great and complete man,
> That all the Greeks begin to worship Ajax;
> Since things in motion sooner catch the eye
> Than what not stirs [*Tro.* 3.3.180–84].

Ulysses' vision of the order of degree is preferable to the chaos of appetite, but it is an artificial order, produced by great effort, and a man's position in this order can only be maintained by constant striving. It is the antithesis of the natural order, or chain of being, where a man's position is located by what he is, not by what he does.

Appetite, the Universal Wolf

Along with the absolute value of intrinsic worth (expressed by Hector), and the value of relative worth (expressed by Ulysses), there is a third source of value in *Troilus and*

Cressida, which ultimately dominates and controls human action. This is appetite, the "universal wolf." Most of the characters in *Troilus and Cressida* act to achieve what they desire or have appetite for.

Ruth Anderson explains in her study of Elizabethan psychology that the appetites are

> inclinations by which the soul likes or dislikes whatever comes to it.... The second form of appetite, that which arises without touch, follows imagination or thought. It possesses a desiring or concupiscent and an angry or irascible inclination from which spring the affections of the heart. These affections, especially in their initial stages, are also called motions. They are impulses, which incite the soul to reach out for the good and to withdraw from the evil [18–19].

Anderson goes on to describe the relationship of appetite to will and reason: "Like the sensitive appetite, will is blind, ordained to follow the light of reason.... Appetite may desire anything that seems good ... but will does not incline to possess or to do whatever reason pronounces good unless reason also teaches a way to obtain or to do the good" (22).

Appetite is at the heart of the problem in *Troilus and Cressida.* The appetite is a faculty of the soul, which responds to stimuli, whether external or internal. It is supposedly attracted to what seems good and repelled by what seems evil. Ideally, appetite's impulses are guided by reason. However, there is no absolute value, which would allow reason to discriminate between what is good and what is less good. Consequently, although the will, guided by reason, is supposed to be able to discriminate between more- and less-good objects of desire or appetite, it cannot function properly. This is why Ulysses warns that if degree is neglected,

> Then everything includes itself in power,
> Power into will, will into appetite;
> And appetite, an universal wolf,
> So doubly seconded with will and power,
> Must make perforce an universal prey,
> And last eat up himself [*Tro.* 1.3.119–24].

No rational choice can be made between two desired goals — peace and the keeping of Helen, for example — because there is no way to discriminate between their values. In the Council debate, Hector has assigned intrinsic value to Helen — she is not worth keeping; she is not worth the loss of Trojan lives. However, he can not finally decide to return Helen to Greece because Hector also has assigned intrinsic value to dignity. He is not able to set the two values into a scale or hierarchy of values by means of which he could rationally conclude that the proper and best action would be to return Helen. Instead, Hector says that the Trojans ought to return Helen and that they ought to keep Helen. Without a scale of values, rational decision-making is impossible. Unfortunately, the only scale of values available in the world of *Troilus and Cressida* is in the artificially constructed hierarchy of the Greek army, which Ulysses strives to maintain.

Without degree, without a recognized scale of values, there are no criteria by which reason can guide the will and appetites. Following the appetites leads to chaos, which is akin to madness. In the first scene of Act I, Troilus tells Pandarus, "I am mad / In Cressid's love" (*Tro.* 1.1.53–54). Anderson explains that, "In the case of actual madness the world becomes a disorganized state in which the principles of justice and morality no longer hold" (106). Both Troy and the Greek camp are such disorganized states because people act out their passions without regard for the effects of their actions on others. Even when people mean well, their capacity to act on their good intentions is limited. There is no need of pagan demons, Fate, or gods to harm people in *Troilus and Cressida*. Human beings alone, acting out their appetites, are quite enough to ruin Troy and all the people in it.

The theme of appetite is developed throughout the play, beginning with an extended comparison of Troilus' love for Cressida as appetite for a cake. (*Tro.* 1.1.14–18) Troilus fears that his indulgence in the appetite of love could destroy his ability to discriminate.

> death, I fear me,
> Swooning distraction, or some joy too fine,
> Too subtle-potent, tuned too sharp in sweetness.
> For the capacity of my ruder powers;
> I fear it much, and I do fear besides
> That I shall lose distinction in my joys,
> As doth a battle, when they charge on heaps
> The enemy flying [*Tro.* 3.2.22–29].

The unbridled appetite of love produces emotional chaos, which threatens social stability once the chain of degree is broken. Appetite, not reason, controls human behavior. Troilus, anticipating spending the night with Cressida, shows more concern with the infinity of his desire than interest in her value as a person. He tells Cressida, "This is / the monstruosity in love, lady — that the will is infinite / and the execution confined; that the desire is boundless / and the act a slave to limit" (*Tro.* 3.2.79–82). Troilus seeks Cressida because of his appetite for her, and yet he attempts to elevate her into an absolute of beauty.

When Troilus finally must confront his failure to elevate the object of his appetite into an absolute value, his response is to insist that if Cressida is false, there can be no absolute value.

> This she? No; this is Diomed's Cressida.
> If beauty have a soul, this is not she;
> If souls guide vows, if vows be sanctimonies,
> If sanctimony be the gods' delight,
> If there be rule in unity itself.
> This is not she [*Tro.* 5.2.137–42].

This passage expresses the crux of Troilus' problem and of all the value systems examined and discarded in the play. Troilus has attached the absolute values of beauty, soul, sanctimony, the gods, and unity itself to Cressida. However, she is unfaithful. Therefore, if these absolute values exist, then Cressida is not Cressida. Since Cressida in fact is Cressida, the logical conclusion is that these absolute values do not exist, and that there is not even "rule in unity itself."

Troilus continues, recognizing that he has gotten himself into a logical trap of conflicting absolutes, where nothing makes sense anymore:

> O madness of discourse,
> That cause sets up with and against itself!
> Bifold authority! Where reason can revolt
> Without perdition, and loss assume all reason
> Without revolt. This is, and is not, Cressid! [*Tro.* 5.2.142–46].

Troilus and Cressida presents a world in which there are no standards for making rational judgments. In the Trojan Council debate, Hector is able to set up reason against itself, claiming that it is right to return Helen, and yet they should keep Helen. For Troilus, Cressida is both the absolute person implied by the limit of her name and a creature composed of changeable attributes. She both is and is not Cressida. She is the creature perceived as having absolute intrinsic being and value, and she is the creature perceived as having value relative to her actions and to the opinions of men.

Troilus quickly moves from questioning Cressida's nature to questioning the nature of the universe. The faithlessness of Chaucer's Criseyde was a sign that men should turn from love of women to love of God, since the world and all in it were unstable and unreliable. Shakespeare's Troilus, however, takes Cressida's unfaithfulness to be proof that the very bonds of the heavens have "slipped, dissolved and loosed" [*Tro.* 5.2.156]. This is a catastrophic disorder of universal proportions. The objects of perception and appetite (e.g., other people) do not prove to be what they seem to be, and there is no possibility of right judgment or right action.

Troilus and Cressida uses the metaphor of appetite to express hatred as well as love. Love and hatred are both based on people acting to gratify their desires, not their rational minds. As already noted, Ulysses compares appetite to a "universal wolf." The Trojan Council opens with Priam relaying a message from Nestor in which he speaks of "the hot digestion of this cormorant war" (*Tro.* 2.2.6). Appetite is a universal wolf that even consumes itself; the war is a greedy beast that digests all those things dear to human beings. Ulysses remarks to Achilles, "How one man eats into another's pride, / While pride is fasting in his wantonness!" (*Tro.* 3.3.136–37). Time devours the deeds of men, as Ulysses comments: "Those scraps are good deeds past, which are devoured / As fast as they are made" (*Tro.* 3.3.148–49).

If appetite is the motivation for behavior, if desire is the source of value, and if the rational mind is baffled by the lack of hierarchical intrinsic values, then Pandarus is indeed the most fitting of intermediaries. He is the stimulator, the facilitator of appetite. In the Epilogue, Pandarus speaks not of the fall of Troy, but of "Pandar's fall" (*Tro.* 5.10.47). Love as appetite has fallen but hatred as appetite survives. The war goes on.

The focus of *Troilus and Cressida* on appetite as the source of value, and hence the cause of action, is a natural continuation of the ancient tradition of Troy stories. The original causes of the Trojan War had dissolved over time. By Shakespeare's time, the gods were long gone, as were various other causative elements such as Destiny, Fate, baleful planets and Fortune. The only remaining causes for the Trojan War were human actions based on human appetites.

There had always been problems at Troy — Greek heroes such as Agamemnon, Odysseus and Achilles behaved badly, while Trojan heroes such as Hector, Troilus and Aeneas exercised poor judgment. Whatever the version, Troy always fell, and both the winning Greeks and the losing Trojans faced future hardships. Yet, until Shakespeare, there was always an excuse. Some external force — the gods, Fate, Destiny, Fortune, Amors — had intervened to cause the destruction of basically decent people.

Along with these external forces, there also was a long tradition of bad decisions at and about Troy. The problem of how to do the right thing when one could not know for sure what to do was already thoroughly developed in Virgil's *Aeneid*. As Troy stories were rewritten in the Catholic Middle Ages, the issue of free will became very important. However, the irrational force of the remaining pagan god — Love or Amors — counterbalanced free will.

The Greeks and Trojans had made unfortunate decisions, but key actors such as Achilles, Paris and Troilus had been carried away by Love, which could not be resisted. Shakespeare's *Troilus and Cressida* is the first truly modern version of the Troy story, as it unequivocally faces the anguish of inadequate human decision-making in the context of a disorderly universe. No malice other than human malice, rooted in unbridled appetite, has caused the fall of Troy.

13

Improving Iphigenia
Racine and Goethe Modernize Evil

Re-motivating Iphigenia: Replacing the Pagan Gods with Inner Drives

Chapter 6 discusses the two Iphigenia plays written by Euripides, who was working within his own culture's historical and mythic tradition. Later writers, although attracted by the power of Euripides' Iphigenia plays, often had difficulties with the demands of the ancient gods for human sacrifice, the lack of clear motivation for Artemis to demand the sacrifice at Aulis, and the extreme barbarism of the Tantalid family. Euripides' *deus ex machina* (god from the machine) endings also became uncomfortable for European Christian writers who thought of human impulses and actions, not pagan gods, as the causes of events. Consequently, Iphigenia's story needed to be modernized to suit European audiences.

In seventeenth-century France, Racine wrote an Iphigenia play based on Euripides' *Iphigenia at Aulis*; in eighteenth-century Germany, Goethe wrote an Iphigenia play based on Euripides' *Iphigenia in Tauris*. Racine's *Iphigenia at Aulis* (*Iphigénie en Aulide*, 1674) retells the story of Iphigenia's near-sacrifice at Aulis. But this Iphigenia is too lovely a being to be sacrificed, so Racine provides a second woman, Eriphile, to be the actual victim — a suicide, not a human sacrifice. This leaves Iphigenia able to love and obey her father without having to be sacrificed to prove her loyalty and obedience. Goethe's *Iphigenia in Tauris* (*Iphigenie auf Tauris*, 1787) goes even further in improving Iphigenia. Goethe's Iphigenia cannot tell a lie, so instead of deceiving the Taurian King Thoas in order to rescue her brother Orestes, she tells the King the truth and asks him to behave humanely, which he does.

Although pagan gods still lurk in the background of both of these modernized Iphigenia plays, the gods never enter directly into the action. The origin of the problems may lie with the gods; the solutions must be human. The characters' inner struggles and personal excellence (or malice) become the wellsprings of action as well as the focus of interest in each play. In the absence of external divine or supernatural motivation, human character becomes destiny. Character as destiny is not necessarily an improvement for those born with bad character, such as Eriphile, but it is closer to modern ideas of psychological motivation. Lilian Furst argues that replacing the pagan gods with inner motivation is the essence of each play's modernization. Both Racine and Goethe replaced Euripides' *deus ex machina* endings with internal psychological motivation, a "god/demon within" (11).

161

Racine's Iphigenia *(at Aulis)*

This story involves the following characters:

Achilles: Noble lover, chivalric soul; seeks glory at Troy; equally seeks to protect his fiancée Iphigenia; loved by his captive Eriphile

Agamemnon: Noble king torn between the proper realm of kings—patriotism and glory—and the proper realm of a father—love for his daughter; sole weakness is kingly pride

Arcas: Attendant to Agamemnon

Calchas: Manipulative priest seeking Iphigenia's sacrifice

Clytemnestra: Loving mother; attacks Agamemnon to protect Iphigenia; accuses him of barbaric behavior

Doris: Eriphile's confidante and fellow-captive

Eriphile: Daughter of Helen and Theseus; does not know who her parents are or her own real name; bitter, envious, spiteful, negative version of Iphigenia; was on a journey to Troy to discover her true origins when Achilles captured her; loves Achilles secretly and obsessively; not in Euripides' version

Iphigenia: Good, loving, dutiful, beloved, perfect daughter; willingly accepts death because it is her duty to obey her father

Ulysses: Clever and sneaky, as usual in his post-homeric career; manipulates Agamemnon by playing on his kingly pride

ACT I

Scene 1. The Greek camp at Aulis. Agamemnon explains how, when the favorable wind stopped, leaving the Greek fleet stuck at Aulis, he had offered to make a sacrifice. Calchas had responded that the Greek fleet would not be able to sail to Troy unless Agamemnon sacrificed Iphigenia, "A maiden pure of Helen's race" (1.1.59) to Diana (Roman name for Artemis). Agamemnon claims he was horrified, but Ulysses persuaded his "regal pride" with talk about honor, patriotism and protecting Greece from Asia. Agamemnon has sent a letter ordering Iphigenia to come to Aulis to marry Achilles. Achilles is away, so he does not know what Agamemnon has done.

Now Agamemnon wants to send another letter, telling Iphigenia not to come because Achilles wants to postpone the marriage. Agamemnon tells his letter-bearer Arcas to say there are rumors that Achilles is in love with Eriphile.

Scene 2. Achilles returns unexpectedly. He is delighted to hear that Iphigenia is coming to Aulis to marry him. Ulysses chides that this is time for war, not a wedding, but Achilles proclaims his eagerness for both.

Scene 3. Ulysses warns Agamemnon that he owes his daughter's life to Greece. If Agamemnon tries to avoid sacrificing Iphigenia, Calchas will tell the army, which will become a frenzied mob and destroy them anyway. Ulysses plays on the ideals of honor, patriotism, and glory that Agamemnon responds to. Agamemnon says that if Iphigenia comes to Aulis, he will sacrifice her, but if destiny keeps her away, he will not.

Scenes 4–5. A messenger announces that Clytemnestra and Iphigenia are almost at the camp. Agamemnon bemoans the "Sad destiny of kings! Slaves that we are / Of fortune's rigour and the schemes of men" (1.5.365–6). Ulysses is sympathetic, but insists on the sacrifice. Agamemnon reluctantly agrees but wants Ulysses to help him hide the sacrifice from Clytemnestra.

ACT II

Scene 1. Eriphile, seriously depressed, talks with Doris. An oracle had told Eriphile that she must die to find out who she is. She had been on her way to Troy, where she would have discovered her true name and family, but she never got there because Achilles captured her in a raid. Worst of all, she is in love with Achilles, who is indifferent to her. Eriphile hopes her ill luck may damage Achilles and Iphigenia. If they marry, she will kill herself.

Scenes 2–3. Iphigenia encounters Agamemnon, who equivocates about the wedding. Iphigenia feels uneasy about her father's welcome and worries that Achilles has not come to meet her.

Scenes 4–8. Clytemnestra has read Agamemnon's second letter, postponing the marriage, and she has talked to Arcas, who implied that Achilles loved Eriphile, not Iphigenia. Clytemnestra prepares to leave Aulis with Iphigenia. There are various encounters between Iphigenia, Eriphile and Achilles, the outcome of which is that Achilles loves Iphigenia and Eriphile hopes for the worst.

ACT III

Scenes 1–2. Agamemnon commands Clytemnestra to stay away from the wedding ceremony because they are in a war camp.

Scenes 3–5. Achilles is looking forward to his marriage. Iphigenia asks Achilles to release Eriphile from captivity, and he assents. Arcas announces that Agamemnon is preparing to sacrifice Iphigenia. Only Achilles can defend her.

Scenes 6–7. Achilles wants to save Iphigenia, but she refuses his help because she wants to obey her father; however, she will talk to Agamemnon about the situation.

ACT IV

Scene 1. Eriphile is jealous of the gods paying attention to Iphigenia by requesting her as a sacrifice. Eriphile fears that Iphigenia will live and only she, Eriphile, will die. Eriphile plans to upset the wedding by revealing to the Greek army that Iphigenia is going to talk to her father and try to avoid being sacrificed.

Scenes 2–5. Agamemnon tries to pretend there will be a wedding, but Iphigenia and Clytemnestra are weeping, so Agamemnon realizes they know what is about to happen. Iphigenia pleads for her life but says she is ready to die if he commands it. Agamemnon has no idea why the gods are demanding the sacrifice; nonetheless, he tells Iphigenia her time to die has come.

Clytemnestra wrathfully reminds Agamemnon of his cursed ancestors who killed and served their children as food. She points out how worthless Helen is and accuses Agamemnon of being a pitiless father and a barbarous husband.

Scenes 6–11. Achilles argues with Agamemnon, trying to save Iphigenia. Agamemnon becomes furious because Achilles has questioned his prestige. Agamemnon decides that he will not sacrifice Iphigenia, who was obedient and loving; however he will forbid her to marry insolent Achilles. Agamemnon tries to save Iphigenia, telling her mother to secretly flee with her, so Calchas will not know she is leaving; but Eriphile goes off to tell Calchas that Iphigenia is fleeing the camp.

ACT V

Scenes 1–2. Iphigenia is ready to be sacrificed since her father has forbidden her to ever talk to Achilles again. Iphigenia and Achilles argue about love versus duty. He loves her and wants to rescue her. She feels bound to respect and obey her father. She'd sooner kill herself than run off to marry Achilles against her father's will.

Scenes 3–5. The army is rioting because Eriphile has betrayed Agamemnon's plan to send Iphigenia away. Calchas is in control. Clytemnestra is still struggling, but Iphigenia is ready to die. She tries to comfort her mother and leaves willingly for the altar.

Scene 6. Ulysses enters to explain that Iphigenia is alive and "the gods content" (V.vi.1720). Achilles had been fighting to protect Iphigenia at the altar, when Calchas suddenly announced that there was another Iphigenia, daughter of Helen (from her liaison with Theseus), hidden under the assumed name Eriphile. She was the victim the gods demanded. Eriphile ran to the altar, grabbed the knife and killed herself. The gods sent thunder and lightning, favorable winds blew, and the unlit pyre burst into flame. Perhaps Diana appeared. Iphigenia is the only one to weep over dead Eriphile. Achilles and Agamemnon are friends again, and all is well.

CHARACTER AND DESTINY

Eriphile is the most interesting character in Racine's *Iphigenia*. Racine had found the story of this "second Iphigenia" in Pausanius. Eriphile makes it possible for Racine's play to have a victim and still preserve Iphigenia, whom Racine found too "virtuous and loveable" to kill ("Preface to *Iphigenia*" 49–50). Eriphile's suicide is both motivated and just, especially when contrasted to Euripides' versions of the sacrifice of Iphigenia (actual or aborted). Not only is Eriphile the daughter of Helen, cause of the Trojan War, but Eriphile is also a hostile, ungrateful, spiteful, obsessive, destructive human being.

Racine was educated at Port Royal by Jansenists, fervent Catholic followers of Cornelius Jansen, who put more emphasis on predestination than on God's grace (Clark 58). Jansen "openly embraced the harsh doctrine that the majority of mankind was condemned to perdition and he taught that the few who were privileged to receive God's grace should immediately renounce the world that their salvation not be impaired" (Maland 178).

While certainly not a Jansenist document on predestination and salvation, Racine's *Iphigenia* seems to present both aspects of Jansenist doctrine: Eriphile is the destined evil victim; she behaves badly because she has a bad character. Iphigenia is among the happy few, a destined virtuous heroine. She behaves well because she has a good character. Each gets what she justly deserves because of her character and actions, as well as because of the will of the gods. There are many references in this play to the "cruel gods," the ancient pagan destinal gods; however, these gods mostly act through the character of their destined victim, Eriphile. Her character is as negative as her fate; child of Helen, she was born to be a victim. She has an obsessive love for Achilles, rooted in the terrible moment of her capture by him. She confides to Doris that she loves Achilles,

> Whose bloodstained hand carried me off in chains,
> Who robbed me of your father and my birth,
> Whose very name should have a hateful ring,
> He is the mortal whom I cherish most [Racine, *Iph.* 2.1.473–6].

Orphaned, of unknown parentage, under a prophecy that she must die to find out who she is, Eriphile is truly a cursed creature of a cursed family. She is the anti–Iphigenia, rejecting all the positive, lawful virtues of healthy love, family love, and love of duty that are so strong in Iphigenia's character. Eriphile "is governed by lawless and unbridled passion" (Koch 170). She is even named after Eris, the goddess of strife, who started the conflict of the Trojan War by tossing the golden apple labeled "for the most beautiful" into the wedding party of Thetis and Peleus. Eriphile's character seems to have absorbed all the curses laid upon the House of Tantalus, leaving the remaining Atreus family free to pursue a better life, although anyone who remembers the old stories might still suspect that bad times were ahead for Agamemnon and his family.

Eriphile, the "other Iphigenia," allows Racine to provide a happier character, and hence a happier fate, for his improved Iphigenia, member of the improved House of Atreus. This Iphigenia is given a noble lover in Achilles, a loving father in Agamemnon, and a way out of her sacrifice by the revelation of Eriphile's true identity as another Iphigenia.

Goethe's Iphigenia in Tauris

This story involves the following characters:

Arkas: Taurian intermediary between Iphigenia and King Thoas
Iphigenia: Simply perfect; naive, innocent, unsullied by experience with the world, despite her near-death experience at Aulis; has a natural intuitive knowledge of right
Orestes: Iphigenia's brother; suffers madness because he murdered his mother
Pylades: Cousin to Orestes and Iphigenia; best friend and traveling companion of Orestes
Thoas: King of the Taurians; has stopped the practice of human sacrifice because of Iphigenia; loves Iphigenia; wants to marry her

ACT I

Iphigenia is the priestess of Diana in Tauris. Iphigenia feels unhappy and useless. Arkas points out that she is responsible for ending the practice of human sacrifice in Tauris, which has improved all their lives. Arkas warns Iphigenia that if she refuses to marry King Thoas, he will resume human sacrifices. Iphigenia finally tells King Thoas her origins in the cursed house of Tantalus (ancestor of Agamemnon), so that he will stop pressuring her to marry him. Iphigenia says that Tantalus' guilt against the gods was a human excess of pride (he had cooked his son Pelops as a dinner dish for the gods), but the gods have been cruel and unjust, cursing his descendents with madness.

Iphigenia recites the history of her family's treacheries and murders. Thoas asks how she could have come from such a family. According to Iphigenia, her father Agamemnon was "the paragon of men" (Goethe, *Iph.* 1.403). She tells the story of her near-sacrifice at Aulis as if Agamemnon had nothing to do with it, only naming Diana, Calchas, and the army. The sacrifice is another example of the gods' unjust anger toward the house of Tantalus.

Thoas still wants to marry her, but she refuses, saying she is dedicated to the goddess and longs to return to Greece. Angered, Thoas decides to re-institute human sacrifices to Diana, which he had neglected while under Iphigenia's influence. Iphigenia objects that people mistakenly attribute their "own cruel will" to the gods (Goethe, *Iph.* 1.525). Thoas replies that he is sending two strangers to her for sacrifice.

ACT II

Orestes is tormented by the family curse (he killed his mother Clytemnestra to punish her for killing his father Agamemnon). Apollo has sent Orestes to Tauris to fetch his "sister" (which Orestes presumes to be a sacred statue of Diana/Artemis, sister of Apollo). Orestes is now a prisoner and feels abandoned by Apollo. He's willing to die as yet another sacrificial victim of the Tantalid family.

However, cheerful, heroic Pylades wants to escape and live. He has faith that the gods will not abandon them. Pylades reminds Orestes how as children they dreamed of doing mighty deeds. But Orestes, passive and depressed, feels that while the gods may bestow excellent heroic deeds on some men, the gods hate him and are seeking to destroy him. Pylades says that the gods do not curse families and each action has its own reward or punishment. Pylades schemes while Orestes despairs.

Iphigenia enters, not revealing her identity. Pylades tells her lies about himself and Orestes. He claims they are brothers and the Fury is pursuing Orestes because he killed their third brother. Pylades also mentions Troy's fall. This is the first Iphigenia has heard of that. She asks for more news about Troy and those who returned home, and he tells her of Agamemnon's death.

ACT III

Orestes tells Iphigenia of Clytemnestra's death. Finally, Orestes rejects Pylades' scheming and tells Iphigenia the truth about himself since he cannot bear to deceive her, a "great soul" (Goethe, *Iph.* 3.1076). Orestes is cursed, guilty, and ready to die.

Iphigenia reveals her identity to Orestes, but he is in a maddened frenzy. She cannot calm him, and he welcomes being sacrificed. Iphigenia prays to Apollo and Diana to release Orestes from the curse, and the curse is lifted; Orestes becomes rational.

ACT IV

Iphigenia says that the gods provide help for those who need it. The gods have provided Pylades to help Orestes and herself. Yet, she is bothered because Pylades has recommended deceit. Arkas arrives and she tells him a false story about how the image of Diana has been polluted by contact with Orestes and now must be bathed in the ocean. Arkas asks her again to marry the King; she again refuses. He accuses her of failing the Taurians, who will be harmed by the King forcing them to reinstitute human sacrifice.

Iphigenia feels remorse for failing the Taurians in order to save her brother. She begins to waver, hating the fact that she has lied to Arkas. Iphigenia argues with Pylades that Thoas has treated her well and deceiving him is ungrateful. Pylades argues that in the real world, people must act and cannot remain pure. Iphigenia's hesitations are threatening all their lives. Pylades says, "It is in vain that you refuse; the iron Hand of Necessity commands…" (Goethe, *Iph.* 4.1680–81).

As she ponders her choice, Iphigenia wonders whether the curse will "endure forever" (Goethe, *Iph.* 4.1694). Necessity would have her steal the statue and lie to the king who befriended her. Such actions would commit her to the terrible traditions of her Tantalid family. Then Iphigenia recalls the song the Parcae (Fates) sang while Tantalus fell. The gods remained on high, feasting, with no pity for the descendents of the Titans. The ancient gods have nothing to offer those who seek justice.

Act V

King Thoas suspects Iphigenia's story about the pollution of Diana's image. Thoas is angry that she has betrayed him. Iphigenia confesses the truth to Thoas, despite the consequences to herself, her brother and her cousin. She relies on Thoas' human decency to treat them with mercy. He wonders that she expects a barbarian to hear "the voice / Of truth and human decency." She replies,

> All men hear it, born
> Beneath whatever sky they may, and through
> Whose bosoms flows the fountainhead of life
> Pure and unhindered (Goethe, *Iph.* 5.1938–39).

Iphigenia then recalls Thoas' promise to return her to Greece if possible. Orestes enters, armed. Iphigenia tells Orestes and Pylades to put down their swords and revere the king, her "second father" (Goethe, *Iph.* 5.2006). Orestes wants to prove his identity by single combat, and Thoas is ready to fight, but Iphigenia stops them and identifies Orestes by a birthmark and a scar. There is still the statue to fight over, but Orestes solves the problem of stealing the statue by realizing that he had made an error interpreting the oracle: Apollo really meant not the statue of Apollo's sister Artemis, but Iphigenia, the living sister of Orestes. Thoas tells them to go, but he is angry. Iphigenia refuses to leave except as friends. Thoas finally agrees, saying, "Farewell!" (Goethe, *Iph.*5.2174).

A Pure Heart Can Destroy Ancient Evils

Goethe represents ancient evil, the power of the past to control the present, in the curse on the Tantalids, the cruel indifference of the ancient gods, the barbaric ritual of human sacrifice, and the iron hand of necessity. These indeed are the dominating factors in ancient Greek representations of the Tantalid family problems.

Goethe's answer to the problem of ancient evil is a pure heart, freely acting. Reason alone is not sufficient to free human beings from the weight of the past. Pylades the rationalist argues for deception as the correct way to escape, but Iphigenia, having a pure heart, rejects deception as an element of the ancient evils enslaving human beings. Only Iphigenia's truth and love can save her brother and cousin, as well as heal King Thoas, so that he will not reinstitute human sacrifice in Tauris.

Discussing Iphigenia's pure heart, Passage remarks that for Goethe the human heart is "the mid-region in which Reason and intuitive Love join in indissoluble union to guarantee the highest type of humanity…" (18). Goethe emphasizes that emotions process thought, and therefore Iphigenia's pure heart is more important than Pylades' rational mind. Goethe's idea of Iphigenia's pure heart seems closer to modern ideas of motivation than Euripides' god in a machine. Indeed, the human heart, freely acting, sounds rather like twentieth-century existentialism, which holds that human beings acting freely create the world they experience. Goethe has replaced the power of the irrational gods with the power of irrational human emotions. And when a heart is pure, as is Iphigenia's, it can intuit and choose good actions, which in turn can improve the behavior of others.

However, while Goethe's concept of the impact of emotion on thinking seems sound today, the "pure" part is less believable, especially after Freud's insights into the unconscious. Racine split Iphigenia into two characters: Iphigenia the Good and Eriphile the Evil; but Goethe claims to have found the cure for evil. All it takes is one pure woman to cure the evils in men's hearts. This stance may be as much Christian as humanistic (Cottrell 163). Unfortunately, pure goodness no longer seems convincing as a cure for the evils that cause human suffering. Further, although it was eagerly embraced in the nineteenth and early twentieth centuries, the notion of one pure woman elevating men from barbarism to higher forms of humanity seems downright silly these days.

Julie Prandi points out that Goethe "helped create the new myth of pure redeeming femininity…" (29). In fairness to Goethe, Prandi explains that much of Iphigenia's idealized character is based on how the men in the play see her, and Iphigenia herself expresses feelings of being trapped and struggles to escape from her condition. Nonetheless, Prandi asserts that "Goethe is at least in part responsible for the over-idealized image of Iphigenie and the myth of a mystical eternal feminine associated with her in the historical reception of the play" (29). Goethe's *Iphigenia* became a primary model of excellent literature in German schools for well over a century. Irmgard Wagner remarks, "School curricula had instituted *Iphigenie* as textbook for idealism, as guide for right behavior…" (31). Up until 1918, German references to this play use "Iphigenie" as a code word for "right attitudes." This play became almost a German bible, which young soldiers carried in their backpacks as they went to World War I. However, "after 1918, the profound disillusionment of defeat trashed the erstwhile ideals like so many false idols, and *Iphigenie* was one of them" (31).

Goethe's *Iphigenia* is packed with ideas, and the style is talky and abstract. Each character declaims his or her feelings and philosophy without much attention to the others. There is little character development and not much action, which is probably why it has not been particularly successful on stage (Wagner 8, 18). However, Goethe's *Iphigenia* is a key expression of Enlightenment humanism as well as of early Romantic ideals of pure feminine nature, human freedom, ideal humanity, the power of truth, and how one good woman could civilize barbaric men. As such, this play is interesting to read as a humanistic, optimistic counter-example to the generally downbeat tradition of Troy stories. Goethe takes the ancient tradition of the destruction of Troy and charts a path that leads to redemption, not destruction.

Free choice is probably the most enduring concept in Goethe's *Iphigenia*. A good heart freely choosing is Goethe's solution to the problem of ancient hereditary evils. Iphigenia is able, despite bad heredity and terrible experience, despite fear of harm to herself and her loved ones, to freely choose to be truthful. She rejects Pylades' deceitful strategies and risks all of their lives to act nobly and truthfully, trusting that her truthfulness will positively influence the king. Her idealism is extreme, basically unbelievable, and yet ... if people cannot choose to move beyond the heavy weight of their past influences and experience, what hope is there for improvement?

14

James Joyce's *Ulysses*
A Mind Trip

Homer and his many literary descendents told stories about the Trojan War objectively, as stories had always been told, narrating events and describing settings and characters. Characters would speak, but mostly to others, so their speech could not be entirely trusted — it always had a purpose: to inform other characters; to tell the audience specific information designed to reveal and explain the character's motivations; to move the story forward; or to provide a clearer understanding of events. The main exception was monologues, such as Lavine's in *Eneas* about love and Achillès' in *Le Roman de Troie* about the madness of his love, but such monologues, like those in Shakespearean plays such as *Hamlet*, were still aimed at the unknown audience and had a direct focus and purpose that functioned to explain the characters, highlight themes, or move forward the events of the story.

Ulysses (1922) by James Joyce offers a radical departure from that ancient tradition of storytelling, because almost all of the adventures of his modernist Ulysses — Leopold Bloom — occur in Bloom's mind during a single day while he wanders the city of Dublin. Joyce puts his readers directly into the mind of Leopold Bloom using a fairly new narrative device called stream of consciousness which captures the perceptions and free associations of a human mind as it encounters and notes the outer and inner worlds, present and past, and attempts to make sense of those experiences. This technique was not developed by Joyce, who credited Édouard Dujardin as his source (Mercer, 209). But Joyce mastered stream of consciousness, which he combined with objective narrative to create a novel that is remarkably readable for the most part despite the sections representing inner waking consciousness as well as the phantasmagorical experiences of dreams and hallucinations. Parts of *Ulysses* offer a focused, purposive narrative which grounds the novel in very specific times, places, and events, but the core of the story occurs inside the wandering mind of Bloom as he goes through one specific day, June 16, 1904. Some of Bloom's thoughts relate obliquely to his role as a modern-day Ulysses, but many do not. In this intimately subjective method of storytelling, readers do not learn of the heroic feats of Ulysses, but of the essential being of Bloom as refracted through his perceptions and memories. The reader also enters two other minds, those of Bloom's adulterous wife Molly (Calypso as well as Penelope) and Stephen Dedalus (Telemachus), the young alienated artist who was the hero of Joyce's previous semi-autobiographical novel *A Portrait of the Artist as a Young Man* (1916).

When I first read *Ulysses* as a Troy Story my questions were: Why Odysseus? Why

Troy? Why Dublin? Why Leopold Bloom, Molly and Stephen? This seemed to me like the oddest mismatch in the long history of Troy stories. Odysseus was a great returning warrior, a master mariner and man of many devices and much suffering, one of the few survivors of the Trojan War. He had offended Poseidon and consequently was forced to voyage around the Mediterranean for ten years trying to get home to his notoriously faithful wife Penelope. During this time his son Telemachus matured into a brave man and warrior and together with help from Athena they killed all the suitors who had been besieging the palace, devouring their stores of food and wine, and pressuring Penelope to declare Odysseus dead and marry one of them.

Without help from Athena, the goddess who loved him, Odysseus would never have reached home, Telemachus almost certainly would have been killed by the suitors, and Penelope would have been forced to marry one of the suitors or return home to her parents, leaving the palace to the usurping suitors. What does this great ancient hero have to do with Leopold Bloom? The time of faith and gods was over. There were no gods or goddesses left to protect Bloom, who had been consecutively Jewish, Catholic, and Protestant and believed in nothing. Bloom, like many modern men and women, was profoundly alone in the world. He did the best he could and like Odysseus he survived. After great loss (his father's suicide, his dead infant son Rudy and his wife's adultery), he achieved the small personal victory of returning home to a semblance of peace and a more or less intact marriage.

Troy had become a powerful metaphor for the end of the Bronze Age, the destruction of a great and ancient civilization. By the time Odysseus achieved his return home, Troy had been destroyed for a decade, many of Odysseus' warrior peers were dead, and one of the few peaceful spots left on the map of the ancient Greek world was Sparta where the proximate cause of the war, Helen, resided comfortably in a no-fault re-marriage with Menelaus. The memory of Troy exists in Joyce's *Ulysses* as a faintly glimpsed metaphor for the destruction of the lives, values and culture of the ancient world, Troy and Greece as well as Ireland. *Ulysses* was composed during the years of World War I and shortly after. The world of Europe was being destroyed as surely as the world of the ancient Bronze Age had been. This war is never mentioned in *Ulysses*, which is set in 1904, but the stresses of a fragile, decaying civilization appear in Bloom's vulnerability, the anger of the Irish nationalists, and the failure of Parnell, as well as in Stephen's rejection of the powers that be, both Church and State.

Dublin is not mapped onto Troy, which was dead, but onto the living Mediterranean, where Odysseus wandered for a decade. Bloom's wanderings during one day in Dublin loosely parallel Odysseus' ten years of wandering the exotic and unknown islands of the Mediterranean. Dublin was the world that Joyce knew intimately, although he spent most of his life in exile from it, and he reproduced Dublin with remarkable naturalistic detail as Stephen and Bloom roam through its streets. Each street and bridge, building and shop, and many of the people mentioned in *Ulysses* were actually there in Dublin in June of 1904 (Kain, 37). Don Gifford with Robert J. Seidman published a very large book, *Ulysses annotated: Notes for James Joyce's Ulysses* (1989), which identifies all of the places and people that Stephen and Bloom encounter during their day and night in Dublin. Very little of this information actually makes the story easier to follow, but it does offer an amazing sense of how grounded in facts *Ulysses* is. While Bloom is wandering the physical streets of Dublin, his mind is wandering much more widely across the Mediterranean, into the Orient, into worlds of curiosity and speculation. He is a born adventurer who never got the opportunity to travel, so he travels in his imagination. Stephen, on the other hand, wanders Dublin as if stuck in a maze seeking an escape. And Molly does not need to wander at all. She is grounded comfortably in her bed. Men come to her.

The Main Characters

Leopold Bloom is an intelligent, likeable, prurient, tolerant and compassionate man. He is curious about all aspects of life and science. Perhaps because he is not very successful as a sales representative for advertisements, he is constantly thinking of schemes for making money. Bloom, like Odysseus, is a man of sorrows. He suffers from his father's suicide, his wife's adultery and the death of his infant son Rudy. These are not imitations of Odysseus but oblique reflections. Odysseus' mother died pining for him, he was captured by Calypso for seven years while his wife Penelope was in danger of being forced to remarry, and his son Telemachus had to grow up without protection from his father. Bloom, like Odysseus, is aging and weary from wandering, has an ever fertile imagination and basic good will, and keeps on going despite difficulties (many in his imagination) until he finally reaches his ultimate goal—home in bed with Molly, as Odysseus's goal was home in bed with Penelope.

Bloom has a complex yet uncertain identity as a Jew, a Christian, an Irishman in anti–Semitic Dublin, a "womanly man" in a macho pub culture, an intellectual with an inadequate formal education, and a cuckold who loves his wife and ultimately tolerates, or perhaps facilitates, her adultery. Bloom and Molly have an intimate but sad marriage. He loves Molly and finds her beautiful and desirable, but he has not been able to satisfy her sexually since their infant son Rudy died ten years earlier. Molly seems fond of Bloom, but craves sexual satisfaction and is determined to get it with another if not with him. Bloom if not impotent is at least impaired in his sexual life. He is fascinated by a distant glimpse of a woman's legs, fantasizes about prostitutes, checks out the Greek statues in the museum to see if they have anuses, and corresponds flirtatiously under the assumed name Henry Flower with a woman Martha whom he has never met. He masturbates to the sight of Gerty's thighs (he stays at a distance and does not know the girl) and kisses Molly's bare rump, but does not seem able to have intercourse with her. Bloom is ambivalent about his gender as well as his sexuality. He is tormented by guilt, goes through an imaginary trial about his sexual behavior, is tempted by masochism, and temporarily succumbs to the angry power of the dominatrix Bella Cohen (Circe) to abuse and humiliate him while she morphs into a man and he morphs into a woman.

Molly is both Calypso and Penelope, a seemingly improbable combination. The reader first encounters Molly in her role as Calypso, luxuriating in bed while Bloom tidies up and brings her breakfast. She has finished reading a pornographic novel and asks Bloom to buy her another one. Bloom is very much her captive, her servant, her obedient husband, who readily agrees to do whatever she asks. Molly is a singer and is preparing to go on a concert tour organized by Blazes Boylan, her newest lover. As Calypso she holds Bloom's heart firmly in thrall when he leaves her after breakfast to wander the city for the day, taking extra care to be away at four when Boylan is due to come, ostensibly to plan for the tour, but in fact to have sex with Molly. She stays firmly at the center of Bloom's life, her bed is the island of Ogygia, and he can only travel around the environs of Dublin and return. This is why he is an adventurer who never went to sea. He is bound by Molly/Calypso. Once he is finally back at home, Bloom wipes away the crumbs in the bed left by Boylan, muses on the naturalness of sex and how one cannot control the sexuality of another person, and goes to sleep with his feet at the head of the bed while Molly sleeps with her feet at the foot of the bed. They have an upside down sort of relationship, and their bed jingles and rattles — it is not solid like the bed of Odysseus and Penelope that was built on a rooted tree. Keri Ames argues that Leopold and Molly indeed have an upside-down relationship: "In Dublin, Molly is able to become the heroine that Penelope could never be in Ithaca. By taking full advantage of this historical shift, Joyce has manufactured a full inversion of sex roles: the wife now cheats while the husband wanders nearby, instead of the wandering husband cheating afar while the faithful wife waits at home" (163).

The last episode of *Ulysses* is an almost entirely unpunctuated monologue by Molly as Penelope. Molly's name reflects the magical herb *móly*, which protects Odysseus from being turned into a swine by Circe. Molly as Penelope protects Bloom from the kind of terrible loneliness that Stephen suffers. Molly's episode opens with "Yes" and it closes with "Yes." Molly is the great female earth-mother spirit that affirms life and ignores conventional morality. As she is falling asleep, Molly rambles in her mind over her girlhood on Gibraltar, her lovers, her dissatisfaction with Bloom as he is now and her pleasure in him years ago, especially the day when they were embracing among the rhododendrons and she manipulated him into proposing to her and said "yes." Molly is true to Bloom in her fashion (she will probably never leave him), but she is not willing to do without sex when he cannot provide it, nor would she have waited twenty years for Bloom to come home. The early hours of the morning are as late as she tolerates. Bloom has reluctantly accepted Molly's sexual nature as natural, unavoidable, and of prurient interest. In one of his fantasies, Bloom acts as Molly's pimp and watches through the keyhole as Boylan and Molly have sex. Molly thinks that Bloom may have deliberately facilitated her affair with Boylan by sending away their daughter Milly to apprentice to a photographer so Molly would have more freedom. This is an unusual marriage, an adulterous one, where both partners seem to be invested in the situation, and both are getting at least some kind of satisfaction from it.

Stephen Dedalus is the third member of this modern Odyssean family. Stephen is not actually related to Bloom, although Bloom is friendly with Stephen's father Simon Dedalus. Stephen is a brilliant, bitter, confused young artist and intellectual who assumes the role of Telemachus, searching for his spiritual father (his "real" father, although alive in Dublin, does not meet his needs). Just as Molly is the spirit of "yes," Stephen is the spirit of "no." In *Ulysses*, Stephen rejects God, the Church, Ireland, his friends and his family. He only says "yes" to his art. Joyce's previous novel, *A Portrait of the Artist as a Young Man,* was centered on Stephen Dedalus, an autobiographical stand-in for Joyce himself. At the end of that book, Stephen rejects the Church and Ireland and goes into exile to create his art. At the start of *Ulysses*, Stephen has recently come back from France because his mother was dying. He refuses her dying wish for him to pray and he is tormented by guilt, anxiety and obsessive thoughts of death and his dead mother.

Richard Ellmann has pointed out that "Stephen is unique in literature in that he is the son of two fathers, Odysseus and Dedalus" (4). Stephen is fascinated by ideas about Shake-speare as a cuckold and how that influenced his creation of *Hamlet* as a story about adultery. It is not entirely clear why this fascinates Stephen except that if his ostensible father Simon Dedalus was a cuckold, perhaps he, Stephen, has another "real" and unknown father, one who is less ordinary and incompetent. Stephen teaches at a local school and shares living space with a vulgar, cynical, high energy medical student Buck Mulligan. Stephen is no longer the developing center of Joyce's novel as he was in *Portrait*. He is a stressed, unhappy young man who drinks too much, spouts exceptionally learned and too-clever theories about Shakespeare as a cuckold, and seems to have lost his sense of direction. If there is a "hero" of *Ulysses*, it is the more mature and grounded Bloom, not Stephen.

While Bloom and Stephen are both wandering through Dublin on June 16, 1904, they cross paths more than once but do not meet until the evening. Bloom feels a bond with Stephen, worries about him because he is drunk, and follows him into the Dublin Nighttown (red light district) to protect him from his rowdy friends and his own poor judgment. Bloom goes after Stephen into Bella Cohen's brothel late in the night, intending to protect him. Stephen is very drunk, nearly broke, hungry and has no place to sleep. When they leave the brothel, Stephen gets into a quarrel with some soldiers over the question of patriotism (he does not want to die for his country) and one of the soldiers knocks him to the ground. Bloom helps the fallen Stephen, persuades the police to leave him in peace, gets him a cup of coffee to clear his head, and then brings him home for a meal in the early morning hours. During their time together, Bloom and Stephen have a long conversation about their opinions, values and interests; they agree on much, but they do not really satisfy one another's needs for a father and son and only temporarily resolve one another's loneliness. Bloom, longing for a son, even considers inviting Stephen to stay with them in the spare room; he could teach Molly Italian pronunciation which would help her singing (and of course Molly wonders about having an affair with Stephen). But the immediate problem is that Stephen refuses to return to his rooms with Mulligan or to his family home. Bloom offers Stephen a bed for the night, but Stephen refuses the offer and leaves before dawn. There is no place in Dublin for him and one expects that he will shortly leave Ireland entirely.

The plan of *Ulysses* is distributed over the scaffolding of the *Odyssey* as well as over the map of Dublin. Joyce used working section headings that were either directly from the *Odyssey* (e.g., the first three episodes were the "Telemachia") or reflected aspects of the *Odyssey* (e.g., "Circe" for a midnight phantasmagoria in a brothel). When Joyce was working on *Ulysses*, each episode heading included a name, a time, an art, a body organ, a color, a symbol, a technique and the corresponding names of the Odyssean characters represented in the episode. Joyce had these headings removed at publication (Kain, 35), but they still are used in some editions and are helpful to readers wandering through the maze of *Ulysses*. Here are the episode headings, settings and times adapted from the more detailed lists in Kain's *Fabulous Voyager* (38) and the Everyman edition of *Ulysses* (1086–7):

I. Telemachia

    Episode 1. Telemachus; Stephen's breakfast 8 A.M.

    Episode 2. Nestor; Stephen teaching 10 A.M.

    Episode 3. Proteus; Stephen on beach 11 A.M.

II. Bloom's Adventures

    Episode 4. Calypso; Bloom's breakfast 8 A.M.

    Episode 5. Lotus Eaters; to baths 10 A.M.

    Episode 6. Hades; to funeral 11 A.M.

    Episode 7. Aeolus; newspaper office noon

    Episode 8. Lestrygonians; lunch 1 P.M.

    Episode 9. Scylla and Charybdis; library 2 P.M.

    Episode 10. Wandering Rocks; people in streets 3 P.M.

    Episode 11. Sirens; Ormond Hotel 4 P.M.

    Episode 12. Cyclops; Saloon 5 P.M.

    Episode 13. Nausicaa; beach 8 P.M.

    Episode 14. Oxen of Sun; hospital 10 P.M.

    Episode 15. Circe; brothel midnight

III. The Homecoming

    Episode 16. Eumaeus; cab-shelter 1 A.M.

    Episode 17. Ithaca; Bloom's kitchen 2 A.M.

    Episode 18. Penelope; Bloom's bedroom 2:45 A.M.

At times the mapping of *Ulysses* onto the *Odyssey* is fairly clear. For instance Episode 6, "Hades," is about Bloom going to the funeral of Paddy Dignam, Episode 17, "Ithaca," is about Bloom bringing Stephen home for a cup of cocoa and a long discussion, and Episode 18, "Penelope," is a long interior monologue by Molly Bloom. Other episodes are far more obscure in their connections to the *Odyssey*, such as Episode 14, "Oxen of the Sun." In the *Odyssey*, Odysseus had been warned by Tiresias that if his men ate any of the Oxen of the Sun, they would all be destroyed and only he would survive to return home to Ithaca. Joyce's version takes place in a lying-in hospital while a woman is going through extended labor and Stephen is getting drunk with a group of rowdy vulgar medical students. The connection seems to be women as "cows" and the insatiable, cynical, drunken men as devouring/impregnating the cows without compassion or limit. Only Bloom expresses pity for the woman (Mrs. Purefoy) in the agony of her extended labor. Episode 7, "Aeolus," is another section that connects rather obscurely to the *Odyssey*, where Aeolus was the king of the winds. He gave a bag of winds to Odysseus and told him to keep them shut if he wanted to get home safely. Members of Odysseus' crew opened the bag, letting out all the contrary winds, which drove them back to Aeolus' island. Aeolus was furious and refused them further help. In *Ulysses* this section takes place in a newspaper office. There are many references to wind and blowing and the place is noisy because of the presses and all the people talking. The connection is thin and feels artificial.

    Following is an overview of the relevant sections of the *Odyssey* and their representation in *Ulysses*:

    Telemachus. Telemachus was the son of Ulysses, raised without his father, threatened by the aggressive suitors, and trying to become master in his own home. Stephen as Telemachus lives in a Martello tower overlooking the sea, one of many built in Ireland for fortification but no longer used for that purpose. His roommate Buck Mulligan is shaving, breakfast is put together, an Englishman, Haines, is staying with them, and old milk woman comes with the milk for breakfast. Stephen is angry at Mulligan for a rude remark he made about Stephen's dead mother, saying she was "beastly dead." Mulligan insists that death is simply "beastly" from a doctor's point of view. They go down to the beach to bathe and Stephen leaves his key with Mulligan, who wants Stephen to meet up with him after he gets paid so they can go for a drunken outing.

Nestor. Nestor was a wise old advisor in the *Iliad.* He told long tedious stories that had useful lessons underlying them. In the *Odyssey* Nestor had returned home safely to Pylos and Telemachus visited him there seeking information about Odysseus. The Nestor in this chapter is Mr. Deasy, the headmaster of the school where Stephen teaches. Mr. Deasy pays Stephen his wages and lectures him tediously on how to plan his life better. Mr. Deasy and Stephen talk of Stephen leaving the post. Mr. Deasy gives Stephen a letter to the press with advice for dealing with a cattle disease. He wants Stephen to take the letter to his friends at the newspaper and arrange to get it published.

Proteus. Proteus was the Old Man of the Sea who was able to constantly change shape. Proteus was not an important character in the *Odyssey.* However, he is representative of the constantly changing nature of the sea, which is important in this episode. Stephen walks along the shore, trying to imagine that the world exists without him by shutting his eyes and then opening them again — the world is still there. He muses on death, still very disturbed by the death of his mother, sees a dead dog being sniffed by a live dog, sees a pair of gypsies and imagines their gypsy sex life outside at night, starts to write a poem, and decides he will not return to his Martello Tower. This section is more difficult to read than the surrounding episodes because much of it records Stephen's stream of consciousness and he has an extremely well-educated, poetic, and complicated mind. Thus there are all sorts of obscure references, strange words, and transforming metaphors. The best way to read this section is aloud as poetry. The sound greatly enhances the sense.

Calypso. Calypso was the goddess who held Odysseus captive on Ogygia for seven years, trying to persuade him to be her husband and become immortal. He resisted, only wanting to return home to Ithaca and Penelope. This episode opens with Bloom preparing breakfast, while Molly is still in bed and she stays there throughout the episode. Bloom goes out to buy himself a kidney for his breakfast, prepares tea and toast for Molly, picks up the mail and takes her breakfast and the mail up to the bedroom. Bloom straightens up the room, Molly reads a letter from Blazes Boylan who will come by at four, and she gives Bloom a pornography book she has finished, asking him to get her another one. She asks him the meaning of a word, "metempsychosis," which Bloom explains means the transmigration of souls. This is a clue to all of *Ulysses*, where the souls of the Homeric characters have been transmigrated into Dublin in 1904 (Ramey, 97), but they have lost their memories as well as their bodies. At the end of the episode Bloom has a bowel movement in the outhouse and then leaves for the day, planning to go to Paddy Dignam's funeral.

Lotus Eaters. This was one of the early places Odysseus visited on his voyage away from Troy. Odysseus sent three of his men on shore to explore, and they ate the lotus fruit. It made them indifferent to all cares and forgetful of any duty or goals. Odysseus forced them onto the ship, tied them down until the drug wore off, and left the port immediately. In this Lotus Land of Dublin, Bloom looks in the window of an oriental tea shop and imagines the warm and lovely places where the tea comes from. He goes to the post office to pick up a letter from Martha, with whom he has been amorously corresponding as "Henry Flower." He admires legs in silk stockings across the road, while chatting about poor Paddy's funeral. He mentions that his wife will be on a concert tour arranged by Boylan. He visits a church and thinks about the women he can see there. Then he goes to the chemists where he gets soap and orders a lotion made up for Molly. Finally, he wanders towards the "mosque of the baths," to indulge himself in yet one more oriental pleasure, a bath before the funeral. Much of this episode is narrated via Bloom's stream of consciousness, but it is much easier to follow Bloom's mind than Stephen's. Bloom is interested in everything and everybody around him, and his constant thinking about what he sees, what he imagines, and what he remembers is couched in ordinary language, not the complex scholastic language of Stephen's mind.

Hades. Hades was where Odysseus went to visit Tiresias to get advice on how to get home safely. Odysseus also talked to the shade of his mother and various others until the press of shades became overwhelming and he and his men fled. In Joyce's version of Hades, Leopold Bloom gets into a carriage with three other men to go to the funeral of a friend, Paddy Dignam, who died suddenly of a heart attack. On the way they pass a funeral carriage carrying a child's coffin and Bloom thinks of his dead son Rudy, who died soon after birth. The men in the carriage meditate on death and Mr. Power says the worst is "the man who takes his own life." Mr. Cunningham, knowing of Bloom's situation, says "Temporary insanity, of course…." This creates painful silence, since Bloom's father had recently committed suicide. Bloom remembers the inquest for his father's death. Then they pass cattle being driven down the street to the slaughterhouse. Bloom wonders what would happen if the carriage hit a bump and Dignam's coffin fell to the ground and his corpse flew out. Then they pass a place where a man was murdered, and finally come to the cemetery. Bloom is concerned about whether Dignam was insured and worries about the fate of his family. Bloom indulges in hostile thoughts about the priest who has a "toad's" belly, while he performs the service, wonders about bad gasses escaping from the corpses, and has various other gruesome thoughts about corpses. He and his friends are very glad to leave the cemetery.

Aeolus. In the *Odyssey*, Aeolus was the king of the island of the winds. When Odysseus first visited him, he was friendly and gave Odysseus a sack of winds which he warned him to keep sealed. This would allow him to have only helpful winds as he sailed home. However, while Odysseus slept, his men opened the bag of winds and a violent storm blew them back to Aeolus' island. The king was furious and refused to help them again. Joyce's "Aeolus" takes place in a newspaper office in short segments, each initiated by a capitalized "headline." Bloom is in the office dealing with an advertisement. It is a noisy place, full of noisy people and noisy machines. Ellmann remarks that "[t]he role of the god Aeolus is filled in part by the printing press, which cranks out on steel tablets its potent ephemera with sublime, godlike indifference" and the editor who controls the presses is irascible like Aeolus (51). Bloom leaves seeking to sell an ad and Stephen comes in with the letter from his headmaster seeking to get it published. The editor asks Stephen to write something for the paper. There is a lot of clever talk, most of it purposeless and noisy. These are the "windbags" or newsmen trying to be witty and impress one another. Eventually Stephen suggests they adjourn to a local pub. After Stephen leaves, Bloom returns with the ad renewal.

Lestrygonians. After Odysseus left the island of Aeolus for the second time, he went to the land of the gigantic Lestrygonians and sent out scouts. King Antiphates promptly ate one of the scouts and other giants came running down to the ships, eagerly spearing and eating the men. Odysseus was able to escape with his ship, but all the other ships were destroyed and the men eaten. Joyce's Episode 8, "Lestrygonians," takes place at the lunch hour, and it is about all kinds of hunger, from the child's hunger for candy to the poor's hunger for food to the hunger of gulls to Bloom's hunger for lunch to the hunger of memory for happier times past. Bloom remembers how happy he and Molly were until ten years ago when their infant Rudy died. He thinks of various things from pregnant women to Parnell, and muses that everyone is being born and everyone is dying, everything is changing, nothing is what it was. Bloom remembers bits from his happy times with Molly before Rudy died. That was evidently the end of their sexual relationship. Hungry, Bloom goes into the Burton restaurant, but he is repelled by the gross slovenliness of the eaters and leaves thinking "Eat or be eaten. Kill! Kill!" (254). Then he goes to Davy Byrne's and has a cheese sandwich while thinking about cannibals. While Bloom eats, Blazes Boylan comes up in the conversation, adding to Bloom's misery. He remembers the joy of sex with Molly. That was then and this is now. Finally Bloom, heart palpitating, goes into the museum to avoid encountering Boylan.

    Scylla and Charybdis. In the *Odyssey*, these were two monsters on either side of a narrow sea passage. Scylla had six heads on long necks and grabbed and ate a sailor with each mouth. Charybdis was a whirlpool that sucked ships down and drowned all the men aboard. Odysseus wisely steered closer to Skylla, not warning his men that six would be eaten, and thus they passed through the strait. Later, after the Oxen of the Sun episode (see below) Odysseus' ship was destroyed by Zeus and he made a raft out of the mast and some debris. He was carried back to Charybdis and clung to a fig tree while Charybdis swallowed and disgorged the raft. Odysseus then regained the raft and continued on his journey. Joyce's Episode 9, "Scylla and Charybdis," takes place in the National Library where Stephen and various intellectual and poetic friends enjoy an esoteric discussion starting with philosophical ideas about what is real. Then Stephen offers an elaborate analysis of Shakespeare's life and its implications in *Hamlet,* asserting that Shakespeare identifies with the Ghost of Hamlet's Father, not with Hamlet. But nonetheless, Hamlet's anger at Gertrude does reflect the real unfaithfulness of Ann Hathaway, which is why Shakespeare left her for many years while he lived in London and she remained in Stratford. Stephen identifies many Shakespearean characters with members of Shakespeare's extended family. Shakespeare created plays out of his life rather as God created life itself. Stephen seems to identify himself with both Shakespeare as a creator of art and Hamlet as a suffering son. Kain remarks that "[t]he parallels between Hamlet and Stephen are striking. Both feel a conscious duty to perform, yet are incapable of action; both sense the injustice and the indifference of an alien world. Both are deprived of normal family relationships" (94). This section is full of obscure references to Shakespeare's plays as well as his life. Its connection to Scylla and Charybdis is thin, and can perhaps best be seen in the danger of unfaithful women, especially Ann Hathaway and Queen Gertrude. Bloom shows up at the library to research an ad, but he does not encounter Stephen.

    Wandering Rocks. Odysseus was warned by Circe in book 12 that his path home could either go by the Wandering Rocks or by Skylla and Charybdis. Odysseus chose to avoid the Wandering Rocks which clashed together to destroy ships. Instead, he sailed close to Skylla, sacrificing six of his men rather than losing them all. Joyce chose to take Stephen on the path between Skylla and Charybdis (the scholastic discourse about Shakespeare and cuckoldry in the library) in Episode 9. Episode 10 of *Ulysses* is the only one based on an event that did not take place in the *Odyssey*, so now Joyce is exploring a path that Odysseus avoided. Joyce's Wandering Rocks are the people of Dublin moving about on their various affairs. The episode is divided into nineteen brief vignettes, each dealing with a different character in the novel, some overlapping, all wandering around Dublin between three and four in the afternoon. The tone is objective, the narrative clear and enjoyable. The reader is given a tour of Dublin and its characters. Among them briefly is Boylan, buying a gift package for Molly, while flirting with the salesgirl. The obvious question is who is avoiding what? Bloom is avoiding his home and Blazes Boylan, because Boylan is due at his house at four. Stephen is trying to avoid being sucked back into his needy family. Stephen and Bloom are not avoiding one another, but they continue passing by without encountering one another. This offers an oblique connection to a non-section of Homer's *Odyssey*.

Sirens. Homer's Sirens were *femmes fatales* who hung out by the shore and sang amazingly, luring sailors to crash on the rocks and die. Odysseus was curious to hear them, so he had the ears of all the sailors stopped up with wax and he was tied to the mast so they could sail past safely while he could hear the dangerously beautiful song. Joyce's Sirens' episode takes place in Ormonds, a Dublin saloon. Bloom eats his dinner there with Simon Dedalus and other friends while an impromptu concert takes place in the connecting music room. The two sirens, "bronze and gold," are two pretty flirtatious barmaids. At one point Blazes Boylan shows up. It is now four and Bloom, painfully avoiding Boylan, unable to oppose him, wonders what he is doing there. Soon Boylan is off for his tryst with Molly in his "jaunting" car that jingles rather like the fastenings of Bloom and Molly's bed. This episode is full of musical language, bits of songs, discussions of music, etc. It is dangerous music because it goes on while Boylan is on his way to Molly's bed. Bloom, like Odysseus, listens to the music but cannot act. Ellmann comments that "[f]iguratively, Bloom is lashed to the mast, incapable of vengeance or — to his later remorse — of returning home" (81).

Cyclops. Homer's Cyclops, Polyphemus, a son of the sea god Poseidon, was a one-eyed, uncouth giant who lived alone in a cave and raised sheep. Odysseus and some crewmembers took a full wine skin and set out to explore the Cyclops' island. They found Polyphemus' cave, and he returned while they were in it. Odysseus greeted him civilly, saying his name was "Nobody." Polyphemus promptly snatched up two crewmembers and ate them. The rest could not escape because he had blocked the entrance of the cave with a boulder. Odysseus got him drunk and then put out his single eye with a sharpened stake. When Polyphemus called out from the cave for help, the other Cyclopses asked who was harming him and he said "Nobody," so they went away. In the morning Odysseus and his crewmembers escaped clinging to the stomachs of sheep which Polyphemus let out of the cave to graze. Once they had escaped the island, Odysseus yelled his true name to the Cyclops who hurled boulders after them. Polyphemus then complained to his father Poseidon, who created massive storms to harm Odysseus. The most important qualities of Homer's Cyclops were his incivility and barbarism in a culture where the proper welcoming of guests was a paramount virtue. Joyce's Cyclops is named "Citizen," he is a big brute of a man who hangs out in Barney Kiernan's Pub with his old dog Garryowen instead of sheep. Citizen's dominant qualities are barbarism, violent Irish nationalism, and virulent anti–Semitism. This episode is narrated by an anonymous "I" who has been identified as Thersites (Ellmann 86), the bitter-tongued man from the *Iliad*. Bloom comes in looking for Martin

Cunningham, whom he wants to see about Paddy Dignam's insurance to help his widow. Citizen is immediately angry at Bloom as a Jew. Bloom's response to Citizen's anti–Semitism is a speech about life and love as the opposite of hatred and he declares that many great men including Christ were Jewish. Instead of being "Nobody," Bloom affirms his Jewish identity. He escapes without a fight; Citizen throws a biscuit tin after him but misses. The episode is complex to read because of the use of elaborate news reporting language of the day, pastiche and parody. There are riffs on Irish nationalism and sports as well as the art of hanging. Although there are plentiful references to eyes and eyes nearly poked out, etc., there is neither physical violence nor cannibalism. Bloom, like Odysseus, escapes. Citizen, like Polyphemus remains in the Pub, blinded by his furious ignorance, mindless nationalism, and rabid anti–Semitism.

Nausicaa. In the *Odyssey*, Nausicaa was a lovely young woman who found Odysseus naked and half dead cast up on the shore of her home island of Scheria. She offered him clothes and good advice about how to approach her parents, the king and queen of Scheria. Nausicaa had marriage on her mind, but Odysseus only had getting home to Ithaca on his mind. Joyce's Nausicaa is Gerty, a pretty, longing young woman with a game leg. At first all Joyce exhibits of Gerty is her romantic longing, in the language of ladies romance magazines, and she is fascinated by Bloom (standing at a distance) in the manner of those romance magazines. Bloom sees her much more sexually and she becomes entranced by his intense interest in her (still from a distance) and as he becomes more sexually aroused, so does she. She realizes he is masturbating while looking at her, sees no harm in it, and leans back so he can see up her legs. At the same time, Molly and Boylan are having sex in Bloom's house. Gerty is kind and generous to Bloom's need but also meeting her own need for sexual excitement. Bloom has an orgasm as a fireworks rocket goes off nearby. The episode ends with a comment about Odysseus coming ashore on a plank after a shipwreck. After his orgasm, Bloom is limp and exhausted, and he sleeps briefly, as did Odysseus after landing on Scheria.

Oxen of the Sun. This was a critical moment in Odysseus' journey home. In Hades, Tiresias had warned Odysseus that if he left the Oxen of the Sun untouched he and his crew would return home safely to Ithaca, but if the Oxen of the Sun were eaten, the crew would be destroyed and only Odysseus would eventually return home to face many troubles. Stranded, the hungry crew ignored Odysseus' warning, they killed and ate some of the Oxen of the Sun, and consequently they were destroyed at sea. Only Odysseus survived to eventually return to Ithaca. Joyce's "Oxen of the Sun" episode takes place in a hospital, where an acquaintance of Bloom, Mrs. Purefoy, is in her third day of agonizing labor. At the hospital Bloom encounters Stephen and a group of carousing medical students, who are gross and uncontrollable like Odysseus' crew with the Oxen of the Sun. Throughout the episode there are plentiful references to various bulls ranging from Irish bulls to the Minotaur as well as many references to insemination, womb, birth, and death. The baby is born while the students carouse. Bloom, aware of the connections between sex, birth and death, thinks of Rudy and how he misses having a son. The students, increasingly drunk, head off at the end for more carousing in Nighttown, Dublin's red light district. The language in this episode is elaborate and artificial, creating a kind of playful history of the evolution of the English language. The episode starts with English imitating the phrasing of Latin, then Medieval Latin, then Anglo-Saxon, Middle English, etc., up into the present English language of 1904 (Gifford, 408, note 1 and intermittently throughout the section on "Oxen of the Sun," 408–449).

Circe. In the *Odyssey*, Odysseus sent members of his crew to explore the island of Circe, a beautiful witch/goddess, who transformed Odysseus' scouting party into pigs. The god Hermes gave Odysseus a magical flower, *mōly*, which protected him from being turned into a pig and then Odysseus was able to pressure Circe to transform his crew back from pigs into human beings. Once they were all human again, they enjoyed a year-long party at Circe's palace before resuming their voyage. Circe advised Odysseus that he had to go to Hades to see Tiresias and get instructions for the rest of his journey home. She told Odysseus how to get to Hades and explained the rituals necessary for talking to the dead. Joyce's Episode 15, "Circe," is a phantasmagoric trip to a hellish brothel. Bloom follows Stephen, who is very drunk, to try and protect him, but Bloom too is drunk and hallucinating. Bloom catches up with Stephen in Mrs. Cohen's brothel, the setting of Bloom's main hallucinations which deal confusedly with issues of identity — being a Jew, sexual ambivalence, voyeurism, and masochism. Mrs. Bella Cohen morphs into a man Bello and Bloom morphs into a woman. Bello torments Bloom sadistically. Bloom rather enjoys being punished. In one part he is a woman giving birth. But he snaps out of Bello/Bella's control when he starts to help Stephen. Stephen's hallucinations deal mostly with guilt and terror. His dead mother appears ghastly trying to get him to accept the Church. He utterly refuses both church and country: he declares "non serviam" (785), smashes the chandelier, and staggers out of the brothel. Bloom pays for the chandelier, follows after him and when Stephen gets into a brawl with a soldier, Bloom protects him and waits until he wakes up. This section although very long and intricate, is amusing and surprisingly readable. It is set up like a play with stage directions and has been produced successfully as a play (*Ulysses in Nighttown*, 1958).

Eumaeus: Eumaeus was the faithful old swineherd who offered Odysseus warm and generous hospitality. Eumaeus, poor though he was, was a model host. After offering him roast pork and wine, Eumaeus told Odysseus (whom Athena had made unrecognizable as a withered old man) about his wonderful master Odysseus and how the greedy suitors were devouring all of his supplies. Odysseus, in turn, told Eumaeus elaborate false tales about his adventures as a sailor, pirate, and warrior at Troy. In Joyce's version, Bloom helps Stephen, drunk and battered, to get to a cabman's shelter and gives him coffee. The old sailor Murphy shows up. He is the Odysseus Pseudoangelus or false messenger (Ellmann 124). Murphy tells all sorts of presumably false stories about his voyages, paralleling the way Odysseus told Eumaeus false stories about himself. Bloom and Stephen leave for Bloom's house; they are talking about all sorts of things, but Stephen does not seem very alert or responsive.

Ithaka: Ithaka was the long-sought home of Odysseus. He had been away for twenty years, his palace was filled with hostile greedy suitors devouring his stores, proposing to his wife, and plotting to kill his son Telemachus. Once landed, Odysseus was disguised by Athena, hid and plotted how best to kill the suitors, which he did with some help from his son and Athena. He finally purged the palace of all the blood and went to bed with Penelope, while Athena made peace among the families of the slain suitors. Joyce's Ithaka is Bloom's home on Eccles Street, sullied, imperfect, but greatly desired. Bloom has spent the entire day staying away from home, knowing that Boylan would be going there for an assignation with Molly. Now, well past midnight, Bloom and Stephen arrive at Bloom's house. He does not have his key so he has to sneak in and then let Stephen in. This is a strangely "objective" chapter written in catechism format with simple questions and extremely wordy and big-wordy answers. Bloom invites Stephen to sleep over, but Stephen leaves. They go into garden and pee while looking at the light in Molly's window. Stephen goes on his way and Bloom muses on various scientific and economic schemes. Then he remembers his father Rudolph Virag, who killed himself. Finally, Bloom goes up to bed, aware of the adultery, but accepting of it as a natural and unavoidable element of his marriage. He has not had complete sex with Molly in over ten years (since Rudy was born). At any rate, Bloom settles into bed, clearing away the crumbs left by Boylan, lies head to foot with Molly, gets mildly excited, kisses her rump, tells her a bit about his day, and goes peacefully to sleep, thinking of Sinbad the Sailor. Readers are informed of Bloom that "He rests. He has travelled" (1005).

Penelope: Homer's Penelope was the ancient world's model of a perfect wife, one who was loyal and faithful and protected the home and family while the men were out pirating or away at war. Odysseus left for Troy when Penelope was a young woman and Telemachus just an infant. Over the ensuing twenty years Penelope managed to resist the constant pressure of the numerous embedded suitors who wanted her to declare Odysseus dead and marry one of them so he could become king of Ithaka. Penelope was able to protect and raise her young son in this difficult environment, although she could not force the suitors to leave and the laws of hospitality forced her to deplete the palace stores to feed them. She was clever and deceptive, necessary traits in the Odyssean world, and used devices such as weaving a shroud for her father-in-law Laertes, stating that she would only marry after the shroud was completed. Then, each night she would secretly unravel the work she had done during the day. Joyce's "Penelope," is an amazing monologue by Molly. There are only eight extensive unpunctuated "sentences" in the entire section (Gifford, 610), yet it is wonderfully readable. Molly's mind wanders through her experiences and desires as she lies in bed, head to foot, next to Leopold Bloom. She thinks about her affair with Boylan and how they are going away on the concert tour together; she wonders whether Bloom actually sent Milly away to facilitate the affair; she considers that she has not had regular satisfying sex with Bloom in over ten years (since Rudy died); she imagines that she would like having Stephen live in the house and having an affair with him; she remembers her girlhood on Gibraltar and her first lover. Molly suspects that Bloom has been to a prostitute; she is curious not angry about it, and mostly concerned that he not waste money or get diseased. Molly thinks about the low quality of Bloom's friends and how he has failed at many jobs and ventures. And yet … she admires his kindness and intelligence and decency and at the end after all her rambling about other lovers, she remembers the moment on Howth when Bloom proposed to her and she said yes. In some strange way she loves the man.

In conclusion, *Ulysses* is the sad and funny story of a fond and tolerant marriage with serious sexual problems and ongoing adultery. It is also in its oblique and complex fashion a modern Troy story. Bloom is both the Judeo-Christian urban Everyman and the Greek adventurer Odysseus/Nobody. His tour of Dublin avoiding home and adultery is a modern miniature reflection of Odysseus' ten years traveling around the Mediterranean seeking home. Odysseus slaughtered the suitors and purified his palace; Bloom can only try to avoid and ignore Boylan while painfully conscious of him throughout the day. Penelope remained the model of a faithful wife, which Molly certainly did not, but each woman ultimately offered home and bed and a semblance of peace to her wandering spouse. Athena was able to repair Odysseus when he was weary and damaged, but Bloom remains damaged as a sexual being. Just as he has the mind of an adventurer and never goes anywhere other than around Dublin, he has the soul of a romantic but fails at having sex with a woman. Bloom, our modern Ulysses, fails at work, fails at love, fails at parenting, and yet … is a curious and compassionate person and readers too, along with Molly, become very fond of him.

15

The Firebrand and
The Gate to Women's Country
Women Revise the Trojan Past

The maturing women's movement of the 1980s was full of hope for the future of women and full of anger at the violent, male-dominated past — male wars, male domination of women, male gods, male anything. It was a time of righteous female anger as women scrambled to achieve the kind of power and status that had previously belonged only to men. Women, new to power, believed that if they had power they would make better, more humane use of it than men did. Women said to one another, "If only women ruled, there would be no more war."

The women's movement had been spreading out in various directions since the 1970s. While some women sought status and power through education and jobs, other women (and sometimes the same women) sought spiritual equality by reviving worship of the ancient Great Goddess, a feminist replacement for the Judeo-Christian God the Father (Eller 58). Revival of Amazon lore was also important to some members of the women's movement. Amazons, whether actual or mythical, offered role models of women who had lived without men, fought like men, and gloried in their independence.

Interest in the Great Goddess was rooted in nineteenth-century anthropological studies (Eller 152–3).[1] For J. J. Bachofen, an important nineteenth-century pioneer in studies of the ancient Goddess, the story was one of historical progress from the very ancient, primitive and emotional Mother Goddess religion to the more civilized, rational Father God religion. He hypothesized that the Mother Goddess was worshipped in societies organized by "mother right," the principle of women inheriting and controlling power and property through the maternal line. He also asserted that these female-dominated societies were more "primitive" than the supplanting patriarchal, patrilineal society of the Greeks. For Bachofen, history was a steady march forward to the high civilization of the European nineteenth century (69–71). However, late twentieth-century feminists such as Merlin Stone turned Bachofen's ideas upside down. They claimed that the matriarchal, goddess-worshipping past had been the good old days, ruthlessly destroyed by male gods and male dominance. According to this feminist re-vision of history, ancient civilizations had been matrilineal, matriarchal, peaceful, and goddess worshipping — before the invasion of the warlike, male-dominant, Zeus-worshipping Aryan Greeks (Stone 61; Gadon xii–xiii, 24, 40).

This re-visioning went far beyond mere historical analysis. Women who felt oppressed

184

by the male patriarchy wanted a female deity to express their religious impulses. Some members of the women's movement actually revived mother goddess spirituality to replace the dominion of male sky gods, from Zeus and Yahweh to modern "God the Father" Christianity. Cynthia Eller documents this process in her fascinating sociological study of the women's spirituality movement, *Living in the Lap of the Goddess.*

> By the mid–1970s … feminists were able to invent their religion…. The publication of Merlin Stone's *When God was a Woman* in 1976, a study of representations of prehistoric goddesses woven together with a story of their overthrow in historical times … inspired more women to search out the supposed surviving remnants of ancient goddess worship in neopaganism. Feminist inquiry went beyond talking about witches and goddesses as symbols of female power, and started to … worship them [58].

Both Marion Bradley's *The Firebrand* and Sheri Tepper's *The Gate to Women's Country* offer well-developed examples of this feminist revision and revival of ancient goddess worship, linked in time and place with the Trojan War. Since the Trojan War represented a spectacularly famous collapse of the "old" goddess-worshipping civilization, it became an ideal venue for feminist speculations about the conquest of the mother-goddess religion by the religion of Zeus. Merlin Stone, citing Robert Graves, blames the weakening of the matrilineal tradition on the invading Achaeans of the thirteenth century BCE, and then on the Dorians:

> With these northern people came the worship of the Indo-European Dyaus Pitar, literally God Father, eventually known in Greece as Zeus…. This transitional period of the change from the worship of the Goddess to the male deity, [was] the change most intensively brought about by the Dorian invasions… [51].

Bradley sets *The Firebrand* in Troy and Colchis in the years leading up to the destruction of Troy by the Greeks. This Troy is a locus of power shifting from mother right to father right, from the Great Goddess (here called Earth Goddess) to Apollo and then Zeus. Tepper's *The Gate to Women's Country* is set in the post-nuclear-war future, but she includes a play within the novel, "Iphigenia at Ilium," that offers a powerfully disturbing look at the Trojan War's destructive impact on women and children. In the play, set in Hades shortly after the fall of Troy, dead Achilles tries to control dead Iphigenia and dead Polyxena, but he cannot, because a man cannot control or oppress a dead woman. In this version of "Iphigenia," the only escape from male dominance and male violence is death. This terrible message, the lesson of the Trojan War and three thousand years of male-dominated history, is used to justify the women's radical restructuring of post-nuclear-war society described in the novel proper.

The Story of The Firebrand: Mother Right and Earth Mother *versus* Father Right and Zeus

The main characters of *The Firebrand* are as follows:

Agamemnon: King of Mycenae; husband of Klytemnestra; killed by her; leader of the Greek armies against Troy

Hecuba: Queen of Troy; wife of King Priam; born and raised an Amazon; mother of Kassandra

Imandra: Queen of Colchis; one of the last upholders of mother right

Kassandra: (Cassandra); Trojan Princess; daughter of Hecuba and Priam; priestess of Apollo; loves Aeneas; pursued by Khryse; survives the fall of Troy; becomes Agamemnon's concubine; eventually goes off with Zakynthia/Zakynthos to start a new life in the west

Khryse: (Chryses); a priest of Apollo; pursues Kassandra

Klytemnestra: (Clytemnestra); Queen of Mycenae; kills Agamemnon when he returns home from Troy

Penthesilea: Amazon leader; Kassandra's aunt

Priam: King of Troy; father of Kassandra

Zakynthia/Zakynthos: A man dressed as a woman; acts as nurse to Kassandra's infant; later reveals himself as a man in love with Kassandra

The Firebrand tells the story of Troy and its fall, from Kassandra's perspective. In Greek myth, Cassandra had been promised to Apollo. When she refused him, he cursed her with the gift of knowing the future but never being believed. She is a powerful, pathetic character in the *Agamemnon* by Aeschylus. After the fall of Troy, Agamemnon had claimed Cassandra as his war-prize concubine and taken her home to Mycenae. When they arrived at the palace, Cassandra had a wild fit of prophecy, seeing and warning of her own and Agamemnon's deaths. True to Apollo's curse, Agamemnon did not believe Cassandra's warning, and his wrathful wife Clytemnestra and her lover Aegisthus murdered them both.

In *The Firebrand*, Kassandra has a much better chance at life. She is a princess of Troy, daughter of a lapsed Amazon (Queen Hecuba), and niece of the Amazon Penthesileia (Hecuba's sister). The story starts with Kassandra's childhood in Troy. She is raised to be a proper princess, marry a noble man and live like a lady, although she is not comfortable with the constraints of that life. As a young woman, Kassandra has a vision of Apollo claiming her for his own. Thereafter, Kassandra has semi-epileptic prophetic fits during which she sees and warns of the fall of Troy. This unseemly behavior greatly annoys her parents, so Kassandra is sent away for an extended visit with her Amazon aunt Penthesileia. Kassandra joins Penthesileia's small band of Amazons as they travel slowly, with substantial hardship, to the ancient city of Colchis, where Kassandra learns about the ancient ways from Queen Imandra.

Queen Imandra rules Colchis by mother right, taking attractive young male consorts when it suits her fancy, and she has some interesting theories about why women are losing control to men. Imandra explains that Helen's "crime" was that she left Sparta, which allowed Menelaus to seize control. Helen had ruled Sparta by mother right. By running off with Paris, Helen abdicated her power to a man. Imandra also theorizes that Agamemnon deliberately invoked false oracles to justify the sacrifice of Iphigenia because he wanted to destroy Klytemnestra's line of maternal descent to her daughter. Kassandra is fascinated by this interpretation of women's history and asks Imandra, "So, then, it is all a matter of whether the land shall be ordered by Kings or Queens?" She replies,

> What else? Why should men rule the hearth or the city, where woman has commanded since first Earth Mother brought forth life? The old way was best, wherein the King was led out every year to die for his people and there was no question of any man setting up his son to follow him. For thousands of years, until these Akhaian [Greek] savages came to try to change our ways, that was the rule of life... [*FB* 331].

Queen Imandra speculates on what might be causing this change, and she concludes it has been the fault of women.

> And then, who knows? Perhaps there was war and a King was too skilled a leader to be made to die; or some foolish woman like myself did not wish to lose her young lover.... Then these horse-folk came, and the first Kings, and set up their arrogant Gods — even the Sun Lord, who claimed to have slain Serpent Mother.... The world is changing, I tell you — but it is the fault of the women who did not keep their men in place [*FB* 331].

Bradley examines the Trojan War as a time of change; her Kassandra is caught between the old and new cultures. Kassandra's mother Hecuba had been a backsliding Amazon girl who chose to marry Priam, King of Troy. Since Hecuba prefers the restricted, luxurious life of a queen to the free, impoverished life of an Amazon, she tries to raise Kassandra to be a good Trojan woman. However, the controls and decorum of palace life at Troy irk Kassandra, who harks back in character to her brave Amazon aunt Penthesileia.

Kassandra lives in a Troy that is still linked to the ancient ways even though ruled by a King and worshipping the male sky god Apollo. There is still respect in Troy for Earth Mother. Apollo is Sun Lord (life giving), not Thunderer (dominant and warlike). Worship of Apollo is more Oriental than Greek. Apollo's priesthood includes priestesses, and his temple includes sacred snakes, even though he "claimed" (*FB* 331) to have slain Serpent Mother. However, Apollo is weaker than Zeus, so he is unable to protect Troy from the fury of Poseidon, who destroys Troy by earthquake under direct orders from Zeus Thunderer (*FB* 540).

Colchis represents the failing mother-right–dominated world of the past. Queen Imandra rules, but she is fat, aging, and uncertain of her successor. Colchis is walled and rich but surrounded by impoverished lands and starving Amazons and Kentaurs (the men on horseback that are the non-partners of the Amazon women on horseback). This ancient way of life is dying out. Its last major stronghold had been the Minoan civilization on Crete, which had already fallen before the time of the Trojan War (*FB* 322). Aside from Colchis, Bradley mentions two other centers of mother right: Sparta, which Helen failed to protect from Menelaus, and Mycenae, where Helen's sister Klytemnestra is still trying to preserve the old ways of mother right and the Goddess after Aegisthus killed Agamemnon (*FB* 599).

At Colchis, Kassandra is initiated into the rites of Serpent Mother. During the initiation ceremony, Kassandra has a vision/experience of the real presence of Serpent Mother and becomes her priestess. Kassandra studies with the priestesses of Serpent Mother, who teach her the ancient lore of raising and handling the sacred snakes. Kassandra actually hatches and raises a snake using her own body warmth, and she takes her snake back to the Temple of Apollo in Troy, where the tradition and understanding of sacred snakes has been dying out.

Thereafter, Kassandra is torn between allegiances. She serves two deities: Troy's own Apollo Sun Lord and Earth Mother of the Amazons. She loves a man she cannot marry (Aeneas), while she is obsessively pursued by, and firmly rejects, Khryse, a slimy priest of Apollo. Unfortunately, Khryse is at times a true manifestation of Apollo. Thus, Kassandra reenacts her rejection of Apollo many times over by repeatedly refusing Khryse's advances. She is also caught up in three different modes of civilization: the Amazon society of free women; the Trojan city ruled by a King, but not unfriendly to women; and the Greek world where, in Kassandra's opinion, a "wife to any Akhaian was no less a slave than any slave in

Troy"(*FB* 576). She is as marginal as any "liberated" woman of the late twentieth century, caught between the conflicting rules and patterns of two worlds, before and after the women's movement of the 1970s.

After Troy falls, Agamemnon seizes Kassandra as his war-prize concubine. She is pregnant, either by her lover Aeneas or by Agamemnon, who brings her home to Mycenae. After Aegisthus kills Agamemnon, he hands the bloody ax to Klytemnestra, who turns on Kassandra, accusing her of thinking she might be Queen of Mycenae. There is a tense moment, but Kassandra quickly says that she wishes she might have held the ax that killed Agamemnon. Kassandra then speaks of the murder of Agamemnon in the context of mother right: "In the name of the Goddess, you have avenged wrongs done to Her. When a woman is wronged, She is wronged too" (*FB* 599). Kassandra's justification of the murder mollifies Klytemnestra, who replies, "You are a priestess, and I knew you would understand these things…. I bear you no grudge…. We have the old ways returned here. Helen has not the spirit to do so in Sparta, but I do"(*FB* 599). Klytemnestra invites Kassandra to stay, but Kassandra finds her terrifying.

> Through Klytemnestra's features she still saw the hunger for destruction; this woman had avenged the dishonor offered the Goddess, but Kassandra still feared her. The Goddess took many forms, but in this form Kassandra did not love Her….
> Or did she but see in Klytemnestra the ancient power of the Goddess as she had been before male Gods and Kings invaded this land? She could not serve this Goddess [*FB* 599].

Kassandra is greatly relieved when the divine Voice, familiar to her from childhood, calls her to return to Colchis. Klytemnestra, too, seems relieved that Kassandra wants to go and allows her to depart in peace.

The ending is a brief and rather lame attempt on Bradley's part to reconcile the rights of women with their right to love men. As Kassandra, carrying her infant, is about to depart for Colchis, a woman named Zakynthia approaches her and begs to come along as a nurse for the baby. For two years Zakynthia accompanies Kassandra on the long, difficult journey to Colchis. Once there, it turns out that Zakynthia is really Zakynthos, a man who wore women's clothing and lived as a woman to learn of their oppression. He now wants to marry an Amazon and take off to the West to found a country where the old ways are respected and Earth Mother is the supreme deity. Bradley's ending fairly represents many women's longing for a better, more gender-equal civilization. Unfortunately, the ending is tagged on like an afterthought to the ancient tradition of Trojan refugees fleeing west to found new countries. However, truth to tell, no better solution to the ancient problems of men and women, goddesses and gods, dominance and servitude, has shown up since then, so … why ever not?

The Story of The Gate to Women's Country*:*
Male Violence versus *Female Deception*

The Gate to Women's Country involves the following characters:

Barten: Warrior; deceives Myra
Chernon: Warrior; lures Stavia into a dangerous adventure; betrays her

Margot: Council Woman; mother of Stavia and Myra

Michael: Leader of the garrison

Myra: Daughter of Margot; foolish, rebellious; loves Barten

Stavia: Daughter of Margot; sober, well-intentioned; becomes a doctor; goes with Chernon on an adventure

"Iphigenia at Ilium" involves the following characters:

Achilles: Ghost of Achilles, still trying to control dead women

Andromache: Widow of Hector

Astyanax: Ghost of Astyanax, infant son of Andromache and Hector

Cassandra: Daughter of Priam and Hecuba

Hecuba: Widow of Priam; mother of Hector

Iphigenia: Ghost of Iphigenia, daughter of Agamemnon; sacrificed at Aulis

Polyxena: Ghost of Polyxena, daughter of Priam and Hecuba; sacrificed on Achilles' tomb

The Gate to Women's Country is set in a post-nuclear-holocaust world, where the population is greatly diminished and food supplies are barely adequate because much of the land is contaminated. Women, children, and some male "servitors" live inside a few widely spaced, gated towns, which are "Women's Country." Male "defenders" live in garrison camps outside the gated towns, one garrison per town. There are festivals once a year that feature lots of sexual freedom. Medically trained members of the Women's Council supervise the women's hygiene and health during their period of sexual activity and pregnancy. The mothers keep the girl children, but when the boys turn five, each is ceremoniously returned to his warrior father to be raised.

At fifteen, each boy must make a decision: either he can return through the Gate to Women's Country and be despised by his male garrison, or he can renounce his mother and become a full-fledged warrior. Very few young men return to Women's Country. Those who do return must go through the Gate to Women's Country, "a simple sheet of polished wood, with a bronze plaque upon it showing the ghost of Iphigenia holding a child before the walls of Troy" (*WC* 5).

If the young man does choose to return to Women's Country, he becomes a servitor, studies various useful arts and crafts, and works for the women but has no apparent status beyond that of a servant. Readers discover only near the end of the novel that the entire setup is a deception. In fact, servitors are the fathers of the women's children; birth-control implants prevent pregnancy during the warriors' sexual visits, and the women are later impregnated artificially, under the guise of hygiene. The idea is to breed violence out of the population by allowing only the nonviolent, nonaggressive males to contribute to the gene pool. Only a small group of ruling women with medical training (the Women's Council) and at least some of the servitors know the true situation.

Iphigenia is the symbol of the suffering and destruction of women and children because of male dominance and male warfare. A play within the novel, "Iphigenia at Ilium," links the painful self-discipline of the Women's Council to the ancient suffering of women and children at the fall of Troy. All the young women study and rehearse "Iphigenia at Ilium" as part of their education, but it is the women of the Council who perform it each year. Margot, a Council Woman, remarks when giving up her son to the warriors:

> We accept the hurt because the alternative would be worse. We have many reminders to keep us aware of that. The Council ceremonies. The [Iphigenia] play before summer carnival. The [radioactive] desolations are there to remind us of pain, and the well [of Surcease] is there to remind us that the pain will pass [*WC* 12].

"Iphigenia at Ilium" presents the story of women and children who have been destroyed by the Trojan War. It draws on Euripides' *Iphigenia at Aulis* as well as two of his dramas about the terrible aftermath of the Trojan War, *The Trojan Women* and *Hecuba*. However, while Euripides wrote about the living victims of war, this Iphigenia play is about the dead. There are four ghosts: Iphigenia, sacrificed by her father Agamemnon to revive the winds so his army could sail to Troy; Polyxena, sacrificed at the tomb of Achilles, who had loved her; the infant Astyanax, murdered by Odysseus; and Achilles, killed by Paris. Along with this tragic material are elements of farce, recalling Aristophanes' *Lysistrata*, such as Achilles' grotesquely overbearing behavior and the artificial large erect penis that is part of his costume. The scene is set outside the destroyed town of Troy. Astyanax, infant child of Hector and Andromache, has just been killed, as in *The Trojan Women*. The ghost of Iphigenia is carrying Astyanax's ghost when they encounter his still-living mother.

> *Andromache.* Do warriors have no pity that they do these things? What stomachs them? Are men made up of iron? What do they use for hearts? Do they not see we are the same as they, our children like their children, and our flesh like that of the women whom they left behind?
> *Iphigenia.* What difference would it make? They do the same to their own.
> *Andromache.* Who calls? Is that my child?
> *Iphigenia.* Your child? Or some other's child? Two children dead. One virgin girl, one suckling boy. See, here we are, wandering together... [*WC* 34].

These dead characters, modeled on the ancient Greek shades in Hades, are insubstantial and extraordinarily poignant — there are no possible resolutions or new beginnings in Hades.

One of the ways that the women resist the illusions of war is by returning to the ancient Great Mother religion. The Great Mother eschews all romantic ideals, such as those that lead to war.

> There wasn't any reason to make promises or seek changes because the Great Mother didn't bargain. The deity didn't change her mind for women's convenience. Her way was immutable. As the temple servers said, "No sentimentality, no romance, no false hopes, no self-petting lies, merely that which is!" [*WC* 9].

The men, however, cherish ancient romantic idols, including statues of Telemachus, "the ancient one, the ideal son, who defended the honor of his father..."(*WC* 16) and Odysseus, his brilliant but untruthful father. Tepper's point is that the women have gone back to the elemental reality of the Great Goddess, while the men are still romanticizing violence as heroism. A huge statue of a penis stands in the men's parade ground as a "victory monument" (*WC* 59). Tepper tends to overdo the links between male sexuality and male violence; however, her many interesting thoughts about the roots of war and gender issues, as well as a good story, encourage the reader to continue.

The problem in the austere utopia of Women's Country is that women, especially young women, fall in love with men, thus becoming vulnerable to the men they love; many of these men are awful. Girls are taught to recite a lesson on this topic: "Infatuation makes otherwise reasonable women behave in unreasonable and illogical ways. It is a result of biological forces incident to racial survival" (*WC* 41). Tepper's point is that women do have these feelings and must tolerate them in others, while trying to restrict the damage such infatuations can bring about.

Tepper's analysis of the vulnerability of women in love recalls Bradley's analysis of the cause of the fall of the matriarchy and the Earth Mother, as explained by Queen Imandra: women love men; when they love men, they may behave weakly; and this weakness may have undermined the dominion of mother right and Earth Mother (*FB* 331). In Tepper's case, this weakness threatens to undermine the woman-controlled government of Women's Country. Both Tepper and Bradley assert that women are ultimately responsible for their own destinies. The responsibility for the destruction of war and the loss of women's' rights has been shifted from men coveting and oppressing women to women coveting men who abuse their love and trust.

The vulnerability of young women to the men they love is exploited by Michael, the leader of the garrison. He enlists young warriors to court girls from the ruling Council families because he is convinced that the women have a secret weapon, which he needs to know about before he can take over the town by force. Although the women are the warriors' mothers, lovers and daughters, Michael scorns such connections: "'Warriors don't have daughters. They may beget an occasional girl, my friend, but we don't have daughters. You ought to know that! No, you've got to use girls for what they're good for. Forget daughters'" (*WC* 69).

Councilwoman Margot has two daughters affected by this deceit. Giddy Myra becomes infatuated with Barten, and her behavior under his influence becomes so intolerable that her mother asks her to leave home. Margot's other daughter, sober Stavia, also goes through a period of infatuation, with Chernon, and she has a long, eventful adventure with him, during which she finally learns that he is no good. Chernon initiates this relationship by begging Stavia to sneak a forbidden book to him. The laws of Women's Country stipulate that only women and servitors may receive a formal, book-based education, while warriors are trained in their craft of war by discipline and experience. Stavia, feeling sorry for this nice young man who craves book learning, passes one book to Chernon, and then becomes hooked by the compulsion of their mutual deception.

Their relationship, mostly at a distance, continues over a number of years, until Stavia is a grown woman, back from medical school. She is supposed to go on a trip to explore some outlying areas and gather useful information about the local plants. However, Chernon convinces her to go on an adventure with him. She agrees to meet him part-way on her trip, and he rapes her on their first night together. Stavia is horrified and disgusted, but before she can get away from him, some truly horrid men capture both of them and take them back to their farmstead. This is a nightmare land of insane religious fundamentalism, where women are considered evil beings, requiring strict control in the name of God. Each elder has several young wives, whom he controls and abuses, while the younger men have no wives at all. Only Chernon's insistence that Stavia is his wife and pregnant keeps her from being married off to one of the elders. Chernon likes the notion of women being controlled, and he starts cooperating with the men to seize more women from a nearby sheep camp. When Stavia tries to escape, she is caught, beaten, and nearly killed. Stavia eventually is rescued and returns to Women's Country, cured once and for all of her inclination to love a worthless man.

While Stavia and Chernon are away on this painful adventure, Michael and his cronies have been planning a forcible takeover of the women's town. The Women's Council finds out what they are up to and lures them into a trap, where they are slaughtered in a battle with the warriors of another garrison. This battle ends the rebellion and lowers the warrior population, one of the Council's secret goals. Since the men they arrange to destroy are their own sons and lovers, however, there is no joy in the victory for the women of the Council, who keep their dirty secrets to themselves.

These insurrections have happened before, and they will happen again until the women have bred violence and the desire to control out of the gene pool. The women's ultimate secret weapon, which Michael never discovers, is manipulating the gene pool to kill off the sperm of the warriors, not some bomb or other weapon that would kill the warriors directly. Remaking the world is a dirty, painful, secret business for the women of the Council. These women identify with Polyxena and Iphigenia because they too are in Hades.

The Council can find no solution to the problems of male dominance and violence, combined with the infatuation of young women for aggressive, dominant men, except by secretly breeding this male dominance out of the human race. "Iphigenia at Ilium" serves to remind the women of the Council why they must continue their deceptive eugenics program. The most powerful argument for eliminating the warriors as a breeding population is made in the play through the repulsive character of dead Achilles.

> *Achilles.* I seek my servant, Polyxena!
> *Iphigenia.* Oh, mighty warrior, she is not here.
> *Achilles.* She's supposed to be here. They spilt her maiden blood upon my Tomb so she would be here.
> *Iphigenia.* But they didn't ask her if she would serve you, Achilles. Now that the warrants of warriors no longer run, she is her own ghost.
> *Achilles.* She is my slave! It's all been arranged. Spill a maiden's blood, heart's blood, or maidenhead, and she's yours. Everyone knows....
> *Iphigenia.* She is no one's slave, Achilles. In the place of shades, we are all equal... [*WC* 51].

Achilles can't control Polyxena's ghost, so he next tries to control Iphigenia's ghost since they were once betrothed at Aulis. However, Achilles has no better luck with her. Iphigenia's ghost explains bitterly that she was indeed sacrificed at Aulis, while Achilles hid until the sacrificial ritual was over. Then poets made up the story about how a deer had been substituted for her at the moment of sacrifice (*WC* 52). Iphigenia has the definitive last word: "'You may as well forget it, Achilles. There is no fucking in Hades'" (*WC* 57). The ability of men to control women through infatuation and sexuality goes as far as death, but no further.

However, there is an up side to the Council's controlled breeding program. The servitors, men who freely choose to return to Women's Country when they turn fifteen, are increasing in number. Each year more return, and each returnee is assigned to a woman's family, ostensibly as a servant. Servitors are not only more peaceful than the warriors, they are also developing another excellent trait — the ability to read minds. The servitors, while quiet and gentle, are able to fight as well as any warrior, if need be, but they keep a very low profile, so they won't arouse the jealousy and anger of the warriors. These new, improved men, bred beyond the excesses of testosterone overload, live peaceful, satisfying lives, masked as servants, but in fact responsible members of their families.

Tepper, like Bradley, ends her novel not with a total rejection of men, but with a rejection of male-dominated history, focused at the turning-point of the Trojan War. Both authors make the point that until gender roles change markedly, there will be no change in the oppression of women and the violence of warfare. While Bradley offers the hope that men can learn to understand the oppression of women and thus change the way they relate to them, Tepper goes further, asserting that there must be fundamental genetic modifications in males before that change can come about.

16

The Tradition Continues
Troy in the Media and Popular Culture

More than 3200 years after the fall of Troy, new stories of the Trojan War continue to be written, adapting readily to new conditions and new media, starting with movies. *The Return of Ulysses* was made in 1909 (IMDb). Classically trained British soldiers thought of Troy in World War I, especially when they were at Gallipoli, across the Dardanelles from Troy (Vinaver). Mainstream European and American literary authors such as H.D. (Hilda Doolittle), James Joyce, Nikos Kazantzakis, Eugene O'Neill and Jean-Paul Sartre continued the ancient tradition of writing narratives and plays about Trojan themes. However, this was only a part of the flourishing of Troy in the twentieth century. Derek Walcott brought Troy to the Caribbean with his epic poem *Omeros*. Rex Stout wrote a tough-guy Troy novel, *The Great Legend*, as a magazine serial. Television serials such as the very popular shows about Xena and Hercules used Trojan themes. Public television presented documentaries about Troy, including Michael Wood's wonderful series *In Search of the Trojan War*. At the start of the twenty-first century, Disney Studios was creating interactive computer games using Trojan material, based on the animated film *Hercules*. Troy is amazingly present on the Internet, both in its classical (electronic texts of Greek and Latin Troy epics and dramas) and its postmodern (cartoons, interactive games and ads galore) modes.

This chapter will focus on Troy in popular culture in order to show that, although there may indeed have been a major break in the classical European and American literary culture and education, stories of the Trojan War have neatly jumped that gap. Students today may not take Greek or Latin in high school or read Homer or Virgil in the original, but they still learn a surprising amount about the Trojan War, often as entertainment.

The Break in Cultural Continuity

For two thousand years, education in Europe and then in the United States centered on the study of Latin and Virgil. Thus, every schoolboy (there were very few schoolgirls for most of this time) knew about the Trojan War and how the exiled Trojans led by Aeneas went to Italy, where their descendents founded the Roman Empire. Rome became the eventual seat of the Catholic Church and the center of developing European civilization. Ruling families in England and Europe claimed descent from Aeneas. Thus there were continuous links from the Trojan War to European history.

In more recent years, especially since World War II, Latin has been less studied than contemporary languages, math, science and, increasingly, technologies. While Homer was (according to modern taste) the greater poet, Virgil was the lynchpin that bound Troy to Europe — and to its rebellious offspring, America. Unfortunately, while the *Aeneid* is wonderful in Latin, it can be difficult to read and appreciate in translation. The consequence is that few schools and colleges teach the *Aeneid* anymore, except to the elite students who study Latin. Conversely, students who do encounter Homer often lack the Virgilian link between Homer and their own contemporary civilization. Therefore, few students learn about the Trojan War as the start of Western Civilization.

THE CANON WARS

Not only is Virgil little studied in schools at present, the very notion of what should be taught is intensely politicized. Women, ethnics (i.e., anyone whose ancestors didn't come willingly from Western Europe), and other minority interest groups such as gays, and people who identify with the working class rather than the upper class, together make up the majority of Americans at the start of the twenty-first century. These groups are quite legitimately challenging the ancient, male-dominated, white European upper-class literary tradition that previously determined what was important and what should be taught — the "canon" (Jan Gorak, 223). As Paul Lauter remarks, "the past, the bodies of knowledge we teach, is not something that simply exists, but rather, is something we construct — and we construct that past on the basis of our visions of the future" (256–7). Just as Americans no longer agree as a people on any one vision of the future, so do they disagree on what pieces of the past should be taught to mold that future.

In the late nineteenth century, most educated Europeans, Britons, and Americans would have been able to agree, in a gentlemanly fashion, on a list of what should be taught, easily including such literary giants as Homer, Sophocles, Virgil, Chaucer, Shakespeare, Racine and Goethe. Each of these poets, not coincidently, wrote at least one Trojan War story, so a literary education meant learning about Troy. This general agreement no longer holds, partly because many groups reject the tradition of the canon, but even more practically because each time a new work is added to the list, something must be taken away. There is simply not enough time to teach everything.

MASS EDUCATION

Another factor confounding the transmission of the ancient tradition of Troy, or indeed any ancient tradition, is mass education. Latin and Virgil are still being taught to elite students in some secondary schools. But in America, public secondary schools are for everyone, and most students do not study Latin and Virgil. A very large number of these graduates go on to some kind of post-secondary education, quite unprepared to encounter the classics in their traditional mode of presentation. Nonetheless, these classics, especially because they are both ancient and continuing, can teach a valuable sense of then and now, there and here, and everything that flows in between. So for the tradition of Troy to continue thriving, it needed to (and did) find rich and varied ways to reach the masses, not just the chosen few.

For the past twenty-five years I have been teaching classical texts and their contexts to nontraditional students in a community college. Although unprepared in Greek, Latin, Homer and Virgil, they are prepared to relish tales of the Greek heroes and gods and appreciate the story of the Trojan War. They do not relate to Virgil because he upholds the vision of the Roman Empire. They do relate to Aeneas as a good leader and a brave man, although almost all of them think that he was a rat to leave Dido, despite the gods and Fate. Dido's vow of faithfulness to her dead husband, and Aeneas' commitment to his destiny, don't make much of an impression on them; and of course, they could care less about Rome. They tend to dislike Achilles because of his gigantic ego, and they almost never see greatness in Agamemnon, only his failures as a general and his outrageous sacrifice of Iphigenia. They often think Clytemnestra was quite justified in killing Agamemnon because he sacrificed their daughter. They very much enjoy stories of the gods, who are rather like the superheroes they grew up with on Saturday morning cartoons. Indeed, at times I suspect that book 21 of the *Iliad* (the furious battle among the gods and heroes) has provided a prototype for many cartoon battles of superheroes against universal opposition, with the very fate of "life as we know it" in the balance.

Troy and Popular Culture

Thanks to the movies and television, entertainment is readily available to almost everyone, and it does not consist of reading Homer or Virgil. The mass media aim at the largest possible audience by simplifying the content of their presentations while increasing their emotional intensity. It is difficult to imagine a print version of Homer competing with an action movie that uses major stars, surround sound, death-defying stunts, exciting car chases, gigantic explosions, intimate sexual encounters, and computer-generated end-of-the-world violence. People simply do not spend as much time or effort reading the classics as they did before there was such diverting entertainment so easily available. Consequently, if the memory of Troy is to survive and thrive, it will probably have to do so in popular culture, especially if the continuity of the literary culture has been broken.

Troy is remarkably well represented in popular culture. Trojan themes are frequently used in films, popular fiction and cartoons. A new film of Homer's *Odyssey* was released in 1997; a blockbuster film *Troy*, largely based on the *Iliad*, was released in 2004, many current popular novels use Troy materials. There are Bronze Age comic books and for a while there was a wonderful *Ilios* cartoon on the Internet in both Japanese and English (I cannot find it currently). The Internet contains an incredible wealth of Troy-related materials, not only from the ancient literary tradition but also from new uses of that tradition in various forms. One sign of the enduring life of Troy is that people continue to name their children after famous characters from the Trojan War, such as Helen, Hector and Achilles, as well as after Troy itself.

Troy on Film, Television, Video and Audio

A brief search of the Internet Movie Data Base (IMDb) in December 2012 brought up many Troy-related titles and I have selected a representative few ranging from 1909 to

2012. As can be seen from this brief list, in the early years of film classical elements of the Troy story were made directly into movies. Gradually, the use of Troy stories became more freely varied, especially as cartoon series (*Hercules*) and TV series (*Xena*) picked up mythic themes from the matter of Troy. There are many other movie and TV titles of Troy stories than those I have selected, and there are far more that use names and themes from Troy, but not the actual content of the Troy story. Currently there are innumerable uses of the names of the Troy characters and themes, but in distant parallels to the original stories. For example, there is a 1997 Hollywood film, *The Trojan War*, which is about teenage love conflict, not the war at Troy. The concept of the Trojan War is used frequently as a familiar metaphor for conflict. There are also a number of IMDb entries under "Trojan Horse," but most are stories of espionage, not of the original horse at Troy. The concept of the Trojan Horse has become a common metaphor for infiltration into the enemy camp, and by extension, spying in general, as well as for a computer virus. I have not included any of these extensions of ideas about Troy made into films and TV series, but it is worth a look if you are curious.

The Return of Ulysses (1909); *Le retour d'Ulysse* (original title)
Dido Forsaken by Aeneas (1910); Didone abbandonata (original title)
Homer's Odyssey (1911); *L'Odissea* (original title)
The Fall of Troy (1912); *La Caduta di Troia* (original title);
The Love of Penelope (1913)
Helen of Troy (1927)
The Private Life of Helen of Troy (1927)
Helen of Troy (1956)
Popeye's Trojan Horse (1960); TV episode
The Adventures of Hercules: The Trojan Horse (1961); *La guerra di Troia* (original title)
La Leggenda di Enea (1962)
The Last Glory of Troy (1962)
The Wooden Horse of Troy (1962)
Fury of Achilles (1962); *L'ira di Achille* (original title)
Der trojanische Krieg findet nicht statt (1964); TV movie
Hercules and the Princess of Troy (1965)
Le troiane (1967)
Dr. Faustus (1967); *Elizabeth Taylor plays Helen of Troy, the ideal woman of all time*
Trauer muß Elektra tragen (1970); TV movie
The Trojan Women (1971)
Hector the Mighty (1972); *Ettore lo fusto* (original title); the Helen of Troy story in a modern Roman criminal setting
The Return of Ulysses to His Homeland (1973); TV movie; *Il ritorno d'Ulisse in Patria* (II) (original title)
Iphigenia (1977)
Iphigenia auf Tauris (1978)
King Priam (1985); TV movie
Ulysses 31 (1981–2); TV cartoon series; Ulysses in the 31st century
Purcell's Dido and Aenaes (2 Feb. 1986); TV Documentary

Dido & Aeneas (1995)

To Vlemma tou Odyssea (1995); *The Gaze of Odysseus* (1995) (English title)

Dido & Aeneas: (1996); Great Performances: Season 25, Episode 4, TV episode; Purcell's music

The Return of Ulysses (1997) *Iepistroti tou Odyssea* (original title) Documentary

The Odyssey (1997)

Crayola Kids Adventures: The Trojan Horse (video 1997)

Hercules and the Trojan War (1998); TV episode

Mythic Warriors: Guardians of the Legend: Ulysses and the Trojan Horse (1999); TV episode (and many other episodes in this series that deal with the matter of Troy)

Helen of Troy (2003); TV movie

Troy: The Passion of Helen (2004); TV movie

Imagining Ulysses (2004); Documentary

Dido and Aeneas (2005); TV movie; *Dido und Aeneas* (original title)

The Yearning of Troy Helen — War or Love (2005); Documentary; *O kaimos tis Oraias Elenis — Polemos i erotas?* (original title)

The Trojan Women (2004); English language version of *Le troiane* (1967)

Troy (2004)

Helen of Troy (2005); TV Documentary

Penelope (2009); *Penelopa* (original title); an Australian-Croatian co-production

Homer and Penelope (2012)

Some of these Troy movies, such as the brilliant *The Trojan Women* and *Iphigenia*, are filmed productions of specific Greek tragedies. Others, such as the 1956 *Helen of Troy,* are uninspired Hollywood flicks. Still others, such as the slow-moving, profoundly sad *The Gaze of Odysseus* take an aspect of the ancient Trojan War story, the wandering of Odysseus, and apply it to a modern issue — a modern controversial filmmaker searching for reels of a mythical early film made in the troubled Balkans. And of course there are many uses of the Troy material that are strictly for fun, such as children's and young adults' cartoon and TV series.

Troy on Educational Television and Video

Many educational videos are available on Trojan themes. The best and most comprehensive historical overview is Michael Wood's *In Search of the Trojan War*, which was shown frequently on the Public Broadcasting System in the 1980s. Wood also wrote an excellent book, full of wonderful pictures and reliable information, to accompany the videos, making this a mixed-media event. However, new archaeological digs at Troy begun in the late 1980s under the direction of Manfred Korfmann turned up a greatly enlarged periphery to the city of Troy (Wood, 260). This put Wood's videos out of date in their information about Troy itself. Wood did prepare an updated version of the book reflecting this new information, but he did not update the video. Consequently, *In Search of the Trojan War* is rarely shown anymore on public television, although thankfully the video has recently been reissued and is well worth watching.

Troy on Audiobooks

In the past few years, audiobooks have become an increasingly popular means of delivering books to their audiences. My local library is giving increasing space to CD sets of novels, biographies, histories, religious studies, drama and poetry. In our mobile society, a book can be consumed on the road, as a bedtime story, or while trying to avoid anxiety in the middle of the night, by people whose eyes are weary from staring at computer screens much of the day. In 2006 at least three different audiobooks of the *Iliad* were published: one read by the translator, Stanley Lombardo, another (abridged) read by Derek Jacobi, and a third read by Anton Lesser. Yet another audio *Iliad* was published in 2010, read by Michael Page. Similar results can be found for the *Odyssey* and *Aeneid*. Since Homer was known orally long before he was known in print, this is in many ways an exciting development for the transmission of ancient epic poetry to a modern audience.

Some Twentieth-Century Troy Books:
A Short Bibliography

There were a number of fine, literary Troy-based books written and published in the twentieth century. The following list aims to include the not-so-great as well, because my purpose is to indicate how deeply Troy stories have penetrated into both the literary and the popular consciousness. This list is not at all comprehensive, but tries to give a sense of the variety of books published on Trojan topics in the twentieth century. Although there are many fine works of academic scholarship on Troy, I have not included most of them here, because my topic is the living popular continuity of Troy, not its afterlife in the universities.

Ackroyd, Peter. *The Fall of Troy*. Nan A. Talese (Doubleday), 2007.
A short novel based on the misadventures of Heinrich Schliemann (here called Obermann), his clever young wife Sophia, and mysteries surrounding both Obermann's past and his experiences and discoveries at Troy.

Adams, Hebron E. *The Burodyssey of H.O.M.E.R.* Reston, VA: Foxon, 1994.
A spoof of the adventures of Odysseus as reflected in bureaucratic memos. Recommended for anyone who enjoys Homer and has worked for the government.

Atwood, Margaret. *The Penelopiad: The Myth of Penelope and Odysseus*. New York: Canongate, 2005.
Atwood retells the story of Odysseus from the points of view of Penelope (the narrator) and the treacherous palace maids (the chorus). Worth reading if you feel dismayed by the way that Odysseus, after killing the suitors, has the maids scrub the blood from his palace before they are hanged.

Byers, Richard McCulloch. *The Winning of Andromache,*1987; *Andromache's Hector and Helenus*, 1989; *Andromache: Beneath the Load of Life*, 1989. Fairfield House.
Three self-published novels about Troy.

Clarke, Lindsay. *The War at Troy*. Thomas Dunne Books. New York: St. Martin's Press, 2004.
A modern prose retelling of the events of the Trojan War. This earnest, carefully researched, but rather prosaic novel, narrated by the Ithacan bard Phemius, begins with Aphrodite and the

Golden Apple of Discord and ends with the fall of Troy and the division of the spoils (women) among the victorious Greeks.

Bailey, Hilary. *Cassandra: Princess of Troy*, 1993. Rpt. Pan Books, 1995.

An aged Cassandra, hiding on a farm in Thessaly, writes her memoirs of the Trojan War. This version is unusual because Bailey uses late 20th century archaeological findings about the connections between Troy and the ancient Hittite Kingdom at Hattusa to create a very up-to-date historical context for the story of the Trojan War.

Bradley, Marion Zimmer. *The Firebrand*. 1987. Rpt. New York: Pocket Books, 1991.

Kassandra narrates the Fall of Troy. *The Firebrand* is discussed in detail in Chapter 15 of this book.

Cargill, Linda. *To Follow the Goddess*. Charlottesville, VA: Cheops Books, 1991.

The story of Troy is told from Helen's point of view. She explains how she really wasn't a bad woman after all. Helen loved Menelaus, was seized by Paris against her will, and was held in Troy against her will because the Trojans believed her to be an incarnation of Inanna, the ancient Near-Eastern goddess of fertility.

Doolittle, Hilda (H. D.). *Helen in Egypt*. 1961. Rpt. New York: New Directions, 1974.

This Helen was spirited away to Egypt, and only her *eidolon*, or image, appeared at Troy. Helen encounters or remembers her lovers — Theseus, Menelaus, Paris, and Achilles — in a series of lyrics with brief narrative commentaries.

Douglass, Sara. *Hades Daughter: Book One of the Troy Game*. A Tor Book, 2003.

The first of a four part fantasy series based on the notion of "The Troy Game" being a witchcraft and labyrinth power trip that is played out by Brutus, descendent of Aeneas, among others.

Fischer, Norman. *Sailing Home: Using the Wisdom of Homer's Odyssey to Navigate Life's Perils and Pitfalls*. Free Press, 2008.

A Zen Buddhist uses the story of the *Odyssey* as a metaphor for the journey of self-knowledge. It is interesting, pleasant and informative, if not exactly classical Homeric scholarship.

Fleishman, Paul. *Dateline: Troy*. Cambridge, MA: Candlewick, 1996.

This retelling of the story of the Trojan War for young people juxtaposes modern news clippings about contemporary wars and the events of the ancient war.

Franklin, Sarah B. *Daughter of Troy: A Novel of History, Valor and Love*. New York: Avon Books, 1998. The author is Dave Duncan, writing under a pseudonym.

Briseis narrates this well-researched story of the Fall of Troy, from her idyllic girlhood through her love affair with Achilles to her old age as a survivor of the war.

George, Margaret. *Helen of Troy*. New York: Viking, 2006.

This version of Helen is perceptive, likeable, and believable; she narrates the events of her life in an interesting, lively manner, from her girlhood in Sparta through her marriage to Menelaus, running off with Paris to Troy, life in Troy, the fall of Troy, and returning home with Menelaus after a stay in Egypt. I found the last part of the book especially poignant as the aging Helen and Menelaus evolve from enemies into comrades and finally into death. This Helen is no goddess, although her father is Zeus. Achilles and Agamemnon are the bad guys in this version.

Giradoux, Jean. *The Tiger at the Gates* (translated from *La Guerre de Troie n'Aura pas Lieu*, 1935). First American Edition. New York: Oxford University Press, 1956.

Although the Greeks and Trojans (reflective of the French and Germans) try to achieve peace, chance or fate intervenes, and the war goes on.

Graves, Robert. *Homer's Daughter*, 1955. Rpt. Chicago: Academy Chicago Edition, 1982.

This rather stodgy novel is narrated by the young Sicilian noblewoman, Nausicaa, who says that she composed the *Odyssey* from a mixture of an old tale, "The Return of Ulysses," and her own experiences. Interesting for its content; rather difficult as a novel, because Graves was writing his mythological dictionaries at about this time, and there's an excess of mythic and historical information.

Gumpert, Matthew. *Grafting Helen: The Abduction of the Classical Past.* Madison: University of Wisconsin Press, 2001.

A scholarly examination of the uses of Helen since the Bronze Age.

Herbert, Brian, and Kevin J. Anderson. *Dune: House Atreides.* New York: Bantam Books, 1999.

This is a "prequel" to the Dune books by Frank Herbert, Brian's father. The story focuses on the House Atreides, the descendents (after 12,000 years) of the House of Atreus. Mention is made of Agamemnon; Helena (like the ancient Clytemnestra) arranges the murder of her husband, Paul Atreides, and the "House Play" *Agamemnon* is performed. Leto Atreides takes on the role of Orestes, but he banishes his mother instead of killing her. All in all, the Agamemnon material is more decorative than integral to the story.

Hill, Reginald. *Arms and the Women.* New York: Dell–Random House, 1999.

This is a nifty British mystery wrapped around a first novel being written by one of the characters. The novel in the mystery is about Odysseus and Aeneas, who meet on their respective wanderings after the fall of Troy. This Odysseus is close kin to Andy Dalziel, a fat and clever Detective Superintendent (with some nods to Falstaff).

Hughes, Bettany. *Helen of Troy: Goddess, Princess, Whore.* New York: Alfred A. Knopf, 2005.

If you want to know all about Helen, from the Bronze Age down to the present, and if you enjoy lively, elegant writing, this is a splendid book to read and enjoy. It is perhaps not as scholarly as some studies of Helen, but it is comprehensive, witty, thoroughly documented, and investigates Helen from every angle, from her putative roots as a Bronze Age Goddess on down to her later role as the despised and adored sex-goddess who led/lured men into their doom at Troy. There are a number of great images of Helen through the ages included. Hughes has not only read all of the relevant texts, but she has traveled in the footsteps of Helen and tells us of the sights and feel of the world that Helen may have once lived in.

Joyce, James. *Ulysses*, 1922. Rpt. New York: The Modern Library, Random House, 1946.

Jewish Dubliner Leopold Bloom is the wandering Ulysses of the title, and Dublin is the maze through which he returns home to his Penelope, Molly Bloom. Probably the greatest modern Troy story, this complex novel redeems the character of Ulysses/Odysseus from many centuries of suspicion and downright dislike.

Kazantzakis, Nikos. *The Odyssey: A Modern Sequel*, 1938. Trans. Kimon Friar. New York: Simon and Schuster, 1958.

This *Odyssey* stands alongside Joyce's *Ulysses* in the renovation of the character of Odysseus.

Komar, Kathleen L. *Reclaiming Klytemnestra: Revenge or Reconciliation.* Urbana: University of Illinois Press, 2003.

An excellent study of the importance of the character of Clytemnestra to feminist authors, especially in the 1980s. Feminists of that time were looking to the past for strong woman role models, before some mythic time when women lost their power. The issue was not so much approving of Clytemnestra as trying to understand a powerful ancient woman. Komar's study is objective and balanced. Interestingly, in the 1990s, feminist authors turned more to stories of Iphigenia and Electra, the daughters of Clytemnestra.

Le Guin, Ursula. *Lavinia: A Novel.* New York: Harcourt, 2008.

The story of the *Aeneid* as told by Lavinia, the woman Aeneas marries in Italy. She has almost no role in the *Aeneid*, but here she tells how she grew up in rural Italy, daughter of King Latinus and crazy Queen Amata, who tried desperately to force Lavinia to marry Turnus. Then she tells about the wars in Italy (as told in the *Aeneid*) and about her marriage to Aeneas. The last part goes beyond that marriage to her three years of living with Aeneas, his death, and her life as a widow raising their son Silvius. This book is suitable for young adults or adults and like other women's retellings of Trojan stories, adds the voices of women to their ancient silence.

Logue, Christopher. *All Day Permanent Red: An Account of the First Battle Scenes of Homer's Iliad.* New York: Farrar Straus & Giroux, April 2003.

> An amazing version of an extremely violent battle scene in the *Iliad* done in very modern terms. This is not a translation, but a new vision based on Homer's vision.

Matturro, Richard. *Troy.* New York: Walker, 1989.

> This retelling explains the events at Troy in the euhemeristic tradition of Dictys and Dares. Almost all events are rationalized into rather boring, pedestrian occurrences. The dialogue is stilted and except for Odysseus the characters are undeveloped. The story covers the period from after the quarrel between Agamemnon and Achilles through the destruction of Troy and the flight of Aeneas and his friends.

McCullough, Colleen. *The Song of Troy: A Story That Will Outlast History.* 1998. London: Orion Paperback, 1999.

> McCullough has retold the story of Troy as historically real and rather dull, in the tradition of Dictys and Dares: no gods, no destiny, nobody larger than life. Odysseus and Deiphobos are lovers, as are Achilles and Patroclus. Achilles is a very nice man. Briseis is a sweet woman who kills herself in Achilles' tomb. The "quarrel" between Achilles and Agamemnon is a stratagem of Odysseus to draw the Trojans out of Troy.

McLaren, Clemence. *Inside the Walls of Troy: A Novel of the Women Who Lived the Trojan War.* New York: Laurel-Leaf Books, 1996.

> Helen and Cassandra narrate the events at Troy. This readable book is aimed at a young-adult audience.

McLaughlin, Ellen. *The Greek Plays.* New York: Theatre Communications Group, 2005.

> This collection includes McLaughlin's feminist trilogy *Iphigenia and Other Daughters*, consisting of *Iphigenia in Aulis*, *Electra*, and *Iphigenia in Tauris*. The plays are loosely adapted from the ancient Greek plays of the same names by Euripides and Sophocles. McLaughlin uses ancient Trojan themes to deal with contemporary ideas about war and the roles of women. Her Clytemnestra is especially interesting — heroic, not evil.

Mee, Charles. *History Plays.* A Collection of Six Plays, including *Orestes* and *The Trojan Women: A Love Story.* Baltimore: Johns Hopkins University Press, 1998.

> Mee's contemporary versions of Greek tragedies are interesting to read and wonderful to watch. He has his plays posted on the Web, too! The current (2013) Internet address is http://charles mee.org/html/plays.html#trag

Merlis, Mark. *An Arrow's Flight.* New York: St. Martin's Press, 1998.

> The Greek soldier Philoctetes had been bitten by a snake and his wound stank so badly that the Greeks left him on the island of Lemnos while they went on to Troy. However, the prophecy was that until he brought the bow and arrows of Hercules to Troy, the Greeks could not conquer Troy. So, dead Achilles' son Pyrrhus, who works as a go-go boy, is sent to persuade Philoctetes to come to Troy, where he will be healed and help to conquer the citadel. There is a good deal of rough gay sexual material in this novel, so it is not for every reader, but the story is powerful and offers a perspective on the conquest of Troy from the era of AIDS.

Miller, Madeline. *The Song of Achilles.* New York: Harper-Collins, 2012.

> An outstanding retelling of the story of Achilles from his childhood up to his death and burial, narrated by Patroclus. We all know the story, but this version is freshly imagined and psychologically convincing. The author is well-trained in the classics and she stays very close to the classical mythic and Homeric material. Thetis is a scary and convincing Greek goddess, not a friendly water nymph and Patroclus is Achilles' lover.

Molinaro, Ursule. *The Autobiography of Cassandra, Princess and Prophetess of Troy.* 1979. Rpt. Kingston, NY: Mcpherson; 2nd edition, 1992.

> This brief, interesting retake on the Troy story expresses the classic 1970s feminist line with a sharply minimalist narrative. The core of Cassandra's story is that when she rejected Apollo, he spat in her mouth, so that no one would believe her. This Trojan moment was the turning point in the shift from female independence to female servitude. She is narrating the story after being dead for 3,000 years, so she has a modern perspective and explains that Homer wrote "five centuries after the fall, when knowledge had become unbecoming, for a woman.... Poor Helen. Legend has made of her the sample type of the new woman that came about with male supremacy. Placidly beautiful, without a mind of her own."

Myers, Amy. "Aphrodite's Trojan Horse." In *Classical Whodunits.* Ed. Mike Ashley, 1996. New York: Barnes and Noble, 2000: 1–24.

> This story is a tongue-in-cheek, rather silly murder mystery. Aphrodite is accused of the death of Anchises, father of Aeneas, and she responds by doing some detective work in Troy.

O'Neill, Eugene. *Mourning Becomes Electra,* 1931. Rpt. in *Three Plays: Desire Under the Elms, Strange Interlude, Mourning Becomes Electra.* New York: Vintage Books, 1959.

> *Mourning Becomes Electra* is a trilogy (*Homecoming, The Hunted,* and *The Haunted*) in which the American playwright reinterpreted the *Oresteia* of Aeschylus as a New England tragedy.

Pomery, Sarah. *Spartan Women.* Oxford: Oxford University Press, 2002.

> Sparta was remarkably different from Athens in many ways, perhaps most in the roles of women, who were raised to be athletic and educated, could hold and inherit property, and in general were valued as human beings. Helen, of course, was Spartan, and some of her negative qualities (such as running off with Paris and causing the Trojan War) may well have come from Athenian men viewing the freedom of Spartan women with horror.

Prescott, Michael. *Comes the Dark.* New York: Signet, 1999.

> This is a retelling as a modern murder mystery of the story of Orestes, son of Clytemnestra.

Sartre, Jean-Paul. *Les Mouches* (*The Flies*), 1943. Trans. Stuart Gilbert. In *No Exit and Three Other Plays.* New York: Vintage, 1989.

> This play reinterprets the story of Orestes as an existential dilemma.

Shanower, Eric. *Age of Bronze: A Thousand Ships.* Orange, CA: Image Comics, 2001.

> A collected series of high quality, seriously researched, carefully detailed, and beautifully drawn "comic" books retelling the events of the entire Trojan War.

Shay, Jonathan, M.D. *Achilles in Vietnam: Combat Trauma and the Undoing of Character.* New York: MacMillan, 1994.

> This commentary on the *Iliad* is part of the current-issues reading list for the U.S. Marine Corps' Professional Reading Program.

Simmons, Dan. *Ilium.* New York: Random House, 2003.

> One of the most intriguing and complicated modern retellings of the Troy Story, set on a future Earth and other places. The Greek Gods are mysteriously cruel and powerful creatures who dwell on Mons Olympus on Mars. There are well-intentioned robots who obsess over Shakespeare and Proust, Hockenberry, a resurrected classics professor from the 20th century, and a wealth of other characters.

_____. *Olympos.* New York: Harper Collins, 2005.

> The sequel to *Ilium.* The Greek Gods get their come-uppance, Hockenberry, the classics professor, messes up the outcome of the Trojan War, Achilles falls in love with the Amazon Penthesliea, one Odysseus (there are two of him) goes off with Circe/Sycorax to explore new worlds and make love in all of them, Prospero (perhaps the incarnation of Shakespeare) and the well-intentioned robots fix up many messes, and human life gets more or less back on track. Personally,

I found this volume contrived, excessively complicated, and less compelling than *Ilium*, but I am sure that many readers will enjoy it.

Stout, Rex. *The Great Legend*. Originally published fairly early in the twentieth century in *All-Story* magazine (n.d.). Rpt. New York: Carroll and Graf, 1997.

Idaeus, son of Dares, narrates this hardboiled version of the Fall of Troy.

Tepper, Sheri S. *The Gate to Women's Country*, 1988. Rpt. New York: Bantam, 1989.

Tepper describes a future civilization where the women live in walled cities and the warrior men live outside. It uses a play, "Iphigenia at Ilium," as a central device to utterly reject the heroic values of Achilles. The book is discussed in detail in Chapter 15 of this book.

Tuchman, Barbara W. *The March of Folly: From Troy to Vietnam*. 1984. Rpt. Ballentine edition, 1985.

Tuchman aims at the folly of the Vietnam War, but she develops her argument starting with a generous section on Troy and the incredible folly of the Trojans bringing the Trojan Horse into their city. Perhaps because of her purpose, Tuchman concludes that the Trojans were free to decide to bring the horse in or not, which goes against many versions of the story, but is a nice prelude to her discussion of the history of bad political judgments, culminating in Vietnam.

Walcott, Derek. *The Odyssey: A Stage Version*. New York: Farrar, Straus and Giroux, 1993.

This delightful play takes Odysseus, his family, and crew to the Caribbean.

_____. *Omeros*. New York: Farrar, Straus and Giroux, 1990.

The story of the *Odyssey* is retold as an epic poem set in the Caribbean.

Waswo, Richard. *The Founding Legend of Western Civilization: From Virgil to Vietnam*. Wesleyan University Press, 1997.

Virgil's take on the trek from Troy to the founding of Rome is the core legend for Western expansion according to Waswo.

Wolf, Christa. *Cassandra: A Novel and Four Essays*. 1983. Translated by Jan Van Heurck, 1984. 1st Farrar, Straus and Giroux paperback edition, 1988.

An East German feminist retells the story of Troy from Cassandra's point of view, focused on patriarchy, corruption and war.

World War I and Troy

A number of World War I poems refer to Troy stories. According to Eileen Gregory,

The matter of Troy was very much in the imagination of leaders, soldiers, and intellectuals before and during World War I, because a major engagement of the Allied forces was the attempt to seize the Dardanelles from Turkish forces.... In March, 1915, the flagship *Agamemnon* was among the British fleet bound toward the shores of ancient Ilion in the land assault on Gallipoli [23].

Troy was deeply embedded in the minds of the young British soldiers. In her essay, "'Millions of the Mouthless Dead': Charles Hamilton Sorley and Wilfred Owen in Homer's Hades" Elizabeth Vandiver explains that, because the study of the classics was so central to Victorian and Edwardian education, the Greco-Roman Homeric and classical tradition had a profound influence on the Great War poets. Here are a few World War I poems echoing Trojan themes.

Guillaume Apollinaire, "Prologue, Les Mamelles de Tirésias"
Robert Graves, "Escape"

Wilfred Owens, "Strange Meeting" and "Arms and the Boy"
Charles Hamilton Sorley, "When You See Millions of the Mouthless Dead"
Isaac Rosenberg, "A Worm Fed on the Heart of Corinth" and "Girl to Soldier on Leave"

Some Other Twentieth Century Poems about Troy

Margaret Atwood, "Siren Song"; "Helen of Troy does Countertop Dancing"
W. H. Auden, "The Shield of Achilles"
Stephen Vincent Benét, "First Vision of Helen" and "Last Vision of Helen"
Rupert Brooke, "Menelaus and Helen"
Louise Glück, "The Queen of Carthage" and "Penelope's Song"
Rachel Hadas, "The Fall of Troy"
Seamus Heaney, "The Cure at Troy"
Bernadette Mayer, "HELEN HYPATIA BAILEY BAYLY"
Sara Teasdale, "Helen of Troy"
Dimitris Tsaloumas: *Helen of Troy and Other Poems*
William Butler Yeats, "No Second Troy," "When Helen Lived," and "Leda and the Swan"
Herbert Zbigniew, "About Troy"

Troy and Music

Margaret Scherer lists several interesting musical connections to Troy in her very useful book *Legends of Troy in Art and Literature* (229–231), such as the following:

Camille Saint-Saëns' opera *Hélene*, 1904
Richard Strauss, music for Trojan and other librettos by Hugo von Hofmannsthal (*Elektra*, 1903; with music, 1909; *Egyptian Helen*, with music, 1927)
George Antheil, music for Erskin's *Helen Retires* [n.d.]
Jerome Moross, music for *The Golden Apple*, 1954
Michael Tippet, words and music for the opera *King Priam*, 1962

More current musical uses of Troy as a theme or name are available on the Internet. Here is a sampling:

Charles L. Mee, *The Trojan Women: A Love Story* (Based on the works of Euripides and Berlioz)
Led Zeppelin lyrics for "Achilles Last Stand"
Pop singer Dido's song, "My Lover's Gone," which seems to be about Aeneas, leaving in a ship at dawn, although he is not mentioned by name
Sinead O'Connor lyrics, "Troy"
TROY! The Musical. By Burnt Nightingale Productions, 2012, Minnesota Fringe Production.

Web sites for popular singers with Trojan-related names include the following:

Post-hardcore trio, The Fall of Troy formed in Mukilteo, WA, in 2002.
Hard rock group, Troy
Popular singer, David Troy
Guitarist and instructor *Troy Stetina*
Southern Gospel singer (The Inspirations), Troy Burns
Blues band, Dr. Hector and the Groove Injectors

Troy on the Internet

Troy has found a welcome home on the Internet, where patient searches bring up an amazing variety of Troy-related items, ranging from the sublime (paintings of Troy through the ages) to the ridiculous (Trojan condoms, Trojan Horse computer viruses and a LEGO Trojan Horse). Museums in Greece and Turkey show images of precious objects from the Mycenaean Bronze Age and a doll maker offers a gussied-up Helen of Troy doll for a substantial sum.

I have developed and maintain a substantial Internet site called TROY. The web address is: http://novaonline.nvcc.edu/Eli/Troy/BbVersion/Troy/index.html. My TROY site gathers and organizes Internet links related to the Trojan War and its stories. This site also contains student activities, essays, bibliographies, and lots of other information on Trojan topics. Most of the sources mentioned below are linked to TROY. Since Internet addresses change rather often, and since I update the web addresses of my links on a regular basis, the best way to find these sites is to go through TROY. Following is a list of various kinds of Troy materials you can examine on the Internet.

ART ABOUT TROY

There are a number of sites that exhibit paintings about Trojan themes. I have links to many on the TROY website. The Perseus Digital Database is probably the most comprehensive place to explore Trojan images, although it is complex to navigate. Perhaps a better approach is to use your search engine to type in the names of Troy characters and events, add the term "art," and see what comes up.

TROJAN ARTIFACTS

Many museums (including the Museum at Nauplion and the Topkapi Museum in Istanbul) have Internet sites that display wonderful Mycenaean Bronze Age artifacts.

TROJAN ARCHAEOLOGY

There are photos of digs, photos of architectural remains such as the Lion Gate and "Treasury of Atreus" at Mycenae, logs of digs, lists of archaeological groups, and so on. One of the most thorough and reasonably current archaeology websites is *Project Troia*. There are even college courses on Ancient Mediterranean Archaeology, such as an excellent one, "Aegean Prehistoric Archaeology" from Dartmouth.

Tours of Troy (Real or Virtual)

Troy is still there, and many tours take people to Hisarlik and environs. Several travel bureaus, as well as the Turkish Government, have great sites with lots of information about visiting Troy. Check out their websites if you are thinking of taking a trip to Troy.

E-texts

There are many free Troy-related electronic texts in English on the Internet, including Homer's *Iliad* and *Odyssey*; all of the Greek Trojan dramas; Virgil's *Aeneid*; Chaucer's *Troilus and Criseyde*; Henryson's *Testament of Crisseid*; Shakespeare's *Troilus and Cressida*; Goethe's *Iphigenia in Tauris*; a number of obscure Renaissance and later plays from the University of Virginia's Chadwyck-Healey English Verse Drama Full Text Database (only available to subscribing institutions), various pre–twentieth-century poems about Troy; Gerhardt Hauptmann's *Bow of Odysseus*; a full text of Joyce's *Ulysses*; and a number of poems about Troy by modern poets such as Auden, Atwood, H.D. and Teasdale. There is not much in the way of longer contemporary Troy literature online because of copyright issues. The MIT Internet Classics Archive is a great place to locate free, searchable, mainly Greco-Roman texts in translation. Project Gutenberg is another good source for free online texts about Troy. Of course free texts generally are older translations, and not necessarily the most pleasant to read.

If you have an e-reader, you can download almost all of this material for free and read it at your leisure.

Lists of Books About Troy to Buy Online

Searching online booksellers brings up hundreds of Troy-related books. They range from scholarly studies to children's stories.

Bibliographies of Virgil Online

There is a good one on Classical Virgil by S. Werner and another substantial bibliography on the medieval and Renaissance reception and imitation of Virgil by David Scott Wilson-Okamura.

Disney's Hades' Challenge

This is an interactive online "Game of Strategy and Adventure Set in the Ancient World of Greek Mythology!" It has sections on Odysseus, the Trojan Horse, etc. The game is a follow-on to the Disney animated film, *Hercules*.

Maps and/or Home Pages

For towns and cities with names like Helena, Montana; Helen, Georgia; Troy, Alabama; Troy, Illinois; Troy, Maine; Troy, Michigan; Troy, New York; Troy Ohio; Troy, Pennsylvania; Troy, Tennessee; and, of course, Paris, France.

A LEGO TROJAN HORSE

This model includes a ladder, Greek soldiers, and several views of the construction.

MYTHOLOGY GUIDES

There are several good ones. I love the illustrated Bulfinch's *Mythology*. It includes substantial sections on Trojan characters and stories. An excellent more recent site is the *Greek Mythology Link*, an extensive collection of myths retold by Carlos Parada.

THE PERSEUS DATABASE

This huge collection of classical texts, history and images, heavily annotated in hypertext, linked to just about everything, is challenging to use but a wonderful source for Trojan materials.

What Tradition?

Surely, the foregoing are not the indicators of a lost tradition. The tradition of Troy stories may have gone underground, along with much other classical learning, so that it does not readily appear in school curricula. Not many people study Greek or Latin or even read Homer or Virgil anymore. However, to borrow from E. B. White, the once and future Troy remains firmly fixed in the popular imagination, in its films, novels, cartoons, ads and place names. Students are fascinated by Troy because they first learned about it in popular media such as the animated Hercules series. Young people love contemporary retellings of Troy stories, so long as the new versions are either adapted to contemporary media such as film, or at least clearly presented in current styles of language. They may not think of the ancient Greeks and Trojans as their personal ancestors, but these superheroes are the story ancestors of "Western" civilization, which by now includes people from just about everywhere, including the kid from Taiwan watching a Saturday cartoon in Virginia about Hercules and the Princess of Troy.

The events of the Trojan War had been narrated orally for several centuries before they were compiled into the Homeric epics. The value was in the performance, which transmitted historical memories as beautifully as possible. Hearing a Troy story must have been both instructive and delightful, or who would have bothered to listen for so long? Perhaps the reason we still have the texts of Homer, but not the other Troy epics, is that they were not as well composed, not as cherished. Over millennia, Troy stories have been endlessly recomposed into epics, dramas, lyric poems, histories, plays, romances, operas, novels, films, cartoons, interactive games, advertisements, and who knows what next? They have been used to name cities and football teams. Europeans who never came near Troy have claimed Trojan ancestors. These stories have life, and life keeps changing. I cannot even begin to imagine what uses the twenty-first century will find for Troy.

Conclusion: The Trojan Problem

The problem of Troy is the problem of war. Human beings simply do not seem to be good enough, wise enough, kind enough, self-disciplined enough to manage their affairs without periodic explosions of violence that destroy armed cities, powerful states, women and children, entire civilizations. When I began this project many years ago, I thought I would find "solutions" to the problem of the Trojan War, why people destroy one another. I hoped that some of the great authors I was planning to explore would offer the kind of wisdom that could help people avoid future catastrophes. I was wrong. If Troy is the problem, the answer is always something like, "if only...."

For Homeric Greeks, the Trojan War marked the end of the Greek mythic/heroic past and the beginning of their history. Perhaps Homeric Greeks thought of it as their last good war (rather as Americans regard World War II). Certainly, life had been different before the Trojan War. As the centuries passed, Troy became a metaphor for the pain of war, the danger of lust, the destruction of civilization, the suffering of women and children. Euripides was exquisitely sensitive to the suffering caused by war, and he wrote plays that presented the Trojan War not as heroic, but as cruel and pathetic in its consequences.

Just as Troy became a metaphor for war, the sacrifice of Iphigenia became a powerful metaphor for the way war destroys the innocent. Euripides may have saved Iphigenia by substituting a deer for her at the moment of sacrifice (or the ending may have been added later). Certainly, when Euripides wrote *Iphigenia at Tauris*, he was presenting a final resolution of the sacrifice of Iphigenia, by subjugating the barbaric Tauric rituals of human sacrifice to the lawful Athenian controls of Athena.

Virgil's *Aeneid* offered the fortunate-fall approach to Troy: If Troy had not fallen, its refugees would not have journeyed to Italy to prepare for the founding of Rome. This approach treats the fall of Troy not as a metaphor for war, but as a metaphor for the fall and eventual triumphant rebirth of civilization. In the *Aeneid*, the Greeks represent a barbaric interval between the civilization of Troy and the civilization of Rome.

The European Middle Ages loved the *Aeneid* and embraced the rise of Rome as the destined outcome of the fall of Troy. However, medieval Troy romances such as Benoît's *Roman de Troie* and Chaucer's *Troilus and Criseyde* could not offer any happy ending to the suffering at Troy because they were about the ancient pagan past. Troy was interesting because it was part of human history, even part of Anglo-Norman and British history. The fall of Troy was at the beginning of recorded time, it was very sad, and it was immutable. For medieval Europeans, Christianity, which did not arise for more than a thousand years after the fall of Troy, was the only possible "solution" to the essential problem of Troy — not that it was destroyed by war, but that it was pagan.

Sex, however, was another matter. Medieval Troy romances picked up the themes of passionate behavior and sexual misconduct. Everyone knew that the lust of Paris and Helen lay at the heart of the Trojan War. However, medieval thinkers allowed for two kinds of earthly love — positive love and negative lust. Thus Benoît wrote of the destruction of Achillès through misplaced passion, while the anonymous *Eneas* poet wrote of the earthly redemption of Eneas through legitimate love. Chaucer, a more balanced author, showed first how love elevated Troilus and then how the limits and betrayal of love destroyed him.

Guido delle Colonne transformed the story of Troy into the prose history of a sad and dangerous time. He more than most Troy story authors kept asking, "what if," and "if only." As a judge, he was acutely aware of the connections between human choices and actions and their unavoidable consequences. And yet, he had no solution to offer other than that life was very dangerous and one should, if possible, avoid most experience.

Other times found other interesting issues to deal with at Troy. Racine was attracted to the pathetic story of Iphigenia, yet reluctant to deal with the ancient pagan issue of human sacrifice, so he created a second bad Iphigenia, Eriphile. Her suicide eliminated the need to sacrifice Iphigenia. Eriphile offered a local solution to a local problem, not a general solution to the problem of Troy, which was the problem of war, human weakness, and the destruction of civilization.

A century later, Goethe tried not only to save Iphigenia, but to refashion her into a pure, strong, new woman, who could resolve the ancient pagan curse on the House of Atreus through her personal integrity and truthfulness. Goethe was a humanist and an optimist; he thought of history in terms of what human beings did. Thus, people could choose to behave more ethically, and that improved behavior could in turn change the course of history.

James Joyce did not attempt to save Troy, but he did manage to redeem one of the Trojan War's most disliked heroes, Odysseus, in the form of Leopold Bloom, a curious, decent, rather ordinary man, a Jewish-Irish version of the ancient Greek wanderer. Instead of wandering the Mediterranean for ten years, Joyce's Bloom wandered through Dublin during a single day in June 1904. The Great War had not yet arrived in 1904, but Joyce wrote *Ulysses* in the midst of the war and surely was aware of the destruction of civilization that had followed the Trojan War and was currently tearing apart Europe.

Bradley and Tepper were humanists as well as feminists, and both of them sought solutions to the tragedy of history, the tragedy of Troy. They not only saw the Trojan War as a problem, but each struggled to offer a solution, whether it was founding a new colony in the West, or breeding a gentler, more egalitarian kind of man, who could live with women without trying to dominate and go to war over them. Bradley's analysis of the roots of male domination and war was close to Tepper's. Women who love men may behave weakly, and this weakness undermines the dominion of Mother Goddesses and mother right (or, in Tepper's case, the Women's Council). This feminist reading of the causes of war created a profound modern shift in the ancient links among Troy, war, and the women men fight over.

Troy seems infinitely adaptable to the needs of each culture. In the late twentieth century, gay presence in literature became significant, and sure enough, there were Troy novels that dealt with this theme. For example, Colleen McCullough's *Song of Troy* developed love relationships between Odysseus and Diomedes and between Achilles and Patroclus. The suggestion of Achilles and Patroclus as lovers was ancient, but the relationship between Odysseus and Diomedes was more unexpected. And Mark Merlis wrote a novel on Philoctetes, *An Arrow's Flight* which tells a part of the Troy story in an unequivocal, roughly sexual gay idiom.

Popular culture generally treats Troy not as a problem to be solved, but as material to be mined to satisfy the enormous appetite of the mass media. The names are familiar, the myths are fascinating, and the events are world-class. Troy suggests ancient times, mystery, power, unearthly beauty, superheroes, ancient gods and heroic quests. And if the story does not contain something that is needed, people can and will just make it up, adding their new imaginings to the ancient legacy of Troy materials.

Future times will have their own, as yet unimagined, uses for the story of Troy, which will enrich the twenty-first century and beyond, just as it has the previous three millennia.

Whether the Greeks win or the Trojans lose, whether or not mother right is destroyed by father right, whether Iphigenia is sacrificed by her father or escapes to Tauris, whether Odysseus is a brilliant hero or a slimy scoundrel, whether Achilles is the greatest of the Achaeans or the most disgusting bully, rapist and murderer, the story, surely, will continue...

Chapter Notes

Chapter 1

1. Based on information in Finley 62; Vermuele, "'Priam's Castle Blazing'" 85, 91; Mellink 94; Mee 52; Vermeule, *BA* 270, 277; Chadwick 184–5; Latacz, 11; Fields, 5, and Bryce, xiii–ix. The dating of the Troy levels is taken from Latacz, who is using Korfmann's dating (the dates vary depending on the source used).

2. Based on information in Finley 67, 74, 126; Snodgrass 365–7, 429; Coldstream 298, 341–56; Desborough 9, 354; Latacz 11, Bryce viii–ix, and Wood 16.

Chapter 9

1. All English translations are taken from *Eneas: A Twelfth-Century French Romance*, translated with an Introduction and Notes by John A. Yunck, Number XCIII Records of Civilization Sources and Studies (New York: Columbia University Press, 1974).

2. All translations from Benoît's *Troie* are mine. The cited line numbers are from the Constans French text.

Chapter 10

1. Material in this chapter is based on a substantially longer version, "New Learning and Old Anxieties" (209–62)," chapter five of my dissertation, "Human Responsibility and the Fall of Troy," CUNY, 1981.

2. Guido de Columnis, *Historia Destructionis Troiae,* ed. By Nathaniel Edward Griffin (1936; rpt. New York: Kraus Reprint Co., 1970). This edition will be cited as *Historia*. English translations from Guido are from the *Historia Destructionis Troiae* by Guido delle Colonne, trans. By Mary Elizabeth Meek (Bloomington: Indiana University Press, 1974), cited as Meek.

3. Elmer Atwood, in "English Versions of the *Historia Trojana*," Diss. Univ. of Virginia, 1932, expresses the view that Guido "was probably the most successful plagiarist in the history of literature" (19). Meek modifies this viewpoint in her excellent Introduction to her translation of Guido by examining Guido's role as a serious medieval historian who was attempting to restore the Troy material to a more reliable historical state than he found it in Benoit's romance (xiv ff.).

She feels that Guido may have believed Benoit's assertions that his sources were Dictys and Dares, and that he had followed them closely, and as a consequence, may have cited only Dictys and Dares, and not Benoit, believing that they were the more ancient and hence, respectable sources for his history (xvii). Further, as Benson points out, Guido's prose version "de-emphasizes the love stories and drops, reduces, or doubts Benoit's marvels. Guido never names his real source, but insists he is keeping alive the full account of the two original reporters [Dictys and Dares]" (4).

4. Meek xi.

5. Meek indicates the popularity and importance of the *Historia*, pointing out that there may be as many as one hundred and fifty extant mss., and that it was translated into many languages as well as serving directly or indirectly as a source for Boccaccio's *Filostrato*, Chaucer's *Troilus and C riseyde*, and Lydgate's *Troy Book* (xi).

6. Benson comments that Guido's despair "...becomes an important element in the two best poems about Troy in Middle English, poems that otherwise use the medieval history of Troy very selectively — Chaucer's *Troilus and Criseyde* and Henryson's *Testament of Cresseid*" (31).

7. Alistair Crombie remarks in *Medieval and Early Modern Science*, Vol. I (1953; rev. ed. New York: Doubleday Anchor Books, 1959) that the "Most influential of all the contributions of Greco-Arab learning to Western Christendom was the fact that the works of Aristotle, Ptolemy and Galen constituted a complete rational system explaining the universe as a whole in terms of natural causes" (56).

8. See Charles Homer Haskins, The Renaissance of the 12th Century (1927; rpt. Cleveland: The World Publishing Co., 1964), 283–84 on the Arab role in Sicily. Dorothee Metlitzki, in *The Matter of Araby in Medieval England* (New Haven: Yale University Press, 1977), discusses the tolerance of the Norman rulers in Sicily as well as in England, which produced a rich cultural diversity.

9. Meek comments: "Guido's interest in astronomy may stem from his being associated with a court at which Michael Scot held the position of Court Philosopher" (xxvii). Michael Scot was especially famous as an astrologer. Jean Seznec, in *The Survival of the*

Pagan Gods, 1940, trans. Barbara F. Sessions, Bollingen Series XXXVIII (1953; rpt. Princeton: Princeton University Press, 1972) remarks that astrology "stood as an integral and essential element of culture ... it had intimately invaded the science of the late pagan world — to such a degree, in fact, that it dominated all the natural sciences" (45). He also comments that "'*Astra inclinant; non necessitant.*' With this reservation, astrology continues as the foundation of profane culture and the underlying principle of all science" (49).

10. According to Metlitzki, "What the Latin translators of the twelfth century transmitted in the body of their Arabic texts, in a scientific framework, was an affirmation of prognostication. But it did not imply a denial of divine providence. The philosophical and theological complications relating to Christian doctrine do not acquire momentum until the middle of the thirteenth century, with the process of assimilating the Aristotelianism of Arab and Jewish scholars into the Christian system" (59–60).

11. L. J. Elmer, in "Demons [Theology of]," *New Catholic Encyclopedia*, Vol. IV, comments that "The belief that idols were inhabited by demons was, of course, a commonplace among the Christians of the first 5 centuries" (754).

12. Seznec comments that "strong in its new prestige, astrology inspired new fears. Furthermore, the Arabs had developed one of its most threatening aspects in the theory of planetary conjunction.... There was a growing sense of inexorable doom threatening from the skies ... the fear of demons revived at the same time. In all these threats which hung over them, men felt evil presences at work, and looked to the magicians for means of escape or propitiation" (52).

13. Thorndike is quoting from *De Consolatione Philosophiae*, IV, 6.

14. Vincent Cioffari, commenting on Boethius, says: "It is Fate, then, that makes the lines of Fortune *concurre* and *confluere*. But Fate, which governs Chance, is itself in turn ruled by Providence" (*Fortune and Fate from Democritus to St. Thomas Aquinas* [New York: Columbia University Press, 1935], 87).

15. Waller B. Wigginton comments that "The association of unquietness with evil was traditional in the Middle Ages" (223, note 47). In "The Nature and Significance of the Late Medieval Troy Story: A Study of Guido delle Colonne's *Historia Destructionis Troiae*" (Diss. Rutgers, 1965).

16. Saint Thomas Aquinas, "The Summa Theologica" in *Introduction to Saint Thomas Aquinas*, ed., with an Intro. by Anton. C. Pegis (New York: The Modern Library, 1948). Q. 9, Art. 6, 507.

Chapter 12

1. An abbreviated version of this chapter, "Study Guide to Shakespeare's 'Troilus and Cressida,'" was published in *A Groat's Worth of Wit. Journal of the Open University Shakespeare Society*. December 1999, Volume 10, No. 4: 56–61.

2. Sexist language: although Cressida is discussed throughout the play as part of the human problem, the language in *Troilus and Cressida* is overwhelmingly centered on the nature of "man." Consequently, the language of this chapter reflects that concern with the nature of "man," although these days we would write of "human" nature.

Chapter 15

1. See also Eric Neumann, *The Great Mother: An Analysis of the Arch*etype, 1955 (Princeton: Bollingen, 1974); Robert Graves, *The White Goddess: A Historical Grammar of Poetic Myth*, 1948 (New York: Farrar, Straus and Giroux, 1999); and perhaps the most influential of all, Marija Gimbutas, who published a number of books on the archaeology of the Goddess, ending with the posthumous *The Living Goddesses* (Berkeley: University of California Press, 1999). Eller remarks, "Gimbutas was the first archaeologist to suggest that artifacts from post–World War II excavations in Europe and the Near East supported the conclusion of widespread ancient goddess worship in this area of the world" (159). For a critique of universalizing goddess-think, see Lucy Goodison and Christine Morris, Editors, *Ancient Goddesses: The Myths and the Evidence* (Madison: University of Wisconsin Press, 1999).

Works Cited

Introduction

Baldwin, Marshall W., Ed. *The First Hundred Years*. Madison: University of Wisconsin Press, 1969.

Berschin, Walter. *Greek Letters and the Latin Middle Ages: From Jerome to Nicholas of Cusa*. Revised and expanded edition. Trans. Jerold C. Frakes. Washington, DC: Catholic University of America Press, 1988.

Cameron, Averil. *The Mediterranean World in Late Antiquity AD 395–600*. London: Routledge, 1993.

Faral, Edmund. *Recherches sur les Sources Latines des Contes et Romans Courtois du Moyen Age*. Paris: Librairie Honoré Champion, 1967.

Fox, Robin Lane. *Pagans and Christians*. New York: Knopf, 1989.

Frazer, R. M. Jr., trans. *The Trojan War: The Chronicles of Dictys of Crete and Dares the Phrygian*. Bloomington: Indiana University Press, 1966.

Geanakopolos, Deno John. *Byzantium: Church, Society and Civilization Seen Through Contemporary Eyes*. Chicago: University of Chicago Press, 1984.

Geoffrey of Monmouth. *History of the Kings of Britain*. Trans. Sebastian Evans. 1903. New York: Dutton, 1958.

Kazhden, A. P., and Ann Wharton Epstein. *Change in Byzantine Culture in the Eleventh and Twelfth Centuries*. 1985. Berkeley: University of California Press, 1990.

Lawman. *Brut*. Trans. Rosamund Allen. New York: St. Martin's, 1992.

Lumiansky, R. M. "Structural Unity in Benoît's *Roman de Troie*." *Romania* LXXIX (1958): 410–24.

Owen, D.D.R. *Eleanor of Aquitaine: Queen and Legend*. Oxford: Blackwell, 1993.

Sommer, H. Oskar, ed. Preface. *The Recuyell of the Historyes of Troye*. William Caxton. Trans. Raoul Lefevre. 1894. New York: AMS Press, 1973. vii–x.

Wood, Michael. *In Search of the Trojan War*. 1985. New Edition. Berkeley: University of California Press, 1996.

Chapter 1

Bouzek, Jan. "Bronze Age Greece and the Balkans: Problems of Migrations." Crossland and Birchall 169–177.

Bryce, Trevor. "Homer at the Interface." In *Anatolian Interfaces: Hittites, Greeks and Their Neighbors*. Eds. Billie Jean Collins, Mary R. Bachvarova and Ian C. Rutherford. 2008. Paperback rpt. Oxford: Oxbow Books, 2010: 85–92.

_____. *The Trojans and Their Neighbors*. New York: Routledge, 2006; transferred to digital printing, 2010.

Burkert, Walter. *Greek Religion*. Trans. John Raffan. Cambridge, MA: Harvard University Press, 1985.

Butterworth, E.A.S. *Some Traces of the Pre-Olympian World in Greek Literature and Myth*. Berlin: Walter de Gruyter, 1966.

Chadwick, John. *The Mycenaean World*. Cambridge: Cambridge University Press, 1976.

Cline, Eric H. "Troy as a 'Contested Periphery'" Archaeological Perspectives on Cross-Cultural and Cross-Disciplinary Interactions Concerning Bronze Age Anatolia." *In Anatolian Interfaces: Hittites, Greeks and Their Neighbours*. Eds. Billie Jean Collins, Mary R. Bachvarova and Ian C. Rutherford. 2008. Paperback rpt. Oxford: Oxbow Books, 2010: 11–20.

Coldstream, J. N. *Geometric Greece*. New York: St. Martin's, 1977.

_____. "Linguistics and Archaeology in Aegean Prehistory." Crossland and Birchall 5–15.

Crossland, R. A., and Ann Birchall, Eds. *Bronze Age Migrations in the Aegean: Archeological and Linguistic Problems in Greek Prehistory*. Park Ridge, NJ: Noyes, 1974.

Desborough, V. R. d'A. *The Greek Dark Ages*. New York: St. Martin's, 1972.

Drews, Robert. *The End of the Bronze Age: Changes in Warfare and the Catastrophe ca. 1200 B.C.* Princeton: Princeton University Press, 1993.

Fields, Nic. *Troy c. 1700–1250 BC*. Illustrated by D. Spedaliere and S. Sulemsohn Spedaliere. Great Britain: Osprey, 2004.

Finley, M. I. *Early Greece: The Bronze and Archaic Ages*. New York: Norton, 1970.

Foxhall, Lin, and John K. Davies, Eds. *The Trojan War: Its Historicity and Context: Papers of the First Greenbank Colloquium, Liverpool, 1981*. Bristol: Bristol Classical Press, 1984.

Latacz, Joachim. *Troy and Homer: Towards a Solution of an Old Mystery*. 2001 (*Troia und Homer*). Trans. by Kevin Windle and Rosh Ireland. Oxford: Oxford University Press, 2004

Hertel, Dieter, and Frank Kolb. "Troy in Clearer Perspective." *Anatolian Studies* 53 (2003) 71–88.

Korfmann, Manfred O. "Troy in Light of New Research." Keynote lecture (English Edition), Universität Trier (2003).

Mee, C. B. "The Mycenaeans and Troy." Foxhall and Davies 45–56.

Mellart, James. "Troy VIIa in Anatolian Perspective." Foxhall and Davies 63–82.

Mellink, Machteld Johanna. "Postscript." Mellink 93–101.

_____, Ed. *Troy and the Trojan War: A Symposium Held at Bryn Mawr College, October 1984*. Bryn Mawr, PA: Bryn Mawr College, 1986.

Millard, A. R. "Events at the End of the Late Bronze Age in the Near East." Foxhall and Davies 1–15.

Redford, Donald B. *Egypt, Canaan, and Israel in Ancient Times*. Princeton: Princeton University Press, 1992.

Sandars, Nancy K. *The Sea Peoples: Warriors of the Ancient Mediterranean 1250–1150 BC*. London: Thames and Hudson, 1978.

Snodgrass, A. M. "Metal-work as Evidence for Immigration in the Late Bronze Age." Crossland and Birchall 209–213.

Warren, Peter. *The Aegean Civilizations (The Making of the Past)*. 1975. First American Edition, NY: Peter Bedrick Books, 1989.

Wood, Michael. *In Search of the Trojan War*. 1985. New edition, Berkeley: University of California Press, 1996.

Vermeule, Emily T. *Greece in the Bronze Age*. Chicago: University of Chicago Press, 1964. Cited as *BA*.

_____. "'Priam's Castle Blazing': A Thousand Years of Trojan Memories." Mellink 77–92. Cited as "PC."

Zangger, Eberhard. *The Flood from Heaven: Deciphering the Atlantis Legend*. Foreword by Anthony Snodgrass. New York: William Morrow, 1992.

Chapter 2

Chadwick, John. *The Mycenaean World*. Cambridge: Cambridge University Press, 1976.

Coldstream, J. N. *Geometric Greece*. New York: St. Martin's, 1977.

"Eris." *Oxford Classical Dictionary*. 2nd Ed. Eds. N.G.L. Hammond and H. H. Scullard. Oxford: Clarendon, 1970.

Finley, M. I. *Early Greece: The Bronze and Archaic Ages*. New York: Norton, 1970.

"Heracles." *Oxford Classical Dictionary*. 2nd Ed. Eds. N.G.L. Hammond and H. H. Scullard. Oxford: Clarendon, 1970.

Lord, Albert B. *The Singer of Tales*. 1960. New York: Athenaeum, 1973.

Parry, Milman. "The Traditional Epithet in Homer." 1928. Trans. of *L'Épithète traditionelle dans Homère: Essai sur un problème de style homérique*. Paris. *The Making of Homeric Verse: The Collected Papers of Milman Parry*. Ed. Adam Parry. Oxford: Clarendon, 1971. 1–190.

Stanford, W. B. *The Ulysses Theme*. 1963. Dallas: Spring Publications, 1992.

Whitman, Cedric H. *Homer and the Heroic Tradition*. 1958. New York: Norton, 1965.

Vermeule, Emily T. *Greece in the Bronze Age*. Chicago: University of Chicago Press, 1964. Cited as *BA*.

_____. "'Priam's Castle Blazing': A Thousand Years of Trojan Memories." *Troy and the Trojan War: A Symposium Held at Bryn Mawr College, October 1984*. Ed. M. Mellink. Bryn Mawr, PA: Bryn Mawr College, 1986. 77–92. Cited as "PC."

Chapter 3

Homer. *Iliad*. Trans. Robert Fagles. Introduction and Notes by Bernard Knox. Harmondsworth, Middlesex, England: Penguin Books, 1990. Cited line numbers are from this edition.

Kim, Junyo. *The Pity of Achilles: Oral Style and the Unity of the Iliad*. Lanham, MD: Rowman and Littlefield, 2000.

King, Katherine Callen. *Achilles: Paradigms of the War Hero from Homer to the Middle Ages*. Berkeley: University of California Press, 1987.

Whitman, Cedric H. *Homer and the Heroic Tradition*. 1958. New York: Norton, 1965.

Chapter 4

Homer. *The Odyssey*. Trans. Robert Fagles. Harmondsworth, Middlesex, England: Penguin, 1997. All line numbers and quotations are from this edition, cited as *Od*.

Lattimore, Richard. Introduction. *The Odyssey of Homer*. Trans. Richard Lattimore. New York: Harper, 1968. 1–24.

Stanford, W. B. *The Ulysses Theme*. 1963. New Edition, Dallas: Spring Publications, 1992.

Chapter 5

Adkins, Arthur W. H. *Merit and Responsibility: A Study in Greek Values*. 1960. Chicago: University of Chicago Press, 1975.

Aeschylus. *Agamemnon*. Grene and Doniger O'Flaherty 34–93.

_____. *Eumenides*. Grene and Doniger O'Flaherty 233–249.

Grene, David, and Wendy Doniger O'Flaherty, trans. *The "Oresteia" by Aeschylus*. Introductions by David Grene, Wendy Doniger O'Flaherty, and Nicholas Rudall. Chicago: University of Chicago Press, 1989. Quotations from and reference to the plays are from this edition.

Harsh, Philip Whaley. *A Handbook of Classical Drama*. 1944. Palo Alto: Stanford University Press, 1979.

Jones, John. *On Aristotle and Greek Tragedy*. New York: Oxford University Press, 1962.

Lefkowitz, Mary R. "The Last Hours of the Parthenos." Reeder, *Pandora* 32–38.

Lloyd-Jones, Hugh. *The Justice of Zeus*. Berkeley: University of California Press, 1982.

Pomeroy, Sarah B. *Goddesses, Whores, Wives, and Slaves: Women in Classical Antiquity*. New York: Schocken, 1975.

Powell, Barry B. *A Short Introduction to Classical Myth*. Englewood Cliffs, NJ: Prentice Hall, 2002.

Reeder, Ellen D. Introduction. *Pandora* 13–18.

_____, ed. *Pandora: Women in Classical Greece*. Baltimore: Walters Art Gallery, 1995.

_____. "Women and Men in Classical Greece." *Pandora* 20–31.

Rosenmeyer, Thomas G. *The Art of Aeschylus*. Berkeley: University of California Press, 1982.

Sourvinou-Inwood, Christiane. "Male and Female, Public and Private, Ancient and Modern." Reeder, *Pandora* 111–120.

Stewart, Andrew. "Rape?" Reeder, *Pandora* 74–90.

Vickers, Brian. *Towards Greek Tragedy: Drama, Myth, Society*. London: Longman, 1973.

Chapter 6

Dimock, George E. "Introduction." Merwin and Dimock 3–21.

Euripides. *Iphigenia at Aulis*. Merwin and Dimock 23–96. Quotations and line numbers are from this edition, cited as *IA*.

_____. *Iphigenia in Tauris*. Trans. M. J. Cropp. Warminster, England: Aris & Phillips, 2000.

Foley, Helene P. *Female Acts in Greek Tragedy*. Princeton: Princeton University Press, 2001.

Girard, René. *Violence and the Sacred*. 1972. Trans. Patrick Gregory. Baltimore: Johns Hopkins University Press, 1977.

Grube, G. M. A. "Euripides and the Gods." (Original title: "The Gods"). *The Drama of Euripides* by G. M. A. Grube. 1941. *Euripides: A Collection of Critical Essays*. Ed. Erich Segal. Englewood Cliffs, NJ: Prentice-Hall, 1968. 34–50.

Hamilton, Richard. Review of *Human Sacrifice in Ancient Greece*. By Dennis D. Hughes. *Bryn Mawr Classical Review* 03.01.25 (1992). http://ccat.sas.upenn.edu/bmcr/1992/03/01.25.html.

Harsh, Philip Whaley. *A Handbook of Classical Drama*. 1944. Palo Alto, CA: Stanford University Press, 1979.

Lefkowitz, Mary. *Women in Greek Myth*. Baltimore: Johns Hopkins University Press, 1986.

Lübeck, Maria Holmberg. *Iphigeneia, Agamemnon's Daughter: A Study of Ancient Conceptions in Greek Myth and Literature Associated with the Atrides*. Stockholm: Almqvist & Wiksell International, 1993.

Merwin, W.S., and George E. Dimock, Jr., Trans. *Euripides: Iphigenia at Aulis*. New York: Oxford University Press, 1978.

Michelakis, Pantelis. Review of *Die Opferung der Iphigeneia in Aulis: Di Rezeptions des Mythos in antiken und modernen Dramen* by Susanne Aretz. *Bryn Mawr Classical Review* 2002.01.05 (2002). http://ccat.sas.upenn.edu/bmcr/2002/2002-01-05.html.

Rabinowitz, Nancy Sorkin. *Anxiety Veiled: Euripides and the Traffic in Women*. Ithaca: Cornell University Press, 1993.

Rohde, Erwin. *Psyche: The Cult of Souls and Belief in Immortality Among the Greeks*. 1925. Vol. II. Trans. W. B. Hillis. New York: Harper Torchbooks, 1966.

Chapter 7

Bailey, Cyril. *Religion in Virgil*. 1935. New York: Barnes and Noble, 1969.

Camps, W. A. "Aelius Donatus' *Life of Virgil*." Appendix I. *An Introduction to Virgil's Aeneid*. Oxford: Oxford University Press, 1969. 115–120. Cited as "Aelius Donatus."

_____. *An Introduction to Virgil's Aeneid*. Oxford: Oxford University Press, 1969. Cited as *Introduction*.

Harrison, S. J. "Some Views of the *Aeneid* in the Twentieth Century." *Oxford Readings in Vergil's Aeneid*. Ed. S. J. Harrison. Oxford: Oxford University Press, 1990. 1–20.

Knight, W. F. Jackson. Introduction. *Virgil: The Aeneid*. Trans W. F. Jackson Knight. 1956. Harmondsworth: Penguin, 1964. 11–24.

Olgivie, R. M. *The Romans and Their Gods in the Age of Augustus*. Ancient Culture and Society Series. Gen. Ed. M. I. Finley. New York: Norton, 1969.

Starr, Chester. *Civilization and the Caesars: The Intellectual Revolution in the Roman Empire*. 1954. New York: Norton, 1965.

Veyne, Paul. "The Roman Empire." *A History of Private Life: I. From Pagan Rome to Byzantium*. Ed. Paul Veyne. Trans. Arthur Goldhammer. Cambridge, MA: Harvard University Press, 1987. 5–234.

Virgil. *The Aeneid*. Trans. Allen Mandelbaum. 1961. New York: Bantam, 1978. All quotations and line numbers are from this edition, cited as *Aen.*

Chapter 8

Baswell, Christopher. *Virgil in Medieval England: Figuring the "Aeneid" from the Twelfth Century to Chaucer*. Cambridge, England: Cambridge University Press, 1995.

Berschin, Walter. *Greek Letters and the Latin Middle Ages: From Jerome to Nicholas of Cusa*. 1980. Trans. Jerold C. Frakes. Revised and Expanded Edition. Washington, DC: Catholic University of America Press, 1988.

Boardman, John, Jasper Griffin and Oswyn Murray, Eds. *The Oxford History of the Classical World*. Oxford: Oxford University Press, 1986.

Cameron, Aevril. *The Mediterranean World in Late Antiquity: AD 395–600*. London: Routledge, 1993.

Chuvin, Pierre. *A Chronicle of the Last Pagans*. Trans. B. A. Archer. Cambridge, MA: Harvard University Press, 1990.

Curtius, Ernst Robert. *European Literature and the Latin Middle Ages*. Trans. Willard R. Trask. 1953. First Princeton/Bollingen Paperback Edition. Princeton: Princeton University Press, 1973.

Dares the Phrygian. "The Tale of Troy." *Medieval Narrative: A Book of Translations*. Trans. Margaret Schlauch. 1928. New York: Gordian, 1969. 243–280.

Daretis Phrygii. *De Excidio Troiae Historia*, recensuit Ferdinandus Meister. Leipzig: B. G. Teubner, 1873.

Dictys Cretensis. *Ephemeridos Belli Troiani*. Ed. Werner Eisenhut. Bibliotheca Scriptorum Graecorum et Romanorum Teubneriana. Leipzig: B. G. Teubner, 1973.

Ehrhart, Margaret J. *The Judgment of the Trojan Prince Paris in Medieval Literature*. Philadelphia: University of Pennsylvania Press, 1987.

Fox, Robin Lane. *Pagans and Christians*. New York: Alfred A. Knopf, 1989.

Frazer, R. M., Jr. *The Trojan War: The Chronicles of Dictys of Crete and Dares the Phrygian*. Bloomington: Indiana University Press, 1966.

Geanakoplos, Deno John. *Byzantium: Church, Society, and Civilization Seen Through Contemporary Eyes*. Chicago: University of Chicago Press, 1984.

Highet, Gilbert. *The Classical Tradition: Greek and Roman Influences on Western Literature*. 1949. Oxford: Oxford University Press, 1970.

Millar, Fergus. *The Roman Near East: 31 BC–AD 337*. Cambridge, MA: Harvard University Press, 1993.

Singleton, Charles S., Trans. and Commentary. *Dante Alighieri: The Divine Comedy. Inferno 2: Commentary*. 1970. Princeton: Princeton University Press, 1989.

Thompson, Diane. "Human Responsibility and the Fall of Troy." Dissertation City University of New York, 1981.

Chapter 9

Adler, Alfred. "*Militia et Amor* in the *Roman de Troie*," *Romanische Forschungen* 72 (1960): 14–29.

Allen, Peter L. *The Art of Love: Amatory Fiction from Ovid to the Romance of the Rose*. Philadelphia: University of Pennsylvania Press, 1992.

Baldwin, Marshall W., ed. *The First Hundred Years*. Madison: University of Wisconsin Press, 1969.

Benoît de Sainte-Maure. *Le Roman de Troie*. Publié d'après tous les manuscrits connus. Ed. Léopold Constans. Société des Anciens Textes Français. 6 vols. 1904–1912. New York: Johnson Reprint, 1968.

Blacker, Jean. *The Faces of Time: Portrayal of the Past in Old French and Latin Historical Narrative of the Anglo-Norman "Regnum."* Austin: University of Texas Press, 1994.

Cormier, Raymond J. *One Heart One Mind: The Rebirth of Virgil's Hero in Medieval French Romance*. University, MS: Romance Monographs, 1973.

Denomy, A. J. *The Heresy of Courtly Love*. New York: D. X. McMullen, 1947.

Dronke, Peter. *Medieval Latin and the Rise of European Love-Lyric I: Problems and Interpretations*. Oxford: Clarendon Press, 1965.

Economou, George D. "The Two Venuses and Courtly Love." *Pursuit of Perfection: Courtly Love in Medieval Literature*. Eds. Joan M. Ferrante and George D. Economou. Port Washington, NY: Kennikat, 1975. 17–50.

Faral, Edmund. *Recherches sur les Sources Latines des Contes et Romans Courtois du Moyen Age*. Paris: Librairie Honoré Champion, 1967.

Fiero, Gloria K., Wendy Pfeffer and Mathe Allain, eds. and trans. *Three Medieval Views of Women: La Contenance des Fames, Le Bien des Fames, Le Blasme des Fames*. New Haven: Yale University Press, 1989.

Geoffrey of Monmouth. *History of the Kings of Britain*. Trans. Sebastian Evans. 1903. Revised Charles W. Dunn. New York: Dutton, 1958.

Jones, Rosemary. *The Theme of Love in the Romans d'Antiquité*. Dissertation Series V. London: Modern Humanities Research Association, 1972.

Kelly, D. *Medieval French Romance*. New York: Twayne, 1993.

Lumiansky, R. M. "Structural Unity in Benoît's *Roman de Troie*." *Romania* 79 (1958): 410–24.

Menocal, Maria Rosa. *The Arabic Role in Medieval Literary History: A Forgotten Heritage*. 1987. Philadelphia: University of Pennsylvania Press, 1990.

Owen, D. D. R. *Eleanor of Aquitaine: Queen and Legend.* Cambridge, MA: Blackwell, 1993.

Parry, John Jay. Introduction. *The Art of Courtly Love.* Andreas Capellanus. Trans. John Jay Parry. Ed. and abridged by F. W. Locke. Milestones of Thought. New York: Frederick Ungar, 1957. iii–vii.

Preminger, Alex, et al., eds. "Troubadour." *Princeton Encyclopedia of Poetry and Poetics.* 1965. Princeton: Princeton University Press, 1972.

Wigginton, Waller. "The Nature and Significance of the Late Medieval Troy Story: A Study of Guido Delle Colonne's *Historia Destructionis Troiae.*" Dissertation Rutgers University, 1965.

Yunck, John A., trans. *Eneas: A Twelfth-Century French Romance.* New York: Columbia University Press, 1974.

Chapter 10

Atwood, Elmer Bagby. "English Versions of the *Historia Trojana.*" Diss. University of Virginia, 1932.

Benson, C. David. *The History of Troy in Middle English Literature*: Guido delle Colonne's *Historia Destructionis Troiae* in Medieval England. Suffolk: D. S. Brewer; Roman and Littlefield, 1980.

Cioffari, Vincent. *Fortune and Fate from Democritus to St. Thomas Aquinas.* New York: Columbia University Press, 1935.

Crombie, Alistair. *Medieval and Early Modern Science.* Vol. I. *Science in the Middle Ages: V–XVIII Centuries.* This is a revised version of the first four chapters of *Augustine to Galileo* (London, 1952). Revised ed. New York: Doubleday Anchor, 1959.

Guido de Columnis. *Historia destructionis Troiae.* Ed. Nathaniel Edward Griffin. The Mediaeval Academy of America. 1936; rpt. New York: Kraus Reprint, 1970.

Guido delle Colonne. *Historia Destructionis Troiae.* Trans. with Intro. and Notes by Mary Elizabeth Meek. Bloomington: Indiana University Press, 1974.

Haskins, Charles Homer. *The Renaissance of the 12th Century.* 1924; 2d ed. Cambridge, MA: Harvard University Press, 1927.

Metlitzki, Dorothee. *The Matter of Araby in Medieval England.* New Haven: Yale University Press, 1977.

Seznec, Jean. *The Survival of the Pagan Gods: The Mythological Tradition and Its Place in Renaissance Humanism and Art.* Trans. by Barbara F. Sessions. Bollingen Series XXXVIII. 1953; rpt. Princeton: Princeton University Press, 1972.

Thomas Aquinas. *The* Summa Theological *of Saint Thomas Aquinas.* Trans. by the Fathers of the English Dominican Province. Revised by Daniel J. Sullivan. In *Great Books of the Western World.*

Ed. R. M. Hutchens. Nos. 19 and 20. Chicago: *Encyclopaedea Britannica*, 1952.

Thorndike, Lynn. *A History of Magic and Experimental Science During the First Thirteen Centuries of Our Era.* 2 Vols. New York: Columbia University Press, 1923.

Wigginton, Waller. "The Nature and Significance of the Late Medieval Troy Story: A Study of Guido Delle Colonne's *Historia Destructionis Troiae.*" Dissertation Rutgers University, 1965.

Chapter 11

Adler, Alfred. "*Militia et Amor* in the *Roman de Troie.*" *Romanische Forschungen* 72 (1960): 14–24.

Boethius. *The Theological Tractates and The Consolation of Philosophy.* Trans. H. F. Stewart, E. K. Rand and S. J. Tester. Loeb Classical Library 74. Cambridge, MA: Harvard University Press, 1973.

Boitani, Piero, and Jill Mann, eds. *The Cambridge Chaucer Companion.* Cambridge, England: Cambridge University Press, 1986.

Carpenter, Thomas H. *Art and Myth in Ancient Greece: A Handbook.* London: Thames and Hudson, 1991.

Chaucer, Goeffrey. *Troilus and Criseyde. The Works of Geoffrey Chaucer.* Ed. F. N. Robinson. 2nd ed. Boston: Houghton, 1961.

Christmas, Peter. "*Troilus and Criseyde*: The Problems of Love and Necessity," *Chaucer Review* 9.4 (Spring 1975): 285–296.

Curry, Walter Clyde. "Destiny in *Troilus and Criseyde.*" *Chaucer and the Mediaeval Sciences.* 2nd ed. New York: Barnes and Noble, 1960. 241–98. In Schoeck and Taylor 34–70.

Denomy, Alexander J., C.S.B. "The Two Moralities of Chaucer's *Troilus and Criseyde.*" *Transactions of the Royal Society of Canada* 3rd ser. 44 (June, 1950): 35–46. In Schoeck and Taylor 147–59.

Gordon, R. K, Ed. and Trans. "Introduction." *The Story of Troilus.* New York: E. P. Dutton, 1964. xi–xviii.

Kaminsky, Alice R. *Chaucer's "Troilus and Criseyde" and the Critics.* Athens: Ohio University Press, 1980.

Lewis, C. S. "What Chaucer Really Did to *Il Filostrato.*" *Essays and Studies by Members of the English Association* 17 (1932): 56–75. In Schoeck and Taylor 16–33.

Mann, Jill. "Chance and Destiny in *Troilus and Criseyde* and the *Knight's Tale.*" Boitani and Mann 75–92.

McCall, John P. "The Trojan Scene in Chaucer's *Troilus.*" *ELH* 29 (1962): 263–75. In *Critical Essays on Chaucer's Troilus and Criseyde and His Major Early Poems.* Ed. C. David Benson. Toronto: University of Toronto Press, 1991. 57–67.

Robertson, D. W., Jr. "The Concept of Courtly Love as an Impediment to the Understanding of

Medieval Texts." *The Meaning of Courtly Love.* Ed. F. X. Newman. 1968. Albany: State University of New York Press, 1972. 1–18.

Schoeck, Richard J., and Jerome Taylor, Eds. *Chaucer Criticism: Troilus and Criseyde and the Minor Poems.* Vol. 2. 1961. Notre Dame, IN: University of Notre Dame Press, 1971.

Steadman, John M. *Disembodied Laughter: Troilus and the Apotheosis Tradition.* Berkeley: University of California Press, 1972.

Stewart, H. F., and E. K. Rand. "Life of Boethius." Boethius xi–xv.

Stroud, Theodore A. "Boethius' Influence on Chaucer's *Troilus. Modern Philology* 49 (1951–2): 1–9. In Schoeck and Taylor 122–135.

Wallace, David. "Chaucer's Continental Inheritance: The Early Poems and *Troilus and Criseyde.*" Boitani and Mann 19–37.

Windeatt, Barry. *Troilus and Criseyde.* Oxford Guides to Chaucer. Oxford: Clarendon, 1992.

Chapter 12

Anderson, Ruth. *Elizabethan Psychology and Shakespeare's Plays.* 1927. New York: Russell and Russell, 1966.

Elton, W. R. "Shakespeare and the Thought of His Age." In *A New Companion to Shakespeare Studies.* Eds. Kenneth Muir and S. Schoenbaum. 1971. Cambridge, England: Cambridge University Press, 1976. 180–98.

Lovejoy, Arthur O. *The Great Chain of Being.* 1936. Cambridge, MA: Harvard University Press, 1973.

Miskimin, Alice. *The Renaissance Chaucer.* New Haven: Yale University Press, 1975.

Shakespeare, William. *Troilus and Cressida. The Works of Shakespeare.* Ed. Alice Walker. 1957. Cambridge, England: Cambridge University Press, 1972. All quotations and line numbers are from this edition, cited as *Tro.*

Tillyard, E. M. *Shakespeare's Problem Plays.* 1950. London: Chatto and Windus, 1968.

Chapter 13

Clark, A. F. B. *Jean Racine.* New York: Octagon Books, 1969.

Cottrell, Alan P. "On Speaking the Good: Goethe's *Iphigenie* as "Moralisches Urphänomen." *Modern Language Quarterly* 41.2 (1980): 162–180.

Furst, Lilian. "Mythology into Psychology: *Deus ex Machina* into God Within." *Comparative Literature Studies* 21.1 (1984): 1–15.

Goethe, Johann Wolfgang von. *Iphigenia in Tauris,* Trans. Charles E. Passage. 1963. Prospect Heights, IL: Waveland, 1991. All quotations and line numbers are from this edition.

Koch, Erec R. "Tragic Disclosures of Racine's *Iphigénie." Romanic Review* 81. 2 (1990): 161–172.

Maland, David. *Culture and Society in Seventeenth-Century France.* New York: Charles Scribner's, 1970.

Passage, Charles E. Introduction. *Iphigenia in Tauris.* By Johann Wolfgang von Goethe. Trans. Charles E. Passage. 1963. Prospect Heights, IL: Waveland, 1991. 5–19.

Prandi, Julie D. "Goethe's Iphigenie as Woman." *The Germanic Review* 60.1 (1985): 23–31.

Racine, Jean. *Iphigenia/Phaedra/Athaliah.* Trans. John Cairncross. 1963. London: Penguin, 1970. All quotations and line numbers are from this edition.

_____. Preface to *Iphigenia. Iphigenia/Phaedra/Athaliah.* Trans. John Cairncross. London: Penguin, 1970: 49–53.

Wagner, Irmgard. *Critical Approaches to Goethe's Classical Dramas: Iphigenie, Torquato Tasso, and Die natürliche Tochter.* Columbia, SC: Camden House, 1995.

Chapter 14

Ames, Keri Elizabeth. "The Oxymoron of Fidelity in Homer's *Odyssey* and Joyce's *Ulysses." Joyce Studies Annual* Volume 14, Summer 2003: 132–174.

Ellmann, Richard. *Ulysses on the Liffey.* 1972. Reprint with corrections 1978. New York: Barnes and Noble reprint, 2009.

Gifford, Don, with Robert J. Seidman. Ulysses *annotated: Notes for James Joyce's* Ulysses. 1974. 2d ed., revised and enlarged by Don Gifford, University of California Press, 1989.

Homer. *The Odyssey.* Translated by Robert Fagles. Intro. and Notes by Bernard Knox. New York: Penguin, 1997.

Joyce, James. *James Joyce's Ulysses in Nighttown.* Dramatized and Transposed by Marjorie Barkentin under the supervision of Padraic Colum. A Modern Library Paperback, 1958.

_____. *A Portrait of the Artist as a Young Man.* 1916. With an Introduction by Herbert Gorman. New York: Modern Library, 1928.

_____. *Ulysses.* 1922. With an Introduction by Craig Raine. New York: Everyman's Library, 1992.

Kain, Richard M. *Fabulous Voyager: A Study of James Joyce's* Ulysses 1947. New York: Viking, 1959.

Mercer, Vivian. "Justice for Édouard Dujardin." *James Joyce Quarterly* V. 4, No. 3 (Spring 1967): 209–13.

Ramey, James. "Intertextual Metempsychosis in *Ulysses*: Murphy, Sinbad, and the "U.P.: up" Postcard. *James Joyce Quarterly,* Volume 45, Number 1 (Fall 2007): 97–114.

Chapter 15

Bachofen, J. J. *Myth, Religion, and Mother Right: Selected Writings of J. J. Bachofen.* Trans. Ralph

Manheim. 1967. Bollingen Series LXXXIV. Princeton: Princeton University Press, 1992.

Bradley, Marion Zimmer. *The Firebrand*. 1987. New York: Pocket Books, 1991. Cited in text as *FB*.

Eller, Cynthia. *Living in the Lap of the Goddess: The Feminist Spirituality Movement in America*. Boston: Beacon, 1995.

Gadon, Elinor W. *The Once and Future Goddess: A Symbol for Our Time*. San Francisco: HarperSanFrancisco, 1989.

Stone, Merlin. *When God Was a Woman*. New York: Harvest/Harcourt Brace, 1976.

Tepper, Sheri S. *The Gate to Women's Country*. 1988. New York: Bantam/Doubleday, 1989. Cited in text as *WC*.

Chapter 16

Gorak, Jan. *The Making of the Modern Canon: Genesis and Crisis of a Literary Idea*. The Athlone Series on Canons. London: Athlone, 1991.

Gregory, Eileen. *H.D. and Hellenism: Classic Lines*. Cambridge, England: Cambridge University Press, 1997.

Internet Movie Data Base (IMDb); www.imdb.com.

Lauter, Paul. *Canons and Contexts*. New York: Oxford University Press, 1991.

Scherer, Margaret R. *The Legends of Troy in Art and Literature*. 1963. 2nd ed. New York: Phaidon, 1964.

Vandiver, Elizabeth. "'Millions of the Mouthless Dead'": Charles Hamilton Sorley and Wilfred Owen in Homer's Hades."*International Journal of the Classical Tradition* Vol. 5, No. 3, "Classical Mythology and Nineteenth-Century English Literature," 1998 Bristol Myth Colloquium (Winter, 1999). 432–455.

Wood, Michael. *In Search of the Trojan War*. 1985. New Edition. Berkeley: University of California Press, 1996.

Index